MW01005619

CORPORATE TREASURY AND CASH MANAGEMENT

Corporate Treasury and Cash Management

ROBERT COOPER

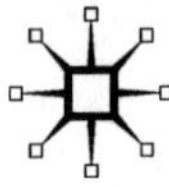

© Robert Cooper 2004
All rights reserved. No reproduction, copy or transmission of this publication may be made without written permission.

No paragraph of this publication may be reproduced, copied or transmitted save with written permission or in accordance with the provisions of the Copyright, Designs and Patents Act 1988, or under the terms of any licence permitting limited copying issued by the Copyright Licensing Agency, 90 Tottenham Court Road, London W1T 4LP.

Any person who does any unauthorised act in relation to this publication may be liable to criminal prosecution and civil claims for damages.

The author has asserted his right to be identified as the author of this work in accordance with the Copyright, Designs and Patents Act 1988.

First published 2004 by
PALGRAVE MACMILLAN
Houndmills, Basingstoke, Hampshire RG21 6XS and
175 Fifth Avenue, New York, N.Y. 10010
Companies and representatives throughout the world

PALGRAVE MACMILLAN is the global academic imprint of the Palgrave Macmillan division of St. Martin's Press, LLC and of Palgrave Macmillan Ltd. Macmillan® is a registered trademark in the United States, United Kingdom and other countries. Palgrave is a registered trademark in the European Union and other countries.

ISBN 978–1–4039–1623–5

This book is printed on paper suitable for recycling and made from fully managed and sustained forest sources.

A catalogue record for this book is available from the British Library.

Library of Congress Cataloging-in-Publication Data

Cooper, Robert, 1945 May 11 –
Corporate treasury and cash management / Robert Cooper.
p. cm. – (Finance and capital markets series)
Includes bibliographical references and index
ISBN 1–4039–1623–3 (cloth)
1. Cash management. 2. Risk management. 3. Corporations–Finance. I. Title. II. Series.

HG4028.C45C5785 2004
658.15'244–dc22

2003062317

Editing and origination by
Curran Publishing Services, Norwich

10 9
13 12 11 10 09 08

Printed and bound in Great Britain by
CPI Antony Rowe, Chippenham and Eastbourne

Contents

List of Figures

List of Tables

Acknowledgements

My thanks to all those who have spent time reviewing individual chapters and for their constructive comments and observations, in particular: Neil Barclay, Nicolas Cinosi, Verity Cooper, Geoff Henney, Keith Phair, Thomas Shippey and Roger Tristam.

PART I

Risk Management

One of the basic building blocks for managing a successful treasury department is the establishment of a comprehensive set of treasury policies. Such policies define the principal financial risks a company is facing and how these risks will be managed by the treasury department. Chapter 1 covers the process of identifying and measuring these risks. What are the typical treasury-related financial risks that most companies have to manage? How are these risks identified and measured? In addition, what is the role of managing these risks in relation to the whole range of other risks facing a company?

Chapter 2 looks at the question of establishing treasury policies by examining financing, foreign exchange and interest rate risk. These are probably the three main financial risks that most companies have to manage. How are these particular risks analyzed? How should treasury policies be established to manage these risks, what are the main elements of such policies and what kind of reports should be produced?

Finally Chapter 3 looks at the question of the debt/equity structure in an organization. What is theoretically the optimum level of debt? More importantly, how does a company practically manage its level of debt, and the risk that debt in the financial structure represents?

CHAPTER 1

Risk Management: Introduction

INTRODUCTION

Most treasurers would consider that their primary role in the organizations they work for is the management of financial risk. This financial risk, as far as it affects the corporate treasurer, can be defined as the extent to which an organization may incur losses as a result of:

- An adverse movement in prices or rates in certain financial market, such as foreign exchange rates, interest rates or commodity prices.
- An adverse change in financial markets. For example, the appetite of lenders in certain debt markets may change so that the company is no longer able to raise finance in its preferred market, or the cost of its finance increases substantially.

WHY MANAGE FINANCIAL RISK?

Corporate finance theory

Broadly stated the Capital Asset Pricing Model (CAPM) indicates that shareholders require compensation for assuming risk. The riskier a share then the greater the return the shareholder requires to compensate for that risk. The risk of an individual security is measured by the volatility of its returns to the holder over and above the volatility of return from the market overall. The volatility of return for a security is affected by three main factors:

- the business sector of the company

- the level of operational gearing (level of fixed costs in its business)
- the level of financial risk.

The objective of managing financial risk is thus to reduce the volatility of return from a security over and above that of the volatility of return from the market. This should increase returns to existing shareholders, since the price of the share should rise to reflect the lower return appropriate to a now less risky share.

Avoiding financial distress

Financial distress is usually reflected in the inability of a company to raise fresh finance, to re-finance existing financial liabilities, or to meet liabilities as they arise. In addition excessive strain may be placed on a company's financial structure as a result of breaches in any financial covenants in its loan documents. Such breaches will have a knock-on effect for the pursuit of the company's strategy.

Preventing an adverse impact on a company's chosen strategy

Most boards of directors need to know that they can continue to pursue key strategies unhindered by unexpected financial losses. Furthermore the boards of most non-financial organizations believe that they have no specific skills in financial markets, and therefore any risks arising from the company's exposure to, involvement in, or access to these markets should be managed. Losses arising from adverse movements in financial markets may, if they are significant, require all or part of an organization's strategy to be modified, put on hold or cancelled.

PRINCIPAL TREASURY-RELATED FINANCIAL RISKS

Companies face a number of different financial risks. The following are probably the most common classifications of the principal financial risks that relate to corporate treasury operations.

Financing risk

This is the risk that a company may either be unable to finance itself in its chosen debt markets, or may have to pay too high a price for its finance and hence reduce returns available to shareholders.

Financing risk is probably one of the most significant risks that the majority of treasurers have to manage. It is a risk that, if it materializes, may result in the company being unable to pursue its chosen strategy. This is particularly the case when a company's strategy involves expansion through acquisition or organic growth, or if it assumes the successful re-financing of existing debt.

Financing risk may materialize from breaches in a company's financial covenants within its loan agreements as a result of an inappropriate financial structure. However, it can equally well result from an inappropriate financing strategy. This may occur when a company fails to diversify its funding sources, or has too high a proportion of its debt maturing at one point in time. As a result of changes in debt markets it may find itself being unable to re-finance existing debt successfully.

Closely related to financing risk are bank relationships and credit rating risks (indeed many companies consider these exposures as part of their financing risk).

Bank relationships

Banks have for some time tried to link the provision of medium and long-term finance to the provision of other 'added value' services. Some banks maintain that the provision of financial support is wholly dependent on their being able to supply these other products. Equally, many companies are concerned to ensure that services and products provided by banks conform to a given level of quality. This leads some organizations to consider that their banking group represents an exposure or risk that needs to be specifically managed to ensure that they can always obtain the right banking products at a desired level of service, quality and price.

Credit ratings

There are few debt markets (other than the bank and private placement markets) that can be accessed without either a short or long-term public debt rating. The cost of finance raised in these markets is often closely related to the credit rating assigned to a company by the rating agencies. A company's strategic or financial actions will have an impact on its public debt ratings and hence on its cost of debt, its ability to access certain debt markets, or its ability to undertake long-term derivative transactions. The relationships with the agencies involved in rating a company's various debt instruments are therefore sometimes considered to require specific management.

Liquidity risk

Closely connected to financing risk, liquidity risk results from insufficient financial resources to meet day-to-day fluctuations in working capital and cashflow (Figure 1.1). The results of inadequate liquidity management are:

- A company making both cash deposits and short-term borrowings, with the result that cash resources are not being used reduce short-term financings. The cost is the difference between the deposit rate and the cost of borrowing.
- The company having insufficient resources to pay its liabilities as they fall due, resulting in penalty costs or loss of reputation.
- The organization incurring losses as a result of either deposits being made with financial institutions that fail, or the purchase of financial instruments that cannot be subsequently sold or realized to meet cash needs.

Foreign exchange risk

This risk is commonly analyzed as transaction risk, pre-transaction risk, translation risk and economic risk.

Transaction risk

This is the risk that a company's cashflows and realized profits may be affected by movements in foreign exchange markets. Generally foreign exchange transaction risk is:

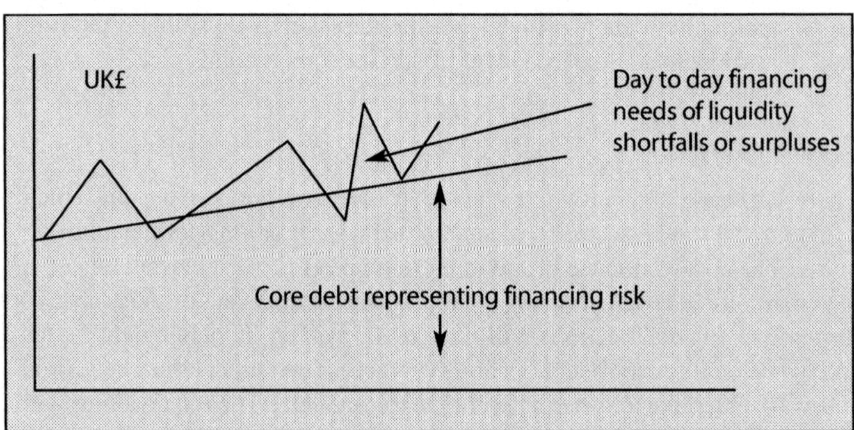

Figure 1.1 Liquidity risk

- short term (although some companies may have long-term transaction exposure)
- revenue in nature
- created where there is a firm commitment to pay or receive in a foreign currency.

Transaction risk represents definite foreign currency receipts or payments where a clear obligation to make a payment or a right to receive a payment has arisen. Examples of transaction risk are payments to be made in a foreign currency for deliveries from an overseas supplier, the receipt of foreign dividends or the payment of royalty and franchise fees.

Pre-transaction risks

These are contingent foreign exchange exposures arising before entering into a commercial contract, which would turn them into transactional exposures. Examples of pre-transaction risks are the publication of a price list, overseas sales not yet made but forecast by the company, or the forecast receipt of foreign dividends not yet declared.

Translation risk

Companies with overseas subsidiaries will find that the domestic value of the assets and liabilities of these subsidiaries will fluctuate with exchange rate movements. In addition the domestic equivalent of the foreign currency earnings of these subsidiaries will also be affected by movements in exchange rates.

Consider a UK company that has an investment in the United States. On the consolidation of this investment the sterling value of these dollar assets will vary depending on UK£/US$ exchange rate ruling at the date of consolidation, and the domestic value of the related foreign currency earnings of the investment will vary depending on the average exchange rate during the year (see Table 1.1).

These movements in the value of the consolidated net assets and earnings of overseas subsidiaries may have significant consequences, depending on financial covenants within loan documents or internal prudential cover ratios such as internal interest cover guidelines. In addition, they may substantially affect published financial results and market expectations.

Table 1.1 Foreign currency earnings and exchange rates

	US$ million	*UK£ million @ 1.60*	*UK£ million @ 1.50*
Gross assets	1 000	625	667
Liabilities	250	156	167
Net Assets	750	469	500
		@1.55	@1.45
Net profit after tax	150	97	103

Economic risk

Companies may be exposed to foreign exchange movements not only through transactional and pre-transactional exposure but also due to their competitive position. Consider a UK-based engineering company exporting to the United States, with its major competitor there being a Japanese manufacturer. Such a company has exposure not only to the UK£/US$ exchange rate on its transactional and pre-transactional exposures, but may also have exposure to US$/JPY. If the JPY weakens against the US$ whilst at the same time sterling strengthens against the US$, that will clearly weaken the company's competitive position vis-à-vis its Japanese competitor.

Again, a London hotel will have all its operating costs in sterling, but nevertheless may find its room occupancy rate affected by UK£/US$ exchange rate. As sterling strengthens against the US$ it becomes more expensive for American tourists to visit London, and they switch their holidays to other venues.

Interest rate risk

Companies with substantial borrowings or deposits will find that their borrowing costs or deposit returns will be affected by movements in interest rates.

Companies with their borrowings at variable rates will be exposed to increases in interest rates, whilst those companies whose borrowings costs are totally or partly fixed will be exposed to a fall in interest rates. The reverse is obviously true for companies with term cash deposits.

Some companies may find that they have a form of natural hedge against interest rate exposure. A common example is the retailing sector, which tends to find that its business is buoyant during periods when interest rates are at the peak of the interest rate cycle as rates are lifted to reduce the level of consumer demand and the inflationary impact that that may have. Equally, low interest rates, designed to boost consumer expenditure, will be linked with lower levels of sales.

Commodity risk

This arises when a company's cost structure is influenced by fluctuations in the price of energy or certain raw materials. An example might be an airline company that needs to purchase substantial amounts of aviation fuel. Equally a mining company, the selling price of whose output depends on the market price for the commodity mined, will have commodity risk exposure.

Counterparty risk

This represents the credit strength of a counterparty in many treasury transactions.

If a company uses derivatives it will find that its exposure to its counterparties will change as the market price of the underlying derivative changes. This exposure may represent:

- The replacement cost of the derivative should the counterparty be unable to fulfill its obligations under the contract. For example, an interest rate swap taken out to swap a bond issue to floating rates, where the corporate receives fixed under the swap, will represent an exposure to the swap counterparty if interest rates subsequently fall.
- The need in some cases for companies under the terms of their derivative contracts to lodge cash collateral if the mark-to-market value of the derivatives contracts with a specific counterparty exceed a stated level. The ability of a counterparty to lodge collateral with a corporate if the market value of a derivative trade moves against it will depend on its credit strength.

Counterparty risk also arises on making cash deposits, or buying negotiable instruments. It represents the possibility of a financial institution that accepts deposits, or a company that issues financial instruments, failing and being unable to meet its obligations.

Equity risk

Manifestations of this include share repurchases, when a company is exposed to the increase in its own share price. It can also arise in mergers and acquisitions, due both to increases in the share price of potential targets and, if a company is contemplating using its own shares to make a purchase, to falls in its own share price. Finally companies that make use of share option schemes are exposed to increases in their share price. The difference between the market price of their shares when an employee or director exercises an option and the cost of the option to the employee or director represents a cost to the company.

Other financial risks

As companies begin to manage and increase their knowledge of treasury financial risk, they may recognize other exposures that can be managed by the treasurer. This may be as the result of the development of new derivatives or because a more extensive analysis of risks identifies exposures that hitherto had lain undetected. A recent example is the development of weather derivatives by some banks in response to companies who identified a relationship between temperature and financial results.

MANAGEMENT OF FINANCIAL RISKS

There are a number of distinct steps in the management of financial risks:

- Identify financial risks within the organization.
- Measure these risks.
- Define the company's risk management policies, which will be enshrined in the company's treasury policies.
- Implement the financial risk management programme.
- Report on the progress of risk management.
- Periodically re-evaluate the whole management process.

Identification of financial risks

In most organizations the treasurer will generally know quite accurately those treasury financial risks to which the company is subject. He or she will either be involved in actively managing these risks, or equally there may be a number of financial risks that the company is aware of but has decided for one reason or another not to manage. In larger companies, where flows are more complex, or where the treasurer or finance director has just been appointed, a separate exercise may be required to identify and map treasury financial risks.

One common approach is to analyze the income statement and balance sheet on a line-by-line basis and identify those financial risks which apply to each line.

This analysis might be conducted as shown below.

Turnover

- To whom does the company sell and in what currency? Are customers price or quality sensitive? Do customers have access to alternative products? What are the standard terms of business?
- Where does the company sell? What is the proportion of domestic and international sales, and which currencies are sales made in? Are exchange controls operating in certain countries? Is there concentration of revenues in certain countries or industries, or is there a default risk of a significant customer?
- Where are the company's competitors based? In what currencies do they sell, and in what currencies do they buy? What is their hedging policy?

Cost of goods sold

- Where does the firm manufacture the goods it sells?
- What goes into what the firm makes or does? A production process may use substantial amounts of raw material or semi-finished goods that must be purchased overseas. Alternatively it may use commodities that fluctuate in price according to market conditions and are priced in a foreign currency such as US$.
- Where are the company's suppliers based? Do the suppliers invoice in their own currency or in the company's currency? If the latter, what financial risk is the company carrying? Do the suppliers use currency variation clauses?

Other general costs

- Does the company operate share option schemes? Do they represent an exposure?
- How significant is interest expense?
- Are premises, equipment or vehicles leased? Are the lease rental payments effectively fixed rate finance?

Balance sheet

- Are receivables concentrated in one or two large customers?
- Does the company provide significant amounts of financing to its customers?
- What currencies are its major assets and liabilities denominated in?
- What is the company's financial structure? What is the maturity profile of its debts? Which markets does it raise its finance in? Has the company issued convertible bonds or debt with warrants, and are they still outstanding?
- What is the fixed/floating structure of its debts?
- Does the company have cash on deposit?
- What is the currency denomination of receivables?

The above approach analyzes the profit and loss and balance sheet. Other approaches may be to identify key business drivers or business processes and analyze the financial risks inherent in those drivers or activities.

Mapping treasury-related financial risks

Once identified, the risks can be mapped as shown in Table 1.2.

Measurement of financial risk

One of the corporate treasurer's concerns is how to actually measure the exposures identified. A company may decide that interest rate risk and foreign exchange transaction and pre-transaction risks are its major treasury-related financial risks, but how do they quantify the size of these risks? This must be done before one can answer the next question: 'How significant are these risks?'

Table 1.2 Mapping treasury risks against profit and loss and balance sheet items

	Financing	*FX transactions*	*FX pre-transactions*	*FX translation*	*Commodity*	*Liquidity*	*Counter party*	*Interest rates*
Turnover		50% overseas sales US$, €, ¥	50% overseas sales US$, €, ¥					
Cost of sales		Purchases from €	Purchases from €		10% energy – electricity			
Admin., selling and interest				US$ revenues				30% fixed 70% floating
Assets				US$ assets		Cash deposits	Derivatives 3 major customers	
Liabilities	£1bn debts			US$ liabilities		Short-term liabilities	Derivatives	

Business planning process

The starting point for most organizations is the annual business planning process, which is usually followed by the budget process. A company with a year ending 31 December may have the following planning and budgeting timetable and process for managing the business.

Three year business plans completed and approved by board	31 August
Annual budget, related to the first year of the business plan, completed and approved by the board	31 November
Monthly reports comparing actual results against budget	Monthly
Reforecast budget	Twice a year (Period 5 and 9)
Rolling 12 month cash forecasts	Every three months

Three-year business plan

In many organizations this is very much a 'blue sky' approach. It consists of identifying the organization's strengths and weaknesses, the economic and business outlook it is likely to operate under, how it will respond to competitor actions, what its major risks and opportunities are. From an assessment of these and many other strategic factors, the company develops its business plan. This will summarize the markets it will operate in, which products or businesses it will develop and which it will sell or reduce, and how it will develop its business. Financial projections are prepared on the basis of the determined strategy, to ensure that the business plan delivers the necessary shareholder value and meets market expectations.

The financial projections normally consist of profit and loss accounts by operating division or subsidiary, together with balance sheets and cash-flows for each year of the business plan.

Annual budget

The annual budget often takes the financial projections for the first year of the business plan and turns them into a detailed financial budget, together with responsibilities for each line. Usually operating divisions/subsidiaries are accountable for achieving financial targets within the budget, such as profit before interest, cashflow and return on asset targets. In addition there may be qualitative targets that need to be achieved, such as like-for-like sales growth.

Some corporate departments may also have major budget responsibilities. The treasury department for example may have responsibility for achieving the rates inherent within the interest budget.

Monthly reports

Monthly reports are submitted by operating divisions or subsidiaries, comparing performance against budgets. These reports contain all the relevant variance analysis and action, together with remedial plans to correct shortfalls or adverse variances.

Forecasts

As the year progresses the actual results will vary from budget. At some point during the year the company will reforecast the remaining months of its budget to reflect these changes.

Basis of exposure identification

It is these financial projections, budgets and forecasts that the treasurer uses to identify the size of various financial risks. For instance, the three-year plan and annual budget will identify cashflows and hence borrowing requirements. The resulting borrowing requirements, when evaluated at assumed interest rates for the plan and budget, will produce planned and budgeted interest costs. The budget will identify overseas sales by currency, and purchases in foreign currencies, which will be used as the starting point for identifying pre-transaction exposure.

It is worth noting that actually measuring financial risks is often one of the more difficult aspects of risk management. Business is increasingly volatile; strategies decided today can quickly become obsolescent. Cashflows are often notoriously inaccurate due to swings in working capital and the timing of the capital expenditure programme. Sales by currency can in some cases be no more than an inspired guess on the part of sales department, let alone the timing of cash receipts from these sales.

Ranking of treasury-related financial risks

The most usual way of ranking treasury risks is by attempting to measure their scale and magnitude. Clearly only those risks that are significant or that might substantially impact on the achievement of an organization's strategy should be considered for active management. There are a number of ways an organization may attempt this measurement.

Notional change in rates or prices

This assesses the impact of a notional change in the market rate or price on the underlying risk. This assessment is often made by comparing the magnitude of such notional changes against a benchmark such as the underlying budget or forecast for the revenue, cost or balance sheet item.

For example, Company A has UK£500 million of borrowings, all at floating rate. It measures the risk of borrowing at a floating rate by assessing the impact of a 1 per cent increase in sterling interest rates: UK£5 million. Budgeted interest expense for the year is UK£27 million, and budgeted profit before tax is UK£100 million. Therefore a 1 per cent increase in interest rates would increase interest expense for the year by almost 20 per cent, and reduce profit before tax by 5 per cent.

The same approach can be applied to foreign exchange, commodity and equity risks, and other financial risks that are denominated by financial prices.

Mathematical techniques such as value at risk (VaR), cashflow at risk or earnings at risk

Simply put, VaR or other related techniques measure the possible adverse change in market value of a financial instrument, on the basis of what is regarded as the largest likely adverse move in rates or prices over a given timeframe. It also includes the correlation between different financial instruments to measure the volatility of a financial portfolio of instruments. These techniques have been adapted by some corporates to measure the significance of market-price-related financial risks.

Qualitative measurement

Not all financial risks are influenced by changes in market rates and prices. Examples of such risks are financing risk, bank relationships, counterparty risk and liquidity risk An organization may assess the significance of these risks by their impact on its strategic objectives should these exposures mature. For instance the prospect of being unable to raise long-term finance is likely to have significant implications for a company with an expansionary strategy involving substantial amounts of new finance.

Whatever the process or technique selected for measuring or assessing financial risk, it should be related to a company's overall risk management process (see page 20). There seems little point in spending large amounts of time and resources in refining risk measurement techniques in treasury, if more significant risks elsewhere in the organization can only be qualitatively assessed.

Establishing risk management policies

What should a company's policy be towards those financial risks that it has identified and measured? A company first needs to consider what its risk management objectives are. Is the organization risk averse or a risk taker? Is its objective to eliminate, as far as possible, all financial risks or are there certain risks it is accepting? If so, how large are they?

Influences on treasury policies

A company's attitude to risk will be influenced among other things by:

- Its corporate philosophy. Some organizations are naturally more cautious, conservative and prudent than others; they may not only try to manage a wider range of potential exposures, they may also manage these risks down to a lower level of exposure.
- Its financial structure and/or volatility of its cashflows. Arguably a company with high financial and operational gearing will be more conservative in its risk management and more risk averse than a company with lower financial and operational gearing, since small movements in financial market rates or prices can have a major negative impact on the former company's financial structure and viability.
- What its competitors do.
- The volatility of the business sector that it operates in. What does the financial community expect it to do regarding risk management?
- What its principal advisers tell it.
- The achievement of its corporate strategy. For instance, companies that have just embarked on a radical change in strategy that may involve acquisitions, disposals or a major capital expenditure programme will be reluctant to accept any risks that may adversely affect this new strategy.

- The size of its financial risks in relation to some benchmark such as the current year's budget or forecast, a 12-month rolling forecast or the three-year strategic plan.
- Natural hedges within its business.

Content of treasury policies

A company will need to determine which risks it wants to manage, the level to which it wants to manage those risks and what its risk management strategy will be. The resulting approach to financial risk management will be enshrined in its treasury risk policy. This will include statements defining:

- what its principal financial risks are
- what its objectives are in managing these risks
- who has responsibility for managing the risks
- what authority levels are and what instruments are authorized to be used
- what reports will be submitted and to whom.

The treasury risk policy will generally be approved by the main board.

Managing risks

Sometimes this is the easiest of all the steps in the risk management process. It is the step that involves the implementation of the treasury policy.

A company may, for instance, have examined and measured the various financial risks to which it is exposed and concluded that the interest expense on its borrowings is a major risk requiring management. Their resulting treasury policy may have established that between 30 and 50 per cent of their forecast borrowings over the next three years should be at fixed rates, with the objective of minimizing the impact of any unforeseen rise in interest rates. The management step involves:

- examining forecast borrowings over the next three years
- determining the level of those borrowings that are at fixed rate
- implementing any necessary hedges, where the level of fixed rate borrowings falls below the 30 per cent level

- making a further decision where the level of fixed rate borrowings is between 30 per cent and 50 per cent.

It should be noted that treasury risks are not always managed through the use of derivatives.

- It may be inappropriate to rely solely on derivative instruments (e.g. counterparty risk).
- Some risks may be netted out (e.g. purchases and sales in the same foreign currency).
- There may be a natural hedge against some risks. For example, a company with foreign currency receipts in two currencies may find that when one currency weakens against its domestic currency the other strengthens.
- Some risks may be altered (e.g. currency adjustment clauses).

It is likely however that substantial reliance will be placed on the use of derivatives, particularly those for managing movements in market prices or rates. It is worth mentioning that most corporates will try to identify other means of managing risks before using derivatives. Business and treasury risks can be very volatile, and risks that exist today may disappear tomorrow as a result of changes in a company's strategy. Derivative contracts however, once entered into, represent contractual obligations that a company may find expensive to cancel later on.

Reporting

A treasury department will need to report regularly on its the risk management process. Most treasury departments produce a monthly treasury report that summarizes:

- Financial exposures outstanding.
- Hedges in place. This may be further analyzed between those brought forward from the last report, those maturing this month/period and new hedges implemented.
- Sensitivity analysis.
- Recommendations as to action.

Some organizations use a treasury committee to review outstanding financial risks periodically. Members of the committee may be the treasurer, the finance director or chief financial officer, and perhaps the director of strategy. The objective of the committee is to bring a group perspective to bear on treasury risk management. Decisions on treasury risks will be made in the light of all risks currently being faced by the company, with the result that treasury risk management is put into the context of the overall company risk management.

Other organizations may just use periodic meetings between the treasurer and finance director to determine what further risk management action needs to be taken.

ENTERPRISE RISK MANAGEMENT

Outline

So far we have been considering risk management from the standpoint of the corporate treasurer, and the concept of financial risk that was used was that which the treasurer has responsibility for managing. In the 1990s the idea of managing risk throughout the organization was relatively new and most companies focused on specific, mainly financial and insurable risks.

Companies have come to pay particular attention to the management of risks throughout their organization due to a combination of: legal and compliance requirements on companies; the increasing need to communicate a company's risk management processes to various stakeholders; and a recognition of the benefits that an active, and corporate-wide, risk management programme can have on achieving the strategic aims of the organization and building shareholder value.

An assessment of the system of internal control is as relevant for the smaller listed company as it is for larger ones, since the risks facing such companies are generally increasing. Risk management is essential for reducing the probability that corporate objectives will be jeopardized by unforeseen events. It involves proactively managing those risk exposures that can affect everything the company is trying to achieve.

A poll of some 200 chief financial officers, treasurers and risk managers conducted in the United States found that more than 75 per cent of the respondents indicated that a major disruption would have a dramatic impact on their companies' earnings or even threaten their business continuity. According to the study, respondents were most worried about property-related hazards such as natural disasters, fires/explosions, terrorism/sabotage/theft, mechanical/electrical breakdowns and service disruptions. More than a third of the respondents believed that their companies' senior management team lacked a complete understanding of what would happen to their companies' earnings and shareholder value if an interruption occurred.

Among the steps involved in implementing and maintaining an effective risk management system are:

- identifying risks
- ranking those risks
- agreeing control strategies and risk management policy
- taking action
- regular monitoring
- regular reporting and review of risk and control.

As can be seen, the process for managing risks on an enterprise-wide basis is essentially the same as that established by the treasurer for managing treasury-related financial risks.

Identifying risks

Risks are often classified into: business, operational, financial and compliance risks.

Business risks

These arise from being in a particular industry and geographical area, and from the strategy the company has chosen to undertake. The risks can range from wrong business strategy, bad or failed acquisitions and inability to obtain further capital, to competitive pressures on price and market share, political risks or the decline of an industry sector.

Operational risks

These relate to the various administrative and operational procedures that the business uses to implement its strategy. They may include skills shortages, stock-out of raw materials, physical disasters, loss of physical assets, quality problems, loss of key contracts or poor brand management.

Financial risks

In addition to those already discussed in relation to treasury risk management, financial risks can also comprise: going concern problems, overtrading, misuse of financial resources, occurrence of fraud, misstatement risk relating to published financial information, unrecorded liabilities and penetration of IT systems by hackers.

Compliance risks

These derive from the necessity to ensure compliance with those laws and regulations that, if infringed, can damage a company. They can include breach of listing rules, breach of Companies Act requirements, VAT problems, tax penalties, health and safety risks and environmental problems.

In identifying risks, it is important to avoid selecting them from some form of generic list. The risks need to be specific to the industry sector and specific circumstances of the company. It is also useful to relate them to the likely obstacles facing the critical success factors that underpin the achievement of the company's objectives.

Quantifying and ranking risks

As with the measurement of treasury-related financial risks, the company is faced with the problem of quantifying or measuring the identified risks. While many treasury financial risks relate to movement in market prices and thus the possible impact of adverse price movements within certain ranges can be calculated, many of the identified enterprise risks are incapable of such direct measurement. Most organizations therefore rank such risks according to:

- High likelihood of occurrence–high impact: Consider for immediate action.
- Low likelihood of occurrence–high impact: Consider for action and have a contingency plan.
- High likelihood of occurrence–low impact: Consider action.

- Low likelihood of occurrence–low impact: Keep under periodic review.

The impacts should be considered not merely in financial terms, but more importantly in terms of their potential effect on the achievement of the company's objectives.

Agreeing control strategies

Various methods can be used to deal with risks identified and ranked. The directors need to ask the following:

- Do we wish to accept the risk?
- What is the control strategy for avoiding or mitigating the risk?
- What is the residual risk remaining after the application of controls?
- What is the early warning system?

Generally there are four main ways of dealing with risks:

- Accept them. Some risks may be inherent to the business (e.g. economic risks or volatility), and investors may actively have sought securities reflecting them. In addition there may be some cases when the costs of managing risks are greater than the benefits from risk reduction.
- Transfer them. This is usually done through insurance or derivatives.
- Reduce or manage them by improving controls within existing processes; for example by improving production control techniques to reduce the likelihood of stock-out of raw materials.
- Eliminate them, generally through the pursuit of existing strategies. For instance, the risk of market share pressures may be handled through an existing strategy of repositioning products and expanding the product range.

Taking action and reporting

Not only does the agreed action need to be taken but a regular reporting procedure needs to be put in place. In a small organization, responsibility for this may be delegated to the finance director or chief executive, but in larger organizations this role is likely to be undertaken by a risk management committee, led by senior executives or board directors.

Implications for the treasurer

What implications does an organization-wide risk management system and process have for the treasurer? It can be seen that the steps adopted in such a process are essentially the same as those adopted by the treasurer in identifying and managing risks within the scope of the treasury department. The treasurer's risk management routines will in most organizations be part of the organization-wide risk management routines. Treasury risks and action to identify, measure, manage and report them need to be set within the framework of corporate-wide risk management.

CHAPTER 2

Treasury Policies for Debt, Foreign Exchange and Interest Rate Exposure Management

INTRODUCTION

The previous chapter discussed how treasury policies flow from the identification and measurement of a company's principal treasury-related financial risks. This chapter starts with a further discussion of these risks as they relate to debt management, interest and foreign exchange risk. It covers such questions as: 'What factors determine a company's treasury policies?' 'How does a company establish treasury policies?' 'What should periodic treasury reports look like?' and 'What information should they contain?'

DEBT MANAGEMENT

The objective of debt management is to ensure that a company has adequate finance to fund its strategic plans and achieve its overall business objectives. The role of treasury policies for debt management is to establish a number of prudential rules, whose purpose is to ensure that the company always has access to the widest possible range of debt markets at the best possible price.

These debt management policies, as with all other treasury policies, will reflect a number of qualitative factors surrounding the company's business.

They will include: the company's strategic aims and objectives, the likely cashflows being generated by the business and the present and forecast volumes of debt, and the risk profile of the business, that is, the extent to which its future is accurately forecastable. Whilst debt policies may vary from company to company, they will have a number of common themes.

Loan maturity profile

A treasurer will always be concerned to ensure that re-financing risk is minimized. This can find expression in a number of ways.

Some projects are financed on a stand-alone basis with each individual project being separately financed. In such a situation the treasurer will attempt to ensure that the repayment profile of the loan package that finances a specific project will match the cashflow profile of that project and that the loan only starts to become repayable once the project starts to generate cash. Companies managing such projects may be those involved in major infrastructure projects where a selection of projects may be financed 'on balance sheet'.

Very few companies however are in such a situation. Most have a whole portfolio of projects, each one having its own specific cashflow profile. To finance each project separately is impractical, since the projects are too small and too numerous. Such companies therefore have to establish a number of prudential rules to ensure that re-financing risk is minimized, and that loans are capable of being re-financed from available free cashflow.

Such rules are designed to ensure that re-financing of existing debt in any one year is kept to 'manageable' proportions and that loans do not fall due for repayment when the company's free cash flow is forecast to be negative or when substantial incremental finance is already being raised to finance new projects. To this end most treasurers try to maintain a relatively smooth maturity profile of their loan portfolio – that is, an even proportion of the loans are due for re-finance on a year-by-year basis. This spreads the burden of re-financing over a period of time. Should any of the debt markets that the treasurer had identified as appropriate be unavailable, another market can be selected without too great an impact on the company's cost of finance or loan structure.

Debt markets

Many companies are faced with a wide range of debt markets from which they can finance themselves. However, the appetite for providing finance from these individual markets can change from time to time. When they do change, a treasurer may find that the availability of finance in any particular market is severely restricted or the price of that finance increases significantly.

The appetite to provide finance is often also linked to scarcity. Lenders are often more enthusiastic to provide finance to a company if they have no exposure to that company already and the company is a strong credit. In managing their portfolios, debt investors will want to ensure they have a broad exposure to a wide range of business sectors, and within each sector to a wide range of individual companies. They want to avoid their portfolios showing excessive exposure to any one sector or company. This spreading of risk prevents the consequent losses that can follow if there is a downturn in one of the business sectors or one of the companies goes into default. Consequently, treasurers need to ensure that they do not over-utilize individual debt markets, otherwise when market liquidity becomes tighter they may find themselves shut out of certain markets, or their cost of funds may rise significantly.

Treasurers will finance their companies through the widest possible range of markets so as to ensure, first, that when they need to undertake a financing they get the best possible reception and terms, and second, that whatever the state of individual debt markets they can always obtain adequate finance.

'Headroom'

A company's need for finance is never static. Continual requirements for finance can arise as a result of:

- the need to effect small to medium acquisitions (often referred to as bolt-on acquisitions)
- an ongoing capital expenditure programme that cannot be financed from existing free cashflow.
- fluctuations in working capital.

The principal aspect of these financing requirements is that the amount of finance required is comparatively small, in the sense that it is impractical to finance them separately. Companies usually decide to keep financial resources to meet these incremental changes in the requirements of finance. These resources can be in the form of cash balances, but more frequently are in the form of the unutilized portion of committed revolving facilities provided by banks. (A committed bank facility is a facility where the bank has an obligation to provide finance up to the level of their commitment during the life of the facility. For instance, a syndicate of banks providing a five-year revolving facility to a corporate for US$500 million is obligated to provide funds up to the facility amount for the five-year period. Many companies cope with the requirement for 'headroom' by establishing facilities for more than their forecast needs. Thus the company may forecast needs of US$400 million, but establish a facility for US$500 million to give US$100 million 'headroom'. Committed revolving facilties and the establishment of 'headroom'are explained in more detail in Chapter 4.)

Equally companies can find that they have unplanned inflows of cash as a result of sales of assets and of fluctuations in working capital. Committed bank facilities that can be drawn upon when required and paid down when cash inflow is positive add flexibility to a company's financial structure.

Currency

Translation exposure has been discussed in Chapter 1 (and see pages 32–4). Many companies handle their translation risk by maintaining a certain level of loans in the currency of their overseas assets. The decision to handle translation risk in this manner may have an implication for planning the loan capital structure. The currency question is usually handled by either the use of currency swaps or the ability to draw advances denominated in foreign currencies under bank facilities.

Other matters

It may be that a treasurer considers it relevant to incorporate other issues into the debt management policies. These items will usually be specific to the company for which the treasurer works, or be an issue on which the board has particularly strong opinions. Examples are described below.

Security

Generally, when a borrower provides security it results in a lower cost of finance (although for companies with a very high credit rating this is not always the case). This is because the provider of finance has a fixed charge over specific assets, or a floating charge over a group of assets, and hence has priority over unsecured creditors in the event of a liquidation. The assets used for providing security are generally those regarded as being easily realizable at or close to their current book value. The usual examples of such assets are freehold land and buildings. The other aspect of such finance is that assets are generally 'overcollaterallized'; in other words, the value of assets charged are more than the value of the loan.

Some companies have balance sheets rich in such asset types: typically property, high street retailers, hotel and leisure companies. While it is natural for such companies to provide security for long-term loans they will always want to put an upper limit to the proportion of assets so charged. This ensures that their ability to sell and trade these assets is not hindered.

Covenants

Does the company have any specific attitude to covenants within its loan documents? Companies might sometimes specify the financial covenants they are prepared to provide or the maximum level at which these covenants can be pitched. For example, a company may specify that the only financial covenant that it will provide will be one related to interest cover, and that the maximum such covenant that it will provide is that interest cover will exceed three times (see Chapter 3). Other companies may specify that 'carve outs' are needed to enable them to issue secured debt, while others may wish to specify the extent to which parent company support will be available to support finance raised at subsidiary company level.

Guarantees

The provision of guarantees is a utilization of the company's financial resources in much the same way as a borrowing. Providers of finance will take note of the amount of contingent liabilities outstanding and will adjust the level or price of the loans they are providing if these levels are significant. For some organizations the provision of guarantees is a related aspect of the business sector they operate in; for example, construction companies have to provide performance bonds for specific contracts. Treasurers of such companies will probably want to design specific policies relating to guarantees; for instance the circumstances when guarantees are provided, who authorizes the guarantees, clauses that are acceptable and those that are unacceptable.

FOREIGN EXCHANGE RISK MANAGEMENT

Transaction exposure

Foreign exchange transaction risk was defined in Chapter 1 as covering those situations where a clear obligation to make, or a right to receive, a payment in a foreign currency has arisen. The exposure spans the period from the obligation or right arising to the final payment or receipt of the foreign currency. The exposure exists because the amount payable or receivable in domestic currency will fluctuate over the exposure period with movements in foreign exchange rates. For example, a Hong Kong company may purchase goods from an Australian supplier and pay that supplier in AU$. From the point at which the obligation to make a payment in respect of a specific purchase from the Australian company arises (say on the placing of an order) to the point at which the supplier is paid for those goods in AU$, the HK$ equivalent of the payment will fluctuate in accordance with movements in the AU$/HK$ exchange rate.

Transaction exposure is usually:

- Revenue in nature. The effects of foreign exchange movements flow straight through to the profit and loss account.
- Cash in nature. Foreign exchange movements are represented by reductions or increases in cash payments or receipts in domestic currency terms.
- Often short term in nature. The time period from the point at which the exposure arises to the point at which it is extinguished is comparatively brief. (For many organizations, however, such as pharmaceutical, aerospace or construction companies, it is worth mentioning that transaction exposures can extend over many months, or in some cases years.)

Transaction exposures often arise from the following:

- Purchases or sales of goods or services in a foreign currency.
- Royalties, management fees or licence fees, where these are payable or receivable in a foreign currency.
- Purchase of capital items (fixed assets) denominated in a foreign currency.
- Dividends on overseas investments, interest on loans payable or receivable in foreign currencies.

Identification and measuring of transaction exposure

One of the challenges facing the treasurer is to identify and measure the scale and timing of transaction exposures. Measuring transaction exposure consists of identifying the following elements:

- Whether the obligation is to make or receive a foreign currency payment. (Where there is an obligation to make a payment this is a short position; where there is a right to receive a payment it is a long position.)
- The currency in which payment is due to be made or received.
- The foreign currency amount of the payment or receipt.
- The timing of the payment or receipt.

There may often be differences of opinion as to when a transaction exposure arises. In the case of the sale of a product to an overseas customer that is invoiced in a foreign currency, does the exposure arise when the order is received from the overseas customer and the company acknowledges its receipt; does it arise when the goods are actually shipped; or does it arise when the invoice is raised and dispatched? Different companies will have different opinions.

Some companies may go even further and consider that the publication of a price list gives rise to transaction exposure. While there may be currency adjustment clauses in a holiday brochure, actually activating those clauses may be something a company is unwilling to do, particularly if the market is very competitive and major competitors have not changed their prices.

The larger the company and the more complex its international flows, the more challenging it is to identify transaction risk as early as possible and then quantify its size. The ability to identify transaction exposures at a very early stage in the order cycle often depends on the systems used by the company. Larger companies tend to have more sophisticated systems and the development and implementation of enterprise resource planning (ERP) systems – by linking order processing, stock control, production and logistics with information that is recorded in finance – has helped to improve control over the identification of many types of transaction exposure. In many organizations these systems are also linked to their customers through electronic data interchange (EDI) or some other electronic link.

Pre-transaction exposure

Pre-transaction risk represents foreign exchange exposures that exist before entering into the commercial contract that will turn them into transactional exposures. Take, for instance, the case of a dividend receivable from an overseas investment; until it has been finally declared, the amount and timing of the dividend can only be anticipated. Up to that point, it remains a pre-transaction exposure. The forecast sale of a product to overseas customers remains pre-transactional until an order has been received, or the goods shipped or an invoice dispatched.

Identifying pre-transaction exposures can be even more difficult than transaction exposure. Very often the sales or purchasing departments cannot know in advance the exact timing of overseas sales or purchases. These dates will continually change as the status of orders changes. In addition, the departments will often be unable to identify the exact quantity of the sales or purchases, which again may be subject to continual change until the final orders are received or dispatched. The further out in time the forecast goes, the more imprecise the data becomes. For instance, amounts receivable in respect of royalties, licences and management fees can only be estimated on the basis of information received on sales to date. Future sales to overseas customers may be susceptible to broad forecasting, but these forecasts may become very inaccurate when analyzed by currency.

The starting point for identifying pre-transaction foreign exchange risk is very often the annual budget. Depending on the detail with which the budget has been prepared, it contains the company's forecast of receipts and costs in foreign currencies for the year ahead. As the financial year progresses the company will need to update the budget with 'rolling forecasts'. These update the budget to reflect changes in the company's business, and will also produce forecasts of foreign currency income and costs for periods outside the current budget period. For example, many companies employ a system of 12-month rolling forecasts. After say, six months of the existing financial year have passed the budget will be updated for the remaining six months of the financial year, and in addition forecasts will be produced for the first six months of the next financial year. Together they produce a new 12-month forecast of foreign currency receipts and payments.

Translation risk

Translation exposure is the risk that the domestic book currency value of assets and liabilities denominated in a foreign currency will alter due to movements in exchange rates. Translation risk arises when these assets and liabilities are converted to the domestic currency and consolidated in the company's group accounts. The assets and liabilities in domestic currency terms will vary between two accounting dates, partly as a result of exchange rate movements. Not only will asset and liability values be affected but so will the profit or loss for the year. The impact of changing exchange rates on the conversion of foreign currency assets and liabilities and profit of overseas subsidiaries was explained in Chapter 1.

Most companies manage translation exposure by borrowing in the currency in which overseas assets are denominated. Using the example in Chapter 1, we find the situation outlined in Table 2.1 below.

In this example, the effect of matching US$ assets with borrowings in US$ has been to offset the movement in foreign currency *assets* when they are converted to domestic currency with the movement in the foreign currency *borrowings* when these are converted to domestic currency. Any movement in the domestic value of foreign currency assets will be offset by movements in foreign currency borrowings when these are converted to

Table 2.1 Example of translation risk

	US$ million	*UK£ million @ 1.60*	*UK£ million @ 1.50*
Gross assets	1 000	625	667
Liabilities	250	156	167
Net Assets	750	469	500
		@1.55	@1.45
Net profit after tax	150	97	103

If the company matched its US$ assets with US$ borrowings, the effect of foreign exchange movements would be as follows:

	US$	*UK£ @ 1.60*	*UK£ @ 1.50*
Net assets	750	469	500
Borrowings in US$	750	469	500
		@1.55	@1.45
Net profit	150	97	103
US$ interest expense	19	12.3	13.1

the domestic currency. To a much lesser extent, the impact on the net profit of changing exchange rates is offset by the change in the US$ interest expense when that is converted to UK£.

Many treasurers believe that translation risk is not an exposure that requires hedging, since the economic worth of a company cannot be affected by movements in the book value of assets. However, while these movements are only 'paper' movements, they may at times have economic consequences for the company:

- Such movements may affect covenants in loan agreements that are based on net worth or interest cover.
- Reported earnings may be affected by foreign exchange movements. The company believes that changes in reported earnings will have some impact on its share price.
- The overseas asset may some day be disposed of and any gain or loss may be 'crystallized'.

Economic exposure

Economic exposure is the risk that future foreign currency cashflows generated by a company will vary in terms of its local currency equivalent. It can be regarded as the impact that exchange rate movements may have on a company's future cashflows. There are a number of situations in which economic exposure may arise.

- Exposure of a pre-transactional nature can extend for a substantial period into the future. One example might be an engineering company based in the United States, selling its goods into Europe and invoicing its customers in euros. Its local currency (US$) will be affected by the €/US$ exchange rate for as long as that trade continues. (While companies often manage pre-transaction exposure extending 12 to 18 months into the future, they often do not go beyond that period.)
- A price list may be issued in the company's domestic economy where goods or merchandise are imported, or may be denominated in a foreign currency in an export market.
- Bid to tender. Once a bid for a contract has been submitted, a company may be exposed until that bid has been accepted or rejected if there is a foreign currency component to the bid.

- A company's local currency cashflows may be affected by the foreign exchange rates of other currencies. In Chapter 1 the example was given of a hotel company whose business was affected by the movements in its local currency and the US$. These currency movements may make its room rates more expensive or cheaper than those of hotels in other countries, depending on the US$ exchange rate with the currency of these countries.

In many cases the distinction between transaction, pre-transaction and economic exposure can be rather blurred. Many treasurers may consider that bid to tender or the issue of a price list belong to the pre-transaction element of foreign exchange risk. The important thing however is that the company considers all risks to which it is exposed and whether they can and should be managed.

Treasury policies for foreign exchange risk

In designing treasury policies to cover foreign exchange, a company will have in mind a number of specific issues relating to its business. Some of these issues are outlined below.

Accuracy of exposure identification

How accurately can the company identify its transaction and pre-transaction exposure? Some companies where there is a consistent trade may be able to calculate pre-transaction exposure by examining sales or purchase volumes from the past and extrapolating these into the future. Companies whose overseas trade is more discrete may be unable to forecast future exposures so accurately.

Natural hedges

Does the company have any natural hedges? For instance, a mining company that sells most of its output on the world markets in US$ may have identified that when the US$ is weak versus their domestic currency, the demand for their commodity-type products is stronger.

A company importing French or German wine may find that, if the euro strengthens versus their domestic currency, wines from other regions such as the United States, Australia or New Zealand can be substituted. This is because the company's customers have a price target for the wine they purchase as opposed to a regional preference.

Ability to pass on price increases

Increasingly, in a competitive world with the emphasis on cost reduction, the ability to even consider passing on price increases becomes less relevant. However, there may be circumstances where cost increases or income reductions due to foreign exchange movements can be recouped through the selling price.

Volatility of currencies

The more volatile the currencies in which it invoices overseas customers or is invoiced by overseas suppliers, then the more likely a company is to take a conservative and cautious approach to hedging overseas foreign currency receipts and payments.

Significance of FX in costs and revenues

The more significant FX is in a company's cost and revenue structure, the more concerned the company will be to adequately manage all FX exposures.

INTEREST RATE RISK MANAGEMENT

Introduction

Interest rate risk management, as explained in Chapter 1, is the extent to which a company's interest expense may increase due to increases in interest rates, or income from cash balances (if these are significant) will be reduced by falling rates.

It is important to note that over the past few years interest rates have consistently fallen around the world. Many companies that locked in their interest expense at what they considered to be low levels have been left with a much higher interest expense than if they had ignored interest rate exposure. Companies now recognize that interest rate exposure is not just the effect of increasing interest rates on their interest costs, but also the opportunity cost of falling or stable interest rates when they lock in their interest cost.

In the case of interest rates the risk management policy will be determined by such things as:

- The level of financial gearing within the financial structure. Generally, the higher the level of financial gearing, then the more conservative the company's approach to interest rate risk management. When financial gearing is high, movements in interest rates can have a significant impact on earnings and cashflow.

- The volatility of the organization's cashflows. Again the more volatile these cashflows, the more a company is likely to want to operate with the interest rate fixed on a higher proportion of its borrowings.
- The level of operational gearing (the level of fixed costs in its operations).
- The importance of achieving the company's determined strategy.
- The nature of any natural hedges. Some companies, such as retailers, find that when interest rates are high in the interest rate cycle, their businesses do comparatively well. This is because these higher interest rates are designed to restrain consumer expenditure and the inflationary impact that this may have, but this buoyant consumer expenditure has benefits for the retailer.

The more volatile a company's cashflows, and the higher the level of its financial or operational gearing, then generally, the higher the level of fixed interest rates the company will want to operate with.

Usually, a company's treasury policies will establish a band within which the organization will want to manage the ratio of its fixed/floating interest costs. A policy may, for instance, state that between 30 and 50 per cent of the next three years' projected borrowings should be at fixed rates. Companies normally establish a band to cater for the volatility in the level of actual borrowings against those planned.

Identifying exposures

In most organizations the starting point for measuring interest rate risk is the annual budget and a three (or five) year business plan. The financial numbers that are put together to support the business plan and the budget will establish the cashflows, levels of borrowing and resultant interest rate cost for the relevant periods. This interest cost will normally be calculated on a currency by currency basis.

In most organizations the annual budget is prepared after the business plans have been agreed. If the company operates with three-year business plans, then the budget when it is prepared normally reflects the first year of the business plan and replaces that year. The three-year business plan then becomes: year one the budget, years two and three the business plan.

CASE STUDY

Identifying selected financial risk at IDI

The following case study is intended to be illustrative of the steps involved in identifying, measuring, setting policies for, managing and reporting on financing, foreign exchange and interest rate risk.

Introduction

International Dynamic Industries (IDI) is based in the UK and manufactures and supplies high-quality components to the aircraft and defence industries. The company sells to customers in approximately 20 countries around the world. Their principal competitors are local manufacturers based in the countries in which they sell, but they have one major international competitor based in United States.

Sales

Manufacturing is undertaken primarily at plants in the United Kingdom, United States and Taiwan. In addition to this the company operates a number of warehousing units as well as sales offices. The plants supply their own geographical region: the UK plants supply the UK and European customers, US plants supply North America, and the plant in Taiwan supplies the Far East. The company supplies customers either:

- Directly from the manufacturing plants.
- From warehousing operations.
- Via sales operations. The deliveries are direct to customers, with the manufacturing plants invoicing the sales unit who then invoice the customer.

Deliveries to customers are made against contracts. These contracts are at a fixed price and payment is usually received 50 per cent on receipt of the contract and 50 per cent 90 days after the conclusion of the contract. Most contracts are for periods up to six months; that is to say, deliveries are made over a six-month period against contract specifications. All overseas sales are invoiced in foreign currencies; thus sales from the plant in Taiwan to a customer in Singapore will be invoiced in SG$. Approximately 35 per cent of sales are to overseas customers.

Global sales are shown in Table 2.2.

Table 2.2 IDI global sales

	Actual UK£ million Y/E 31/12/2002
UK	600
Europe	500
North America	700
Australia, Japan and Far East	500
	2300

Supplies

Most raw material and semi-finished components are sourced within the country where the manufacturing plant is situated. The exceptions are the United Kingdom, where some supplies are sourced from Germany, and Taiwan, where some supplies are sourced from Japan. All these supplies are invoiced in foreign currency. Details are shown in Table 2.3.

Table 2.3 IDI supply costs

	Estimated UK£ million Y/E 31/12/2002
Germany	50
Japan	25
	75

In addition there is a certain amount of trade among the company's operating subsidiaries.

Capital Employed and Profitability for year end 31/12/2002

Table 2.4 gives details of IDI's assets and profits.

Table 2.4 IDI assets and profits

	Assets UK£ million	*Profits before interest and tax UK£ million*
UK	900	130
North America	800	115
Far East	600	75
	2300	**320**

Loan capital

At 31 December 2002 the repayment details of the loans were as shown in Table 2.5. The revolving credit facility is UK£1 billion.

Approximately 40 per cent of the loan capital – the Eurobond and the leases – is at fixed rates. The weighted average rate of these fixed rate borrowings is 7.0 per cent. The company has one financial covenant in its loan documentation: *Earnings before interest, tax and dividends and amortization (EBITDA)/net interest must exceed 3.5 times.*

Risk philosophy

The company has a conservative attitude to risk. It also operates in a business sector with a pronounced cyclicality, as a result of which earnings and cashflow can be volatile.

Strategy

The company has recently undertaken a major acquisition by acquiring a company based in the United States. The objectives of the acquisition are:

Table 2.5 IDI loan repayments

		UK£ million 31/12/2002
Bank debt – revolving credit	Matures 30/9/2004	900
Eurobond	Matures 31/12/2005	400
Financial leases	Amortising to 31/8/2006	200
		1500

- To expand its product range. The company can now supply a complete product range and is the world's leading supplier.
- Establish a manufacturing and major sales and marketing presence in the United States, one of the most significant markets for its products.

The company considers that a key element in successfully implementing its strategy is a tight control over its cost base. In addition, since the acquisition was greeted with some scepticism by the markets, the company considers it imperative to meet and exceed the market expectations for its financial results.

Question

Design the company's treasury policies covering debt management, foreign exchange and interest rate risk (the summary financial results are given overleaf).

INTERNATIONAL DYNAMIC INDUSTRIES

SUMMARY FINANCIAL RESULTS

YEAR ENDING 31 DECEMBER 2002

Profit and loss	*UK£ million*
Turnover	2300
Cost of sales	1340
	960
Distribution and administrative expenses	640
Profit on ordinary activities before interest	320
Interest	95
Profit after interest	225
Taxation	40
	185
Balance sheet	
Fixed assets	1900
Current assets less current liabilities	400
Net debt	(1500)
Net Assets	800
Cash flow	
Net cash flow from operating activities	420
Servicing of finance and taxation	(105)
Capital expenditure and acquisitions	(150)
Cash flow before financing and dividends	165
Note:	
Depreciation	80
Maintenance capital expenditure	105

SOLUTION

Financing risk

- The company operates with a relatively high level of financial gearing. For the year ended 31 December 2002:
  EBITDA/net debt = 0.27
  EIBTDA/interest = 4.2 times
  Free cashflow/net debt = 0.14
  Note: EBITDA is calculated profit before interest plus depreciation. Free cashflow is calculated as cashflow from operations less maintenance capital less servicing of finance and taxation.
- 60 per cent of its loan structure is represented by a revolving credit facility provided by banks. In addition, the financial leases may well be with banks. The company is therefore exposed on the re-financing of these facilities.
- Currently there is only UK£100 million of available headroom under its revolving facility.

Interest rate risk

Interest rate risk is one of the significant financial risks identified by the company.

- The interest cover ratio in their loan documents is a minimum EBITDA/interest of 3.5 times. Prudentially however, the company's target is to get back to a minimum of five times cover. EBITDA(320+80)/interest (95) was 4.2 for the year to 31 December 2002 and is forecast to be 4.5 times for the next financial year. Should interest costs move adversely by more than UK£9 million, this cover will reduce to below four times. Such a movement represents only a 1 per cent movement in interest rates.
- Control over interest cost is critical to achieve the financial results anticipated by the market. The company forecast pre-tax results next year of UK£250 million.

Foreign exchange exposures

The process for analyzing the foreign exchange risks facing the company is very similar to that used to analyze interest rate risk.

Transaction risk

This would normally be considered to arise when the contracts are signed. Since payment is made 50 per cent on signature of the contract, the major exposure is for the remaining 50 per cent, which is payable 90 days after completion of the contract or order. Since contracts normally extend over six months, the exposure period is approximately nine months.

At any one time, the exposure to foreign exchange movements is broadly:

Total sales	UK£2300 million
Of which, 35 per cent are sales in foreign currencies	UK£805 million
The exposure on each contract lasts nine months, so on average the exposure on each contract outstanding at any one point in time is 4.5 months	UK£805x 4.5/12 =302million
Amount receivable in foreign currency in respect of current outstanding contracts	UK£302 x 50 per cent = 151 million
A further offset is the fact that some sourcing is done overseas. Since each contract lasts approximately six months, at any one time approximately 50 per cent of the annual projects are being worked on. Annual overseas sourcing is UK£75 million, and thus a broad offset to the above.	UK£75 x 50 per cent = 37 million
(This is very much the maximum offset however, since the currency of receivables may not be offset by the currency of payables)	

A 5 per cent movement in foreign exchange rates could therefore affect cashflow and reported earnings by between UK£7.5 million and UK£5.8

million. This represents approximately 3 per cent of profits before taxation, and over 3 per cent of free cashflow. Offsetting this is the fact that the exposures would be in a range of different currencies. A strengthening in one currency of exposure may be offset by a weakening in another.

Pre-transaction risk

This is a more difficult area for the company to assess. At any one time the company may be in negotiation to conclude a number of different contracts or orders. These negotiations may take many weeks to conclude. Much depends on its ability to adjust the contract price to reflect any foreign exchange movements before the contract is finally signed.

However, budgets and forecasts that the company is working to achieve will be based upon some assumption of sales by country by currency, and of exchange rate levels. To this extent the company may consider that it has pre-transaction exposure that it wishes to manage. The ability to hedge pre-transaction risk also depends on the extent to which the company can forecast sales by currency with any accuracy.

Translation risk

The UK-based company has 60 per cent of its net assets and 60 per cent of its profits before interest and tax being earned from overseas operations. A 5 per cent movement in foreign exchange rates against the UK£ would therefore have a significant impact on reported earnings and on capital employed.

Treasury policies covering the above exposures

The following could be an extract from IDI's treasury policies:

> ***Debt management***
>
> *Objectives of debt management*
>
> The objectives of debt management policies are to ensure a continued availability of funds to finance its strategic aims at the lowest cost.
>
> *Debt profile*
>
> The group's objective is to maintain a smooth maturity profile to its

outstanding long-term debt. To achieve this the company will observe the following:

- No more than 30 per cent of the group's long-term debt shall be re-financeable within the following 12-month period.
- No more than 50 per cent of the group's debt shall be re-financeable within the following three years.
- No more than 75 per cent of the group's debt shall be due for repayment within seven years.

Sources of debt

To prevent excessive exposure to one debt market the company will try to finance itself in the widest number of markets practicable. In particular, bank finance shall not represent more than 50 per cent of outstanding debt while outstanding debt is more than UK£1 billion. In meeting this target the company will use the following instruments: private placement, Eurobonds and medium-term notes.

Headroom

To ensure there are always sufficient financial resources available to meet the capital expenditure programme, small acquisitions and fluctuations in working capital, the company will always maintain sufficient unutilized committed finance to meet the monthly forecast or budgeted cash outflow before financing for the next 12 months, plus further headroom of UK£100 million. If these cashflows are positive, then available headroom will not be less than UK£100 million.

Foreign exchange

Objectives of foreign exchange management

The objectives of hedging foreign exchange exposures are:

- To protect the projected profit and cash generated from customers' contracts and orders from foreign exchange movements.

- To provide some measure of stability to budgeted and forecast earnings where these have been based on sales contracts and orders being awarded at specific exchange rates. This recognizes that the company operates in a competitive environment and has limited immediate ability to adjust pricing on overseas contracts and orders in response to a change in foreign exchange rates.
- To ensure that interest cover, one of the major measures of the company's borrowing capacity, remains broadly similar by currency.

Transaction exposure

- All contracts/orders invoiced in foreign currencies must be hedged back into the domestic currency at the point at which these contracts are awarded. Contracts and orders are awarded at the point at which signed authorized orders and contracts are received from a customer.
- All purchases from foreign suppliers must be hedged into the domestic currency as soon as the liability is established. Liabilities are established once authorized orders are dispatched, either electronically or by mail, to the supplier.
- Payments and receipts in the same currency must be netted in establishing the currency exposures above, including currency-denominated interest costs.

Pre-transaction exposure

Estimates of foreign currency receipts (sales to foreign customers that have not yet been converted to contracts) may be covered or hedged as follows:

50 per cent for estimated sales over the next six months

25 per cent of estimated sales covering the period 6–12 months.

Cover can only be taken where there is a consistent underlying sales trend in that particular currency. No cover may be taken for estimated sales beyond 12 months without specific approval of the Finance Director or Main Board.

Translation exposure

The company will match overseas assets with relevant foreign currency borrowings. In establishing the relevant level of foreign currency borrowings to match an overseas asset, regard will be had to the level of total borrowings, and the proportion that the overseas asset bears to total assets. For example if euro-denominated assets are 25 per cent of total assets, then 25 per cent of total borrowings will be in euros.

Interest rate risk

The objective of the interest rate risk policy is to enable the company to achieve a high level of confidence that any increases in interest rates will not adversely affect the achievement of its strategic and financial objectives.

Short-term interest rate risk

The company may take out interest rate hedges for up to 100 per cent of forecast net interest expense risk for the following rolling 12 months. Treasury is authorized to take out these hedges without prior reference to the risk committee.

Long-term interest rate risk

Between 40 per cent and 70 per cent of forecast net interest rate risk over the following four years may be hedged, and between 40 per cent and 25 per cent of net interest rate risk for the following four years.

Authorized instruments

In managing interest rate and foreign exchange exposure the treasury team may use the following instruments:

- forward rate agreements
- interest rates swaps
- interest rate caps

- forward FX
- foreign currency options.

Certain exotic derivatives such as barrier options or digital options can only be used with the express agreement of the treasury committee. Exotic options should not consist of more than 20 per cent of outstanding derivative hedges.

The company does not believe that combinations of derivatives such as interest rates collars add significant value to the hedging process and their use is forbidden unless authorized by the treasury committee.

Reports

Reports are designed to show how treasury activities are aligned to implementing treasury policies. Among the reports produced are:

- debt management
- headroom within banking facilities
- maturity profile of the company's debt
- analysis of debt source.

Interest rate risk

Total net borrowings analyzed by fixed or floating borrowings: Borrowings are further analyzed between fixed and floating rate borrowings by month/period, by currency over a rolling 12-month period and year-by-year for the next three years.

Hedges in place: Hedges are analyzed by derivative by month/period over a rolling 12 months and year-by-year for the next three years. Derivative hedges are further analyzed by notional derivative amount and by average strike rate or fixed rate under the derivatives:

Foreign exchange risk

- transaction exposures analyzed by period by currency

- hedges in place against transaction exposure by period by currency
- reasons for the non-hedging of any transaction exposure
- pre-transaction exposure by currency by period
- hedges against pre-transaction exposure by currency by period
- details of hedges in place (forwards, options)
- foreign exchange rates or exercise prices of hedges in place
- sensitivity analysis
- analysis of translation exposure: overseas net assets and profits
- hedges in place against translation exposure.

Transaction and pre-transaction exposure are usually reported monthly, while translation exposure is usually reported quarterly or semi-annually.

Sample Reports

Debt Maturity

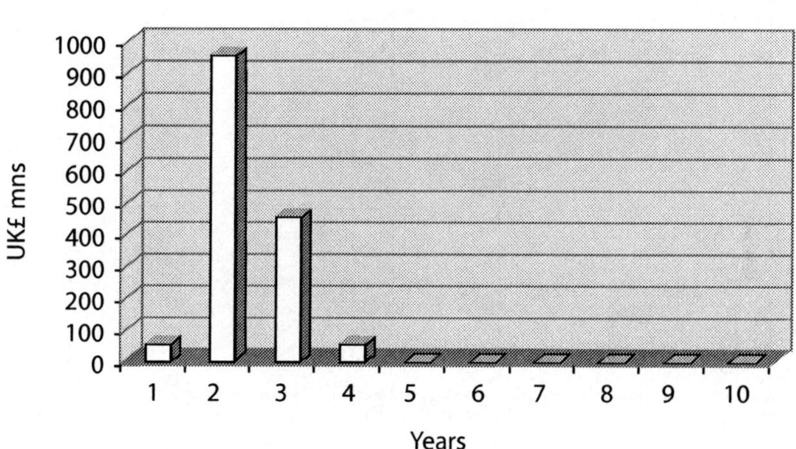

Headroom

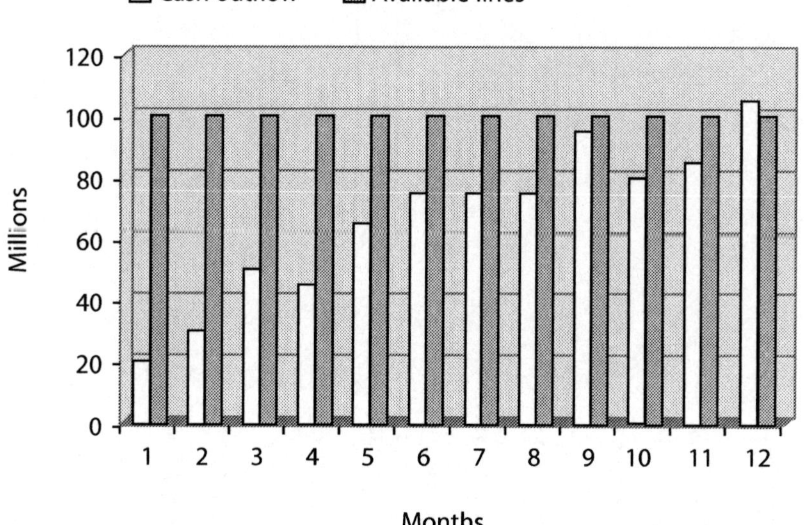

Foreign exchange report

FOREIGN EXCHANGE EXPOSURE – BUDGETED

Budgeted exposure – SG$m	Periods							
	1	2	3	4	5	6	7	8
Committed orders SG$ receivable	28	25	32	18	16			
Forecast receivable but no committed orders received				17	16	28	28	30
Total forecast SG$ income	28	25	32	35	32	28	28	30
Cover taken	26	20	15	15	15	10	8	5
Net forecast exposure to SG$	2	5	17	20	17	18	20	25
Analysis of cover already taken								
Forward FX	26	20	15	15	10	5	3	
Vanilla options					5	5	5	5
Average forward FX rate	1.81	1.81	1.81	1.8	1.8	1.78	1.78	
Strike rate on options					1.8	1.8	1.8	1.78
Budgeted FX rate	1.83	1.85	1.85	1.85	1.85	1.85	1.85	1.85
Current market rates	1.8302	1.8282	1.8267	1.8249	1.8230	1.8212	1.8194	1.8175

Excerpt from a typical foreign exchange exposure report showing budgeted SG$ receivables for a US company. The receivables are split between orders received and those forecast. Hedges are analyzed between instruments and the rates at which the hedges have been taken out are shown against budget. Further analysis could be provided by showing the effects of a given movement in US$/SG$ exchange rate, and the effects on the budget of hedging at the current exchange rates.

SAMPLE REPORT FOR INTEREST RATE EXPOSURE

All currencies	*Months* 1	2	3	4	5	6	*Years* 2	3
Forecast borrowings	1560	1575	1585	1555	1540	1500	1400	1250
Hedges in place:								
Drawings	900	750	500	250	100			
Fixed rate borrowings	400	400	400	400	400	400	400	400
Derivatives:								
FRAs			150	250	250	200		
Interest rate swaps			200	200	200	200	150	150
Caps		100	100	100	100	100	80	60
Other								
Total hedges	1300	1250	1350	1200	1050	900	630	610
Proportion fixed	83.33%	79.37%	85.17%	77.17%	68.18%	60.00%	45.00%	48.80%
Average rate under FRAs, swaps and Eurobond	6.50%	6.60%	6.70%	6.60%	6.70%	6.90%	7.00%	7.00%
Strike rate under caps		6.50%	6.50%	6.50%	6.50%	6.50%	5.50%	5.00%

CHAPTER 3

Debt Capacity

INTRODUCTION

One of the questions that a corporate treasurer is often asked is: 'How much debt can we raise?' This question is usually posed when the company is planning either a major expansionary capital expenditure programme or a significant acquisition. The result of either of these activities may be to push debt levels up to or beyond those levels that have hitherto been considered normal, or that the company has been used to operating with.

An associated question that the treasurer is also often involved in solving is: 'What should our financial structure be? How much debt and equity should we have on our balance sheet?'

This chapter examines the various aspects of debt and equity and attempts to provide some guidance in answering the above questions.

DEBT VERSUS EQUITY

Introduction

Equity comprises share capital and reserves, and these are controlled by shareholders. Except under highly circumscribed conditions, share capital is not redeemable at the discretion of the shareholders or the company's management. Reserves in the profit and loss account are distributable at the discretion of the shareholders through powers given to their appointed directors.

Shareholders receive a return out of the residual amount of all profits after prior charges have been met. They have to bear all costs up to the extent of their limited liability, and have no return due to them other than that what remains after all others have received their entitlement. Shareholders may or may not receive a dividend, and current levels of dividend payouts may in the future be cut as well as increased.

Debt is that part of a company's financing where the rights to income are independent of the company's financial profitability. Debt has the following characteristics:

- It is repayable on a fixed date in the future.
- The amount repayable is fixed.
- It carries a rate of interest. The interest rate may be fixed or floating.

Tables 3.1 and 3.2 compare debt and equity from the standpoint of both investor and issuer.

Table 3.1 Aspects of equity and debt from the standpoint of shareholders and lenders

	Ordinary shares	*Debt*
Voting rights	✓	
Known redemption date		✓
Prior claim over ordinary shareholders in the event of liquidation		✓
Investors share in the profits of company	✓	
Certainty of annual coupon/dividend payment		✓
Potential for capital gain	✓	✓
Unlimited potential for capital gain	✓	
Information on company publicly available	✓	✓
Pre-emptive rights	✓	
Choice of credit risk, maturity and instrument		✓

Note: If debt is raised through publicly traded bonds there is potential for capital gains and capital losses by the bondholder.

Table 3.2 Aspects of debt and equity from the standpoint of the managers of the company and borrowers

	Ordinary shares	*Debt*
No legal obligation to make payouts, giving more flexibility	✓	
A potentially useful tool for motivating employees	✓	
Requirement to obtain permission for major corporate actions	✓	✓
Acquisition currency	✓	
Current owners (possibly founders) do not have to give up future capital gains		✓
No obligation to repay capital	✓	
Does not increase financial risk	✓	
Lower cost of capital		✓

General

From the point of view of the issuer, since dividends may be reduced or eliminated altogether and equity is not repayable, equity provides greater flexibility as it is a lower burden on operating cashflows. However, many directors believe that 'cutting' the dividend payout can have major implications for the company's share price. While debt also creates risk due to the requirement to pay interest on specified dates, it also has flexibility in the ease with which it can be created and repaid.

THE IMPACT OF DEBT ON FINANCIAL RETURNS TO SHAREHOLDERS

There are a number of ways of examining the question of debt capacity and the correct debt/equity mix. One is to examine the return to shareholders with different levels of debt in the financial structure. (It is a principle of corporate finance that, since shareholders are the ultimate risk takers in a business – i.e. they only receive their returns after all other stakeholders have been paid out – any examination of the debt/equity structure should be examined from the standpoint of the impact on the returns available to them with different structures.)

Assuming no taxes

A company makes US$400 million in pre-tax profits. Under scenario one in Table 3.3 it is financed with 100 per cent equity. Under scenario two it is financed with 50 per cent debt/50 per cent equity. The interest cost on its borrowings is 5 per cent. In this situation the returns on the book value of shareholders equity are 50 per cent higher under the 50 per cent debt/50 per cent equity structure.

Introducing volatility of earnings

However, when volatility of earnings is brought into consideration, the riskiness of debt becomes apparent.

What happens to the returns to shareholders if operating profits increase by 25 per cent?

In Table 3.4. the pre-tax return on shareholders' book equity increases by 33 per cent under the 50 per cent debt/50 per cent equity scenario, and only 25 per cent under the 100 per cent equity scenario.

If pre-tax operating profits before interest fall by 25 per cent, the effect under the two financial structures is that shown in Table 3.5.

Financing with debt therefore has the following attributes: the greater the level of debt in a financial structure, the greater the return on the book

Table 3.3 The difference in return to shareholders between different financial structures

	100 % equity	*50 % equity*
Operating profits before interest	US$400 million	US$400 million
Cost of debt	–	US$100 million
Available to shareholders	US$400 million	US$300 million
Book value equity	US$4 billion	US$2 billion
Book value of debt	–	US$2 billion
Return on shareholders equity	10 %	15 %

Table 3.4 Pre-tax operating profits before interest increase by 25 per cent

	100 % equity	*50 % equity*
Operating profits before interest	US$500 million	US$500 million
Cost of debt	–	US$100 million
Pre-tax operating profit	US$500 million	US$400 million
Book value equity	US$4 billion	US$2 billion
Book value of debt	–	US$2 billion
Pre-tax return on shareholders equity	12.5%	20.0 %

value of equity. However, when the possible volatility of earnings is considered, debt financing becomes much riskier.

Conclusion

Given the above, it would seem that the best approach to financing would be for a company to finance itself with as much debt as possible. In doing this, and in setting the outer limits of its debt financing, it needs to consider the volatility of its earnings and the stability of returns it wants to earn for its shareholders. However the problem with the above examples is that they all relate to the past return to a shareholder, and they relate these past returns to the book value (accounting value) of shareholders' equity. They take no account of future cashflows, and the risks associated with different financial structures. As such the examples cannot help us say whether,

Table 3.5 Pre-tax operating profits before interest decrease by 25 per cent

	100 % equity	*50 % equity*
Operating profits before interest	US$300 million	US$300 million
Pre-tax cost of debt	–	US$100 million
Pre-tax operating profits	US$300 million	US$200 million
Book value equity	US$4 billion	US$2 billion
Book value of debt	–	US$2 billion
Pre-tax return on shareholders equity	7.5 %	10 %

economically, shareholders benefit from increasing amounts of debt in the financial structure. Corporate finance theory attempts to relate a company's capital structure to its economic value.

DEBT EQUITY STRUCTURE: THEORY

The capital asset pricing model

The value of a company is the net present value (npv) of its future after tax cashflows. The rate to use to discount these cashflows is the company's weighted average cost of capital (WACC). The WACC can be calculated as follows:

$$\frac{\text{Cost of debt} \times \text{Market value of debt} + \text{Cost of equity} \times \text{Market value of equity}}{\text{Market value of debt} + \text{Market value of equity}}$$

It is one of the central features of the capital asset pricing model (CAPM) that the cost of equity is greater than the cost of debt. This is fundamentally because equity holders are the ultimate risk takers in a company (they only receive their return after all other stakeholders have been paid). If the cost of debt is lower than the cost of equity, then at first sight a company can increase the market value of its equity by financing itself with increasing amounts of debt. This is because the lower a company's discount rate (weighted average cost of capital), the greater the net present value of its after tax cashflows.

Calculating the weighted average cost of capital

This can be illustrated in Table 3.6.

If debt was increased to 75 per cent of the financial structure then with no other adjustments WACC becomes:

$$\text{WACC} \quad \frac{5\,\% \times 3 \text{ billion} + 10\,\% \times 1 \text{ billion}}{4 \text{ billion}}$$

$$= 6.25\,\%$$

(It is of course important to note that while CAPM is used to calculate the WACC, CAPM is really a model used to calculate required project returns.

Table 3.6 Calculating the weighted average cost of capital

Company's cost of debt	5%
Company's cost of equity	10% (There is a 5% equity premium to reflect the higher risk of equity.)
Company's beta (ß)	1.0 (This measures the riskiness of a company's equity against that of the market as a whole. A beta of 1.0 means that the company's shares are as risky but no riskier than the market as a whole. Risk is measured by volatility of returns.)
Market value of equity	US$2 billion
Market value of debt	US$2 billion
Company's cost of equity	10 % (5 % + ß × cost of equity)
Weighted average cost of capital (WACC)	$\frac{5\,\% \times 2 \text{ billion} + 10\,\% \times 2 \text{ billion}}{4 \text{ billion}}$
	= 7.5 %

In theory the correct discount rate to use is the return available on a competing investment; in practice, a simple rate has to be calculated, and most companies use WACC derived from CAPM.)

Impact of debt/equity on the riskiness of shares

However, increasing the amount of debt in the funding structure of a company also increases the riskiness of its shares. This was first propounded by Modigliani and Miller, who maintained that changing a company's capital structure could not in itself increase the market value of a company. Only investment in projects yielding a return over the company's hurdle rate (WACC) could do that. As a result, increasing the proportion of debt in a company's financial structure can have no impact on the WACC and hence on the market value of a company. Therefore from an economic standpoint the financial structure of a company can have no impact on the market value of its shares.

By increasing the proportion of debt to 75 per cent of the financial structure, the company's beta increases to reflect the increased riskiness of the shares, as already discussed.

Lower levels of debt

It is now, however, generally held that at low levels of debt increasing the amount of debt funding will not increase the cost of equity. However after a certain point more debt starts to increase the cost of equity. Furthermore, there is another point where higher levels of debt result in higher costs as lenders get more concerned about financial distress. There is usually a point beyond which lenders refuse to allow more borrowing. Thus the WACC is saucer shaped when increasing amounts of debt are plotted against WACC (Figure 3.1).

In an ideal world, a company would measure its cost of equity and cost of debt at different levels of gearing. It would then identify that level of gearing where its WACC is at a minimum and establish a financial structure with that appropriate amount of debt. In practice a company cannot do this, since the cost of equity at different levels of gearing is not directly identifiable.

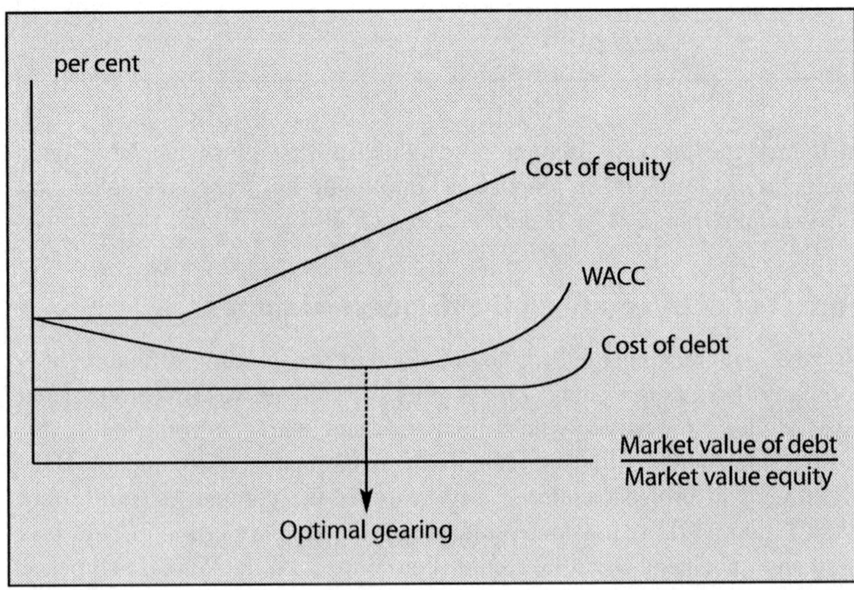

Figure 3.1 Optimal capital structure when the cost of financial distress is included

Introducing tax into WACC

So far the analyses of debt versus equity have been made on a pre-tax basis. One of the benefits of debt finance is that in most countries the interest cost of debt is deductible in computing a company's taxable profits, whereas dividends are not.

CAPM looks at the net present value of a company's after-tax cashflows. Since debt is tax deductible the WACC should be calculated on a company's after-tax cost of debt. Introducing this into the previous example with 50 per cent debt/50 per cent equity and assuming a 30 per cent tax rate WACC becomes:

$$\frac{3.5\ \% \times 2 \text{ billion} + 10\ \% \times 2 \text{ billion}}{4 \text{ billion}}$$

$$= 6.75\ \%$$

Taxation has lowered the discount rate and hence has a positive benefit on the value of a company. The general proposition of CAPM is that, due to the tax deductibility of interest, it is better to finance with debt than equity up to the point at which financial distress could impact. Indeed the trade-off theory of capital structure predicts that firms will choose their mix of debt and equity financing to balance the costs and benefits of debt. The tax benefits of debt and control of free cashflow push firms to use more debt financing, while bankruptcy costs and other associated problems provide firms with the incentive to use less. The theory describes a firm's optimal capital structure as the mix of financing that equates the marginal costs and benefits of debt financing.

Debt capacity: practice

It would seem from the above that, due to the impact of taxation, it is best to have as much debt in the debt/equity mix as possible consistent with a company's risk tolerance. However CAPM is a theoretical model. Companies, while recognizing the importance of CAPM need some practical way of identifying, first, how the cost of debt will increase as the level of debt increases, and second, whether there is a level of debt beyond which the risk of financial distress becomes significant.

In thinking about, planning and managing their level of gearing, companies will have regard to the qualitative factors discussed below.

Financial flexibility

The ability to respond to a changing business environment is critical for many management teams. Acquisition and investment prospects continually present themselves and companies need the financial strength to grasp these opportunities as they arise. Retaining an element of 'fire power' can be essential to the achievement of an organization's strategic aims. Similarly a company needs to heed the impact that a downturn in its business sector or in the overall economy may have on its financial position. What may be a satisfactory financial structure when the business environment is buoyant may prove more burdensome to maintain when a business downturn arises and cashflows are reduced.

Avoiding financial distress

Financial distress is not merely the risk of bankruptcy. It also represents the risk that business opportunities, corporate objectives and strategy must be curtailed because the company's cashflows are severely reduced and those that are available must be dedicated to servicing debt. Such companies may also be at risk of breaching financial covenants within their loan agreements. In such cases the organization usually has to reorganize its affairs, dispose of assets and prune capital expenditure to stabilize its financial position.

No company wants to run its financial structure so near the margin that small changes in its cashflows may have a significant impact on its ability to service its debts and meet its financial obligations.

Credit worthiness and credit ratings

It may be a central plank in a company's financing strategy that it maintains a given credit rating or a given level of credit worthiness. This credit rating may enable it to access certain debt markets or maintain its cost of debt at certain levels. Generally companies like to have access to the widest possible range of debt markets. To achieve this they have to maintain a given level of financial strength as measured by certain financial ratios that indirectly affect their credit ratings.

Other qualitative business considerations

A company will also consider a number of other qualitative business factors in determining its debt/equity structure. Amongst these considerations are:

- The level of operational gearing. Does it operate with a high level of fixed costs?
- Its market position. Does it have a dominant market position and is it able to protect its profits and cashflow in adverse conditions?
- The competitive environment. Does the company operate in a business with low barriers to entry?
- The business sector it operates in. Is it in a cyclical business sector where cashflows are subject to fluctuation?
- Its management team. Are they experienced in the business and the sector it operates in?

These qualitative factors determine how well the company can maintain its cashflows in an adverse business environment. Generally the stronger its market position and the lower its operational gearing, the higher level of debt that a company can tolerate.

FINANCIAL RATIOS

These various qualitative considerations will often find expression in internal financial ratios. These ratios represent the level of financial strength a company considers it should maintain in order to achieve those qualitative factors such as financial flexibility and credit worthiness described above.

There are two classes of ratios, those that are balance-sheet-based and those that are earnings and cashflow-based.

Balance sheet ratios

Net borrowings: tangible net worth

Tangible net worth is calculated as shareholders' funds less intangible items such as goodwill. It is a crude measure of what might be realized in a winding-up situation.

Net borrowings: net assets

Net assets are calculated from total assets less total liabilities. Another term for this is debt gearing or leverage.

Both the above are crude measures of the amount of cover for debt providers in the event of liquidation or winding up. Arguably this is hardly something to concern the treasurer or finance director. Also, many providers of debt have found that in wind-up situations the realizable value of assets bears no relationship to their book value. Increasingly therefore, more emphasis is being placed by both borrowers and providers of finance on ratios that measure a company's ability to meet its financial obligations on an ongoing basis.

Earnings and cashflow-based ratios

Interest cover

This is a simple measure of a company's ability to pay the ongoing interest cost of its debts. The philosophy behind this measure seems to be that provided interest costs can be met, existing debt can always be re-financed with fresh debt.

$$\frac{\text{Profit on ordinary activities before interest}}{\text{Net interest before substracting capitalized interest}}$$

In calculating the above ratio a company needs to consider whether adjustments need to be made for such items as:

- One-off exceptional items such as gains and losses on disposal of businesses. These can introduce large fluctuations in profit and hence on interest cover from year to year.
- Interest income. Does interest income arise from temporary cash balances that will be used to pay down borrowings and hence reduce interest expense, or does it arise from long-term lending such as customer finance leases? Should interest income be netted against interest expense in calculating net interest?
- Operating leases. Some companies decide to lease equipment as opposed to purchasing it. Should adjustments be made to operating profits and interest expense to reflect this?
- Profit from discountinued operations.

Interest cover is a ratio that is easily understood and calculated. As such it is a popular measure in some companies. However it takes no account of the various provisions, charges and other non-cash items charged or credited in calculating operating profits.

EBITDA interest coverage

This ratio attempts to overcome the disadvantages of interest cover by adjusting that ratio for the two largest regular non-cash items usually charged in calculating operation profit before tax, namely depreciation and amortization (generally of balance sheet goodwill). It attempts to measure the one true factor of a company's ability to pay interest expense: its cashflow.

$$\frac{\text{Profit on ordinary activities before interest, taxes, depreciation and amortization (EBITDA)}}{\text{Net interest expense before substracting capitalized interest}}$$

EBITDA interest coverage is a simple calculation that gets closer to a company's ongoing cash resources to service its debt. Again, it is a simple ratio to calculate and is easily understood. However, it still takes no account of a number of other provisions and non-cash items that may be charged or credited in the profit and loss account. Nor does it take account of a company's ability to repay its debts as they mature.

Funds from operations/net debt

It is not only a company's ability to pay interest expense on its debts that is important in assessing financial strength and borrowing capacity, but also its ability to repay its loans as they fall due. Debt providers are equally concerned with the question of 'How are we going to get repaid?' The calculation below attempts to measure the company's ability to repay loans from its cashflow.

$$\frac{\text{Profit on ordinary activities after tax plus depreciation, amortization and other non-cash items}}{\text{Long term debt (including current maturities) plus short term borrowings (total debt)}}$$

While it is a simple ratio to calculate and understand, the calculation takes no account of the maturity profile of a company's debts. Take two companies, both with the same cashflow and level of debt:

	Company A *US$ million*	*Company B* *US$ million*
Funds from operations	250	250
Total debt	1,000	1,000

Funds from operations/total debt is the same for both companies, namely 0.25 times. However, if the average weighted life of debt for Company A was five years and that for Company B was ten years, Company B would have less re-financing and repayment pressure than Company A.

Again the calculation takes no account of the other non-cash items involved in calculating operating profits before interest.

Free operating cashflow/total debt

This is calculated as:

$$\frac{\text{Funds from operations minus maintenance capital expenditure minus (plus) the increase (decrease) in working capital}}{\text{Total debt}}$$

This is a more complex calculation than the earlier ones, since a company needs to know what its maintenance capital expenditure is. (Maintenance capital is that capital expenditure that must be incurred in order to maintain the fabric and earning capacity of the business.) In addition, working capital can show some major fluctuations from year to year in some organizations. This can introduce an element of instability into the calculation.

Technically this is a more precise calculation. It relates the real cashflow of the business to its financial obligations. However, it suffers from the same disadvantages as EBITDA/net debt; that is, it takes no account of the maturity of a company's debts.

What ratios should we operate with?

As explained earlier, the appropriate ratios to be used by a company and the precise level they should be set at are specific to that company. A whole range of factors to do with the company's business and financial structure are relevant. However, Standard and Poor's publish key ratio medians for US corporates, and these can be useful guides. For instance, the three-year median for US industrial companies for 1998 to 2000 was an interest cover of 6.1 for A rated companies and 3.7 for BBB, while A rated companies had an EBITDA/interest of 9.1 and BBB companies had a ratio of 5.8 (see Chapter 5, on credit ratings). This provides some kind of target for those companies that want to establish or retain a credit standing at investment-grade level.

Use of financial ratios within a business

Usually a company will have two 'layers' of financial ratios:

- Financial ratios in its key financing documents. These ratios are usually set at a very low level. If they are breached, it sends a signal to the lenders that there has been a significant change in the underlying financial health of the company. Lenders are therefore put on notice that the credit quality of the company they originally lent to has now substantially deteriorated, and that unless action is taken their capital is at risk. Breaches of these covenants are normally expressed as events of default, allowing the providers of finance to request immediate repayment of their loans. In practice borrowers and lenders have to agree on effective plans of action to redress the deterioration in the company's financial position.
- Internal ratios that the company establishes to manage its financial stability. A company may have a guideline that interest cover should not fall below four times. Should it breach these internal guidelines, it needs an action programme to rectify the position. This programme may consist of asset disposals, reduction in capital expenditure or a postponement of planned acquisitions. Internal ratios will normally be set at levels well in excess of the ratios in the financing documents.

Most companies will try to ensure that they operate comfortably within their internal guidelines. This is generally because the remedy for breaching such guidelines can have negative impacts on their business. Thus a company may have an interest cover guideline of four times, but for prudential reasons may not want to see it fall below five times.

DEBT CAPACITY: CONCLUSION

When looking at the level of financial returns available to shareholders on the book value of their investment, it would seem that a company should finance itself with as much debt as possible subject to the volatility of its earnings. Debt increases financial leverage and hence returns, and the interest expense of debt is tax deductible.

Corporate finance theory states that altering the financial structure of a company cannot in itself increase company value, but that when taxation is introduced there is a benefit from debt in the financial structure. Companies should consider an appropriate level of debt in their funding structures due to the 'tax shield' of debt.

In practice there is no way of identifying what the theoretically optimum debt/equity level actually is. As a result companies have to adopt a number of common sense rules in establishing and controlling their capital structure. These rules tend to find expression in financial ratios. When answering the question of how much debt can be raised, the treasurer's first reaction is to look at the impact of the increase in debt on the financial ratios established by the company. Generally, a company can support breaches of these ratios for comparatively short periods of time provided there are feasible action plans for correction.

CASE STUDY

Introduction and background

Leisure Time plc is a UK FTSE 250 company involved in the leisure sector. Its operations include the ownership and management of:

	% PBT	*% Assets*
Old people's homes (residential homes)	20	25
Health clubs	30	30
Budget and 4-star hotels	30	30
Film production and distribution	20	15

It has recently made two acquisitions. One is a company that operates health clubs in the Far East, and the other a company operating budget hotels in Europe. Leisure Time plans to develop its existing businesses primarily in Europe and the Far East. The company judges that in many European countries there is a lack of budget hotels offering consistent standards, and that health club offerings in the Far East are underdeveloped in comparison with Europe and North America.

Financial structure

A profile of its debt at 31 December 2002 was:

	UK£ million		
Bank debt:			
Acquisition/revolving facility	800	Matures: UK£400	31/05/04
		UK£400	31/05/06
Eurobond	200	Matures 31/01/08	
Financial leases	105		
	UK£1105		

Questions

1. How do you think the company should finance its expansion programme, with debt or equity?
2. What considerations would you bear in mind in reaching your conclusion?

Profit and loss UK£ million

	Actual	←	*Plan*	→
	31/12/2002	*31/12/2003*	*31/12/2004*	*21/12/2005*
Turnover	2106	2268	2687	3256
Operating profit before interest and tax	200	225	275	335
Net interest expense	– 48	– 86	– 120	– 141
Profit after interest	152	139	155	194
Taxation	– 46	– 49	– 49	– 52
Profit after tax	106	90	106	142
Dividends	– 53	– 45	– 53	– 71
Profit retained	53	45	53	71
Depreciation and amortization	105	147	198	243

Cash flow UK£ million

	Actual	←	*Plan*	→
	31/12/2002	*31/12/2003*	*31/12/2004*	*21/12/2005*
Net cashflow from operating activities	285	72	448	493
Interest and taxation	– 94	– 135	– 169	– 193
Dividends	– 53	– 45	– 53	– 71
Capital expenditure	– 150	– 600	– 725	– 650
Net cash outflow before financing	– 12	– 708	– 499	– 421

Balance sheet UK£ million

	Actual	←	*Plan*	→
	31/12/2002	*31/12/2003*	*31/12/2004*	*21/12/2005*
Fixed assets	2060	2513	3040	3447
Current assets less current liabilities	– 100	200	225	310
Total assets less current liabilities	1960	2713	3265	3757
Debt falling due after one year	– 1105	– 1813	– 2312	– 2733
	855	900	953	1024
Share capital	245	249	254	260
Reserves	610	651	699	764
	855	900	953	1024

SOLUTION

Leisure Time plc

There are no hard and fast rules as to the maximum level of debt that a company can sustain. So much depends on the industry that a company operates in, the strength and certainty of its cashflows, and its ability to react to changes in business fortunes by reducing capital expenditure or introducing economies.

1. Interest cover. Generally most companies would want to maintain this above three to four times.
2. EBITDA/interest. This would usually be maintained above five to six times.
3. EBITDA/net debt. How long would it take to repay net debt out of operational cashflows? A ratio not below 0.20 to 0.25 is often regarded as an ideal target.
4. Free cashflow/net debt. This attempts to look at operational cashflows after interest, tax and maintenance capital have been paid.

Debt to cashflow ratios obviously have to be used in conjunction with the average life of the debt.

Based on these ratios, Leisure Times debt ratios are:

Balance sheet UK£ million

	Actual	←	*Plan*	→
	31/12/2002	*31/12/2003*	*31/12/2004*	*21/12/2005*
Interest cover				
Operating profit before interest and tax/ Net interest expense	4.17	2.62	2.29	2.38
EBITDA/Net interest				
Operating profit before interest and tax+ depreciation and amortization/ Net interest expense	6.35	4.33	3.94	4.10

Balance sheet UK£ million (continued)	*Actual* 31/12/2002	← *Plan* 31/12/2003	31/12/2004	→ 21/12/2005
EBITDA/Net debt				
EBITDA/Debts falling due after more than one year	0.28	0.21	0.20	0.21
Free cash flow/Net debt				
Debts falling due after more than one year/Net cash flow from operating activities less interest and tax depreciation	0.08	– 0.12	0.04	0.02

Note: Free cashflow was calculated using net cashflow from operating activities less interest and tax less depreciation (which might approximate to maintenance capital spend).

Many companies would regard these ratios as being too tight to finance the expansion programme purely from debt, and would seek some equity funding, particularly since the deterioration in the ratios lasts for a number of years.

PART II

Financing Alternatives

A company is faced with a wide range of financing options when considering its financial structure. Its first consideration might be:

Debt or equity? A consideration of the factors that determine the level of debt and equity in a company's financial structure has already been considered.

When considering debt alternatives, its may consider a range of options:

- Bank funding:
  - term loans to fund discrete one-off projects
  - revolving facilities to cover working capital fluctuations and small acquisitions
  - acquisition financing
  - leasing
  - standby facilities.
- Bond markets
  - public or private markets
  - Eurobond or domestic issues.
- Commercial paper to manage fluctuations in liquidity.
- Non-recourse financing, comprising project finance and asset securitization.
- Quasi-equity such as convertible bonds.

A company will choose different markets depending on its existing debt structure, treasury policy and strategic objectives. Whichever market is chosen, the successful exploitation of that market depends in part on a good understanding of how it works. The treasurer needs to understand what the mechanics of issuing debt in the market are, who the market participants are with whom he or she will have to deal, and the important factors to negotiate over.

The following four chapters examine aspects of debt financing and the mechanics of funding through the bank and bond markets, and non-recourse funding in the form of asset securitization. They are designed to give the reader an understanding of some of the issues that are involved in issuing debt in these markets. Why select a particular market? How are bonds valued and what is the role of the rating agencies? With whom will the treasurer have to deal? What information must be provided? What documentation must be negotiated? What fees are generally payable? How can one judge whether an issue is successful or not?

CHAPTER 4

Bank Finance

INTRODUCTION

It is often said that every company should have bank finance as part of its core debt. The reason for this is generally the very flexible nature of bank finance. This flexibility is reflected in the different maturities, currencies, availability, repayment options and structures available with bank finance. The object of this chapter is to provide a background to the principal elements of bank finance and how it is used by the corporate treasurer.

FORMS OF BANK FINANCE

Bank finance comes in many different forms and structures, with the principal ones outlined below.

Committed facilities

Under a committed facility a bank is obligated to provide finance to the borrower. The nature of this obligation or commitment is defined in the loan agreement, lasts for the duration of the facility (364 days, three years, five years etc.) and extends to the amount of the commitment. For instance if a bank enters into a three-year committed facility with a customer for US$50 million, the bank is obligated to advance funds up to the amount of US$50 million for the period of three years, provided the customer observes the conditions and obligations in the facility. Committed facilities are characterized by the following:

Loan documentation

They have extensive loan documentation that sets out each party's rights and obligations together with the situations under which the borrower will be in default and the bank can reclaim any funds it has advanced before the maturity of the facility.

Interest rate for advances

An agreement as to the method of calculating interest rate and the margin thereon for all funds advanced under the facility.

Commitment fee

A fee (calculated daily) paid by the borrower for any commitments not drawn.

Uncommitted facilities

Uncommitted facilities create no obligation on the bank to provide funds. If a corporate requests an advance under an uncommitted facility but it does not suit the bank's position to advance funds (for instance when the advance would fall over a year or quarter end), then the bank can refuse the request. Uncommitted facilities are characterized by the following:

Loan documentation

Generally the briefest of facility documents. The facility is generally renewed annually.

Advances

Advances are for short periods (generally no more than six months).

Interest rate for advances

The interest rate and applicable margin for the funds advanced is agreed at the time of the advance (unlike committed facilities, where the formula for establishing the interest rate applicable to an advance and the size of the margin is established in the facility agreement). There is no commitment fee payable if the facility is not used.

Uncommitted facilities are usually used for funding day-to-day liquidity shortfalls.

Types of committed facilities

Revolving facility

A revolving facility is, as its name suggests, a facility where the funds committed by the bank(s) can be drawn and repaid to suit the borrower's requirements. Multiple drawings, in total up to the facility amount can be made, all of them for different periods. Drawings are for short periods, generally not in excess of six months.

Take, for example, a company with a three-year revolving credit facility for US$500 million from a syndicate of banks. On day X it has drawn the following under the facility:

US$50 million for three months repayable in two months' time

US$75 million for six months repayable in four months' time

US$200 million for three months repayable in one month's time.

It can still draw up to US$175 million for different periods. The repayment of advances can be financed by further drawings under the facility (provided the new drawings do not extend beyond the facility maturity date).

Revolving facilities are typically used to finance fluctuations in working capital, small 'bolt-on' acquisitions and incremental capital expenditure.

Term loans

With a term loan, funds are advanced on the signing of the facility agreement, or can be drawn for a short period after signing, often up to six months (the drawdown period). Funds advanced are outstanding for the period of the loan. Terms loans often have the following characteristics:

Repayment during loan

If any amount of the finance advanced is repaid during the life of the loan, these funds are surrendered and cannot be redrawn by the borrower.

Drawdown period

Any available finance that is not drawn during the drawdown period, usually up to six months, is also surrendered.

Repayment methods

These may be by amortization over a period of time or by bullet (all the facility repaid on one day). Both are common.

Term loans are typically used for core funding requirements where the flexibility of a revolving credit is not necessary. Examples of the use of term loans include acquisition and project finance. In such instances the drawdown period and repayment profile of the facility can be tailored to meet the cash projections of the acquisition or project.

Bilateral versus syndicated facilities

A bilateral facility is a facility arranged between just one bank and the borrower. A borrower could have a number of separate bilateral facilities, each with a different bank. In such a case each individual loan agreement could contain different terms, and the margin applying to drawings under each bilateral could also be different.

Bilateral facilities are usually established where the total amount of funds to be raised is comparatively small or the borrower wishes to restrict the bank's right to assign or transfer.

A syndicated facility is arranged with a number of banks. The aspects of a syndicated facility are:

Common documentation

Only one loan agreement is signed, which operates between the borrower and the syndicate of banks. As a result, the terms of the facility are common to each bank.

Advances

Each bank contributes to advances under the facility in proportion to its individual commitment.

Facility agent

Syndicated loan facilities have an agent to coordinate drawings and repayments between individual syndicate members. The agent also acts as a 'go-between' between the banks and the borrower.

Other forms of committed bank finance

Bank finance can be structured to meet specific requirements. The following are examples of some of these specialist financings:

Backup or standby facilities

It is a often a condition of the credit rating agencies that companies issuing commercial paper should have backup lines. The purpose of these lines is that they can be drawn on should the company be incapable of 'rolling' (repaying commercial paper by issuing fresh commercial paper) outstanding paper.

Bridge facilities

Banks will often provide finance to bridge a company from one event to another. For example, a company may have a loan facility due to mature in three months. The company's intention may be to re-finance the loan by a bond issue, but it may judge the particular bond market unreceptive to a corporate issue at the present moment in time. The company arranges a bridge facility to finance itself from the maturity of the loan to a successful issue in the bond markets. Bridge facilities are generally for short periods of time, usually up to one year, but often have some mechanism to extend the facility life for a further short period. It is usually a condition of the bank providing a bridge facility that it takes a major role in its re-financing.

Acquisition finance

Acquisitions, particularly where the target company is a publicly quoted entity, usually have to be completed in total secrecy and in a very short period of time. They also often require the banks involved in providing the initial finance to advance substantial levels of funds.

Leasing

Many banks have a leasing arm. With leasing, specific assets are financed as opposed to a pool of assets. Assets can be financed through operating leases, where the lessor takes an element of risk on the realizable value of the asset being financed, or finance leases that are effectively amortizing loans.

Project finance

Some banks specialize in project financing. Such financings, particularly of large infrastructure projects with complex cashflows that are financed on a non-recourse basis to the construction or operating companies, require the bank to have specialist skills.

ASPECTS OF SYNDICATED REVOLVING FACILITIES

This section looks at various aspects of a facility that most treasurers at one time or another have to put in place: the syndicated revolving facility. In particular:

- How are such facilities 'put together' or established?
- What are the costs and fees associated with such a facility?
- What are the advantages and disadvantages of this type of facility?
- What are the usual terms that are found in the loan documentation?

Facility size and duration

The starting point is usually to determine the required size and maturity of the facility. For most companies the data for this exercise is derived from the annual planning process when the strategy and the financing requirements flowing from that strategy are determined. Many companies produce an annual financing plan that sets out how the financing requirements arising from the strategy will be managed. Chapter 2, dealing with debt management, has already outlined the policies that a company will establish to handle its loan structure: headroom, maturity profile, currency and debt mix. These policies will help the company to determine its financing needs, the different markets it will use to satisfy those needs, and in the case of bank funding, the type, size and maturity of the facility.

For instance a company may, from its latest three-year business plan, have the data shown in Table 4.1. Given this information, the treasurer may well decide to propose that the existing revolving facility should be

Table 4.1 Calculation of annual funding requirements

	Year one US$ million	*Year two US$ million*	*Year three US$ million*	*Total US$ million*
Net cash inflow (outflow) before financing	(100)	(100)	150	(50)
Repayment of leases	(50)	(40)	(30)	(120)
Maturity of revolving facility (At end year one)	(500)			(500)
	(650)	(140)	120	(670)
Utilization of headroom in existing facility (during year one)	150			150
Annual financing needs	(500)	(140)	120	(520)

Note: Year one cash outflow peaks at US$120 million.

re-financed with another revolver for US$750 to 800 million. This covers the financing needs for years one and two of US$660 million (which includes peak financing in year one of US$120 million) and gives headroom of US$100 million. To cater for the inflow in year three the facility may be structured with a three and five-year tranche.

Selecting the arranger

Every treasurer will want to ensure that the best terms are obtained for the facility. This will probably entail trying to ensure that the facility when finally signed contains:

- margins and fees in line with those applying to deals for similar credits that have recently been announced
- a maturity and structure that is appropriate to the treasurer's financing objectives

- covenants that are appropriate to the company, its financing strategy, credit strength, asset base and cashflow profile
- a syndicate comprising the company's existing relationship banks, and possibly some new banks with whom there is currently no relationship.

The role of the arranger is to:

- suggest the relevant terms (e.g. conditions, structure and pricing) that will be necessary to achieve the client's objectives
- assist the client in marketing the transaction to potential syndicate members
- act as an intermediary between the client and potential participants in agreeing the loan documentation
- possibly underwrite the transaction.

In selecting the arranger, the treasurer will have to be satisfied that the terms being proposed are the best for his/her company and that the arranger will be able to bring the transaction to a satisfactory conclusion The usual route for selecting the arranger is through the process of 'beauty parades'. Core relationship banks who have the specialist skills to arrange syndicated facilities will be asked to present their proposals for arranging the finance and the terms (margin, maturity, covenants) that they consider relevant. A good arranger will have a very keenly developed sense of the current appetite of the market, those banks willing to participate in transactions, and the terms and conditions that are being sought by those banks. As a core relationship bank, it should also have a good understanding of its client's business and strategy, its likely financing needs and the appeal of the company's credit to the bank market.

It is important that the treasurer has objective and disciplined criteria for selecting an arranger. Some of the factors to be considered in making this choice are:

- What is the bank's reputation in the market? Perhaps more importantly, what is the strength of its syndication team in the market? Is it a market leader? Does it have clout? No treasurer wants to select an arranger that appears merely to follow the market.
- How many transactions has the bank arranged? Who were the companies, what was the size and maturity? How were these deals received by the market?

- How do the terms I am being offered compare with other transactions either currently in the market or that have just closed? This includes not just price but also any covenant packages that are being recommended, and the structure of the transaction.
- Does the structure of the transaction meet my company's needs? Is the bank able to suggest other structures that may be more cost effective yet still match my company's cashflow? Can the arranger suggest other structures that may be better received by the market?
- What is the potential arranger's commitment to the relationship? This covers not just the relationship with the company, but the commitment the bank has to getting the transaction completed on terms that suit the client. How much reputation does the manger have to lose for 'getting it wrong'?
- How strong are the arrangers' skills? Can they deliver on their suggestions?

It is also important to handle the relationship with those banks that have not been awarded the mandate.

Underwritten or best endeavours

One of the first decisions is whether the transaction should be underwritten. 'Best endeavours' means that the arranger will use its best efforts to raise the finance required on the terms and conditions agreed. Should the financing target not be reached, then the transaction is concluded for the smaller amount. With an underwritten facility the borrower is guaranteed the target level of funds. If the syndication process fails to reach the target level, the underwriter provides the balance. The disadvantage of underwritten facilities is the underwriting fee payable.

Underwritten facilities are usual with event-driven transactions such as acquisitions and share buy-backs. Generally, smaller facilities that should be capable of being met by commitments from relationship banks are undertaken on a best-endeavours basis.

Invitations and marketing the transaction

Having selected and mandated the arranger and agreed the outline terms and structure of the financing, the next step is to market the transaction and send out invitations to potential participants.

The arranger will first size up the transaction. The treasurer will supply him or her with a list of relationship banks that the treasurer wants to see as members of the syndicate. In addition the arranger will suggest other banks that may be interested in entering into the deal. An estimate will be made of how much each bank may be willing to commit to the financing, which is then compared with the total amount of finance to be raised.

The arranger will consider syndication strategy. This may range from approaching a selected number of relationship banks to participate at a senior level with a substantial take and hold level, to a more widespread syndication. Generally most treasurers like to see the smallest banking group in a syndicated facility, with all the principal relationship banks participating. With most syndications, therefore, it is generally hoped that, first, most of the finance will be provided by relationship banks, with a few new banks to provide any balance, and second, there will only be one round of syndication.

Clearly the above will depend on the size of the transaction being contemplated and whether sufficient liquidity is likely to be available from a borrower's relationship banking group. In the case of significant financings, such as an acquisition finance, there will almost certainly be a need to attract a wider group of banks outside the company's relationship banks.

Invitations

Generally invitations to participate in the transactions are sent out to more banks than will ultimately agree to take part in the facility. For instance, if a company wants to establish a revolving facility for US$500 million, estimates may suggest that eight key relationship banks will commit US$50 million each, with four other relationship banks providing US$25 million each. Invitations however may go out to, for example, another four to six banks, all of whom the arranger believes have appetite for such financings. The object of such a strategy is to provide a safety net and to ensure that the total amount of finance can be raised. Depending on the syndication strategy originally envisaged, it may be regarded as a negative aspect, both for the arranger and the company, if the company has to go on a further round of syndication to try and complete a deal because the initial group of banks did not provide sufficient finance. If the company receives more finance than it needs, then participating banks will be scaled back (their commitments will be reduced, often on a proportionate basis).

Bank presentations

It is a common practice now, especially with larger transactions, for the borrower to make a presentation to all banks invited into the financing. This presentation will not only cover the proposed terms of the transaction but will also summarize the company's strategy, financial profile, uses of the finance being raised and how and from what sources the facility is to be repaid. This is the opportunity for the borrower to establish the soundness of its credit to the banks.

The invitations to participate in the transaction will then explain the terms and fees in more detail, with a date by which invited banks must respond.

Information memorandum

To complement the bank presentation, the arranger and borrower will almost always prepare some form of information package to provide further background on the company and the transaction. The contents of the information memorandum will depend on the complexity of the company and the deal itself. For a straightforward transaction involving only the borrower's relationship banks, this information package may only consist of the latest historical financials plus some brokers reports. For more complex financings it may also include financial models and an in-depth analysis of the company's markets and strategy.

Documentation

After invitations have been sent out, the company and arranger will spend the next couple of weeks in agreeing loan documentation. It is usual for the arranger to review the first drafts of the loan document before providing them to the company for review. The lawyers responsible for drafting the loan agreement will be appointed by the arranger.

At the same time, invited banks will be reviewing the terms of the transaction, assessing the credit and obtaining credit approval. They will also raise queries, most of which can be handled by the arranger. Some questions however, will need to be answered by the treasurer.

At the end of the allocated time the invited banks must reply, either accepting participation, and if so specifying the commitment they are making, or refusing it. At this stage the company will know how much it has raised. If it has raised more than it requires it can usually either decide to increase the facility size or scale back each individual bank's commitment.

Once the company has agreed the loan documentation, it is then handed to the participating banks for their agreement.

Signing

Once the loan document has been agreed between the company and participating banks, it is signed by all parties. Before the company can sign, it will need to conform to the conditions precedent in the loan document. Examples of these conditions precedent are:

- The company has full authority in its Articles of Association and Memorandum to enter into the transaction.
- There are no substantial legal claims outstanding against the company.
- There have been board resolutions accepting the terms of the loan and authorizing certain individuals to both sign the loan document and operate the loan (usually issuing drawdown notices).
- Copies of specimen signatures are provided.

Costs, margins and fees

These will vary from transaction to transaction, and depend on the appetite of the banks to provide such finance. Generally the borrower will expect to pay the following fees, margins and costs.

Arrangement fee

This is a one-off up-front fee, based on the facility size, and is paid to the arrangers for their work in putting the transaction together.

If the facility is being underwritten, underwriting fees will be included in the arrangement fees. The overall up-front fee will also include participation fees.

Participation fee

Participation fees are paid to syndicate banks for their participation. This fee is paid to them by the arranger from the overall arrangement fee. The amount usually depends on the level of their commitment to the transaction.

Margin

A margin is paid on all drawings under the facility. The margin is added to the underlying interest rate applicable to that drawing.

Commitment fee

This is paid on the undrawn portion of the facility and is calculated daily. The commitment fee is generally approximately half the margin, since banks typically have to provide half the capital in respect of undrawn commitments that they need to provide against drawings. Commitment fees accrue on a daily basis.

Legal fees

The borrower will normally expect to pay all legal fees.

Agency fees

Fees are payable to the agent. They can be a flat rate annual fee or payable for each drawing under the facility.

ADVANTAGES AND DISADVANTAGES OF BANK FINANCE

Flexibility

The position of bank finance as part of a company's core financing is due principally to its great flexibility. Most forms of bank finance can be repaid without penalty, by giving the necessary notice laid down in the loan document. This is generally not more than three months. Corporate strategies may change, and as a result capital expenditure programmes may be cancelled. What were regarded as key subsidiaries and assets may subsequently be sold. As a result of such events a company's requirements for finance can alter substantially (it may even find itself with net cash). The ability to adjust the loan capital structure without penalty is therefore an extremely attractive option to have.

Multi-currency

Most revolving facilities give the borrower the ability to make drawings in different currencies (provided these currencies are freely available on the foreign exchange markets). This can have benefits for a company that is managing its translation exposure by borrowing in the currency in which its overseas assets are denominated.

Structuring

Bank finance can be structured to meet different requirements. For instance facilities may be:

- Arranged in different tranches, for example a 364-day tranche, plus a three-year tranche and plus a five-year tranche. This may reduce the overall cost of the facility, and also meet re-financing objectives the company has.
- Repaid in stages over a period of time, for instance repaid evenly over a three-year period. This may match the cashflow profile of a particular project.

Rating

No rating is required. For some companies this may be a substantial advantage over the bond market where credit ratings are required.

Speed

Generally banking facilities can be established quite rapidly A typical outline timetable to establish a revolving facility may be:

	Weeks
Determine outline financing needs. Obtain board approval for the facility	1
Select arranging bank (including beauty parades)	2
Agree terms with arranger	1
Presentation to potential participating banks	1
Review loan documentation. Acceptance/rejection by invited banks	2
Documentation reviewed by banks	1
Signing	1
Total weeks	9

A determined effort from the treasurer can ensure that the process is completed in less time.

Ancillary business

Many banks consider that the return they obtain for providing bank finance is insufficient to meet their cost of capital requirements. The only way that this problem can be addressed is for the bank to obtain more profitable business from the borrower, for example: cash management services, capital market transactions, or treasury products. However, many companies find that the ancillary business they can offer is strictly limited and certainly insufficient to satisfy the appetite of major banks. In such circumstances the corporate treasurer may find some of the banks in the syndicate wanting to transfer their participation to banks with whom there is no existing relationship.

Maturity

Most bank finance is for comparatively short periods and, with the exception of project finance, maturities currently do not extend much beyond five to seven years. Other loan instruments are needed if longer maturities are being sought.

Terms and conditions

Generally the terms and conditions attached to bank finance are more onerous than those for public bonds, particularly in terms of financial covenants, ability to undertake major restructurings and disposal of assets. There are many circumstances where permission may be needed from the banking syndicate to undertake certain transactions, which is not required under public bonds.

DOCUMENTATION

Loan mechanics

This section covers the process, the timetable for which, and the format in which requests for advances need to be received by the agent. The margin applied to the borrowing will be specified together with mandatory costs (the costs of the lender in complying with central bank mandatory deposit rules). In addition there is a means of determining the interest rate for the period of the advance, LIBOR (see Appendix) for example, to which the margin is added.

Representations and warranties

These cover matters such as the power of the company to borrow, the authorization of the borrowing by the company and the enforceability of the company's obligations. The borrower also warrants the fact that there has been no adverse material change in its financial position since the date of its last audited accounts and that the company is not involved in any material litigation.

Representations and warranties are typically repeated at the time of every drawdown.

Covenants

One of the key elements in a banking facility will be the terms and conditions attached to the finance. Covenants provide a framework that lenders use to reach an understanding with a borrower regarding how the borrower will conduct its business and financial affairs. Borrowers will generally seek to obtain the least restrictive covenants they can, so that they will be free to manage their business with the maximum flexibility. Lenders will generally be sympathetic to allowing the borrower to get on with the management of the business with the minimum of interference, but they are concerned to protect the capital that they have put at a company's disposal. Covenants fall into a number of distinct categories.

Preservation of repayment capacity

There are a number of concerns here. First, that the company's shareholders are not enriched at the expense of the lenders. Second, that the borrower does not reduce its ability to service the debt by excessive borrowings. Last, that the earnings base is not diluted through asset sales, where the proceeds of sale are not re-invested back into the business. There may therefore be restrictions in applying the funds raised through the borrowing in repurchasing shares, a restriction to ensure that the proceeds of asset sales are re-invested back into the business, and a prevention of excessive borrowings.

Protection against financial restructurings

Banks are particularly concerned that a company may restructure and divert cash-generating assets away from the lenders and the servicing of the debt. The lenders will be concerned therefore to protect themselves against major restructurings, generally by their consent being required before such restructurings can be effected.

Protection in the event of bankruptcy or default

Lenders are concerned with establishing the following three conditions:

- That should the company fail to meet its obligations under the loan agreement, the syndicate is able to establish a default and claim immediate repayment of outstanding borrowings and the cancellation of all commitments (default).
- That if the company defaults under any other financing or derivative instrument, they have the ability to claim default under their own agreement (cross default). This prevents a situation where some lenders can claim default and realize some of the company's assets, while other lenders have to stand by.
- That in the event of bankruptcy or liquidation, other lenders are unable to claim priority through, for example, exercising security. This is normally reflected in a negative pledge clause (the company being unable to raise secured debt), and pari passu (all unsecured creditors ranking equally).

Signals and triggers

These are designed to provide an early warning of a deterioration in the credit. Most signals and triggers are in the form of financial ratios such as minimum net worth and minimum interest cover that a company must comply with. The purpose of such triggers is to bring the parties together to decide what action may be necessary if a signal or trigger is breached. Such action may be a restriction on dividends and capital expenditure, or a requirement for asset sales or cost reduction measures until the credit worthiness of the company is rectified.

Some covenants, if well drafted, can of course serve more than one purpose. For instance a trigger in the form of a financial covenant may also help preserve repayment capacity. Covenants will also vary according to the credit quality and financial strength of the borrower. Generally, the higher the credit quality, the less stringent the overall covenant pacakage.

The specific covenants appearing in loan documents will vary. However, the more common ones are described below.

Specific covenants

Covenants that will always apply

- information requirements (generally all information sent to shareholders is always provided to the banks)
- default and cross default/cross acceleration
- how modifications to the agreement will be effected.

Covenants that may apply

- a limitation on the ability to raise secured borrowings (negative pledge)
- a limitation on sale and leaseback transactions
- a limitation on mergers or consolidations
- a limitation on sale of assets
- limitations on raising further debt
- restrictions on certain payments. these may include dividends, and share repurchases
- change of control provisions
- triggers including: minimum net worth, minimum interest cover or EBITDA/interest, maximum leverage.

Negotiating the document

In negotiating covenants the corporate treasurer needs to be sympathetic to the concerns and aims of the banks. A company wants the freedom to implement its basic strategy, and the treasurer should always ensure that the loan document provides such freedom. Equally, there may be little point in trying to eliminate covenants that have little impact on the company but are essential safeguards for the lender.

A treasurer needs to be robust in the approach to negotiating loan documentation and ensure that the covenants suggested are those required to get the transaction completed on terms that the treasurer considers necessary. Covenants should match the business profile of the borrower and the way the company is structured and operates.

In negotiating the document, the treasurer also needs to apply a number of common sense tests. Some of these are:

- Is there *de-minimus* applied to cross default so that cross default cannot be claimed for small defaults elsewhere in the organization? Depending on the size of the company, a usual level might be US$10 million.
- Should a creditor waive a default, then the cross default clause should not trigger.
- Is there adequate carve-out in the negative pledge for secured debt that

may need to be issued? Is there also a *de-minimus* level to allow for small amounts of secured debt?

- Does the default clause allow time for the cause of default to be rectified? This caters for the situations that occur, even in the best-run departments, where due to oversights interest or principal is not paid on time.
- Are financial covenants in the form of financial ratios well below internal ratios used for managing the business? If the business is managed with a four times interest cover, then any financial ratios that are covenants within the loan document should be set well below four times.
- Is there a provision for a majority of banks to agree to amendment of the terms?

SPECIALIST FINANCING

Acquisition finance

Acquisition finance is an example of a specialist form of bank financing mentioned earlier. There are certain key aspects to this form of financing.

Certainty of funds

This rule applies in many countries and relates to offers for companies listed (and often unlisted) and resident in that country. The rule requires the financial advisor to the offeror to confirm in the offer document that resources are available to the offeror sufficient to satisfy full acceptance of the offer. The form of certainty is highly dependent on the company's advisors, and also depends on the size of the bid and the relative sizes of the acquirer and target companies. However many advisors interpret this rule to mean that the company must have an acquisition facility capable of being drawn down when the offer for the company is announced. Most advisors require financing available to cover the next 18 months' cashflow (including the acquisition). Certain funds when required are achieved by the lending banks agreeing to waive certain restrictions in the facility agreement such that the acquirer can offer the certainty of funding during the acquisition period (for instance financial covenants may not apply during the offer period).

Secrecy

The acquiring company wants to keep its plans of the acquisition secret until the day the bid is launched. Should news of an impending bid leak out to the market, the share price of the target company is likely to rise. This may result in the acquirer paying substantially more than would otherwise be the case.

Small banking group

Since the acquirer needs to keep the proposed transaction secret, the acquisition finance needs to be provided initially by the smallest possible banking group. This also means that there is no possibility of having a beauty parade of potential providers of finance and thus receiving alternative and competitive bids for the mandate. Depending on the size of the facility, it may be possible for the acquisition facility to be provided by just one bank. Larger facilities will need to be provided by two or more banks, who will underwrite the facility to facilitate the bid, which is then syndicated more widely once the bid is public.

The following case study is intended to provide an example of some of the issues that arise in establishing an acquisition facility.

CASE STUDY: ACQUISITION FINANCE

Background

A major UK multinational company is planning a large acquisition. The target company is quoted on the Frankfurt Stock Exchange. Summary details of the acquisition are:

- Number of shares issued in target company: 200 million. In addition there are a further 10 million shares in unexercised share options.
- Market price of shares: €20. The company is planning to offer a premium of 10 per cent to the market value, but is prepared to go to a premium of 15 per cent.
- The company's cashflow forecasts show an outflow of UK£300 million over the next 18 months.
- The target company has net debt of €2 billion.
- Deal costs are estimated to be €50 million.

- The UK company has net cash of UK£500 million.
- €/UK£0.70.

Questions

1. What would be the size of the acquisition facility that as treasurer you would have to put together?
2. How would you go about raising the finance?
3. What would be the concerns of the banks that provide the initial facility? How would they seek to manage these concerns?
4. What structural issues would need to be considered?

SOLUTION

Acquisition finance case study

1. Funding requirements

	€
Opening net cash	(714)
Equity consideration	4830
Target net debt assumed	2000
Cash outflow over next 18 months	430
Deal costs	50
Total funding requirement	6596

The total funding requirement may be reduced by any cashflow from the time of announcing the deal to its completion.

It is assumed that the target company's loan documents specify that the loan is repayable if there is a change of control.

2. Raising the finance

The treasurer will want to be sure that the necessary funds will be raised within the timetable available, in strictest secrecy and on the best terms possible. A treasurer's concerns will cover:

- Certainty of being able to raise the finance. This is generally the biggest concern. The treasurer can only approach those banks that he/she is certain will provide the funds. It is not desirable to approach a number of banks because of the risk that news of the planned acquisition might leak into the market. Many treasurers try to cover this by identifying, in times when no acquisition is being planned, the capabilities and pricing of those banks that are potential providers of acquisition finance. Banks can be approached to assess how much finance they could provide, how quickly and on what terms. This homework will stand the treasurer in good stead should an acquisition later be undertaken by his/her company.
- The strictest confidentiality must be maintained. While confidentiality letters can be signed these are never the complete answer, and the

treasurer needs to be satisfied that the selected banks are completely secure.

- There is a detailed rationale for the acquisition, together with details of the synergies and proforma profit and loss, cashflow and balance sheets of the combined entities.
- Speed. Most acquisitions are undertaken against very tight time pressures, and establishing available finance is often one of the critical points on the timetable. Usually a treasurer will want a commitment in principle within a couple of days. Again, the treasurer needs to be confident that the banks approached can respond in principle in a matter of two to three days.
- A re-financing plan that will show how a high margin acquisition facility is going to be replaced with more cost-effective instruments.
- The acquisition facility is provided on terms, pricing and structure consistent with the bidding company's credit rating, market standing and financing needs. The treasurer needs to be aware of the alternative structures available and how much they may cost, for example, a 364-day facility with a six-month term out versus a two-year facility.

3. The banks' concerns

Typically, the lead banks' concerns are to manage their exposures as effectively as possible. Many of their concerns will be expressed in the loan document. Typical covenants within an acquisition finance documents are:

- Finance is available from completion of conditions precedent.
- Any funds raised through any re-financing (e.g. bond issues, medium-term note issues) are to be used to pay down the acquisition facility.
- Any proceeds from asset disposals are to be used to pay down acquisition finance.
- The facility is cancelled if the bid is not launched, or if the bid is not concluded.
- The facility is cancellable upon change of control.
- The facility is only available for the contemplated specific acquisition.
- Financial covenants. Depending on the size of the company these are

likely to be cashflow based (e.g. EBITDA/interest and net debt/EBITDA).

- Any changes in market conditions. The lead banks will be looking to syndicate their portion of the facility as soon as possible. They will want protection in the event that there is a change in market conditions between the time that the acquisition facility is provided and syndication starts. The major change would be a change in the applicable margin due to market forces.

Typical income for the banks will include:

- arrangement fee including underwriting
- commitment fee
- margin on drawings
- term-out fee.

Banks providing acquisition facilities also aim to win a significant role in subsequent re-financings of the facility.

4. Other issues

The banks will consider the following in determining the pricing and structure of the facility:

- Who is the borrower, and what is its standing and recognition in the market? Is the borrower well known to the market?
- What is the borrower's credit rating (if any)?
- What ancillary business is available?
- What is the market perception of the acquisition? Will the transaction be well received by the banking community?
- Certainty of funding requirement to meet stock exchange requirement. What is the cashflow profile for the next 12–18 months?
- Maturity of the facility. (Typically an acquisition facility is envisaged as a bridge into capital markets.)
- What will the financial structure of new organization look like (EIBTDA/interest, interest cover etc.)?

- What is the company's re-financing strategy?

Due to their pricing, acquisition facilities are generally comparatively short term. Often they are for tenors of 364 days to two years, but generally with a term out (an ability to extend the facility if re-financing has not been effected on maturity of the facility). Depending on the overall financing and the borrower's longer-term re-financing plans, an acquisition facility may comprise several tranches of varying maturities such as: a short-term, 364 day tranche to be re-financed by capital market transactions or disposals; a three-year bullet revolving facility to provide ongoing working capital finance, and a five-year fully amortizing term loan as further core debt.

CHAPTER 5

Bond Valuation and Credit Ratings

INTRODUCTION TO BOND VALUATION

A bond represents a legally binding obligation on the part of the issuer of the bond to pay interest on the bond on the stated coupon dates and at the coupon rates and to repay the principal on maturity. The majority of bonds that are issued by corporates pay a fixed rate of interest throughout their lives.

Bonds can be brought and sold throughout their life and the market price at which a bond will trade will constantly change throughout its life. These changes in the market price of the bond will be the result of many factors some of which include:

- a change in the demand for bonds
- a change in the market's perception of the issuing company's credit worthiness
- a change in the outlook for interest rates.

Bond mathematics

Calculating the price of a bond

Assume a bond with a face value of US$1 million that pays an 8 per cent coupon and has four years to run to maturity. A purchaser of the bond would receive the following cashflows:

Today	*Year 1*	*Year 2*	*Year 3*	*Year 4*
Pay	Receive	Receive	Receive	Receive
Price	US$80,000	US$80,000	US$80,000	US$1,080,000

The US$80,000 is the annual coupon (8 per cent on US$1 million) and the amount received in year four is the final coupon plus the face value of the bond (US$1 million), which the issuer pays on maturity. The above represent a series of fixed cashflows that the bond purchaser knows will be received once s/he owns the above bond and has the intention of holding it to maturity.

Let us assume that the investor wants to obtain a return on his/her investment of 5 per cent. The price that must be paid for the bond to achieve the 5 per cent return is calculated by discounting all the future coupons plus the principal repaid at the end of four years by 5 per cent. The target return of 5 per cent relates to the market return the investor believes can be achieved on other bonds of similar credit quality and maturity. It is lower than the coupon rate payable on the bond because market rates have fallen since the bond was issued (see Table 5.1).

Table 5.1 Cash flows from a bond with an 8 per cent coupon and four years to maturity discounted at 5 per cent

Year 1	*Year 2*	*Year 3*	*Year 4*	*Total*
$\frac{80,000}{(1+0.05)}$	$\frac{80,000}{(1+0.05)^2}$	$\frac{80,000}{(1+0.05)^3}$	$\frac{1,080,000}{(1+0.05)^4}$	
76,190.48	72,562.36	69,107.01	888,518.67	1,106,378.52

In the table the cashflows from the bond are discounted at 5 per cent, to calculate a net present value of US$1,106,378.52. The result of the above calculation tells us that the investor should not pay more than US$1,106,378.52 for the bond in order to achieve the target yield. In the bond markets, the price of a bond is not quoted as a cash value, but as a percentage of the face value of the bond. This enables a single price to be quoted for a bond regardless of the denomination being sold. In the case of the above bond, the price quoted would be 110.638 per cent, which would apply whether US$10 million was being purchased or US$10,000.

Yield

So far we have assumed that the buyer of the bond has a certain target yield or return. However, an investor may well be faced with the choice of deciding between two different bonds and wanting to know which would give the highest return.

There are five basic variables involved in the valuation of a bond:

- coupon rate
- maturity date
- redemption price (price at which the bond will be repaid)
- present value
- yield (return).

Generally the first three are always known. Provided also that four of the above five variables are known, it is always possible to solve for the fifth. Most financial calculators have facilities to calculate the yield to maturity (YTM) for a bond, as does Exel 97. The CD attached to this book contains a spreadsheet that shows how to calculate YTM.

Price/yield relationship

In the example above, the price was calculated for a bond, for which the required return was below the coupon rate. As the coupon was fixed at the time of the bond's issue, the only way that the return to a subsequent buyer can reflect current market levels of interest rates is for the market price of the bond to change. This, then, gives the buyer of the bond in the secondary market either a capital gain or loss when the purchase price is compared with the principal paid on redemption. If the coupon is high in comparison to current markets rates, a capital loss will be necessary to offset the effect of above market receipts from the coupons. This capital loss will arise because the bond will be sold at a premium to face value (par), but only redeemed at face value (par). Should the coupon be below current market rates, the investor will require a capital gain to offset the effect of coupons below market (Figure 5.1).

Reinvestment of coupons

The method described above assumes that the interest received via coupons on the bond is compounded at the discount rate. In other words, in the example above the assumption is that the coupons received can be reinvested at 5 per cent.

In fact, the coupons received will be re-invested at the different rates of interest ruling at the time they are received. These rates are unknown when the bond is first purchased and so the market needs to make an assumption about what they will be. In reality no single estimate is any better than any other, and so the market works on the simple assumption that coupons can

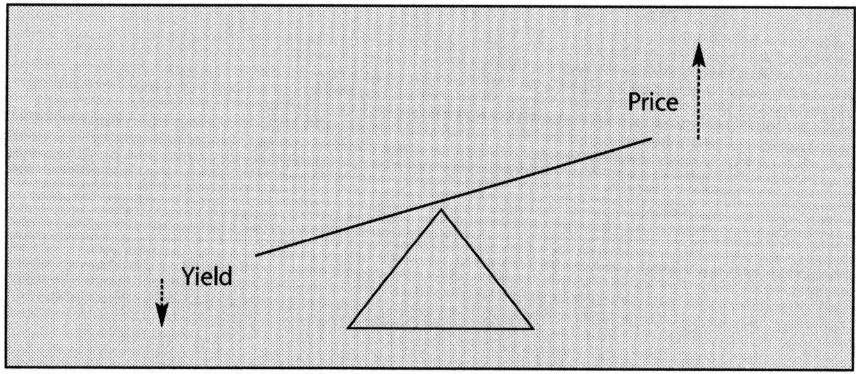

Figure 5.1 Bond yield and price relationship

be re-invested at the discount rate. (However see the chapter on zero-coupon bonds.) This means, therefore, that a bond investment is most unlikely actually to achieve the indicated yield to maturity on its purchase, and the final yield achieved when the bond is redeemed will depend on rates actually available during the life of the bond.

Government bonds

Government bonds are defined as those issued by a government or government-backed entity. They are issued in the domestic market in the domestic currency. In addition to taxation, borrowing is a major source of funds for governments. Examples of US and UK government bonds are as follows.

US Treasuries

These are issued by the US Department of the Treasury. There are three forms of security:

T-bills: have a maturity of less than one year and are issued at a discount.

T-Notes: have maturities of two to ten years and pay a coupon semi-annually.

T-bonds: have a maturity of over ten years and pay semi-annual coupons.

US Treasuries are issued either by using a single price auction, where all securities are awarded at the highest yield (lowest price), or by a competitive (Dutch style) auction, where securities are awarded at successively higher yields (lower prices) until the total is awarded.

Secondary market

1. Treasuries trade in prices of 1/32.
2. Settlement is at T+1 (Transaction date + one day).
3. Coupons are paid semi-annually, and accrued interest is calculated on an actual–actual basis.

UK government bonds

The UK government issues four types of bonds (Gilts):

Straights: these have bullet repayments.

Convertibles: these are generally of short maturity with conversion schedules allowing conversion of the issue into other issues with specified conversion dates.

Index linked: coupons and principal are linked to the retail price index (RPI).

Perpetual: no final maturity, but are redeemable after particular dates on three months notice.

Gilts come in four maturity bands, as shown in Table 5.2.

Secondary market

1. Gilts trade in 1/32.
2. Settlement is at T+1.
3. Coupons are paid semi-annually with accrued interest calculated on an actual–actual basis.

Table 5.2 Gilt maturity bonds

Category	*Maturity band (remaining life)*
Short	0–7 years
Medium	7–15 years
Long	15+ years
Undated	No set redemption date

The yield curve

The term structure of interest rates for UK Gilts is the pattern of yields to maturity for UK Gilts for a number of different maturities. It is commonly called the yield curve for UK Gilts.

The term structure for UK interest rates shown in Figure 5.2 was calculated by plotting the yield for Gilts maturing within the years shown on the graph. For instance the yield for the Treasury 5 per cent maturing in 2008 was 4.30 per cent at close of business on 21 December 2002. That yield gives the number for the six-year yield in the graph.

There are a number of important facts to be recognized about yield curves:

- There are different yield curves for different instruments. For instance, there would have been a yield curve at 22 December 2002 for US Treasuries, Eurobonds, and Japanese Government Bonds. Each of these yield curves would have been different.
- The yield curve for a particular instrument (e.g. UK Gilts) will change from day to day. This change will be due to changing demand for, and supply of, bonds together with changing views on interest rates.
- Yield curves at different times will have different shapes. For instance the yield curve for UK Gilts at 21 December 2002 (Figure 5.2) was gently upwards sloping. The yield on the Treasury 6.5 per cent 2004 (two-year interest rate) was 3.76 per cent, while that on the 6 per cent

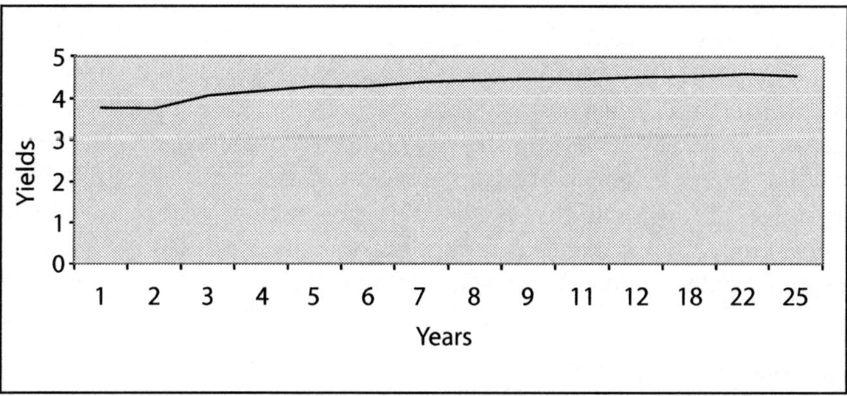

Figure 5.2 Term structure of interest rates based on UK Gilt yields at 21 December 2002

2028 (26-year interest rate) was 4.54 per cent. Some yield curves are flat and others downward sloping. The shape of the yield curve will be based on factors such as the demand for the underlying instrument and the view the market is taking on the future course of interest rates. For example, when the market believes interest rates will rise in the future, the yield curve will generally be upwards sloping.

Corporate bond yields

Corporate bond spreads

For an investor buying a corporate bond denominated in US dollars, the benchmark is the relevant US Treasury Bond with the same maturity. Given the opportunity to buy a US$ five-year corporate bond, the investor will first refer to the yield available on five-year US Treasuries. The difference between the yield that can be obtained on the US Treasury Note and that on the US$-denominated corporate bond is referred to as the spread. Since the US Treasury Note is a risk-free instrument, a corporate bond should provide an investor with a higher yield to compensate for the additional risk. The investor then has a decision as to whether the spread is large enough to compensate for the additional credit risk taken on the corporate bond.

For instance the yield to maturity on the ten-year US Treasury may be 4.00 per cent, and an investor is offered a corporate bond yielding 5.50 per cent to maturity. The spread in this case is 1.50 per cent or 150 basis points, and the investor has to determine whether this additional yield compensates for the additional risks in holding the corporate bond.

When examining corporate bonds, the investor therefore will refer to the yield available from the government bond for the same maturity and the same currency.

It is important to recognize that corporate bond spreads will widen and narrow over time. When the demand for corporate bonds is high, the spread between corporate bonds and the relevant government security narrows. Investors prefer corporate bonds to government securities and will bid up the price of corporate bonds vis-à-vis government securities. When demand for corporate bonds is lower, investors prefer to hold government securities and hence the spread widens (Figure 5.3).

Significance of spread

This concept of the spread between the corporate bond and the underlying government bond is extremely important for the corporate treasurer issuing

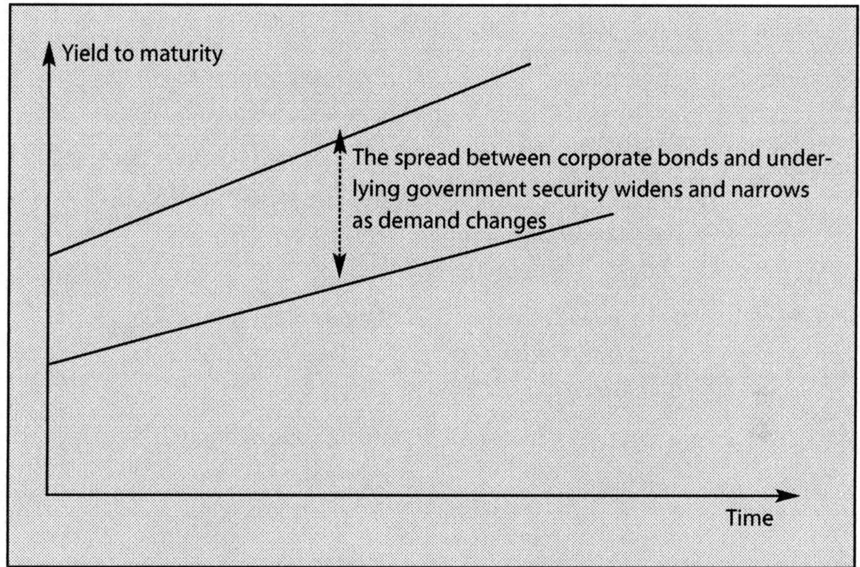

Figure 5.3 Corporate bond spreads

in the bond market. The lead arranger will provide information about the spread over the relevant government security that his/her company should issue at. The treasurer needs to be completely satisfied that the recommended spread is correct. Too wide and the company will be paying too much for the money it is raising.

Accrued interest

Day count conventions

Various markets have different conventions for calculating how much interest accrues day by day on a bond. It is the manner in which days are counted that creates the different bases of calculation of accrued interest. There are four main day count bases, shown in Table 5.3.

Example

Consider a bond with coupons payable on 18 January and 18 July. Interest is to be accrued up to 30 March 2002 or, if that is a Sunday, 31 March, or if 30 and 31 March are Saturday and Sunday, 1 April. The number of days in the current period (18 January, to 18 July is 181). This is outlined in Table 5.4.

Table 5.3 Calculation of accrued interest under different conventions

Day count basis	*Convention*	*Examples of markets where convention is found*
Actual/actual	Actual days elapsed since the last coupon date /2 × actual number of days in coupon period	Government bonds of Australia, Canada, New Zealand, UK, USA and Euro
Actual/365	Actual days elapsed since last coupon date/365	Government bond of Japan, Norway
30(A)/360	• If D1 = 31 then D1 = 30 • If D2 = 31, but D1 is not = 30 or 31 then D2 = 31	US Corporate bonds, US Govt. Agencies & US Municipal
30(E)/360	• If D1 = 31 then D1 = 30 • If D2 = 31 then D2 = 30	Eurobonds

Note: D1 is the first day of interest accrual. D2 is the last day of interest accrual. The number of days between dates is given by (Y2-Y1) × 360 + (M2-M1) × 30 + (D2-D1)

Business day conventions

In the bond markets, if a regular coupon date falls on a weekend or holiday, the payment is generally delayed until the next business day but the amount of the payment is not altered.

Table 5.4 Examples of interest accrual under different conventions

	30 March	*31 March*	*1 April*
Actual/actual	71/362	72/362	73/362
Actual/365	71/365	72/365	72/365
30(A)/360	72/360	73/360	73/360
30(E)/360	72/360	72/360	73/360

Following business day/next good business day

Dates are adjusted for weekends and holidays to the next good business day. For instance if interest was being accrued to the 15 August and that day was a Sunday, then interest would be accrued to the 16 August.

Preceding/previous good business day

As above but dates are adjusted for weekends and holidays to the previous good business day. In the above example interest would be accrued to 13 August.

Modified following/modified business day

Dates are adjusted to the next good business day unless that day falls in the next calendar month, in which case the date is adjusted to the previous good business day. Interest is due to be paid and calculated to 31 August, which is a Sunday. Interest is paid on and calculated to 29 August. This day convention is used in the swap markets.

CREDIT RATINGS

Introduction

In considering their financing strategy and the potential loan structure for their organization, corporate treasurers often have to decide whether their company is likely to be issuing debt either in the public bond markets or via a medium-term note programme. If the answer is yes, then their company will need a credit rating. This section covers questions such as: What are credit ratings and what is their purpose? What is involved in a corporate obtaining a credit rating? What benefits can a corporate expect from having a credit rating?

How do credit ratings operate?

What is a credit rating?

A credit rating is an independent, third-party assessment of the creditworthiness of an obligor with respect to a specific financial obligation. Credit ratings are provided by entities called credit rating agencies. These agencies are independent of any government institution, investment banking firm, bank, or similar institution. There are two agencies that have gained an international reputation over the last century: Moody's Investors Service (Moody's) and Standard and Poor's (S&P). Because of their reputation, investors tend to place great reliance on them. The advantage for the investor is that the assessment by the rating agencies is independent. It is important to emphasize that it is the financial obligation that is rated, not the company.

Credit ratings can be either short or long term. Short-term ratings are assigned to those obligations considered to be short term in the relevant market. In the United States, for instance, that mean obligations with an original maturity of no more than 365 days, and would include commercial paper.

Ratings are typically based on a letter scale. The scale ranges from AAA (Aaa for Moody's) for the highest credit quality down through down to C and D (for default)

Long-term credit ratings

Bond prices closely follow the rating scales (shown in Table 5.5). For this reason ratings receive a great deal of attention from bond traders, analysts and investors.

The credit rating agencies apply modifiers for credit worthiness lying between any of these individual scales. Standard and Poor's use + and – signs (e.g. AA+ lies between AAA and AA) and Moody's uses modifiers of 1, 2 and 3 (its Aa1 is equivalent to S&P's AA+).

Ratings of BBB or above are investment grade category. The term 'investment grade' was originally used in the United States by various regulatory bodies to connote obligations eligible for investment by institutions such as banks, insurance companies and savings and loan associations. Over time the term has gained widespread usage internationally throughout the investment community.

Historical analyses of US corporate default statistics carried out by S&P demonstrate that over a 15-year timeframe, only 0.5 per cent of issuers initially rated AAA defaulted on an obligation. Close to 30 per cent of issuers initially rated B fell into default. The biggest change is between BBB and BB where 15-year cumulative default rates have been roughly 4.5 per cent and 16.4 per cent. Hence the cut-off for investment grade at BBB.

Short-term credit ratings

It can be guessed from the above that the better a company's credit rating the lower the price they will have to pay for debt finance.

Table 5.5 Long-term rating scales for Standard and Poor's and Moody's

Standard and Poor's	*Moody's*	*Meaning (summary)*
AAA	Aaa	Top rating: the best quality, fundamentally strong
AA	Aa	High quality: strong capacity to repay; margin of protection not as large as AAA (Aaa)
A	A	Strong capacity to repay, but more susceptible to changing economic conditions
BBB	Baa	Adequate capacity for payment but protective elements may be lacking, or unreliable
BB, B, CCC, CC, C	Ba, B, Caa, Ca, C	Significant speculative characteristics, with BB (Ba) the least speculative
D	D	Default

Credit watch or review

A credit rating attempts to evaluate default risk over the life of a debt issue. To the extent that they can be anticipated, it incorporates an assessment of all future events. However, the rating agencies recognize that future performance may differ from initial expectations. Ratings appear on credit watch when an event or deviation from the expected trend has occurred, or is expected to occur. Additional information is necessary to make a rating decision. An issue may be placed on special surveillance when events such as corporate restructurings, mergers and acquisitions, or unanticipated operating developments occur. Such rating reviews are normally completed within 90 days. Although being placed on credit watch does not mean that a rating change is inevitable, in some cases it is certain that a change will occur and only the magnitude of the change is unclear.

A rating outlook, which also assesses the potential for change, is assigned to all long-term debt issues. An outlook is not necessarily a precursor to a rating change or a credit watch listing.

Table 5.6 Short-term rating scales for Standard and Poor's and Moody's

Standard and Poor's	*Moody's*	*Meaning (summary)*
A–1+	P–1	Highest grade: extremely strong capacity to meet financial obligation
A–1	P–1	Strong capacity to meet financial obligation
A–2	P–2	Ability to meet financial obligation is satisfactory
A–3	P–3	Adequate protection parameter
B		Significant speculative characteristics

Note: Issuers rated A-1/P-1 correlate generally with long-term ratings of A or better.

What is involved in obtaining a credit rating?

The ratings process

There are a number of steps involved in the process.

The company will make an approach to selected credit rating agencies to request a rating. This is usually done before the debt issue is made, so that the company can receive an indication of what rating to expect.

The rating agencies selected will assign an analyst to undertake the rating assignment. The analyst selected will be the one with the greatest relevant industry expertise. Analysts concentrate on one or two industries and cover the entire spectrum of credits within that industry. The analyst will be supported by a team of colleagues.

The company to be rated should submit background material and a written presentation to the rating agencies. Among other things the background material will include:

- Five years of audited annual financial statements.
- Last five years of interim financial reports.
- If a debt issuance is being planned, a draft of the offering memorandum or the equivalent.

- In addition, the written presentation will cover those items likely to be discussed at a subsequent meeting between the ratings analyst and the company. It will include:
  - A narrative description of the company's operations and products.
  - The industry environment the company operates in.
  - An overview of major business segments including operating statistics.
  - Management's financial policies and financial performance goals.
  - Financial projections. These will include profit and loss and cashflow statements together with balance sheets, plus the underlying market and operating assumptions behind these projections.
  - Capital spending plans.
  - Financing alternatives.

The company to be rated needs to be sure that there is sufficient time between contacting the agency and the meeting with the agency to prepare the presentation.

The rating agency will wish to meet with the company's senior management. This is likely to include the chief executive, managing directors of major operating divisions, finance director and treasurer. The purpose of the meeting is to review in detail the company's key operating and financial plans, management policies and any other factors that the agency considers may have an impact on the rating. It also allows the agency to assess management capabilities to achieve their plans Sometimes a facility tour may be included in the meeting. Meetings typically last about half a day. While management may make a formal presentation they must expect numerous questions from the analysts.

A rating committee is convened. The analyst selected to lead the rating makes a presentation. The committee votes on what the rating should be. Once the rating is determined, the company is notified of it.

How much does a credit rating cost?

Fees are paid once on obtaining an initial rating and then upon issue. They vary from agency to agency, but a broad indication is an initial rating fee of UK£25,000 to UK£40,000, depending on the complexity of the company and analysis. An issue fee would tend to be approximately 3.00 to 3.50 basis points of the issue rated, with a cap on the fee at approximately UK£50,000. The initial fee is usually offset against the issuing fee if an issue is made within a certain time.

Typical questions raised by companies

Companies often have a number of concerns when they go into the rating process. Among these concerns are:

How long does the process take?

This can vary from company to company, but in general most companies should allow at least three months. A lot depends on the complexity of the company, the availability of information and, most significantly, the resources in the company to assemble it.

Is it necessary to employ a ratings advisor?

Many of the major investment banks provide a ratings advisory service. Individuals who once worked as senior analysts at one of the major agencies staff the ratings advisory groups in these banks. When a company employs a ratings advisor it benefits from having advisors who understand how the agencies work, how they conduct their analysis and what processes and analysis they employ in reaching a rating decision. Moreover, the advisors will often prepare the written presentation to the agency and provide dress rehearsals for the meeting with the agencies, so that management are well prepared for the actual meeting. This should ensure that the company makes the best and most appropriate case for its credit strength.

Employing a ratings advisor should ensure that the whole process is undertaken as efficiently and time effectively as possible. Due to the analyst's knowledge of the rating agencies and their processes, it also means the company is able to make the best case possible for its credit.

The disadvantage with employing an advisor is that the investment bank supplying the service will expect to get the lead manager's mandate for any ensuing bond issue. It may be that this is something that the company is not prepared to commit to at the time of the rating. Care needs to be taken therefore over the terms on which the advisory service is provided.

What about confidentiality?

Many companies are concerned about the confidential nature of the information that they provide the agencies. This may comprise not only planned future capital market issues but also, more significantly, future financial projections and business plans, which may also include anticipated disposals or acquisitions. If a ratings advisor is being employed the same information will be supplied to the advisor.

Credit ratings agencies and ratings advisors work under the strictest confidentiality. However, it is often a major test of the company's faith to provide so much sensitive information.

What if we do not like the rating?

Outside the US public market, the issuers have the option not to have the rating published. This does however mean that the company will be shut out of a number of public markets that require the issuer to have a credit rating.

Once issued, will the rating change frequently?

Normally ratings, once assigned, are not expected to change very often. The agencies try to build factors such as cyclicality into their long-term ratings. For instance a company may have very strong financials that would indicate an A rating. However, if it is in a very cyclical industry such as commodity mining, it may only receive a BBB rating in anticipation of a downward part of the cycle when the company may look more like a BB credit. The agencies try to signal short and medium-term changes to the rating through the use of outlooks, these being stable, positive or negative, and typically considering a one to three-year timeframe.

How credit ratings are assigned

As mentioned, credit ratings are assigned to different types of debt instruments. The ratings can vary depending on:

The characteristics of the instrument: For instance a deeply subordinated debt structure would typically have a lower rating than a senior security issued by the same company.

Where the debt is issued within the corporate structure: Holding company debt can often carry a lower rating than subsidiary company debt, since in a number of cases the real assets are at subsidiary level.

The starting point for assigning a debt rating to a security tends to be a fundamental analysis of the group issuing the debt. This is what S&P call its Corporate Credit Rating (CCR) and Moody's call Senior Implied Rating. The rating assigned to the debt issue may then be adjusted to reflect the specifics of the debt issue. For instance a company may be assigned an

A, CCR or Senior Implied Rating. If that company has minimal debt and it issues debt at the holding company level, the new debt would probably be assigned an A rating. If there is substantial debt at subsidiary company level, however, then the debt issued at holding company level would probably be assigned BBB/Baa to reflect the fact that subsidiary company lenders are closer to the assets and cashflow.

What methodology do the rating agencies use?

The ratings agencies focus on the cashflow available to service debt. Most debt instruments require cash to repay principal and interest; the agencies analyze a company's stand-alone ability to generate sufficient cash to run and manage its business and to service its debts.

For an international industrial company the analysis will focus on:

- *Country risk.* No issuer's debt will be rated higher than the country of origin of the issuer ('sovereign ceiling').
- *Universal/country importance.* The company's standing relative to other companies in the country of domicile and globally.
- *Industry risk.* The strength of the industry within the country, measured by the impact of economic forces, cyclical nature of the industry demand factors and cashflow, federal or state legislation etc.
- *Industry position.* Issuer's position in the relevant industry compared with competitors; for example a strong market share within an industry with inelastic demand for its products compared to a company with a small market share in an industry with low barriers to entry.
- *Management evaluation.* The company's planning, controls, financing policies and strategies, overall quality of management and succession, merger and acquisition performance record, record of achievement in financial results.
- *Company strength.* Market position, products, suppliers, expenses, operating margins and cashflow for each line of the business. Most emphasis is placed on major contributors to cashflow.
- *Financial profile.* Both historic and projected profit and cashflow (usually for the next three to five years). The agencies will test these projections for sensitivity to various factors, e.g. interest rates. In addition the agencies employ certain financial ratios with the emphasis on cashflow ratios such as cashflow to interest or cashflow relative to debt. They

also factor in the effect of off-balance sheet liabilities such as operating leases, pensions and sales of receivables.

- *Financial flexibility.* Evaluation of financing needs, plans and alternatives under stress (ability to attract capital), banking relationships and debt covenants.
- *Accounting quality.* Auditor's qualifications (if any), inventory, goodwill, depreciation policies etc.

CHAPTER 6

The Bond Markets

INTRODUCTION

Most treasurers seeking to diversify their debt financing away from the bank market, or aiming to expand the maturity or average life of their company's long-term debts, will need to examine the bond markets. This chapter explains the principal bond markets available to a corporate, how they operate and the advantages and disadvantages of bond markets in relation to bank finance.

ADVANTAGES/DISADVANTAGES OF BOND MARKETS

Terms

Generally the terms in the major bond markets are less onerous than the bank market. Covenants in the public markets are generally more standardized and often less demanding than the bank market. For instance the Eurobond market requires a simple negative pledge, default and cross default.

Better pricing

Companies can often attract cheaper financing in the various bond markets than they can in the bank market. This pricing comparison needs to be made on an 'all-in' basis after accounting for lead management fees and rating agency costs.

Diversification of funding sources

Companies raising finance in the bond markets are able to diversify their funding away from reliance on the bank market. As already mentioned this diversification gives greater security to the provision of finance to fund the company's strategy.

Longer maturities

The bank market is generally limited to five or seven years. Issues can be made in most of the bond markets for maturities out to 10, 25 or even 50 years.

Inflexibility

One of the problems with the bond markets is the difficulty a treasurer may find if the terms of the bond need to be revised to permit a corporate transaction. It is comparatively easy to sit down with relationship banks and discuss the reasons for proposed changes to the loan documentation. Providing the banks can understand the commercial logic of the transaction and they believe that their position is not being jeopardized by the proposed changes, they are normally sympathetic to the proposal. With bond issues the borrower is normally dealing with the trustee on small matters, or having to deal with a meeting of the investors for more significant matters. This involves obtaining a quorum of investors, with all the time-consuming difficulties of issuing notices.

In addition, once bonds have been issued it is expensive to redeem them before their maturity date. As already discussed, bank debt can be repaid without penalty by the borrower on giving the requisite period of notice.

Rating required

For most bond markets other than the private placement market, the issuer needs a rating. For some companies, particularly those for whom the benefits of the bond markets are marginal, this may be yet one more piece of administration and cost.

More time consuming

Issuing in either the public or private markets can often be more time consuming than the bank market. There are generally more parties to the issue, since approval is needed from regulatory authorities, trustees are involved in the transaction, and agreements need to be reached with lead managers on underwriting. There is more documentation to be agreed than with bank finance, where there is generally just the loan agreement.

THE PRICING OF CORPORATE BONDS

Format for new issues

When examining the different opportunities in the various bond markets, the treasurer will need to calculate the all-in cost of funds of any financing being considered. Most investment banks that lead manage corporate bond issues tend to show indicative pricing in a standard format. The calculations are shown in Table 6.1, and explained below.

1. The corporate bond market works with certain benchmark government bonds. For instance the issue of a new ten-year sterling Eurobond will be compared with a Gilt maturing in ten years' time. If there are two or more securities maturing in ten years, then the market will chose the one most recognized by investors (which also tends to be the largest and most liquid). A new benchmark is usually selected every year for that particular maturity. As already discussed, the role of the benchmark security is important since the government securities in many countries represent the risk-free debt security. Any other debt security that investors purchase should, therefore, provide a higher yield than the relevant government security with the same maturity.

Table 6.1 Calculating the all-in cost of a fixed rate corporate bond

Calculating the funding cost of a ten-year EuroSterling issue		
Government security benchmark (ten-year Gilt rate)	(1)	4.56
Spread (95 basis points per annum)	(2)	0.95
Re-offer rate	(3)	5.51
Management, underwriting and selling (40 basis points)	(4)	0.04
All-in fixed rate cost	(5)	5.55
Swap rate (receive fixed pay floating)	(6)	5.15
Floating rate equivalent cost of funds		LIBOR + 40 bp

2. The spread is determined by a number of factors, all of them directly or indirectly related to the corporate's credit standing. Clearly a corporate's credit rating will have a major influence on the size of the spread: the higher the rating the smaller (or tighter) the spread; the lower the rating the wider the spread. However, the size of the spread is influenced by a number of other factors. These may include: whether the corporate has other bond issues in the market and how they are trading; where the bonds of other corporates in the same business sector and with similar credit ratings are trading; and the current sentiment of the market; to name just a few.
3. The re-offer reflects the price at which the lead manager will offer the bonds to investors. The investors will buy the bonds at a price that will provide them with a yield of 5.51 per cent.
4. Corporate bonds are underwritten by the lead manager(s), who buys the bonds from the corporate and re-offers them to institutional investors. In return for the near certainty of being able to issue the bonds at the re-offer price (or yield), the corporate pays a management, underwriting and selling fee. Such fees need to be amortized over the life of the bond to determine the annual cost of underwriting.
5. The all-in cost of funds.
6. Many corporates want to know what the equivalent floating cost of funds is. This is because they will compare the bond markets with other forms of finance that are raised on a floating basis, such as the bank market, or because they have a floating cost of funds target for any finance raised (see pages 230 and 235).

In addition to the above the treasurer also must remember legal, printing and accounting and rating agency fees. However, amortized over the life of the bond, these are unlikely to be significant.

Regular updates

A corporate treasurer contemplating an issue in the bond markets should receive regular indicative pricing schedules similar to the above from relationship banks who are potential lead managers for an issue. (It is important to ensure that these pricing schedules are prepared by the syndicate manager and reflect the bank's view as to the pricing for the treasurer's company.) To maintain consistency and effective comparison between indications, it is important that the treasurer ensures that banks are using the same benchmark security and that the yield/price of this security is taken at the same date.

Most investment banks are always willing to provide indicative pricing for a range of maturities, for instance five, seven and ten years, in the currency and market of the treasurer's choice. It is the quality of this dialogue that will be one of the inputs into the selection of the investment bank to handle any bond issue.

BOND MARKETS: GENERAL

Domestic bonds

The international bond markets consist of two broad sectors: domestic and foreign bonds, and Eurobonds. Domestic bonds are those issued by domestic entities in their domestic currency.

Domestic bond markets are regulated by the domestic authorities, who conventionally impose regulations on the issuance of bonds by both domestic and foreign issuers. For instance a public bond offering in the United States must obey the regulations set out by the Securities and Exchange Commission (SEC). Some of the common restrictions that domestic regulations impose include:

- type of debt structures
- issue size and frequency
- minimum ratings
- waiting period before issuance
- reporting standards and disclosure.

Eurobonds

The key aspect of Eurobonds is that they are issued for international distribution, and consequently are outside the regulatory scope of the country of issue. For instance a sterling Eurobond issued by a UK corporate and listed by the UK Listing Authority is outside the full regulatory scope of the domestic sterling bond market. While domestic bonds are normally registered, Eurobonds are unregistered. The Eurobond market is split into a number of different sectors such as Eurodollar, Eurosterling, Euroyen and euro-Eurobonds. Each sector has its own characteristics in terms of issue size and maturities.

The Eurobond market attracts little regulation from host regulators. Issues are considered 'private placements' that are offered by the underwriters via dealers to institutional and private customers. Most Eurobonds are listed by either the UK Listing Authority or the Luxembourg Stock Exchange. A Eurobond listed by the UK Listing Authority, while subject to the requirements of that authority, is subject to far less regulation and disclosure than that applicable to the sterling domestic bond market. Listing is sometimes important, since some funds have limits on the unlisted securities that they can buy. Although Eurobonds are typically listed on an exchange, most trading takes place OTC (over the counter).

Eurobonds may be held by investors free of withholding tax. In most countries there are restrictions regarding the sale of Eurobonds to retail investors.

ISSUING A PUBLIC BOND: EUROBOND

While it is not important that the corporate treasurer understands the detailed mechanics of the market, it is important that he or she has a good grasp of the fundamentals of the market. This will enable a treasurer to make a more logical approach to undertaking a bond issue. The following is a brief description of the mechanics involved in issuing a Eurobond.

There are five principal steps that the treasurer is actively involved in during the issuing process:

- obtaining internal approvals for the transactions, and determining size, maturity and currency of issue
- selection of the lead manager(s)
- marketing the issue
- price discovery and launch of the bond
- agreeing the documentation accompanying the bond.

Role of lead managers

The role of the lead manager from an issuer's standpoint is varied. Generally most corporate issuers consider the role to include the following:

- *Underwriting.* The treasurer has two basic objectives: that the bond will be fully sold and that the yield is the one appropriate for market conditions on the day of issue. In other words, the company gets the money it needs and pays the right price. To ensure this occurs a bond issue needs to be underwritten. The lead manager buys the bonds from the corporate issuer and then sells them into the market at a fixed re-offer price.

- *Advice.* Treasurers look to the lead manager to provide full and proper advice. This includes which markets are considered the best ones for the treasurer's company to issue in, how these markets should be approached and the issue marketed, and the yield that the bond should be issued at (what margin above the relevant government security should be offered).
- *Roadshows and investor presentations.* The advice provided will extend to helping to put together or advising on the content of the information presented at investor roadshows and presentations, together with how different investors should be marketed.
- *Documentation.* The treasurer will need someone with expertise to manage the documentation process, to help in the preparation of the offering circular and to maintain all the necessary contacts with the exchange authorities.
- *Managing the issue process.* The lead manager will manage the process of selling the bond to investors.
- *Managing the trading* of the bond in the primary market.
- *Secondary market maker.* Lead and co-lead managers for an issue will be expected to be market makers for the bonds.

In short, the lead manager's role is to ensure that the issue is correctly priced and well received in the market, and that all the administrative elements of issuing a bond are efficiently undertaken.

How to select a lead manager

From the above it is clear that the selection of the right lead manger is one of the critical elements in a successful transaction. Selection of the lead manager should follow a rigorous and formal process, and some of the factors to be considered are as follows:

- *Proposal.* The proposals need to be very carefully analyzed. What is the distribution and trading capacity of the bank? What are the recommended pricing and terms for the proposed issue? A treasurer needs a checklist of specific questions and pointers before the banks make their presentations.

- *Corporate relationship.* One important factor for the treasurer is to determine how committed the bank is to the relationship and the potential bond issue. Is it prepared to put resources into the transaction to ensure that the customer's expectations are met, or will the transaction be just another bond issue?
- *The strength of the lead manager's syndicate presence in the market.* A strong house will have the clout in the market to ensure that the deal gets done to the client's satisfaction.
- *Pricing versus comparables.* What pricing is being recommended and by whom? Is the pricing comparable to other issues of a similar size? Where are other issues from companies of similar market capitalization, credit rating and industry sector trading? Who is committing to the pricing (this should be the syndicate manager at the bank)?
- *Flexibility.* Can the bank adapt to changes in market circumstances? One example might where the bank detects better demand and hence better pricing in different maturities or currencies from that original planned. How capable is the bank of switching maturities or currency?
- *Approach.* What is the tactical approach to the proposed deal? What is the proposed distribution for the transaction, which investors will be targeted and why? Does it fit with the corporate's objectives?
- *Derivatives capability.* If the transaction is being swapped, the house needs to have the necessary derivatives ability to give the client the floating rate objectives that have been set.
- *Fixed income coverage.* It is important that the treasurer is confident about the quality and standing of the investment bank's credit research.
- *Secondary market trading.* Fixed income investors require bonds that are tradable. This is dependent not only on the size of the issue, but also on the banks acting as market makers in the bonds. Does the bank trade in a large number of corporate bonds, and what is its share of the secondary corporate bond market? A corporate treasurer needs to be sure that the bond will be well supported in the secondary market.

- *Other intangible factors.* These consist of things like personal chemistry, the importance of the banking relationship, reward for past support and recommendations from other treasurers. However it is important that emotion and relationships do not cloud the issue.
- *Mandate.* A mandate should spell out precisely where the treasurer wants to end up. It may be that certain 'drop dead' aspects need to be clarified, for instance minimum pricing levels that must be achieved.

Marketing the issue

Few institutional investors are prepared to buy a Eurobond without having attended a 'roadshow'. This is the opportunity for the company to sell the strengths of their company's credit and hence the attraction of the bond. In turn the roadshow gives the investor the opportunity to question management about key aspects of their business and its financial performance and profile. Roadshows for bond issues will differ in emphasis from presentations to equity analysts. While equity analysts may want to hear about expansion, growth and the upside to the company's share price, the debt investor is concerned about the downside to the cashflows available to service the bond and other loans. The usual formats for roadshows include:

- *One-to-one meetings.* Usually the largest investors will insist on having a one-to-one meeting.
- *Group presentations.* Formal presentation to a group of investors with questions and answers at the end.
- *Bloomberg roadshows and Internet presentations.* This allows the presentation to be watched by the investors in their own time.
- *Conference calls.*

The one-to-one meetings and the group presentations will generally be made at four or five major financial centres. For instance a corporate wishing to issue a sterling Eurobond is likely to make presentations in London, Edinburgh and, depending on the issue size and the lead manager's distribution, in Frankfurt or Paris.

It is important that the issuer is fully involved in the marketing programme. This includes preparing presentations, assessing the marketing plan in relation to the proposed distribution of the bonds and ensuring that the proposed syndicate structure is appropriate for the distribution strategy.

Price discovery

During the roadshow process the lead manager will be assessing the level of demand for the issue from contact with potential investors. The bookrunner will reference a spread range called 'price talk'. Institutions will indicate to the lead manager the amount of bonds that they are prepared to buy and the price at which they will buy. This process of price talk enables the lead manager to determine the price at which the bond should be sold.

The final price is agreed just before launch and is usually within the price talk parameters. For instance, price talk may be a spread of 150 to 153bps, and the lead manager may recommend an issue spread of 152bps.

This bookrunning process can create problems for the treasurer, who may have awarded lead manager role to a bank whose syndicate manager was showing the best pricing. However, this indicative pricing may be very different from that at which the lead manager subsequently advises that the bond should be issued. This points to the importance of being completely thorough in the selection process, ensuring that the bases for selecting the lead manager are as objective as possible, and that expectations are clearly spelt out in the mandate letter.

Assessing the recommended pricing

At the end of the day the treasurer will need to assess whether the price being shown is correct. Among the factors that need to be borne in mind in reaching this conclusion are:

- What is the comparison with other issues in the market for corporates of similar size and credit standing? If there is a significant difference, why is this?
- What is the investor appetite for the name? Does the company have substantial bonds already out in the market or is this a maiden issue? Is the size enough to ensure good liquidity?
- What has been the history of other issues the issuer has had in the market? Have they been well received or is there a perception that past issues were badly priced?
- What is the perception of the issuer's business sector? Are there any positive or negative factors that should be considered, such as government regulation or review?
- What is the current condition of the market? Has there been substantial issuance recently or is the market hungry for new issues?

Launch

Once the treasurer is confident that the margin being recommended is the correct one for the issue, he or she will need to give the go ahead for the bond to be launched. The issuer's lead manager buys the whole issue on the predetermined terms and price and then places the bonds with its own clients. In addition it will distribute to the co-managers those bonds that they have been allocated. They are not however permitted to place the bonds at a price below the fixed price agreed until the syndicate is broken. The syndicate is only broken by the lead manager when most of the issue has been placed at the fixed price (this will usually be within a few hours). At this point, the issue can be offered by members of the management group below the fixed price re-offer level. The issue now becomes 'free to trade'.

The treasurer also needs to be involved in the allotment of bonds to other members of the syndicate and relationship banks.

Any hedging, for instance a swap to floating rates or a cross-currency swap, needs to be timed and transacted for launch. Otherwise the treasurer is exposed to foreign exchange and interest rate movements after launch.

Payment date

On the payment date, the management group provides the issuer with the funds. Ownership is then assigned to the management group at one of the bond clearing houses. One certificate, called a 'temporary global note', is initially issued and held in the clearing systems. The temporary note is later replaced by a 'global note', which is held by a custodian on behalf of the clearing systems.

Post-issue review

It is important that the treasurer carries out a post-issue review. The bond spread should tighten in by a few (two to three) basis points after issue. Any further tightening and the bond is likely to have been incorrectly priced. Were the distribution objectives met and how is the bond currently trading?

Secondary market trading

The secondary market in the bond is maintained by market makers. These institutions provide liquidity to the investor by committing to quote firm, two-way prices. Good secondary market performance is important in providing a favourable background for future issues by the same borrower. In assessing market performance, an issue is generally judged to have performed well in the initial distribution period if it is trading at the fixed re-offer price or slightly higher. Subsequently, the issue should trade at yield levels similar to those on broadly equivalent bonds issued by comparable borrowers.

Documentation

While documentation in Eurobonds is standard, the treasurer will need to ensure that these standard terms are being recommended for the issue. If changes are being recommended, is it because there is a genuine change in market practice or is the lead manager giving way to pressure from investors?

Typical documentation will include the elements described below.

Offering circular

The information to be disclosed in the offering circular will be subject to the regulatory requirements of the country where the bonds are to be listed. The UK Listing Authority requirements for Eurobonds are set out in the purple book. These cover such matters as:

- *Terms and conditions of the bond.* This includes such items as issue size, currency, coupon rate and payment dates, redemption amount and dates, the terms of early redemption, events of default and status of the bond. In addition it will include details of any covenants such as negative pledge.
- *Description of the issuer.* This will comprise the registered office address, date of incorporation, and details of the issuer's directors (names, and other directorships), and a statement that there is no litigation pending or threatened. It will also include financial statements for the last two years and an indebtedness statement.

Most of the information to be disclosed will undoubtedly be in the company's domain (details of directors, summary of financial information including capitalization and indebtedness statements). Some of this information however may require time to compile (such as the indebtedness statement) and yet other information may require due diligence (such as confirming that there is no legal or arbitration proceedings outstanding against the company).

Subscription agreement

This sets out the basis on which the sale of the bonds will be managed. The agreement is between the issuer, lead manager and co-managers. If the bond is underwritten, the terms of the underwriting are set out in the subscription agreement. Also included in the agreement will be the fees payable for underwriting and selling, and which costs and expenses are to be paid by the issuer.

The subscription agreement also includes certain representations and warranties by the issuer. These ensure that the offering circular contains all necessary information for the an investor to make an informed decision about the offering, that the company has the necessary authority to undertake the transaction, and that there is no material litigation pending against the company.

The obligation of the managers to subscribe for the bonds is subject to certain conditions. The usual ones are that the managers have received a satisfactory legal opinion from their lawyers and a comfort letter from the auditors regarding financial information contained in the offering circular. An officer of the company will need to state that there has been no material adverse change since the date of the offering circular.

Trust deed

This sets out the powers and duties of the trustee. The trustee is essentially an intermediary between the company and the bondholders. The trustee can agree to certain minor modifications to the terms of the bond and is capable of waiving non-material defaults.

Paying agency agreement

This is an agreement between the issuer, paying agent and trustee. It sets out the basis on which interest and principal are to be paid.

MEDIUM-TERM NOTE PROGRAMMES

Once a decision has been taken to borrow in the capital markets, a company can either undertake a one-off transaction via a bond issue, or establish a medium note programme (MTN). An MTN programme is essentially a documentation platform, which will allow the issuance of up to a pre-agreed amount on an opportunistic basis. It has been described as a 'shelf' of debt from which funds are drawn down over a defined period. Some consider such a programme to be one of the most convenient and efficient ways for a treasurer to raise funds in the capital markets.

Aspects of an MTN programme

Specific aspects of an MTN programme are outlined below.

Note issuance

Notes are issued within a programme. A continuous programme is established within a specified limit. The size of the programme can be from US$300 million to US$10 billion, or unlimited. Within the programme, notes can be issued at any time. It is similar to a revolving loan facility in that as maturing notes are redeemed new notes can be issued

Public or private notes

Notes can be issued on the public markets or privately. For instance a company can issue a Eurobond out of its MTN programme with the notes being offered to a wide range of investors. A private placement allows the treasurer to negotiate a more structured deal in comparison to the generally plain vanilla paper issued in the public markets.

The investors buying such structured private deals are usually financial institutions or investment funds that, for instance, need to hedge a particular exposure, or invest in an instrument with an embedded return linked to an underlying index or which contains a particular tax angle. Since the corporate issuing the notes will not want to take on this type of exposure, it will need to undertake a derivative transaction to 'neutralize' the risk. This derivative is usually provided by the dealer.

US$ and European MTN programmes

MTN programmes fall into two broad categories. A US$ MTN programme is registered with the SEC. Notes issued under these programmes are in US dollars and are issued to US investors. Notes under a euro MTN programme can be issued in any currency and go primarily to investors outside the United States. Such programmes are registered with the appropriate listing exchange (usually London or Luxembourg).

Dealers

An MTN programme will usually have a panel of dealers. The selected dealers are usually those members of an issuer's existing bank relationships who have capital market capabilities. An issuer will post levels with the dealers at which it is prepared to issue notes. Issuance is thus by 'reverse enquiry', where a corporate receives an enquiry to issue via a dealer.

Terms and conditions

The issuer agrees with its dealers the price, interest basis and maturity at which it wants to issue. The documentation must be sufficiently flexible to allow for notes to be issued in any form that may be required. This documentation needs to cover, for example, a wide range of currencies, fixed and floating issues, a wide range of maturities, coupon notes and zero-coupon notes, notes issued at par or at discount or premium, and notes with put and call options attached.

Shelf registration

The shelf registration system allows a listed issuer to produce, on an annual basis, a prospectus ('shelf document') that contains most of the information required in listing particulars. If during the following 12 months (in the case of a London listing) the issuer wishes to issue notes pursuant to an MTN programme, all that is necessary is the publication and circulation of a short document (the 'pricing supplement') containing the information required to complete the listing particulars.

Broadly, the prospectus relating to the programme contains all the financial information relating to the issuer. It also contains a summary of the terms and conditions of the notes. This summary has to be very broad to allow notes issued under a programme to be issued in different currencies, in different sizes, maturities, issue prices and coupon bases (fixed, floating or zero-coupon). In addition it will allow notes to be issued at a premium or discount. The notes have to be so broadly defined in the programme as to enable them to be issued to meet a whole range of investor requirements.

The individual issue notes will then contain specific details about the terms and conditions of the notes.

Advantages of an MTN programme

An MTN programme can allow the opportunistic issue of notes to meet specific investor demand. As a result the pricing of these notes is made attractive to the issuer as an incentive to issue. In addition, notes can be issued in a wide range of maturities to manage the maturity profile of the issuer.

The fact that so much documentation has already been prepared allows a company with an MTN programme to respond swiftly to issuing opportunities. Even a Eurobond can be issued through an MTN programme.

One thing for a company to recognize is that significant responsibility will need to be delegated to the treasury department. Once an enquiry has been received from a dealer, the corporate will need to respond promptly. This means that the normal processes of discussion and approvals that many corporates use for financing transactions need to be streamlined.

PRIVATE PLACEMENTS

Summary of market

Essentially, a private placement is the direct sale of debt by a company to sophisticated investors, primarily life insurance companies and pension funds. Since the deal is privately agreed, the bonds are not listed on any stock exchange; there is thus no secondary market and hence no quoted prices at which the bond trades. Finally there is no publicly available information. The bonds are held privately and not traded, and usually the investor holds the bonds to maturity. Since the bonds are not traded and have no liquidity, the initial yield on the bond is higher than that on a comparable traded bond. In addition the terms of the bond, represented by covenants, are more restrictive from the point of view of the issuer than quoted bonds. Foreign issuance in 2002 in the US private placement market was approximately US$11 billion.

What are the advantages?

From the standpoint of the issuer private placements have a number of advantages over a domestic or Eurobond issue.

Credit ratings

There is no need for the issuer to have a credit rating, although it may require an NAIC rating. Since the transaction is privately agreed between issuer and investor, the latter undertakes all due diligence investigation into the credit worthiness of the former. Private placements can therefore be attractive to a small growing company that wants to diversify its funding away from bank debt, or for companies whose credit rating falls below investment grade.

Smaller issue sizes

Issue sizes can range from US$50 million to US$500 million. These issue sizes can be attractive for companies whose issue requirements are too small for the public markets. The public markets tend to have minimum issue sizes that will ensure proper liquidity and hence tradability for the issue. Very often companies' funding requirements may fall below this minimum issue size.

Wide range of maturities

Maturities can range from five years to 25 years. This makes the market an attractive alternative to the bank market where maturities do not generally range beyond seven years.

Structures

Transactions can be structured to meet a particular cash profile required by the issuer or investor. Such profiling is not so easily achieved in the public markets.

How are private placements undertaken?

A private placement requires intermediation via an agent. The agent is usually an investment bank that can exploit its contact with potential investors and issuers. Most of the investors reside in the United States and most issues are made in US dollars, while issuers can reside in other countries. As a result, currency swaps as well as interest rate swaps are often required to back an issue.

Once introduced, the investors will undertake their own credit analysis. This is usually some form of presentation by the issuer, which will often be followed by due diligence trips to the issuer's headquarters and major operating centres. The issuer will formalize the presentation, usually with the preparation of an information memorandum. The agent will provide advisory services on the preparation of the information memorandum.

In addition to the credit analysis there will need to be negotiation and agreement on the covenant package attached to the transaction. It is often felt that the covenant package is broadly in line with what the issuer could expect from a banking transaction.

Generally the timetable for issuing is approximately 6–12 weeks from engagement of the agent to receipt of funds.

How much does a private placement cost?

Typically, because a private placement is less liquid than a public issue, the yield on the private placement is higher than a comparable public issue. However, since private placements are typically smaller than public issues, comparable issues are not always available. The agent's fees may typically range from 40 to 100 basis points up front.

CHOICE OF MARKET

Once a company has decided it wishes to raise funds in the capital markets, it is then faced with the decision of which market to tap. For most companies this decision is based on a number of factors such as: the need for a rating, the size of the issue, the currency required and the information requirements of the regulatory body concerned. The choice of markets is outlined below.

- *US public market.* A very large market with great depth and liquidity. Very considerable issues can be made (over US$5 billion) and maturities can stretch to 100 years. However, registration with the SEC is necessary to issue in the full US domestic bond market. For non-US companies this can be a major disadvantage, since accounts have to be prepared to accord with US GAAP, as well as the disclosure being made of a large volume of firm-specific data together with detailed information on any risks facing the firm and industry. In addition the issuer is required to prepare quarterly financial reports to update the bondholders on the company's funding position. The preparation of the prospectus can be costly and time consuming.

- *Rule 144A.*This was developed as a competitive response by the US authorities to the flexibility of the Eurobond market. Rule 144A allows the issue of a bond in the US domestic market without SEC registration provided the potential investors have expertise in the markets and large capital resources. Although issues under Rule 144A are sometimes referred to as 'private placements', there is no restriction on the number of investors who can buy the securities for any issue. There are several conditions attached to issues under Rule 144A, one being that the seller must take reasonable steps to ensure that a buyer is aware of the exemption from registration, and is a qualified institutional buyer (Qib). A Qib is an institution acting on its own account with more than US$100 million invested in securities. Qibs represent the largest 3500 investors in the United States. Unless the issuer has appeal to retail investors, a 144A issue should not result in any pricing differential.

Issuing under Rule 144A enables the company to issue in the US domestic market without the constraints of SEC registration. However, the potential number of investors in a bond is reduced in comparison with a registered US domestic issue.

- *A company's own domestic market.* A bond issue in these markets will be subject to regulation by the national equivalent of the SEC. Very often disclosure procedures are less onerous. However, domestic bond markets tend to be small and hence issue sizes and maturities can tend to be restricted.
- *Eurobonds.* Usually listed on the London or Luxemburg stock exchanges. Information and disclosure requirements are generally low. With the advent of the euro, a new investor base has developed to rival that in the US markets.
- *Private placements.* As discussed earlier, this market is attractive to companies that want to raise amounts below the minimum practicable size for the public markets. Most private placements are US$-based and carry the benefit that ratings are not required.
- *MTN programme.* The advantage of the MTN programme is that opportunistic issues can be made, often at competitive pricing levels in a wide range of maturities. It can also be an attractive instrument for companies with regular issuing needs.

The final choice of market or instrument therefore comes down to a number of issues. Some of the choices facing the company can be set out in a matrix, as shown in Table 6.2.

Swapping the funds to floating

Very often the treasurer is concerned to swap the funds to floating. This process is described in Chapter 11 (see page 235).

Table 6.2 Relative merits of different bond markets

	US domestic	*Rule 144A*	*Domestic Other marker*	*Private placement*	*Eurobonds*	*EMTN*
Regulatory body	SEC registration	No SEC registration necessary	Official agency approval	No regulation	Minimum regulatory control	Minimum regulatory control
Disclosure requirements	• High initial expense • High on-going expense • Onerous to non-US firms	Less onerous than a full Yankee but still time consuming	Variable Generally less onerous than US Domestic	No public disclosure requirements	Minimum disclosure requirements	Minimum disclosure requirements (as for Eurobonds)
Road show required?	Yes	Yes	Depends on market. Increasingly yes	No but presentation to potential investors	Yes	No unless bond issue planned

Table 6.2 continued

	US domestic	*Rule 144A*	*Domestic Other marker*	*Private placement*	*Eurobonds*	*EMTN*
Credit rating	Yes	Yes	Depends on market. Increasingly yes	For US market not required (although NAIC required)	Yes	Yes
Minimum issue size	US$250–500 million	US$250–500 million	Depends on market	US$25 million	US$250–500 million	US$5 million
Maximum issue size	Approx. US$5 billion	Approx. US$5 billion	Depends on market	US$500 million	Approx.US$5 billion	Approx.US$5 billion Eurobond issued off MTN programme
Maturities	Up to 100 years	Up to 100 years	Depends on market	10 years and beyond	Up to 30 years	Any maturity

CASE STUDY

Examine the following four fictional bond issues. Each one is for a ten-year US$ Eurobond.

Issuer A Financial institution

Rating	Aa2/A+
Amount	US$1.0bn
Maturity	15 February 2013
Issue/fixed re-offer price	99.713
Coupon	4.875%
Spread at re-offer	60 (UST 3 5/8% May 2013)
Launched	Tuesday, 4 February 2003
Spread after launch	58bp

Issuer B Corporate issuer

Rating	A+
Amount	US$250m
Maturity	12 February 2013
Issue/fixed re-offer price	99.139
Coupon	5.0%
Spread at re-offer	80bp (UST 3 5/8% May 2013)
Launched	Friday, 24 January 2003
Spread after launch	78 bp

Issuer C Financial institution	
Rating	Aaa/AAA
Amount	US$500m
Maturity	29 January 2013
Issue/fixed re-offer price	99.512
Coupon	4.50%
Spread at re-offer	25bp (UST 3 5/8% May 2013)
Launched	Wednesday, 22 January 2003
Lead manager	Three lead managers
Spread after launch	25 bp

Issuer D Corporate issuer	
Rating	Bbb/BBB
Amount	US$850m
Maturity	16 February 2013
Issue/fixed re-offer price	99.159
Coupon	5.50%
Spread at re-offer	130bp (UST 3 5/8% May 2013)
Launched	Tuesday, 4 February 2003
Spread after launch	120 bp

Please construct a matrix for each issuer showing:

- rating
- amount
- maturity
- coupon
- fixed re-offer price
- yield at re-offer
- spread at re-offer
- spread after launch.

Bond New Issue Matrix

Issuer	*Rating*	*Amount*	*Maturity*	*Coupon*	*Fixed re-offer price*	*Yield at re-offer*	*Spread at re-offer*	*Spread after launch*
Issuer A	Aa2/A+	US$1.0 billion	10 yrs	4.875 %	99.713	4.91 %	60bp	58bp
Issuer B	A+	US$250 million	10 yrs	5.00 %	99.139	5.11 %	80bp	78bp
Issuer C	Aaa/AAA	US$500 million	10 yrs	4.50 %	99.512	4.56 %	25bp	25bp
Issuer D	Bbb/BBB	US$850 million	10 yrs	5.50 %	99.159	5.61 %	130bp	120bp

Comment: Issuer A and B tighten in four and two basis points after issue and was a good issue from investor and issuer standpoint. Issuer D tightened in ten basis points, this implies that the issue was overpriced by some five to seven basis points. Over the life of the bond this amounts to some US$4.25 million.

CHAPTER 7

Specialist Financings: Asset Securitization

INTRODUCTION

Many treasurers find that at some time in their careers they are required to put some form of specialist financing in place. This financing may be a securitization of some of the company's assets, a sale and leaseback of properties, or the stand-alone financing of a project. This chapter attempts to give the reader a broad introduction to some of the principal considerations that are involved in these specialist types of finance by looking at the basic elements of asset securitization. It does so by addressing the following questions: What are the basic elements in a securitization? Why should companies consider such a financing and what are its benefits? What are the obstacles to a successful securitization?

PRINCIPLES OF ASSET SECURITIZATION

The next section considers, step-by-step, the main elements in a securitization of lease receivables. The principle outlined is applicable to a wide range of financial assets.

Sale of the asset

Consider a motor vehicle distributor that offers leasing packages to its principal customers as a marketing and sales tool to help promote vehicle sales. The customer can either choose to purchase vehicles outright for cash or enter into a leasing arrangement. On the asset side of the distributor's balance sheet will be outstanding amount of leases that have been written, and on the liabilities side the finance raised to fund the leasing programme. Over time, as business expands, the outstanding value of leases shown on its balance sheet will steadily increase. The distributor starts to consider how these leases can be separately financed. Its objective is to finance these assets on a stand-alone non-recourse basis. That is, all finance raised will be repaid solely out of the cashflows generated from the leases. Should the cashflow from the leases prove insufficient for this task, the providers of the finance have no recourse back to the distributor.

In such circumstances, one of the steps that any provider of non-recourse finance would want to achieve would be a separation of the lease receivables from the other assets of the vehicle distributor (originator) (Figure 7.1).

In securitization parlance, the lessees are the obligors. They have the obligation of making lease payments to the vehicle distributor, and it is these lease payments that will repay any debt raised via a securitization of the leases. The vehicle distributor, in turn is the originator of the transaction. Without the distributor wanting to finance the lease receivables separately there would be no securitization.

The Special Purpose Vehicle (SPV) is established solely for this transaction. There are two elements of the SPV:

- It is bankruptcy remote. If the originator's business should fail after the securitization is effected, there must be no possibility that the liquidator

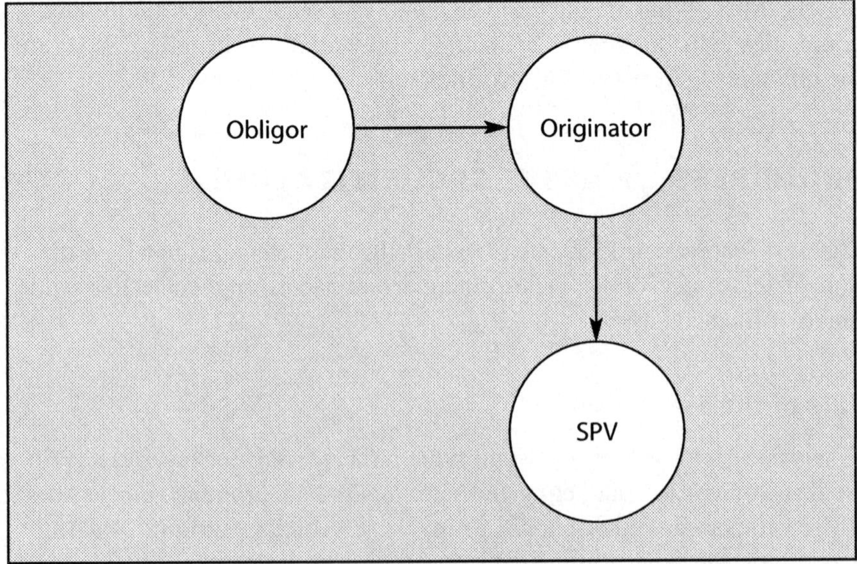

Figure 7.1 Step one: the sale of the assets to an SPV

of the originator's business can claim the assets that have been securitized. For this reason there must be a true legal sale of the assets to the SPV. In addition the management of the SPV must be quite separate from that of the originator's business.

- It is bankruptcy proof. The only assets held by the SPV will be the lease receivables. It will have no other business and have no employees; there must be nothing that could set up a separate claim on the SPV.

The role of the SPV is to hold the securitized assets (in this case the lease receivables), receive the cash from the obligors and use it to pay interest on finance raised and repay principal. In addition there will be a charge over the assets in the SPV in favour of the providers of finance. This charge will normally be held by the trustee for the bondholders.

Credit enhancement

No provider of finance will lend 100 per cent against the assets being securitized unless the credit quality of these assets has somehow been improved. There will always be losses, and due to unforeseen circumstances these may be much greater than anticipated.

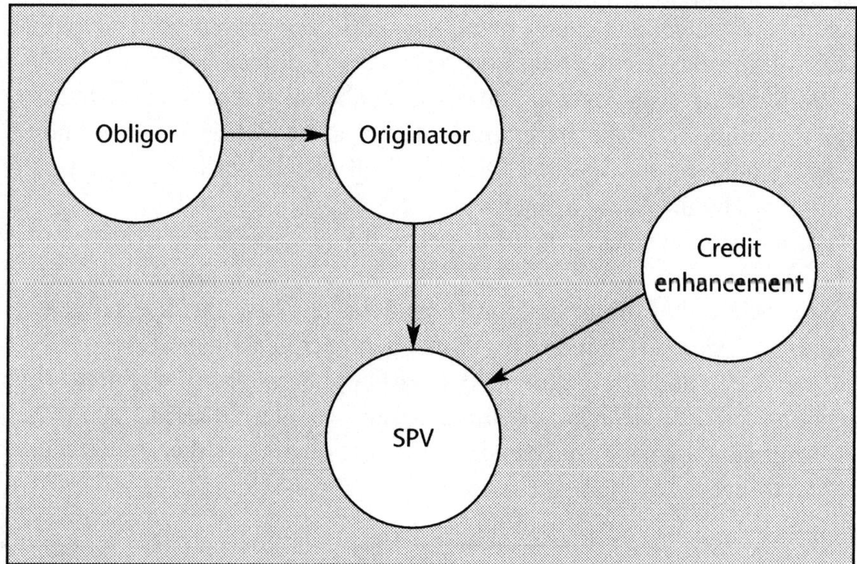

Figure 7.2 Step two: credit enhancement

Credit enhancement can take a number of different forms. Examples are:

- *Over-collateralization.* The originator sells more assets into the SPV than the finance it wants to raise.
- *Guarantee.* A guarantee from a AAA bank or insurance company that they will meet the first percentage of losses.
- *A cash reserve.* This may be a reserve that is put in place by the originator at the outset of the transaction, or is allowed to build up over time (excess spread). In the latter case, the interest charged on the leases by the originator may be greater than the cost of finance provided (more cash is flowing into the SPV than is flowing out).
- *Subordination.* Some of the debt provided to the structure is subordinated to the rest of the debt. Holders of subordinated debt are only paid interest and principal once the other debt holders have been paid. In large transactions, where a whole series of debt instruments may be issued, this is known as tranching, The debt instrument that is paid off first has the lowest credit risk and bears the lowest coupon.

Role of the rating agencies

By itself the credit enhancement is of little value unless there is some measure of its adequacy. Debt providers have neither the experience nor the expertise to judge this. Credit rating agencies have developed a particular expertise in assessing the risks attached to a securitization structure.

Credit rating agencies will address a number of issues in assessing the credit worthiness of the structure. Different asset classes – leases, mortgages, whole businesses and so on – will require different analytical approaches by the rating agencies.

For lease receivables some of the issues to be addressed are:

- Assessment of the originator. Considerations here include: company history, management quality, strategic objectives, financial resources, marketing and origination, underwriting policies and procedures. The objective is to determine if there are any qualitative factors about the originator that may influence the credit quality of the assets being securitized.
- Portfolio characteristics. Some of the considerations are the:
  - Size of the portfolio. Is it large and diversified?
  - Accuracy of data on past defaults and delinquency.

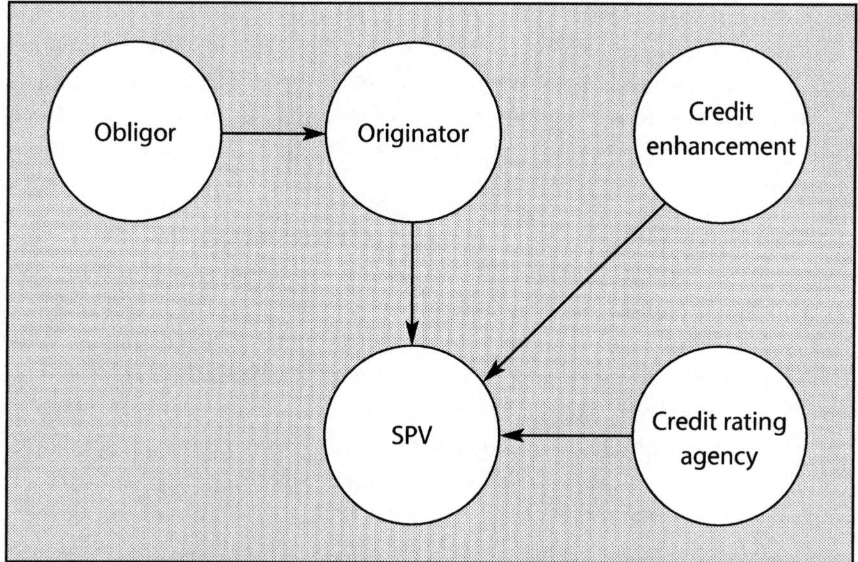

Figure 7.3 Step three: the rating agencies

- Repayment experience. Is there a history of early terminations?
- Yield on the leases. Are these well in excess of finance costs?
- Concentration: geographic concentration, vehicle concentration, manufacturer concentration, lessee concentration.
- Payment terms, e.g. a portfolio with regular payments against one with variable lease rates, skip payments, step up or step down payments.
- Saleablity of the assets.
- Quality of documents recording contractual terms.
- Consistency of application of underwriting criteria.
- Can leases be modified, are substitutions made and are leases ever re-financed?

■ The servicer's or administrator's capabilities (see next step):
- What is the servicer's financial strength and track record?
- What are the collection procedures?
- How will accounts be segregated from non-securitized assets?
- Reconciliation of payments to lease receivables outstanding.
- Ability to analyze the performance of the portfolio (write-offs, prepayments, terminations etc.).

■ Assessment of credit enhancement levels. The level of credit enhancement is obviously a function of past losses and delinquencies and the desired credit rating for the debt raised on the structure. The credit rating agencies analyze past loss data, the originators charge off policy and the credit obtained for recoveries. The rating agencies will analyze losses on a year-by-year basis, as well as taking a portfolio of leases and tracking losses to that portfolio over their lifetime.

- Other factors. There are a number of other factors that the rating agency will need to consider in assessing the soundness of the securitization structure. These include:
  - Liquidity risk. Is there a timing difference between interest and principal being received from obligors and interest and principal payments made to debt holders?
  - Are there any legal and structural risks? Has there been true sale of the assets to the SPV, what is the legal ability of the originator to sell the lease receivables, and what is the ownership of the SPV?
  - Administration. What is the bank account structure and what are the banking arrangements? What reports will be prepared?

Administration

If the SPV has no employees and merely holds the securitized assets, how will cash be collected from the obligors? How, for instance, will records be maintained of outstanding leases, and how will delinquent accounts be chased and handled? The usual procedure is for the originator to take on the role of administrator. The administrator will be responsible, among other things, for maintaining records of outstanding lease receivables and analyzing these between current and arrears, collecting repayments from lessees, analyzing repayments between interest and principal, and pursuing delinquent accounts. In addition payments need to be analyzed between current, repayments in advance and repayment of arrears.

Generally in most securitizations the originator assumes the administrator's role, since s/he has all the base records and documents.

The considerations that the originator needs to consider on assuming the role of administrator are:

- Asset identification. Assets subject to securitization need to be separately flagged on the computer system. Records need to be separated and stored separately. Procedures for administering the portfolio, which may be different from those applied to other assets, need to be well documented. Cash collection procedures may need to be re-organized, and

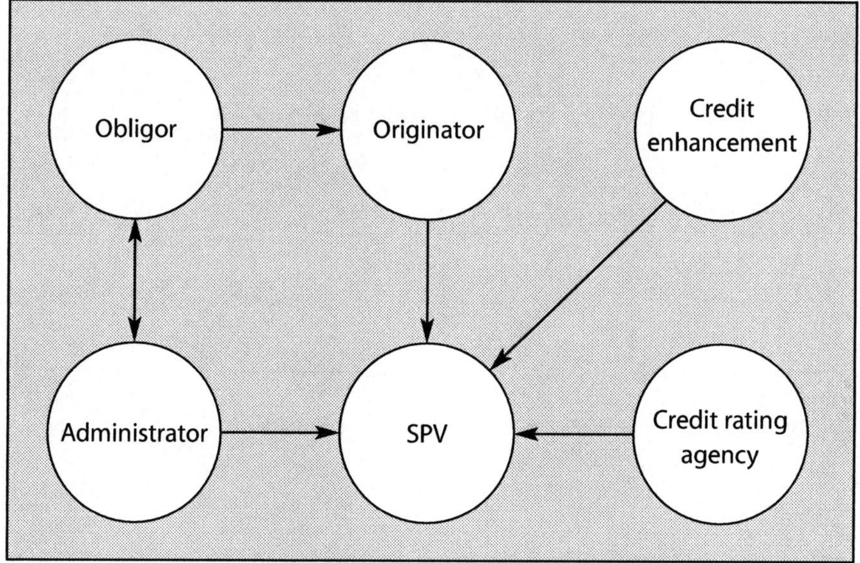

Figure 7.4 Step four: the administrator

collections from obligors in respect of securitized assets separated from other cash. The above can give rise to a whole range of systems issues for the originator.

- Reports will also need to be prepared for the SPV.

Financing

The last part of the basic structure is the financing. It is assumed here that financing is via a publicly issued bond or series of bonds. The yield the bondholders will require will partly be a function of the credit worthiness of the structure as a whole, and the credit quality of the lease receivables in particular. In assessing the credit rating to be applied to the debt capital of the structure, the rating agencies will assess the level of losses suffered by the portfolio of leases over a certain time period. This period usually includes at least one recession. The credit rating for the debt will in part be a function of historic losses. For instance to achieve AAA, the level of credit enhancement in the structure must be sufficient to cover five times the historic losses on the portfolio. Thus if losses have historically been 2 per cent of the portfolio, credit enhancement of at least 10 per cent of the value of the portfolio of assets to be securitized must be established.

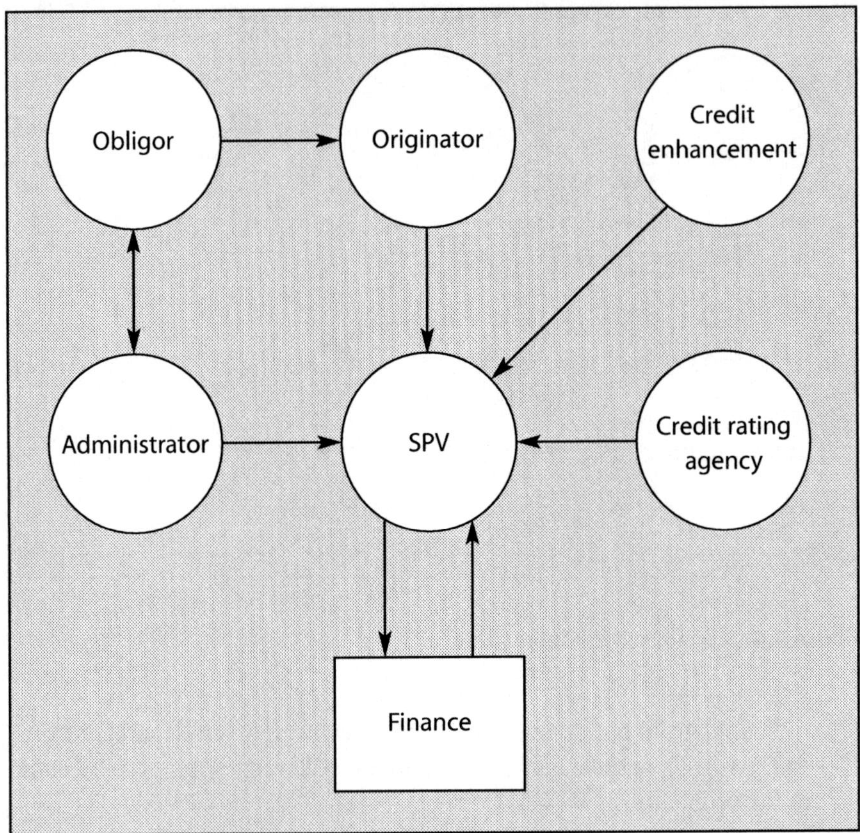

Figure 7.5 Step five: the finance

Summary

Certain basic features of an asset securitization will probably have emerged in the reader's mind by now. These principal features may be summarized as follows:

- There needs to be some selection criteria for a portfolio of assets to establish a securitizable group of assets. Not all the assets within the obligor's original portfolio have the necessary qualities to be subjects of a securitization. For instance, in the example of lease receivables, leases in arrears may not be appropriate to include in a portfolio of leases to be securitized.
- There is a true legal sale of the selected assets to a special purpose vehicle (SPV) that has narrowly defined purposes and activities.

The SPV is insulated from events affecting the condition of the seller.

- Total reliance is placed on the performance of the assets securitized – as opposed to the credit of the originator – for payment of interest and principal. Should the assets not perform, the debt providers have no recourse to the originator. From the originator's standpoint this is essential.
- Credit enhancement provides support for the timely payment of principal and interest.
- A formal rating from one or more agencies.
- There is a prescribed process for the administration of the securitized assets.

What assets can be securitized?

Essentially any asset that generates stable, predictable and regular cashflows and has a low risk of default can be securitized. Examples of commercial or industrial assets that have been securitized are: hotels, public houses, toll road revenues, lease receivables, trains and trade receivables.

WHY SECURITIZE?

There are a number of reasons that can attract a company to consider securitization. Among them are the following:

- Securitization can enable a company to dispose of non-core assets. Many companies believe that assets that are not core to their operations should be securitized so that equity analysts and debt providers can gain a clearer view of their underlying business. A vehicle distributor may believe that its core business is the distribution and sale of vehicles. Its business plans and marketing efforts are directed to establishing a viable distribution network and the franchise of key vehicle brands. The provision of leases to customers is merely a sales tool. By securitizing the lease receivables it can enable markets to understand more clearly its underlying business performance and credit strength.
- Securitization may enable the effective disposal of assets for which there is no ready market, or for which the market price may be well below the value that could be released by securitization.

- Owners of assets may take a different view about the risk attached to certain assets from the rest of the market. Securitization enables the risk burden of owning and operating those assets to be 'shifted'.
- Diversification of funding sources. Securitization of certain assets may enable the originator to access different debt markets or to establish new sources of funding.
- For some companies it may be an effective way of managing their debt duration. The finance raised may match in terms of maturity and repayment profile the cashflow profile of the securitized asset more precisely than traditional recourse finance. This may manage re-financing risk for a block of a company's assets.
- Financial leverage. In the chapter on debt capacity is was stated that many providers of debt finance liked to see EBITDA/net interest of approximately 5.5 to 6 times for a 'good quality' credit. However the finance for a securitization can be raised on much lower multiples and still retain a high credit rating. This is examined in more detail below.

Leverage

The effect of leverage works broadly as follows. Consider a portfolio of lease receivables with a value of US$1000 million and an average lease period of five years. The EBITDA yield from the portfolio is 10 per cent. On a full recourse basis the debt that can be raised against that portfolio is broadly:

EBITDA	100 million
EBITDA/Interest	5.5 times
Assuming financing cost is 6 per cent, total interest cost cannot exceed	18.2 million
Total debt raised on portfolio on recourse basis	303 million

However with securitization the finance that can be raised is broadly:

Asset value	1000 million
Level of credit enhancement for AAA	150 million

Debt that can be raised on securitized asset	850 million
Interest cost at 6 per cent	51 million
EBITDA/interest	2 times

The leverage enables cash to be returned to shareholders or re-invested in the business.

There are of course many who would say that this is an extreme example, and they would be correct. There may be many providers of debt finance that would lend more than EBITDA/interest of 5.5 times against high quality lease receivables without it affecting their view of the credit quality of the borrower.

Others would say that, while greater leverage can be effected on securitized assets, the credit quality of the remaining assets on the originator's balance sheet falls, resulting in the cost of debt finance increasing and/or less debt finance being capable of being raised on those remaining assets. Still others would argue that leverage really counts where whole businesses are being securitized, in which case the EBITDA/interest covers need to be much higher than the example above.

All these are correct. However, in situations where the owner of assets is prepared to relinquish control over the management of those assets and the cashflows they generate can be specifically structured, more debt finance can be raised against those assets. It is for this reason that securitization has become a popular vehicle in certain acquisitions, where small, lightly capitalized companies have been able to effect the purchase of substantial blocks of assets.

SHOULD A COMPANY SECURITIZE ASSETS?

Any company considering a securitization will have a considerable amount of due diligence to undertake before embarking on such a transaction. Its most notable considerations are some of those described below.

What are our commercial objectives?

Some of the principal reasons why a company may want to consider securitization have been outlined above. Are these valid commercial objectives and what will the financial benefits be? It should be clear that a securitization programme may be very costly in terms of time, staffing and money. Do the benefits outweigh the transaction costs? It may be that, in the example of the vehicle distributor, the organization has reached a point beyond which it cannot expand without first reducing the level of debt carried by the company. This debt may in turn be due to the level of leases that the company is writing for its customers. In this case securitization supports the strategic objectives of the company to expand the business.

However, it could be argued that some other objectives are not commercially valid. These might include using securitization to increase the return on assets or to achieve off balance sheet finance. In such circumstances it could be argued that securitization does not help increase company value, but merely improves accounting returns.

The company also needs to consider whether these objectives can be achieved in a simpler and more cost-effective manner. Referring back to the example of the vehicle distributor, it may be more efficient to consider whether all leases, rather than being written by the company, could be written directly by a bank. In such a circumstance, provided the customer met established credit criteria, the lease would be provided directly by a bank. This would represent a positive cooperation between the distributor and a key relationship bank.

What will it cost?

At some early stage in the process the potential originator needs to assess the cost of the transaction. Major costs are likely to include:

- The costs of an advisor. Many investment banks with substantial origination in asset-backed securities will offer their services as an advisor. This will include identifying the assets to be securitized, undertaking a feasibility study for the securitization of those assets, and structuring the transaction to meet the commercial objectives. This advice, often essential for many companies, can be a major cost element in the transaction.
- Costs associated with analyzing the asset pool. It may be that a substantial project team needs to be established to undertake this analysis. The historic data required by the credit rating agencies may not be readily available and so considerable time may need to be spent 'mining' this information.
- If the originator becomes the administrator, will existing systems need to be modified or re-written to cater for the duties of being

administrator? Can existing systems separately identify securitized assets and can all transactions associated with those assets be recorded separately? If not, what needs to be done to the current information and record keeping systems to enable the duties of administrator to be fulfilled?

What are the tax and accounting issues?

The accounting issues often revolve around the question of whether the originator still retains substantial commercial interest in the assets being securitized. If the originator retains certain rights and liabilities in relation to those assets, it may not be possible to account for the transaction as a complete sale of the assets involved. Some of the issues to be addressed in this regard are matters such as remuneration for administration, credit enhancement in the form of cash reserves supplied to the structure, obligations to take back certain assets, payment of dividends from the SPV, or an option to repurchase the assets.

Most companies embarking on a major and costly transaction such as securitization would want to ensure the accounting results reflected what they considered to be the commercial objectives and substance of the transactions.

The objective with taxation is to ensure that the transaction is tax neutral. Among the issues to be considered are questions such as: how the sale of assets to the SPV will be taxed; whether the authorities can adjust the sale value to what they consider a market value; whether stamp and transfer taxes are payable; the tax treatment of the return of cash reserves; and how profit extraction will be handled.

Provided the transaction is not a 'first' in any particular way, tax and accounting issues are normally resolvable. However they can, in certain circumstances, raise issues that stop the transaction.

DEVELOPMENTS IN SECURITIZATION

There have been a number of developments in securitization. For instance, companies in developing countries often have problems accessing international capital markets due to the credit rating of their domestic country. Securitization has been used successfully by such companies with access to 'hard' currency, usually through exports, to access capital markets that otherwise would be closed to them. These transactions are known as 'future flow transactions' (FFT).

The cost and complexity of most securitization structures means that the minimum effective transaction size is approximately US$250 million. Conduits are securitization structures established by the major banks that allow companies with smaller asset portfolios to securitize those assets. Essentially such a company sells its assets to the conduit that receives those assets together with the assets from other companies. The SPV therefore becomes the holder of assets from a number of different originators.

A major development in Europe that has had significant implications for treasurers is the securitization of whole businesses. One of the problems with securitization of a business such as a group of hotels or inns is that the assets need to be managed to continue to generate cashflow. This is different to a financial asset such as a lease, which automatically generates cash through repayment by the obligors. Businesses also have to grow and develop to meet changing circumstances. New hotels or inns need to be acquired, old properties disposed of. The fabric of the businesses needs to be maintained and upheld to ensure that returns from the property are maintained. Therefore the securitization of a whole business looks quite different from the securitization of a financial asset.

Principal aspects of whole business securitization

The assets remain part of the originator's group structure, but the assets are secured in favour of the holders of the securities issued by the structure. This enables the holder of the charge (trustee) to control the securitized assets in any insolvency proceedings through the appointment of an administrative receiver. The receiver will manage the assets for the sole interest of the security holders.

Whole business securitizations need to consider the aspects outlined below.

Cashflow variance

There must be safeguards to ensure that there is no great variance in the business assets and their related cashflows. These include:

- a minimum amount of maintenance capital to maintain the cash-generative capacity of the business
- limitations on permitted disposals

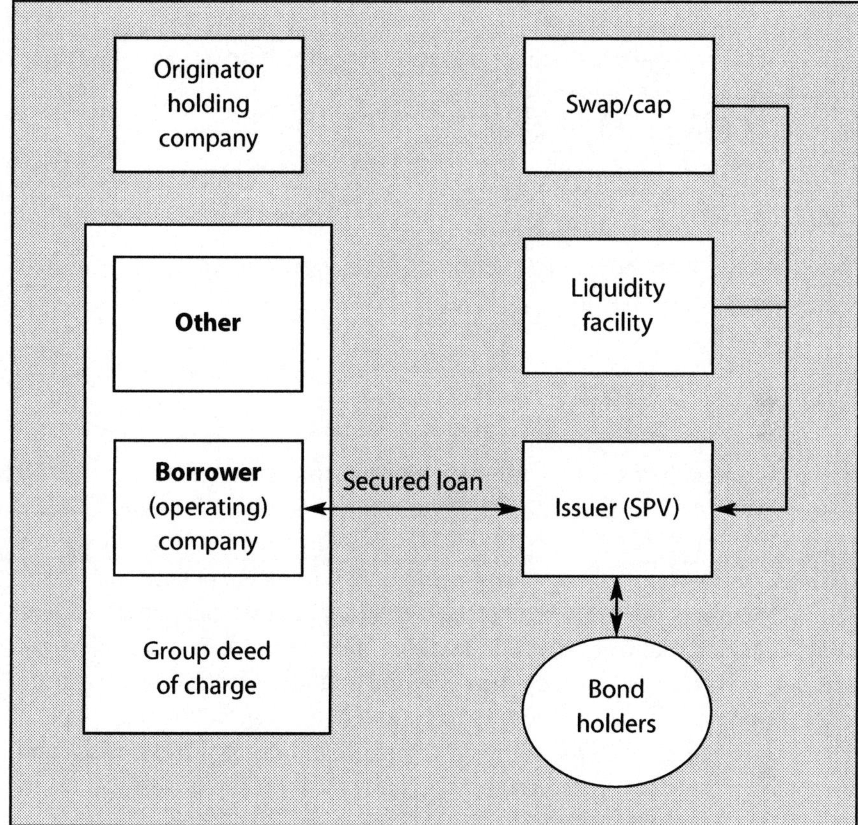

Figure 7.6 Basic structure of whole business securitization

- permitted indebtedness
- permitted acquisitions of new units.

Debt service coverage

In addition there must be restrictions on the use of free cashflow. The debt service coverage ratio is usually expressed as EBITDA less capex less tax/debt service. The objective of this ratio is to ensure that cashflow can cover interest and principal on the securities.

Swap/cap

The swap or cap is required only for any securities that bear interest at a floating rate, to protect against excessive rises in interest rates.

Liquidity facility

This facility is required to cover situations where there are timing differences between cash received by the structure and the due date for the payment of interest and principal.

Finance raised

This will obviously be some function of the net present value of projected cashflows from the business.

SUMMARY

Specialist financing can often involve complex structures, but be regarded by the company as critical to achieving certain strategic objectives. Such a financing will involve the treasurer as either a key member or the leader of a project incorporating many parties from both within and outside the organization. Members of such a project team can include external parties such as rating agencies, valuers, lawyers, auditors and investment bank advisors, together with internal parties drawn from finance, taxation, information systems and operations. The ability to complete the transaction may depend as much on the treasurer's ability to manage and control the project and project team as on that person's ability to analyze and plan the project itself.

CASE STUDY: LEASE SECURITIZATION

A vehicle manufacturer (Wanderer PLC) has a financial subsidiary (Wanderer Finance) whose activity is the provision of financial leases to customers for the purchase of all makes of its vehicles. The activities of the company are carried out through cooperation with a large network of dealers throughout Europe. Wanderer PLC is interested in securitizing the financial leases it has granted to customers.

You have the following information:

- The company has selected the leases to be securitized. At 3 per cent, the net present value of the portfolio of leases is €500 million.
- The originator wishes to achieve AAA on its principal financing. To achieve this, credit enhancement of approximately 8.5 per cent is necessary.

- The leases have a maturity between 12 and 48 months. The minimum remaining maturity of leases to be securitized is 12 months and the maximum is 39 months.
- The notes will be floating rate notes that pay interest and principal on the 17th of the following month. The payments from lessees is due on the first day of the month.

Questions

1. What could the structure look like in outline?
2. What issues would the rating agencies address in determining the credit worthiness of the structure?

SOLUTION

Structure

Credit enhancement

Credit enhancement can be provided in a number of ways. In outline it has been assumed that credit enhancement is provided by the subordination of some of the debt. In this case there are two tranches of notes, A and B notes. The B notes receive interest and principal after the A notes. Credit enhancement for the B notes is provided by cash collateral put into the structure by the originator. The support for the A notes is therefore the B notes together with the cash collateral account. It is only when losses have exceeded €42 million that the A noteholders start to bear loss. This is close to the 8.5 per cent credit enhancement required to get the A Notes to AAA level.

In addition it should be noted that payments are due from lessees on the first day of the month while interest is due on the notes on the 17th of the following month. Therefore there is always approximately six weeks' cash in the system.

One of the challenges for the originator is to match the cost of credit enhancement against its transaction objectives. If the objective is to reduce the cost of finance, then it may well want to get as much of the notes to AAA as possible. If its objective is to securitize as much of the available assets as possible, then the originator will need to consider a lower credit rating on the securities issued.

Legal structure

The assets are sold to an SPV. The SPV is established as a company owned by a charitable trust. The activities of the SPV are limited to acquiring receivables from Wanderer Finance and to obtaining funding through the issuance of notes for the acquisition of such receivables. There is a fixed charge over the receivables sold into the SPV in favour of the noteholders, which are held by the security trustee. In addition there is a charge over the cash collateral.

Valuation of assets

The leases offered to customers are at a fixed rate. The finance however is at floating rate. Two interest rate swaps need to be put in place. In calculating the net present value of the lease receivables the discount rate will be a blended rate of the two swaps. The floating rate on the swaps will match the floating rate on the A and B notes.

Cashflow

Under a collection agreement between the originator and administrator, all cash collected from obligors is paid into a distribution account. This cash will be partly principal and partly interest. The interest received will be at the fixed rate used to calculate the net present value of the leases. The interest rate swap matches this fixed rate with the floating rate under the notes.

Cash balances

As mentioned above, there is approximately six weeks' cash in the system. Usually this cash is paid into a special account in the name of the SPV and there is a charge over the balance in favour of the noteholders. Obviously the cash needs to be deposited with a bank with a minimum credit rating.

Administrator

It is assumed that the originator will become the administrator. One consideration is how the administrator will be remunerated, since the fixed rate at which the receivables have been discounted equals the fixed rate under the interest rate swaps. One way is for the administrator to receive the interest on the cash balances held in the structure.

Credit rating agencies

There are a number of factors that the credit rating agencies will consider in deciding what rating to give the notes. Some of these are outlined below.

Legal issues

The rating agencies will satisfy themselves that the legal structure is sound. The lease receivables as well as title to the leased objects (vehicles) must have been validly transferred, and the sale must be enforceable against Wanderer Finance, including in its insolvency. They will also be concerned to ensure that the assignment of the leases and the cash collateral to the security trustee was valid, and that should the security trustee go into liquidation these assets would not be part of its estate.

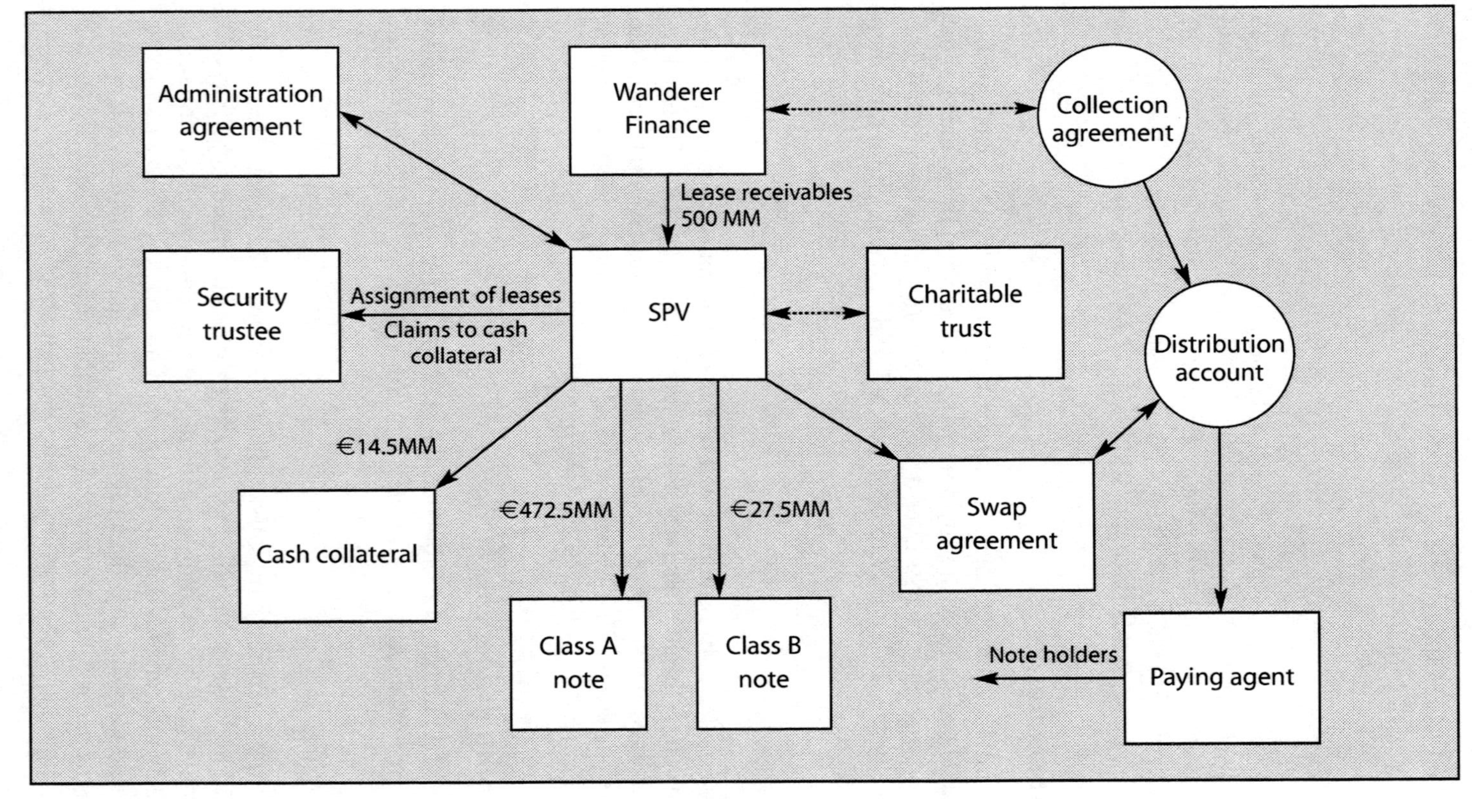

Figure 7.7 Outline of case study structure

Lease receivables

The credit rating agencies will want to receive portfolio data, including loss history going back a number of years. This period may be as high as 15 to 20 years, and will ideally cover two recessions. They will examine the history of losses to determine their pattern and identify any trends. Were the losses similar in the two recessions? These losses will then be stress tested to determine the level of credit enhancement needed for a AAA rating to be assigned to the Class A notes.

They will ask the following questions and undertake the following analysis:

- How large and how geographically widespread is the dealership network?
- How many lessees are there and how many lease contracts? What is the maximum number of lease contracts with one lessee? What is maximum value of one lease contract?
- Is each lease contract seasoned (i.e. have repayments yet been received on the lease)?
- What is the spread of leases between vehicle makes? Is there excessive concentration on any one make?
- Are the lessees geographically dispersed?
- Are all the leases only finance leases with no operating leases?
- How does the lessor handle arrears? There will need to be a process for ensuring that all leases in arrears over a certain number of months are actioned.

Administrator

What is the capability of the administrator to undertake the various obligations within the administration agreement? What is the administrator's credit rating? If the administrator goes into liquidation, is there a substitute administrator?

PART III

The Use of Derivatives to Manage Risk

Different organizations are exposed to a wide range of different risks. In addition to common risks such as foreign exchange and interest rate risk, other risks can range from exposure to the commodity markets and the purchase of power through to exposure to the weather and equity markets. Many such financial risks are managed through the use of derivatives. An effective use of derivatives by a corporate treasury department involves a thorough knowledge of both the markets in which the relevant derivatives are priced and the pricing and structure of those derivatives.

Chapters 9 and 10 cover the use of derivatives to manage foreign exchange and interest rate risk. How do these markets work, how are assets priced in these markets, what derivatives are available to manage these risk and how should a treasury department use such derivatives? Banks display great ingenuity in structuring different derivatives; how should such derivatives be analyzed?

In addition, two chapters in this section look at the mechanics of some derivatives. Chapter 8 gives a broad overview of options, the different options available and the principal elements involved in pricing an option. Chapter 11 provides a summary of how zero coupon rates are calculated, how they are used to value interest rate swaps and how forward rates are calculated. In addition it contains a brief summary of the legal documentation to which derivative contracts are subjected.

The spreadsheets on the CD attached to this book are designed to provide practical guidance, through case studies, as to how derivatives can be used to manage foreign exchange and interest rate risk. Further examples provide guidance on the calculation of zero coupon rates and the use of FX swaps.

CHAPTER 8

An Outline of Options

INTRODUCTION

An explanation of the mathematical basis and methodology used in the calculation of option prices is generally well outside the scope and requirements of most corporate treasurers. Virtually all treasury management systems have modules that calculate option prices upon the input of the necessary parameters, and in addition there are a number of inexpensive stand-alone software applications that perform the same function. It is necessary, however, for the corporate treasurer to understand the basic mechanics of options and above all what drives option prices. This understanding is essential if the company's financial risk policy is to be effectively implemented and the treasurer is to make the correct decision between different treasury products, and to tailor these products to his or her own particular requirements.

This chapter deals with the basic mechanics of options together with what inputs are necessary for an option to be priced. In addition it looks at so-called 'exotic' options.

A BASIC INTRODUCTION TO OPTIONS

Call options

An investment company has just been appointed investment manager of a UK pension fund. The manager for the fund is expecting to receive UK£50 million from the pension fund for immediate investment in the UK stock market. These funds, however, will probably not be received for another three weeks. The manager has identified a number of companies in which to buy shares, and believes that one of them – MegaSystems – is likely to rise substantially before the funds are received. The manager anticipates investing UK£500,000 in this company, and therefore decides to protect the position by buying an option to buy MegaSystems shares. These are currently trading at UK£5 a share.

The details of the option transaction are as follows:

Option type	Call option. Gives the fund manager the right, but not the obligation, to buy Megasystems shares.
Strike or exercise price	UK£5 a share. The price payable by the fund manager under the option contract for the shares s/he has an option to buy.
Number of shares	100,000.
Period	One month. The option expires at the end of one month from the date the option contract is entered into.
Premium	5 per cent. The price the fund manager must pay for acquiring the right to purchase Megasystems shares at UK£5 for the next month. Premium per share is 25 pence (UK£25,000 in total).

While the fund manager has bought the right to buy MegaSystems shares at the option price of UK£5, the bank selling the option has the obligation to sell MegaSystems shares at UK£5. In payment for this obligation it receives an upfront premium.

There are a number of possible outcomes, two of which are summarized below.

Scenario one: MegaSystems share price falls to UK£4. Under this scenario the fund manager lets the option contract lapse. There is no point in buying MegaSystems shares for UK£5, when they can be purchased in the market for UK£4

Scenario two: MegaSystems share price rises to UK£6. The fund manager exercises the option and buys 100,000 MegaSystems shares at UK£5 a share.

The fund manager's strategy of buying the call option does not break even until MegaSystems share price exceeds UK£5.25. At the final market price

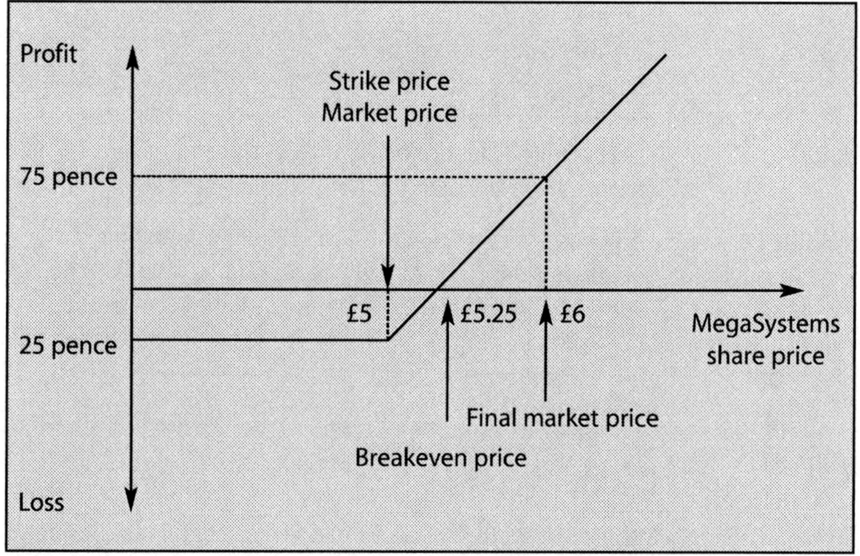

Figure 8.1 Payoff profile for the fund manager buying the call option on MegaSystems shares

of UK£6, the fund manager has made a net gain of 75 pence per share after deducting the cost of the premium (the final market price of UK£6 less the breakeven price of UK£5.25).

The graphical representation of the bank's profit and loss on the contract would look the reverse of the fund manager's. It is shown in Figure 8.2.

Put options

A fund manager can not only buy a call option on MegaSystems, but also purchase the right to sell MegaSystems shares. This is known as a put option. Put options have similar payoffs to call options. However, the purchaser of a put option hopes or expects the share price to fall. The fund manager in this case, after having held MegaSystems shares for some time, is concerned that there may a substantial fall in the price over the next three months. Rather than sell the shares outright, the manager decides to protect the position by purchasing a put option on MegaSystems. Details of the contract are:

Option type	Put option. Gives the fund manager the right, but not the obligation, to sell Megasystems shares.

Strike or exercise price	£6 a share. The price receivable by the fund manager for the shares under the option contract.
Number of shares	100,000.
Period	One month. The option expires at the end of one month from the date the option contract is entered into.
Premium	5 per cent. The price the fund manager must pay for acquiring the right to sell Megasystems shares at £6 for the next month. Premium per share is 30 pence, (£30,000 in total).

Again there are a number of possible outcomes, two potential scenarios being:

Scenario one: Share price rises to UK£7. The manager retains the holding in MegaSystems. There is no point in selling for UK£6 a share that has a market value of UK£7.

Scenario two: Share price falls to UK£5. The manager exercises the option and sells the holding of MegaSystems for UK£6 a share.

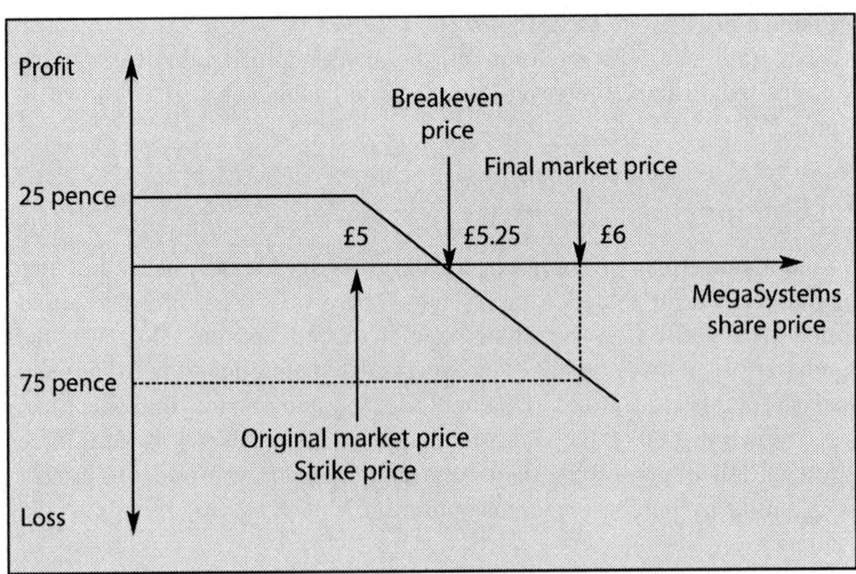

Figure 8.2 Profit and loss outcome for bank selling the call option on MegaSystems shares

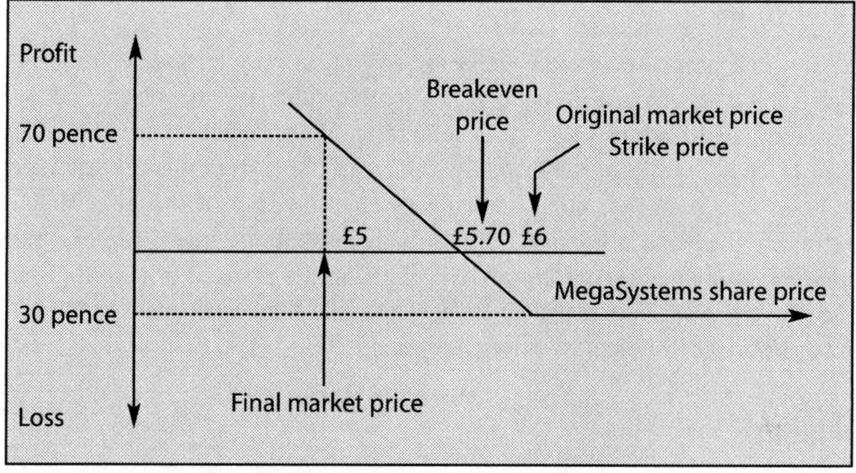

Figure 8.3 The fund manager's payoff under the purchase of a put option on MegaSystems shares

In the money, at the money and out of the money

Options are in the money when they can be profitably exercised, and at the money when there would be neither gain nor loss from the exercise of the option. An option is out of the money when it cannot be profitably exercised. Using the example of MegaSystems:

Call option *Final market price*		*Put option* *Final market price*
UK£4	Out of the money	UK£7
UK£5	At the money	UK£6
UK£6	In the money	UK£5

Intrinsic value

The intrinsic value of an option is the difference between the market price of the underlying asset and the option strike price. Let us refer back to the example of the fund manager who purchased a call option on MegaSystems shares at UK£5. The option period was one month. Suppose after two weeks the price of MegaSystems shares had risen to UK£5.50. The intrinsic value of the option would have been 50 pence.

Time value

At any one point in time the value of an option may be greater than its intrinsic value. This difference between the value of an option and its intrinsic value is time value. It is related to the probability that the final asset price on expiry of the option will exceed the current market price for an asset that is in the money. For an asset that is out of the money, the intrinsic value of a call option represents the probability that the final asset price on expiry of the option will exceed the strike price. (For a put option intrinsic value represents the probability that the final asset price on expiry of the option will be below the strike price.)

Volatility

One of the major inputs to the calculation of the price of an option is the volatility of the underlying asset. Volatility is a measure of the variation in the market price of the underlying asset over a particular period of time. Historical volatility, the variation in prices that has occurred in the past, is often used as a measure of what volatility will be in the future. These variations in return when plotted are normally distributed.

Normal distributions have two principal features: the mean and standard deviation. The mean is the value around which the normal distribution is dispersed, and the standard deviation is a measure of that dispersion. For every normal distribution, when looking at the possible outcomes in an asset's price, it is true to say that:

- 68 per cent of the possible outcomes will lie within +/– one standard deviation
- 95 per cent of the possible outcomes lie within +/– two standard deviations
- 99 per cent of the possible outcomes lie within +/– three standard deviations.

A normal distribution curve is shown in Figure 8.4. The median or mean value is zero and the standard deviation is 1.

Volatility is important in option pricing in the following way. Figure 8.5 illustrates two stocks both trading at a price of 100. Assume that a fund manager holds a call option on both stocks, with an exercise price of 115. It can be seen that the standard deviation, or the volatility, of share A is much higher than that of share B. One must conclude therefore that the

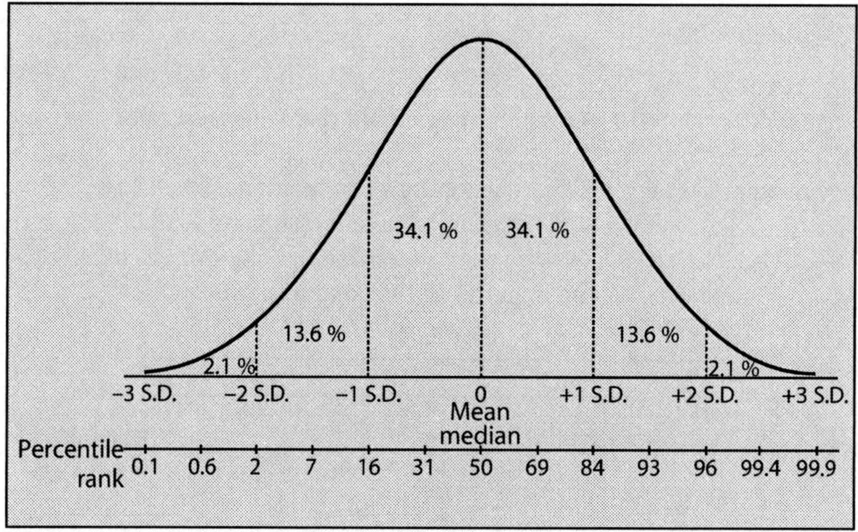

Figure 8.4 Normal distribution curve with a median of 0 and the percentile ranks of standard deviations

probability of share A increasing above 115 is greater than the probability of share B doing so. Assume that the standard deviation (volatility) of share A is 15 and that the standard deviation (volatility) of share B is 5.

The probability of share A increasing above 115 is: (1–68 per cent)/2 = 16 per cent. That of share B is (1–99.6 per cent)/2 = 0.2 per cent. The probability of share A going into the money is 16 per cent; much greater than the likelihood of share B doing so, which is virtually zero. Clearly the value of the call option on share A with an exercise price of 115 is greater than that on share B with the same exercise price.

Other inputs into option pricing

These are:

Strike price	The nearer the strike price to the underlying market price of the asset when the contract is entered into, then the higher the premium. Clearly a call option with a strike price of £5 on a share with an underlying market value of £4.50 is going to be more expensive than a call option on the same share but with a strike price of £5.50.

Expiry	The longer the life of the option contract the higher the price.
Interest rates	Option prices should rise as interest rates rise.
American or European	American options can be exercised at any time during the option contract period. A European option can only be exercised on maturity of the contract.

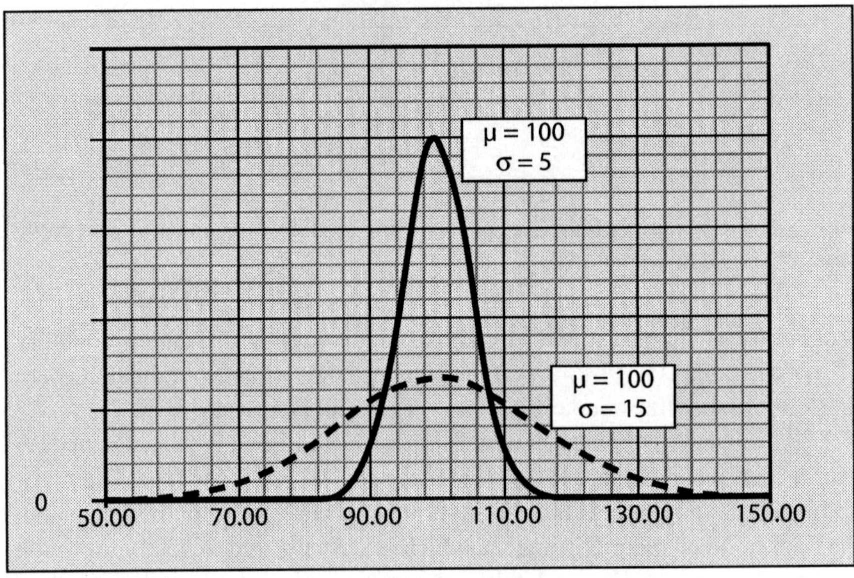

Figure 8.5 Two different stocks, one with a standard deviation of 15 (Stock A) and the other with a standard deviation of 5 (Stock B)

Option pricing with different inputs

Table 8.1 shows different option premiums for a European call option on a share with a market price of UK£5.

Cylinders and collars

Specific option products will be discussed in more detail in the two chapters that deal with foreign exchange and interest rate derivatives. However, it should now be clear that the treasurer can reduce the cost of an option in one of two ways:

Table 8.1 Premium variations consequent to different strike prices, contract periods, volatility and interest rates

	Option 1	*Option 2*	*Option 3*	*Option 4*	*Option 5*
Market price	UK£10.00	UK£10.00	UK£10.00	UK£10.00	UK£10.00
Strike price	UK£11.00	UK£11.00	UK£12.00	UK£11.00	UK£12.00
Contract period	3 months	6 months	6 months	3 months	6 months
Volatility	20%	20%	25%	25%	20%
Interest rates	3%	3%	2%	3%	2%
Premium as % of market price	11.21%	23.99%	16.44%	18.99%	8.05%

- By setting the strike price on the option further out of the money, or by reducing the expiry period of an option. The price of a call option on a share with a market price of UK£5 will be much lower when the strike price is UK£6 and the expiry period is three months, than when the strike price is UK£5 and the period is six months.
- By taking out an offsetting option contract. The price of a call option on a share with a strike price of UK£6 and a market price of UK£5 can be reduced by selling a put option on the same share with, say, a strike price of UK£4. Should the price of the share increase above UK£6, then the call option is exercised. However, if the price of the share falls below UK£4, all gains from buying the shares at a market price below UK£4 are surrendered, since the buyer of the put option will exercise the option. The cost of the call option is reduced by the income from selling the put option.

EXOTIC OPTIONS

Exotic options can be of interest to the corporate treasurer because they change the nature of the option payoff. Sometimes this change in the payoff structure may meet more precisely the specific exposures that a treasurer has. Below, we list some examples of exotic options.

Path dependent options

In the case of path dependent options the payoff from the option is modified by the path taken by the asset price. Examples are:

Asian options

These are often known as average rate options. With a traditional option the payoff at expiry is a function of the difference between the strike price and the underlying asset price at expiry. With an Asian option the strike price is compared to the average price of the underlying asset over the option period. The average may be based on daily, weekly or monthly prices. The average may be also geometric or arithmetic. By averaging out the data, the volatility is smoothed. Average rate options are cheaper than standard options.

Lookback options

With lookback options the strike is set at maturity. The holder of a lookback option can choose the best price achieved in the option's lifetime. For a lookback call option, the strike price will be the cheapest during the option period; for a lookback put option, the strike price will be the most expensive. Because the payoff will always be greater than the standard option, lookback options can be very expensive, sometimes at least twice the price of a standard option.

Contract variation

Bermudan options

A cross between the traditional American and European option, a Bermudan option allows exercise on certain specific dates during the life of the option, for example every week or month.

Digital options

As opposed to the standard option, which pays out the difference between the strike price and the underlying asset price, a digital option pays out a fixed, predetermined amount if the option is in the money. Digital options can come in two variations:

- *One-touch.* This option will pay out if it was in the money at any stage, any time during the life of the option.
- *All-or-nothing.* Only pays out if it is in the money at expiry of the option.

Paylater options

The premium is payable only if the option is exercised. To the option holder the advantage of this option structure is that no premium is payable if the option expires out of the money. These options can be very expensive, and if they expire in the money they must be exercised.

Limit-dependent options

Barrier options

Often called knock-out or knock-in options. With a knock-out option, the option is cancelled if the price of the underlying asset breaches a particular price barrier. A knock-in option only starts to operate when the price barrier is breached.

There are a number of other exotic options, for instance multi-factor options such as basket, compound or rainbow options. However it is very unlikely that the corporate treasurer will use them for routine hedging.

CHAPTER 9

Foreign Exchange (FX) Markets and Derivatives

SPOT FOREIGN EXCHANGE

Base and quoted currency

Foreign exchange (FX) is the exchange of two different currencies on a specific value date. In any FX contract there are a number of variables that need to be agreed upon. These are:

- The currencies to be bought and sold. The two currencies being exchanged are referred to as a currency pair. Within the currency pair one currency is defined as being the base currency and the other as the quoted currency.
- The amount to be bought or sold. Spot deals are symmetrical: one currency is bought and the other is sold.
- The date at which the contract matures. The term 'spot FX' refers to the exchange of one currency for another in two days time, with the exchange rate agreed today. The currency that is bought will be receivable in two days, while the currency that is sold will be payable in two days.
- The rate at which the exchange of currencies will occur. The FX rate is defined as being the number of units of the quoted currency to one unit of the base currency.

For instance, consider the exchange rate of the US dollar against the Singapore dollar. In this currency pair, the US dollar is the base currency and the Singapore dollar is the quoted currency. If the following quote is seen:

US$/SG$ 1.6609

one can say that 1 US dollar = 1.6609 Singapore dollars.

Within the currency pair the base currency is always written first. In general the US dollar is always the base currency in a currency pair, but there are certain exceptions. The following currencies can replace the US dollar as the base currency:

- British pound
- Euro
- Australian dollar
- New Zealand dollar.

There are many cases when a currency pair does not include the US dollar. These pairs are called cross rates, for example, the British pound against the Australian dollar.

The bid offer spread

Market makers display two prices: a buying and a selling price. The selling price is obviously always higher than the buying price. The buying price is the bid price and the selling price the offer. Taking a specific example:

US$/SG$ 1.7390 / 1.7396

In this case the market maker will buy the US$ for SG$ 1.7390 and sell US$ for SG$ 1.7396. The market maker always deals at the most favourable side of the price to him/herself. All this can be represented in a table:

Market maker

	Bid	Offer
Market maker	Buys base Sells quoted	Sells base Buys quoted
Market user	Sells base Buys quoted	Buys base Sells quoted

Market user

So using the above example of US$/SG$ at 1.7390 / 1.7396

Market maker

	Buys US$ Sells SG$	Sells US$ Buys SG$	
1.7390			1.7396
	Sells US$ Buys SG$	Buys US$ Sells SG$	

Market user

Cross rates

As mentioned earlier, cross rates are those currency pairs that do not include the dollar. The first, and most important, step with crosses is to identify which currency will act as the base and which as the quoted. The basic rule is that the base currency is stronger than the quoted; in other words, the exchange rate calculated will be greater than one.

US$/SG$	1.7390 / 1.7396
US$/HK$	7.7980 / 7.7990

While both the SG$ and HK$ are weaker against the US$, the SG$ is stronger against the HK$. Thus the SG$ will become the base currency in the currency pair.

Bid side: Here we are looking for the rate at which the market maker will buy the base currency (SG$) and sell the quoted (HK$). This can be done by considering the trades undertaken to construct this; the market maker will buy SG$ and sell US$, then buy US$ and sell HK$. This uses the offered side in the US$/SG$ and bid side in the US$/HK$.

The market maker:

+ SG$ – US$ @ 1.7396
– HK$ + US$ @ 7.7980

$$\frac{7.7980}{1.7396} = 4.4826$$

Offered side: This is where the market maker sells SG$ (buys US$ @ 1.7390), and buys HK$ (sells US$@ 7.7990).

The market maker:

– SG$ + US$ @ 1.7390
+ HK$ – US$ @ 7.7990

$$\frac{7.990}{1.7390} = 4.4848$$

While it is important to understand and grasp the principle involved in calculating cross rates, the treasurer or dealer need not be over-concerned with detailed calculations. The foreign exchange markets are now so deep and there are so many market makers quoting prices in different cross-currency pairs, that the treasurer is mainly concerned to ensure the best price rather than to work out what the cross rate should be.

Market participants

The main market participants can be grouped broadly into four main groups. First, there are the domestic and international banks that are acting on their own behalf or for their customers. The major banks are market makers, always quoting a two-way price for a number of currency pairs to their customers. Second, there are the central banks. They generally let the market determine the value of their currencies, but there are exceptions to this policy when they may intervene to buy or sell their domestic currency if they believe it is substantially under or over-valued. Third, there are the customers of the banks. These are varied and include corporates settling receipts or payments arising from overseas trade, fund managers buying or selling foreign currency as a result of shifts in their portfolio allocations, government agencies, hedge funds taking positions in currencies or other assets and, finally, high net-worth individuals either entering the market on their own behalf or through the private banking arm of a bank. Last, there are the brokers. Brokers do not trade on their own account, but act as intermediaries.

Why do exchange rates move?

There are a number of factors that determine exchange rate movements.

Economic news: A government's economic policy will have an impact on the market's view of a particular currency. Generally countries seen to be carrying out prudent economic policies, incorporating stable economic growth and low inflation, will find that there is strong demand for their currency.

Statistics: Markets are continually waiting for and then analyzing statistical data on inflation, unemployment, economic growth, government borrowing needs and so on. Each release of data gives a clearer view of the actual course that the government's economic policy is following and what this may herald for the demand for, and hence value of, a country's currency.

Sentiment and rumour: Sentiment seems to play a large part in the short-term movements of many financial markets, as prices often move away from what might be perceived to be fair value.

Forecasting exchange rate movements

Treasurers may need to decide whether to take note of the various forecasts for different currency pairs that are prepared by all kinds of market observers. There are two types of forecasters: fundamental and technical. Fundamental forecasters focus on the economic forces that drive prices to move higher, lower or stay the same. The fundamental approach examines all of the relevant factors affecting the exchange rate between two currencies to determine the intrinsic exchange rate. This intrinsic value may be above or below the current market rate indicating that a currency may depreciate or appreciate against other currencies.

Technical analysts look at past exchange rate movements and from this try to predict future movements. Such analysts are also known as chartists, since their basic tool is a chart of past price movements. They analyze past price movements to determine patterns in them, which they maintain can be used to predict future price movements.

Use of spot market for corporate purposes

Corporate treasuries that sell or purchase small amounts of foreign currency usually use the spot market. Two examples might illustrate this.

- A company pays its creditors at the end of the month. Within the payment run there are a number of payments to overseas suppliers. Some of these payments represent significant transaction exposure and will have been covered using the forward market (see next section).

However there are always a number of small foreign currency payments to overseas suppliers that it has not been feasible to cover on the forward market. The treasury department will purchase these currencies on the spot market.

- A company has a number of small sales to customers in the United States. Customers pay in US dollars to a foreign currency bank account maintained with the company's domestic clearer. Periodically, the treasury department sells the US dollars that have accumulated in this account on the spot market for their domestic currency.

FORWARD FOREIGN EXCHANGE

Forward foreign exchange is defined as being the exchange of two currencies on any date beyond spot with the rate agreed today. To calculate the rate of exchange that applies to any forward date three things are required:

- spot rate for the currencies involved
- base currency interest rates
- quoted currency interest rates.

It is important to recognize that the forward foreign exchange rate does not reflect the market's anticipation of where exchange rates will be in the future, but is a function of the interest rate differentials between the two currencies concerned.

A simple example can illustrate how the forward rate is derived from the spot rate and the interest rates of the two currencies involved.

Example: constructing forward rates – offered rate

A Singapore bank has a customer who is importing from the United States. In one year's time the Singaporean customer has a contract to pay US$1million. The customer wants to buy these US dollars for SG dollars in a year's time, but wants a rate of exchange to be fixed now.

The relevant information is:

US$/SG$ spot rate	1.7380 / 1.7390
One-year US$ money market rates	1.5125 / 1.525
One-year SG$ money market rates	.875 / 1.00

- The bank knows that in one year it will need to have US$1 million to supply its customer. It therefore needs to buy the number of US dollars spot that when invested at the current rate of interest will produce US$1 million in one year.
- The one-year deposit rate is 1.5125 per cent. US$984,896 will, when invested at 1.5125 per cent produce US$1 million in a year (984,896 × 1.5125% × 365/360). To buy US$984,896 the bank will need to exchange SG$1,712,734 (984,896 × 1.7390). It will need to borrow this amount.
- After one year the principal and interest of the amount borrowed will have accumulated to SG$1,730,099 (1,712,734 × 1.00% × 365/360). It therefore knows that the rate of exchange it needs to quote for US$/SG$ forward one year will be the rate that will repay its borrowing of SG$1,730,099. This amount is 1,730,099 / 1,000,000 = 1.7301 (see Figure 9.1).

Example: calculating the forward rate – bid rate

This is the offered side of the one year US$/SG$ forward rate. To calculate the bid the same calculations would be undertaken.

Assume that another customer is an exporter and that in one year it will receive US$1 million which it wishes to sell for SG dollars.

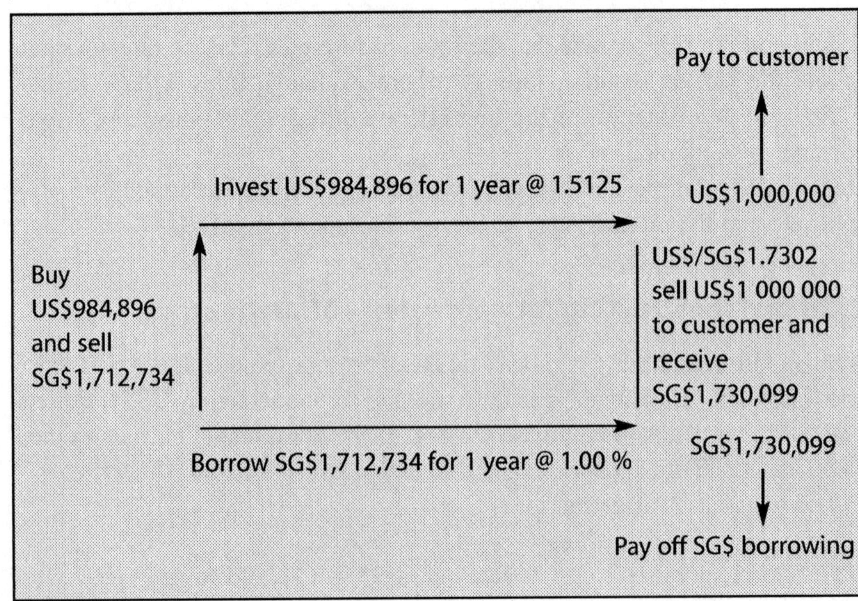

Figure 9.1 Establishing the forward rate

- Buy SG$1,711,535 and sell US$984,773 (spot rate 1.7380).
- Borrow US$984,773 for one year at 1.525 per cent.
- Invest SG$1,711,535 for one year at 0.875 per cent.
- In one year SG$ principal and interest on investment accumulate to SG$1,726,719.
- In one year US$ principal and interest on borrowing accumulate to US$1,000,000.
- One year bid side of forward rate of exchange US$/SG$ = 1.7269.
- The one year US$/SG$ forward rate is 1.7269 / 1.7301.

Formula for calculating forward rates

Expressing this as a formula:

$$F = Sx \frac{1 + r_Q \cdot {}^{d}/_{b}}{1 + r_B \cdot {}^{d}/_{b}}$$

Where: F = outright forward, S = spot rate, r_B = interest rate in base currency, $r_Q =$ interest rate in the quoted currency, d = number of days in the period, and b = day base for each currency.

Forward points

Forward foreign exchange is normally quoted in the form of points, that is, the difference from the spot price.

US$/SG$ Spot	1.7380	1.7390
US$/SG$ 1 year forward	1.7269	1.7301
Forward points	111	89

In the example above the forward points would be quoted as:

1 year US$/SG$ 111 / 89

Although the forward rate is lower than the spot rate, there are no minus signs in the forward points. This is a convention in the market, and market participants can tell whether to add or subtract the points by looking at their bid/offer composition. If the points go down from left to right, the points are subtracted. If they go up from left to right, the points are added.

It is sometimes common to refer to discounts or premiums to spot. In the above example, the US dollar is at a discount forward, and this means that the forward price is lower to the spot price due to higher US dollar interest rates. The SG dollar is therefore at a premium.

Cross rates forwards

Forward cross rates are calculated by using the forwards of the two simple exchange rates, and then calculating the forwards in the cross:

	US$ / SG$		US$ / HK$	
Spot	1.7380 /	90	7.7980 /	90
One year points	111	89	200	230
Outright forward	1.7269	1.7301	7.8180	7.8220

The forward cross rate is then calculated as the same way for cross rates spot.

Bid side: $\frac{7.8180}{1.7301} = 4.5186$

Offer side $\frac{7.8220}{1.7269} = 4.5295$

Use of forward market for corporate purposes

Transaction exposure: It may be clear, if a corporate treasury is seeking to cover transaction exposure, that the forward market is one of the principal mechanisms for doing this. For instance, a Canadian company may have identified a transaction exposure whereby they have to pay US$1 million in 90 days time. Their treasury policies state that all transaction exposure should be covered when identified. The 90-day forward FX rate is US$/CA$1.60. To cover this exposure they therefore enter into a 90-day forward FX contract to buy US$1 million and sell CA$. In 90 days they will pay the requisite CA$ to the bank and receive US$1 million. The US dollars they receive under the purchase are used to pay their US supplier. The advantage of entering into the forward contract to buy US$ is that the cost of the US$ in CA$ terms is fixed, and hence the company's cost structure is protected, when the contract is entered into.

Pre-transaction exposure: With pre-transaction exposure, the exact liability or receipt in a foreign currency very often cannot be identified with certainty but can only be forecast. Companies will often enter into forward FX contracts to manage pre-transaction exposure to give some certainty to the foreign currency receipt or liability in domestic currency terms. For instance, the Canadian company described earlier forecasts that, based on current levels of business activity and hence purchasing volumes, they will have a liability to pay US$1 million in 180 days. Their treasury policies state that up to 75 per cent of pre-transaction exposure forecast within in the next six months may be covered. Since they want to give certainty to some of their costs in the current financial year they enter into a 180-day forward FX contract to buy US$750,000 and sell Canadian dollars.

Economic exposure: There may be situations where a company may consider using forward FX contracts to cover FX economic exposure. A company with London hotels that is very dependent on US visitors notes that there is a clear relationship between the UK£/US$ exchange rate and occupancy rates at its hotels. To counter the effects of a strong UK£/US$ rate, they enter into a forward FX contract to offset the reduction in revenue they would suffer.

The current 180-day UK£/US$ forward rate is 1.50. The company enters into a 180-day forward FX contract to sell US$10 million and buy UK pounds. In 180-days the UK£/US$ spot rate has moved to 1.75.

The company's position is: sell US$10 million and buy UK£6,666,667. The forward contract to sell US dollars is met by buying dollars on the spot market and selling UK£5,714,285, giving a profit on the contract of UK£952,382. This profit offsets the losses arising from lower occupancy rates.

There are obviously numerous pitfalls with such a transaction. How clear is the relationship between occupancy rates and the exchange rate? It is likely that this relationship is not at all definite. Moreover, tax and accounting issues may distort the economic result of the transaction.

FOREIGN EXCHANGE SWAPS

Foreign exchange swaps are a combination of two foreign exchange deals, both transacted on the same day with different value dates. The second deal is a reverse of the first.

Consider the spot sale of US$ for HK$, with a subsequent forward sale of HK$ for US$. The exchange rate of the second deal reflects the interest rate differentials between the two currencies. The FX swap can be interpreted as a borrowing – in this case a borrowing of HK$ – and a loan, in this case a loan in US$. The FX swap can be used to replace a borrowing and a loan in different currencies.

Hedging an outright forward transaction

In the example of the calculation of the outright forward price between US$ and SG$ the concept of hedge pricing was used; in other words, an outright borrowing in one currency and a deposit in the other. The cost of the transaction would be passed on to the customer. The structure is shown in Figure 9.2.

This transaction can be reconstructed using an FX swap, as shown in Figure 9.3.

The different exchange rate used in the second leg of the swap should exactly reflect the interest cost/benefit of the loan and deposit. However, this can only be done if the bid–offer spread is not taken.

Spot	+ US$	– SG$
	Deposit US$	Borrow SG$
1 year	Receive US$ principal + interest from deposit	Repay SG$ principal + interest
	– US$D to customer	+ SG$ from customer

Figure 9.2 Flows involved in creating a hedged outright forward transaction

Spot	+ US$ – US$	– SG$ + SG$	Spot deal FX swap
1 year	+ US$ – US$	– SG$ + SG$	FX swap Outright forward

Figure 9.3 Creating an outright forward transaction using swap market

Use of mid-market rates

Let us take some numbers as an illustration:

Spot US$/SG$	1.7380 / 90
One-year points	111 / 88

FX swap:

Spot	– US$	+ SG$
One-year	+ US$	– SG$

Considering these as two separate trades, the market user would have to pay the bid side in the spot price: 1.7380. He or she would then give the offered side in the forward 1.7302. If this is done, the difference between spot and forward points is 78 points, and therefore the market user is paying over too many SG dollars. In order to realize the 88-point difference in the prices, we must deduct the 88 points from the spot price used in the spot leg of the swap. Because of this, it is usual to use a mid-market rate in the spot leg.

In this case the FX swap would look like this:

Spot	– US$	+ SG$	1.7385
One-year	+ US$	– SG$	1.7297

In market terminology the market user is selling and buying the US$, and buying and selling the SG$. In other words, he/she is selling US$ spot and buying them forward, and buying SG$ spot and selling them forward.

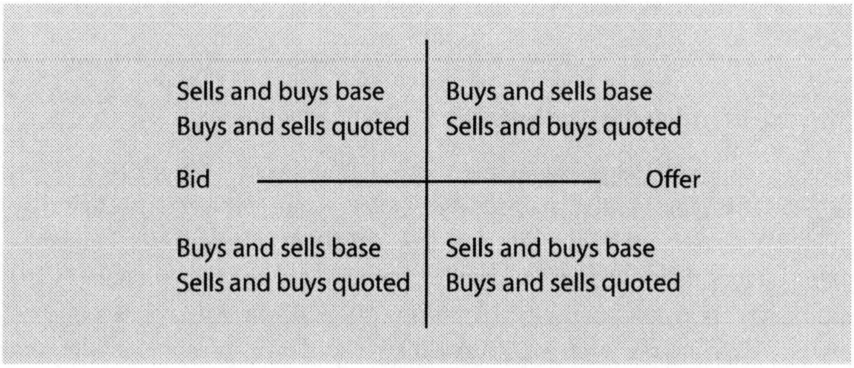

Rolling positions forward

In a business environment one can never be certain when receivables will actually be paid and arrive, nor when payables will finally become due. Very often, a company treasury department will have taken out a forward foreign exchange deal to cover anticipated receipts or payables in a foreign currency. If the receivables or payables are not due on the day the foreign exchange deal matures, the department will be faced with a foreign exchange contract that they cannot fulfil.

For example, a treasury department in Hong Kong takes out a 90-day forward foreign exchange contract to sell US$ and buy HK$. The purpose of this contract is to cover the anticipated receipt of US$, which is due on the same day as the forward deal matures. However, when the forward foreign exchange deal matures, the treasury department discovers that the receipt of the US$ has been delayed. They therefore do not have the US$ to sell to meet their obligations under the forward foreign exchange contract. They are told by the sales department that the anticipated receipt of the US$ is 30 days hence.

They undertake an FX swap as follows:

Spot	– US$	+ HK$	Maturing FX deal
FX Swap:			
Spot	+ US$	– HK$	First leg
30 days	– US$	+ HK$	Second leg

The obligations under the forward foreign exchange deal are met by the receipt of US$ under the first leg of the FX swap. The second leg of the FX swap, the payment of US$, is met by the receipt of US$ from the customer (Figure 9.4).

Example of rolling position forward

An Australian company has entered into a contract to sell US$10 million for AU$ to cover an identified transaction exposure. However on maturity of the FX contract they do not have the US$10 million to meet their obligations under the contract. They undertake an FX swap to buy spot US$10 million for AU$, and sell US$10 million for AU$ in 90 days, when it is forecast that payment of US$10 million should be received under the commercial contract.

Current US$/AU$ spot rate	1.5203 / 1.5213	
90-day forward points	133	140

Buy US$10 million   Sell AU$ @ 1.5208 = 15,208,000

At termination of swap:

Sell US$10 million   Buy AU$ @ 1.5341 = 15,341,000

The first leg of the swap, the purchase of US$10 million enables the company to meet its obligation under the FX contract. The second leg of the swap, the sale of US$10 million will be met from the receipt of US$10 million under the commercial contract. The difference between the sale of AU$15,208,000 on the first leg of the swap, and the receipt of AU$15,341,000 on the second leg of the swap is due to interest rate differentials, between US$ and AU$. Most companies would account for the difference as sale proceeds.

Creating synthetic currency assets and liabilities

Treasury departments are very often faced with the following opportunities:

- An ability to borrow more cheaply in foreign currencies. An obvious example is a non-US company with a US dollar commercial paper

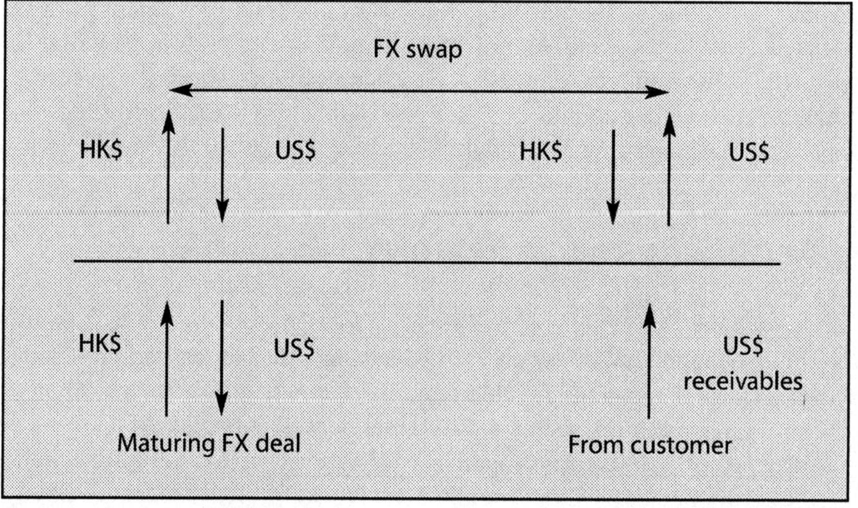

Figure 9.4 Rolling positions forward

programme. The currency in which the borrowing is raised is often different from the currency in which the funds are required.

- An extension of the above is a company that is managing translation risk by borrowing in foreign currencies. However, the company's main borrowing instrument raises funds in its domestic currency. An example might be a UK company with a UK commercial paper programme, needing to borrow funds in euros to match its European investments.
- Overseas operations that have cash surpluses that are not required for certain periods of time.

The FX swap is the typical instrument by which such opportunities are managed. Take the example of an Australian company with a subsidiary in Singapore. The Singapore company has SG$20 million of cash deposits for which it has no business requirements for the next six months. The Australian parent would utilize those funds by means of an FX swap.

FX Swap:

Spot	–SG$	+AU$
Six-month	+SG$	–AU$

The first leg of the FX swap generates AU$, which can be used to pay off short-term borrowings in Australia. The second leg of the swap regenerates SG$, which are used for business needs in Singapore. The AU$ part of the second leg of the swap is met by re-borrowing in Australia. In this case the Australian parent should save the borrow/deposit spread plus the margin that it pays on borrowings in Australia. (See question Short dated FX swaps, page 203.)

FOREIGN CURRENCY OPTIONS

So far we have examined spot and forward foreign exchange. The forward foreign exchange market, when used to manage transaction and pre-transaction risk management, is clearly a market where the two currency amounts involved are fixed at the time the deal is entered into. Currency options in their various forms together with hybrids set up a situation where the option holder has protection against adverse foreign exchange movements, but has the opportunity of benefiting from favourable movements.

'Vanilla' currency options

The buyer of a currency option has the right, but not the obligation, to buy or sell that currency in exchange for another at an agreed price over a specified time period or at a specified date. In exchange for this right, a premium is payable.

A call option gives the option buyer the right to buy a currency. For currency options, the currency exchange is usually against the US$. A SG$ call US$ put option gives the buyer the right to buy SG$ and sell US$. A SG$ put option US$ call option gives the option buyer the right to sell SG$ against the US$. The strike price is the agreed price at which the exchange of currencies takes place.

Consider a Japan-based company exporting to the United States. It has a contractual receipt of US$1 million in six months time. The US$/JPY exchange rates are:

Spot	120.160 / 210
Six-month forward points	800 / 700

The company decides to hedge the receipt of the US$ by means of a currency option. It takes out a JPY call US$ put, at the six-month US$/JPY forward rate –119.360. Expiry is six months from contract date.

Two potential scenarios are shown in Table 9.1. In one scenario the US$ has strengthened against JPY to stand at 130 at exercise date; in the other it has weakened to 115.

Hybrid options

Over the years the banks have marketed a number of hybrid options. These options are based on either combinations of options, or options and forwards. Some common examples are:

- *Break-forward.* This is a forward foreign exchange contract where one party has the right, but not the obligation to terminate the contract at one or more pre-determined times during its life. There is no up-front premium because the costs are incorporated in the forward rate. There is however a fee payable for breaking the contract.
- *Compound option.* Also known as an option on an option. The purchaser has the right to buy a specific option at a predetermined price on a fixed future date. This instrument is designed for contingent foreign exchange

Table 9.1 Exercise decisions at different final market prices

US$/JPY at exercise date	*US$/JPY at exercise date*
130	115
Do not exercise option. Sell US$ in market for 130 JPY	Exercise option Sell US$ for JPY at 119.360

liabilities. The initial option premium will be materially lower than for a standard option.

- *Cylinder option.* This instrument enables the treasurer to reduce the cost of an option by agreeing to forego gains when the hedged currency strengthens above a given level. For example, a treasurer receiving US dollars may buy a UK£ call US$ put at UK£/US$ 1.65, with a floor at 1.55. If the US dollar weakens above 1.65, then the treasurer is protected. However if the dollar strengthens against the pound to below 1.55, s/he gives up any further gains and sells US$ at 1.55.
- *Participating forward.* The purchaser of this instrument has a floor rate of exchange together with an element of upside potential. If the spot rate of exchange moves against the purchaser of a participating forward, the loss is limited to the floor rate. However if the exchange rate moves in the purchaser's favour, he/she enjoys a percentage of that favourable movement. This percentage is determined by the so-called participation rate.

From the treasurer's standpoint, it is not necessary to be knowledgeable about all the hybrid options that are on the market. At any one point of time there may be far too many of these structures to make that feasible. It is far more important, however, to understand how these different instruments can be structured. This enables the treasurer to both test the pricing of different structures being offered, and also, by using first principles, to conceive of different structures that may meet desired hedging objectives.

The reader is invited to examine some of the questions at the end of the chapter, where the uses of some these hybrid structures and the method of their structuring is examined.

Exotic options

The most likely exotic options that the treasurer may meet or want to use for managing foreign exchange are knock-in and knock-out options, and average rate options.

Knock-in, knock-out options

A Canadian treasurer has to make a payment of US$1 million in six months, and is given the information shown in Table 9.2 by the bank:

To save on premium, the treasurer decides to buy the knock-out option.

Scenario one: In six months, the US$/CA$ exchange rate has moved to 1.6160. The treasurer exercises the option and buys US$1 million for CA$1.5607 million. In this situation the treasurer has saved 0.83 per cent of the US$ principal, US$8300, compared with purchasing a standard option.

Scenario two: After three months, the US$/CA$ exchange rate moves beyond 1.52. As soon US$/CA$ spot exchange rate breaches 1.52, the option falls away worthless, and the treasurer may cover the position by buying US$ forward. The three-month forward rate offered is 1.53

The cost/benefit of the knock-out option depends on the ultimate US$/CA$ exchange rate at the expiry of six months. One can compare two situations with the US$/CA$ at 1.48, and 1.53 (after having breached 1.52, the US$ subsequently strengthens to 1.53) in Table 9.3.

Note that the premium payable in CA$ is calculated:

* US$ principal × premium rate × US$/CA$ spot rate at contract date.

Table 9.2 Comparison of standard option and barrier option

US$/CA$ information	
US$/CA$ spot	1.5490
6-month outright forward	1.5607
6-month option:	US$ call CA$ put
Strike	1.5607
Premium	1.96 % of the US$ amount
6-month knock out option	US$ call CA$ put
Strike	1.5607
Barrier	1.52
Premium	1.13 % of US$ amount

Table 9.3 Payoff comparison of standard option with barrier options at different final market prices. The table assumes that the treasurer covers the position with a forward transaction at 1.53 when the barrier is breached at 1.52.

	Payoff with standard option		*Payoff with knockout option*	
US$/CA$ 1.48	CA$ payable	1,480,000	CA$ payable	1,530,000
	CA$ premium*	30,360	CA$ premium*	17,503
		1,510,360		1,547,503
US$/CA$ 1.53	CA$ payable	1,530,000	CA$ payable	1,530,000
	CA$ premium	30,360	CA$ premium	17,503
		1,560,360		1,547,503

Average rate options

There are two types of average rate options: average *spot* rate options and average *strike* rate options.

Average spot rate options: Spot rates are averaged over the option period, and this average is compared to the strike rate chosen by the option buyer.

Average strike rate options: The option buyer selects the expiry date and averaging dates. On the expiry of the option the average rate becomes the strike price of the option.

Average rate options are typically used by companies that have periodic payments or receivables, and wish to gain trend protection against unfavourable currency movements. Alternatively, they can be used by a company with an invoiced cost for materials based on the average of spot rates over a defined period.

Hybrid exotics

In the same way that standard options can be combined, either together or with outright forwards, to create hybrid instruments, so can exotic instruments. The following is an example of such a combination.

A UK company sells to the United States. It expects to receive US$5 million in six months. The outright six-month forward rate of exchange is 1.55. The company purchases a six-month US$ put UK£ call knock-out barrier option, with a strike rate of 1.55 and a barrier at 1.475. It then funds the purchase of the option by selling a six-month US$ call UK£ put knock-in barrier option, with a barrier at 1.475 and a strike of 1.55. The profile of the company's payout is shown in Figure 9.5.

The argument for this instrument is that the treasurer is always protected against adverse movements in the UK£/US$ exchange rate through the knock-out barrier option which has a strike of 1.55. The treasurer benefits from favourable movements in the UK£/US$ exchange all the way to 1.475 at which point the knock-out option falls away and the knock-in option takes effect, making it necessary to sell the US$ at 1.55. This is no worse, so the argument runs, than having sold the US$ at 1.55 forward. Note: the disadvantage of this structure is that the company is uncovered should the exchange rate go below 1.475 and then subsequently move back above 1.55. In this situation the holder of the US$ call would not exercise the option.

USE OF OPTIONS FOR CORPORATE PURPOSES

The use of options to hedge transaction and pre-transaction exposure is not necessarily a passive exercise since there are a number of important questions to be addressed.

Where to draw the strike? The closer the strike price under the option to the current market price, then the greater the option premium but the greater the

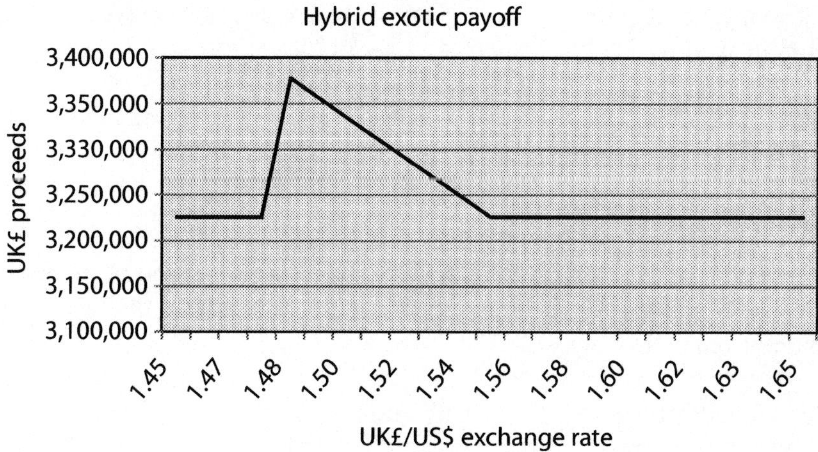

Figure 9.5 Payoffs under hybrid exotic option

protection. The further away the strike price is from the current market price, the lower the premium but the lower the protection. This is a critical decision for a treasury department trying to balance option costs against protection.

What kind of option? It is not necessarily the case that the plain vanilla is best suited to the company. There may be situations where the use of an exotic option or some form of hybrid is more suited to the company, its business and cashflows, and its risk management philosophy. Generally it is true to say that 'you get what you pay for in financial markets, and the less you pay the less you get'. Using exotics because the premiums may be lower is not necessarily a valid decision.

How will options be tracked? What happens if the market runs in the treasurer's favour? For instance, the treasurer of a Singapore company selling to the United States may buy a US$ put SG$ call. What should the decision be when the US$ strengthens against the SG$ and the option becomes further out of the money? Some treasurers argue that the option should be replaced with forwards and the option sold back to extract some time value. Options should not necessarily be left to maturity. A knock-out option needs to be tracked, since once the barrier is breached the hedge that the option represents will fall away. At this point should it be replaced with forward FX.

View of market: In making the above decisions, to what extent is it valid to take views of the market? Probably, for most treasurers, it is virtually impossible to make a risk management decision without taking some view of the market. How does this marry with the company's risk management philosophy, particularly those companies which define themselves as cost-centre treasuries?

EXERCISES

Forward foreign exchange

A Singapore-based company imports a significant proportion of its needs from the United States. It is invoiced in US$. It forecasts the following imports from its US supplier:

In one month's time	US$ 10 m
In two months' time	US$ 17.5 m
In three months' time	US$ 16 m

A bank quotes US$/SG$ spot rate and forward points as follows:

	Bid	Offer
Spot	1.8252	1.8262
One month	52	42
Two months	74	63
Three months	94	82
Six months	120	107

The company decides to use the forward market to cover its FX exposure.

1. Calculate the relevant forward rates to cover the exposures.
2. How much SG$ cash will the importer need to pay?
3. Supposing that in three months the spot rate US$/SG$ has moved to 1.93, what would be your opinion of the above strategy?

Foreign exchange options

The same company forecasts a payment of US$10 million in six months' time. It decides to use options to cover the exposure. It is quoted a premium of 2.5 per cent of the US$ notional amount for a six-month option with a strike price at the forward rate.

1. What will be its breakeven rate for the strategy to work?
2. What will the company do if in six months' time the US$/SG$ exchange rate is:

   a) 1.9210/1.9220
   b) 1.7516/1.7526?

The company's six-month borrowing rate is 2 per cent.

Hybrid options

As treasurer of the same Singapore company you also have the information on strike rates shown on the next page.
Consider how you would therefore evaluate the following structures that have been offered you to manage the exposure of paying US$10 million in six months:

Strike rate	*6-month US$ call/SG$ put*	*6-month US$ put/SG$ call*
1.84	2.18 %	3.56 %
1.83	2.41 %	3.23 %
1.82	2.66 %	2.95 %
1.80		2.40 %
1.79		2.16 %
1.78		1.93 %

Strike rate	*3-month US$ call/SG$ put*	*3-month US$ put/SG$ call*
1.8199	1.90%	1.68%

1. The company is protected against the adverse movement of US$/SG$ beyond 1.84, but can receive 100 per cent of any favourable movement to 1.78.
2. The company can be protected against any unfavourable rate beyond 1.84 but can obtain 50 per cent of any favourable movement in exchange rate below 1.84.
3. The company is able to buy US$10 million at the US$/SG$ at a fixed six-month forward rate but is free to break the contract and buy the US$ on the open market should a more favourable rate be available at maturity.

Experience tells you that the cashflow forecast for the next quarter could be inaccurate by + or – 50 per cent.

Short dated FX swaps

As treasurer of MultiMedia you are presented with the following data:

- Cash balances

Parent	*Pooled Singapore subsidiaries*
US$m	SG$m
(350)	540

- Cashflow forecasts

Month	*Parent*	*Subsidiaries*
	US$m	SG$m
1	(100)	(70)
2	50	(70)
3	(200)	165

- You also have the following data:

US$ LIBOR 1, 2, and 3 month	5.69 / 5.70,	5.81 / 5.93,	5.86 / 5.98
SG$ SIBOR 1, 2, and 3 month	2.00 / 2.37,	2.19 / 2.31,	2.38 / 2.50

Funds for the Singapore subsidiaries can be deposited at the bid rate.
The US parent borrows at a margin of 25bps.
US$/SG$ exchange rates are:

	US$/SG$
Spot	1.6625/1.6635
Forward points	
1 month	52/47
2 month	93/88
3 month	135/128

Question

As treasurer:

1. What action would you take regarding the SG$ balances?
2. What would your strategy be if you believed US$ LIBOR rates would increase more than the market anticipates?

SOLUTIONS

Forward foreign exchange

a) Calculation of forward exchange rates:

One month:

	Spot	1.8252	1.8262
Forward points		52	42
One-month forward rates		**1.8200**	**1.8220**

Two months:

	Spot	1.8252	1.8262
Forward points		74	63
One-month forward rates		**1.8178**	**1.8199**

Three months:

	Spot	1.8252	1.8262
Forward points		94	82
One-month forward rates		**1.8158**	**1.8180**

Note that the spread (difference between bid and offer) gets wider.

b) Payments
The manufacturer is selling SG$ and buying US$ and so must take the offer price, that is, the price at which the bank is selling US$ and buying SG$. The following SG$ amounts will have to be paid:

US$10 ×	1.8220	= SG$ 18,220,000
US$17.5 m ×	1.8199	= SG$ 31,848,250
US$16 m ×	1.8180	= SG$ 29,088,000

c) Strategy result
If in three months the US$ had strengthened against the SG$, then the forward strategy would have been successful, since without forward cover the importer would have had to pay 16,000,000 × 1.93 = SG$ 30,880,000 for its imports.

Foreign exchange options

The cost of the premium in US$ is US$250,000. In addition the company will have to pay the borrowing costs of financing the premium.

The costs of the option strategy will therefore be:

Purchase cost	US$ 10,000,000
Premium	250,000
Borrowing costs (.25 m × .02 × 182/360)	2,528
	10,252,528

For the option strategy to work the US$/SG$ rate needs to weaken to a level where the premium and borrowing costs are recouped.

The six-month forward rate is 1.8132/1.8155. If the option is not taken out, but the importer has covered itself on the forward market, then the SG$ payment for the US$ imports would be:

US$10 m × 1.8155 = SG$18,155,000

The breakeven rate is therefore:

18,155,000/10,252,528 = 1.7708

If the spot rate US$ weakens against the SG$ to 1.7708 the company will be in exactly the same economic position as if it had taken out straight forward cover.

- If the option strategy is adopted then:
  i. If the US$/SG$ exchange rate moves to 1.9210/1.9220, the option would be exercised and US$ purchased at the option rate of 1.8155.
  ii. If the US$/SG$ exchange rate moves to 1.7516/1.7526, the option will not be exercised as the US$ will be purchased spot.

Hybrid options

Structure one

This is a typical cylinder type structure. The cylinder consists of buying an option and selling an offsetting option to reduce the premium.

The first option is a six-month US$10 million call SG$ put with a strike rate of 1.84. If the US$ strengthens against the SG$ beyond 1.84, then the company is protected. The cost of this option is 2.18 per cent. The second option is a six-month US$10 million put SG$ call with strike rate of 1.78. The receipt from this option is 1.93 per cent. The overall cost of the structure is therefore 0.25 per cent (ignoring the bank's spread). The company's payoff is shown diagrammatically in the figure below.

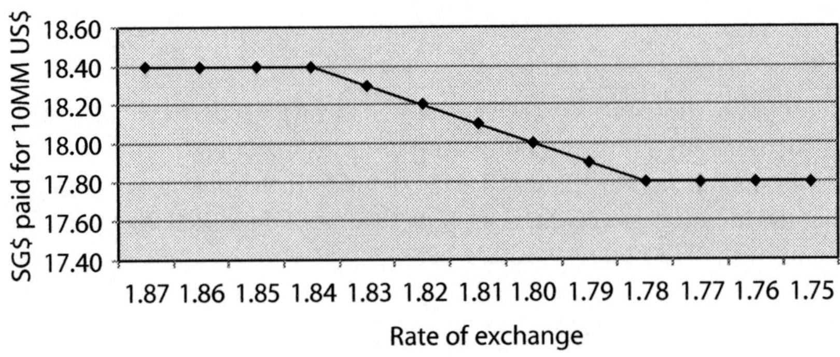

The company is protected against any adverse movement in the US$/SG$ exchange rate beyond 1.84, and between 1.84 and 1.78 is able to purchase the US$ at the more favourable spot rate. However, once the US$/SG$ exchange rate moves beyond 1.78 the company gives up all further gains and must purchase the US$ at 1.78 (since the bank will exercise its US$ put at 1.78).

This strategy compares with the six-month forward rate of 1.8155.

Structure two

This structure again consists of the combination of two standard options. The first is a six-month US$10 million call SG$ put with a strike rate of 1.84. The cost of this option is again 2.18 per cent. The premium is reduced by selling a US$ put SG$ call, but for only 50 per cent of the principal, namely US$5 million. The receipt from this sale is 3.56 per cent on US$5 million, giving a net premium of 0.40 per cent. Essentially therefore the premium has been reduced to 0.40 per cent. The company's payoff is now as shown in the next figure.

Structure three

The six-month US$/SG$ forward rate for buying US$ is 1.8155. The structure proposed can be created by the corporate buying US$ at the forward rate of 1.8155. In addition the corporate should buy a six-month US$ put SG$ call. The strike rate of the optional is variable, but could be set at 1.82.

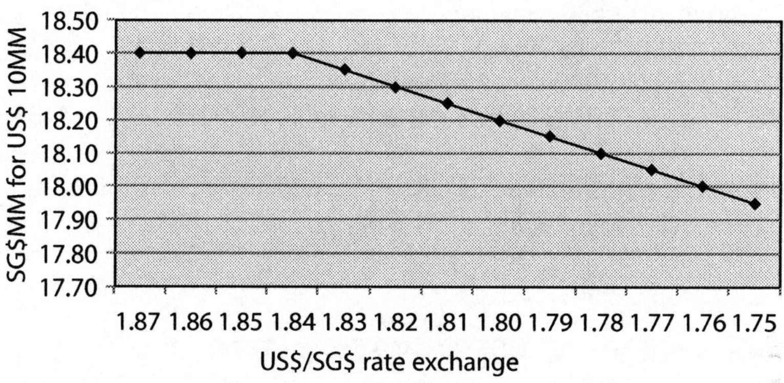

In six months' time, if the US$/SG$ rate has fallen to 1.75, the company would exercise the put option, enabling it to sell the US$ it has purchased under the forward contract. This leaves it free to buy US$ in the market at 1.75.

The cost of the structure is the put option at 2.95 per cent.

It is hard to say why this structure should be entered into as opposed to the purchase of US$ call option.

Short-dated FX swaps

	Parent US$	*Singapore sub SG$*
Current balance	(350)	540
Projected month 1	(100)	(100)
	(450)	(440)
Projected month 2	50	(100)
	(400)	340
Projected month 3	(200)	110
	(600)	440

Maximum to be taken from the Singapore pool SG$340.

Benefits of pooling

SG$340 m at 1.6630 generate	US$ 204,449,789
US$206,123,067* generate	SG$ 340,000,000
Interest foregone 340 m × 91/360 × 2.38	SG$ 2,045,478
Cost of buying SG$ interest 2,045,478/1.6490	US$ 1,240,435

(*This represents the amount of US$ to be sold at the end of three months to generate SG$340 million – 340/1.6495.)

Benefit of transaction

Interest saved on swap US$ 204,449,789 × 91/360 × 6.23*

	US$	3,219,686
Cost of swap (206,123,067 – 204,449,789)		(1,673,278)
Interest purchased		(1,240,435)
Benefit of swap	US$	305,973

If the treasurer believed that US$ LIBOR would rise more rapidly than the market is currently anticipating, then s/he would either cover the position with FRAs or swaps (see Chapter 12) or would take advances for a longer period than three months.

(*3-month borrowing rate 5.98 + margin 25 bps.)

CHAPTER 10

Interest Rate Risk Derivatives and Their Use in Managing Financial Risk

INTEREST RATE SWAPS

Definition

An interest rate swap is a legal arrangement between two parties to exchange interest rate payments or receipts on a notional principal amount, for a specific period of time. The interest obligations are in the same currency. There is no exchange or payment of principal under an interest rate swap.

Example

In the following example, a corporate has borrowed US$20 million under a five-year bank term loan. The loan is at floating rate, whereby the corporate pays six-month US$ LIBOR plus a margin of 50 basis points. The corporate wants to change the interest payment basis from floating to fixed. To achieve this it enters into a fixed–floating five-year interest rate swap with a bank whereby the corporate pays a fixed interest rate on US$20 million for five years, and receives floating rate at US$ LIBOR on US$20 million for five years.

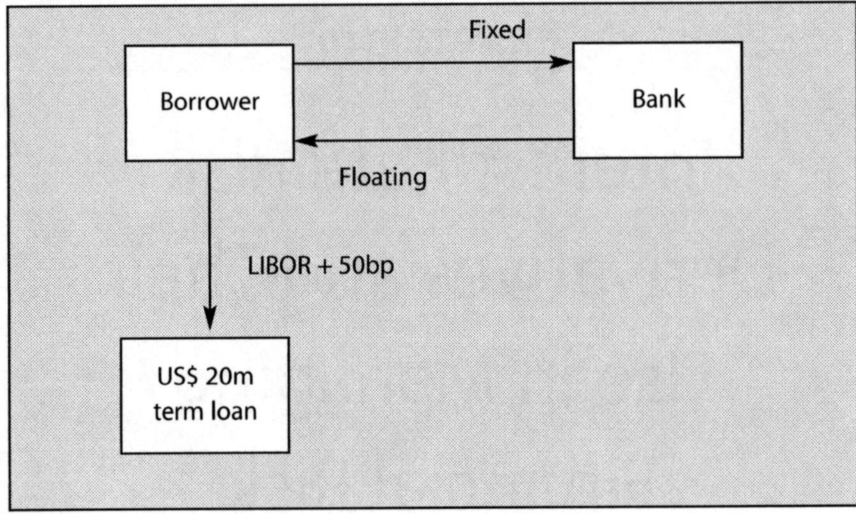

Figure 10.1 Diagram of an interest rate swap with a borrower receiving floating and paying fixed rates

The effect of the swap is as follows:

Term loan	Pay six-month US$ LIBOR + 50bp
SWAP	Receive six-month US$ LIBOR, pay fixed
NET	Pay fixed + 50bp.

There is no exchange of principal, only interest is exchanged.

Effect of interest rate swaps

The corporate treasurer of the organization has now converted the floating rate liability into a fixed rate liability. The two US$ LIBOR flows, one a payment on the loan and the other a receipt under the interest rate swap, cancel each other out. This leaves the fixed flow that is payable under the swap, plus the 50 basis point margin on the loan.

Let us assume that the fixed rate payable under the swap is 5 per cent every six months, and that US$ LIBOR for the first six months of the swap is 4 per cent. At the end of the first six months the net cash paid under the swap and term loan is:

Company pays 5 per cent on US$20 million for six months (5 per cent × 20 m × 182/360) under swap	(505,555)

Company receives six-month US$ LIBOR – 4 per cent on US$20 million for six months (4 per cent × 20 m × 182/360) under swap	404,444
Company pays US$ LIBOR + 50bp on US$ 20 million for six months under term loan	(455,000)
	(556,111)

A net payment under the swap of US$101,111 is payable by the company to the bank. The final net borrowing cost equates to a fixed rate borrowing of 5.5 per cent and is calculated:

Company pays 5 per cent on US$20 million for six months under swap	(5 per cent)
Company receives US$ LIBOR on US$ 20 million under swap	LIBOR
Company pays US$ LIBOR + 50bp on US$20 million under term loan	(LIBOR + 50bp)
	(5.50 per cent)

LIBOR fixings or swap roll-overs

LIBOR (see Appendix) or its equivalent under an interest rate swap can be fixed for different periods (three months, six months or a year being the most common). If LIBOR is fixed every six months, then on a five-year interest rate swap there will be ten fixings. At the beginning of each period, LIBOR for that period is fixed, interest exchange taking place at the end of the period (Figure 10.2).

The five-year term loan is composed of ten LIBOR fixings. The matching five-year interest rate swap, which converts the floating rate borrowings to fixed, also consists of ten LIBOR fixings. There will be ten exchanges of interest during the life of the swap. The dates of the roll-overs under the swap must match those under the term loan to completely cover the exposure to floating rate.

Variations in LIBOR during the life of the swap

During the life of the swap, six-month LIBOR may sometimes be above the fixed rate in the swap. In this case the fixed rate payer will receive a net payment at the end of the LIBOR period. On other occasions six-month LIBOR may be below the fixed swap rate, in which case the fixed rate payer will make a net payment at the end of the LIBOR period.

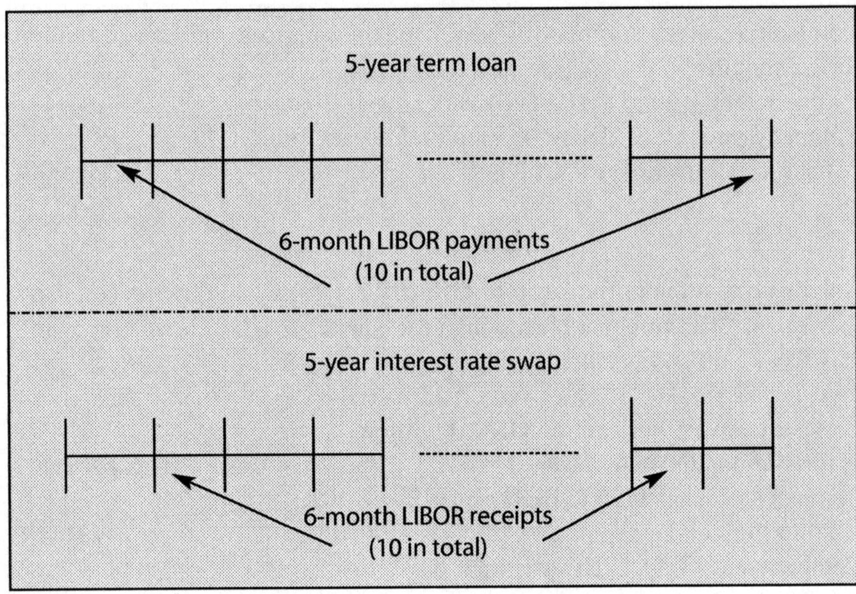

Figure 10.2 LIBOR fixings during a five-year interest rate swap

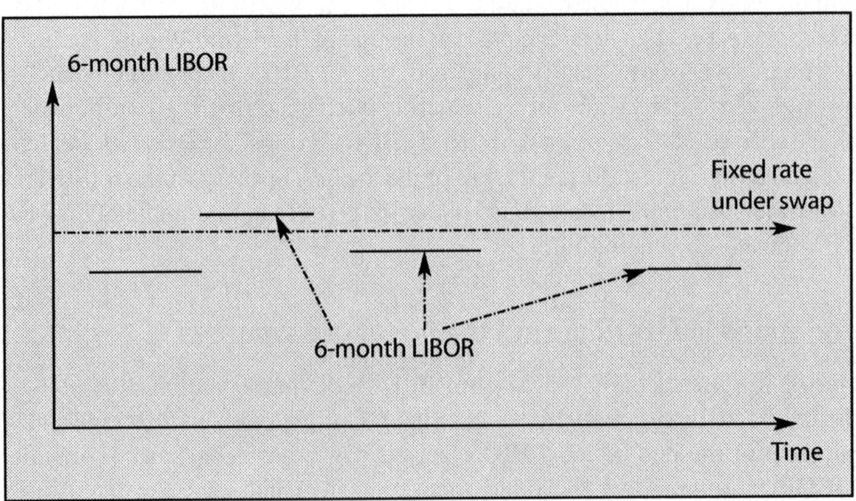

Figure 10.3 LIBOR during the swap in relation to the swap fixed rate

Elements of interest rate swaps

There are a number of elements to an interest rate swap:

- Interest rate swaps are always based on a notional principal amount. In the case of the above example the notional amount is US$20 million.
- Interest rate swaps always have a maturity period. In the above example, the swap runs for five years.
- The floating rate (LIBOR or equivalent) can be for any period up to one year. However three months, six months or one year are the most popular periods.
- Usually both the interest payments are for the same period. If the floating leg is based on six months, then the same will apply to the fixed rate leg.
- Interest is always exchanged at regular intervals, usually at the end of each interest period. The interest exchange is netted; in other words, there is one net interest payment.
- Interest rate swaps can be used to fix the interest receivable on a cash deposit as well as the interest payable under a floating rate loan. (In this case the corporate would pay floating rates under the swap and receive fixed.)
- Interest rate swaps can also be used to swap fixed rate borrowings to floating. (In this case the corporate would receive fixed rates to offset the fixed rate under the borrowing and pay floating.)

Determining the fixed rate under the swap

The fixed rate under an interest rate swap will be determined by the rates ruling in the swap market when the swap is undertaken. It will be established in much the same way as the fixed rate under a corporate bond. The yield on the relative government security (for a five-year swap this is the yield on the five-year benchmark government security used by the swap market) is determined, and the swap spread added.

The fixed rate under a swap will reflect three things:

- The yield curve for the relevant benchmark government bonds used by the stock market. This will change as a result of changes in both the market perception of the outlook for interest rates and the supply of and demand for government bonds.

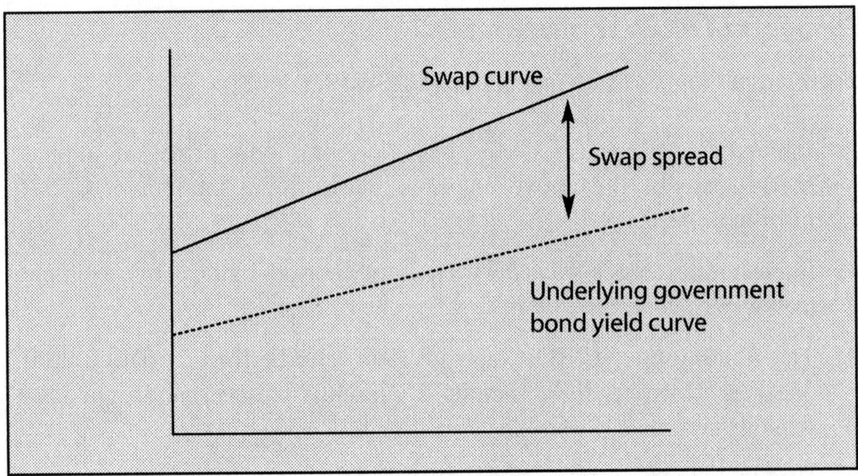

Figure 10.4 Swap yield curve versus the government bond yield curve

- The perception of bank risk relative to the government risk. Banks, who are the principal counterparties to interest swaps, lend to each other at LIBOR. The size of the swap spread reflects the market perception of bank risk relative to government risk.
- The number of counterparties wishing to pay fixed under an interest rate swap. Simplistically, a surfeit of counterparties willing to pay the fixed rate will cause spreads to widen, since banks will increase the price at which they receive fixed to a level where the counterparties no longer have the appetite to pay. Conversely a reduction in counterparties willing to pay the fixed rate will cause spreads to narrow.

For the corporate treasurer seeking the opportunity to undertake an interest rate swap in a particular currency, the significance of the above is that not only must the relevant government bond yield curve be kept under observation but the swap spread also needs to be monitored. This is because both these factors establish the swap yield curve for a currency.

Different types of interest rate swaps

Interest rate swaps, being merely a package of cashflows, can come in as many variations as there are variations in packaging the cashflows. The following are some of the different types of interest rate swaps that a corporate treasurer may use:

Accreting swaps: The notional principal increases at each interest rate setting. Accreting swaps can be used to hedge zero-coupon notes.

Amortizing swaps: The notional principal amortizes over a period of time. Such swaps are used to hedge amortizing borrowings such as leases or term loans that amortize over a period of time.

Basis swap: Enables the corporate treasurer to change the interest basis of a loan, for example a basis swap where one party pays six-month LIBOR and the other pays three-month LIBOR.

Forward starting swaps: Instead of the swap starting today (i.e. spot), the swap starts at some time in the future. Treasurers taking out swaps often have to ensure that the dates of the interest rate fixings in the swap coincide with the interest payment dates in the underlying loan that is being hedged. Very often that next interest payment date on the loan when the swap is transacted may be some months away.

INTEREST RATE OPTIONS (IRO)

Definition

An interest rate option gives its buyer the opportunity to protect the rate of interest payable or receivable on a notional loan or deposit for a specified period. The protection rate is the strike rate under the option. The option will guarantee a maximum interest payable on a loan, or a minimum return on a deposit. A premium is payable by the option buyer.

An interest rate cap protects the rate of interest payable on a notional loan from an upward movement in interest rates, and thereby guarantees a maximum interest payable. An interest rate floor protects the rate of interest receivable on a notional deposit from a downward movement in interest rates, and thereby guarantees a minimum.

Example of an interest rate cap

The corporate treasurer in the previous example decides not to hedge the floating rate borrowing with an interest rate swap. Instead he or she decides to use an interest rate cap to hedge the exposure to rising interest rates that a floating rate borrowing brings. The quotes obtained are shown in Table 10.1.

Table 10.1 Elements of quotations for two alternative interest rate caps (assuming a flat yield curve of 4.75 per cent)

	Alternative one	*Alternative two*
Currency	US$	US$
Notional principal	US$ 20 million	US$ 20 million
Period	5 years	5 years
Roll-overs	6-monthly linked to US$ LIBOR	6-monthly linked to US$ LIBOR
Strike rate	5.00 %	5.50 %
Premium payable	1.81 %	1.21 %
Total premium payable	US$ 362,000	US$ 242,000

Clearly an interest rate cap with the strike at 5.5 per cent will cost less than an interest rate cap with the strike rate set at 5.00 per cent. The treasurer decides to select the cap that provides the greatest protection, namely that with a strike rate of 5.00 per cent.

Let us assume that at the beginning of the third six-month US$ LIBOR fixing that US$ LIBOR has now risen to 5.5 per cent, and that the roll-over period is 182 days. The treasurer will receive under the interest rate cap:

US$20,000,000 × 0.5 per cent × 182/360 = US$ 50,555.55

It may well be that, at the commencement of the fifth six-month US$ LIBOR fixing, US$ LIBOR has now fallen to 4.75 per cent. In that case the interest rate cap is out of the money for that particular roll-over period, and the cap buyer borrows at the lower US$ LIBOR rate (Table 10.2).

Aspects of interest rate options

It is natural for the treasurer to look at the swap yield curve when deciding where to set the strike price. However, it must be remembered that the yield curve consists of a whole series of forward–forward rates. When the yield curve is upward sloping, the curve for forward–forward rates rises more steeply than the underlying par curve, and lies above the that curve. With a

Table 10.2 The effect of an interest rate cap at different interest rates

	LIBOR at 5.5 %	*LIBOR at 4.75 %*
Strike rate under cap	5.00 %	5.00 %
6-month LIBOR	5.5 %	4.75 %
Interest rate on underlying loan	5.50 %	4.75 %
Receivable under interest rate cap	0.50 %	NIL
Net borrowing cost	5.00 %	4.75 %

downward sloping yield curve, the forward–forward rates fall more steeply than the underlying par curve, and lie below it (see Chapter 11).

The calculation of the premium payable under a particular interest rate cap is established by splitting the option into a series of individual 'caplets'. Each individual caplet relates to an individual roll-over period or LIBOR setting. The strike rate under each caplet is compared with the forward–forward rate for that roll-over period in determining the premium payable for the caplet. The premium payable for the option is a summation of the premiums for each caplet.

Table 10.3 shows hypothetical five-year swap rates for US$. The forward–forward rates have been calculated using the formula explained in in Chapter 11.

By setting the strike at 3.50 per cent for a five-year cap, the strike rate for three of the four caplets will all be in the money when established. Therefore the treasurer will need to consider a strike of say 3.25 per cent for year two, 3.75 per cent for year three and so on.

Table 10.3 Swap rates and corresponding forward–forward rates

	Swap rates		*Forward–forward rates*
1 year	2.50 %		
2 years	2.75 %	12 vs 24	3.04 %
3 years	3.00 %	24 vs 36	3.55 %
4 years	3.25 %	36 vs 48	4.09 %
5 years	3.50 %	48 vs 60	4.65 %

Interest rate collars

It should be clear that one of the principal attractions of using options to manage interest rate risk is the flexibility of the instrument. While the downside of adverse interest rate movements (rising interest rates in the case of a loan, or falling in the case of cash deposits) is protected against, the option buyer benefits from any positive movement in interest rates. One of the problems the treasurer faces with using interest rate options is that boards of directors or finance directors often react negatively to the absolute amount of the premium payable. In the example used above, the absolute cost of the interest rate cap at 5.00 per cent was US$462,000. For many this is psychologically too great a price to pay for protection.

Banks selling options to corporates have therefore developed structures that, while trying to keep some of the flexibility of an option, reduce the upfront premium. A common example of this type of structure is the interest rate collar. If one of the problems with an interest rate cap is the premium payable by the corporate buyer, this can be reduced if the corporate, in turn, sells an option to the bank.

A corporate wishing to obtain protection against rising interest rates could reduce the premium payable to obtain that protection by selling an interest rate floor. In such a case, if interest rates fell below the strike rate under the floor, the corporate gives up all further gain.

Sometimes collars are structured to reduce the premium payable to zero, in which case the premium receivable from selling the floor exactly offsets the premium payable on the cap. In other cases collars are structured to reduce the premium payable, but not to zero.

In the scenario given in Table 10.4, assume that the corporate treasurer selects example one. What happens under the two scenarios when six-month US$ LIBOR exceeds the cap rate and when six-month US$ LIBOR falls below the floor rate interest rate? This is shown in Table 11.5.

Payout under different interest rate scenarios

It is probably clear from Table 10.5 that the collar operates something like an interest rate swap operating within bands.

EXOTIC OPTIONS

Exotic options in some cases not only reduce the size of the premium payable, but can also provide a very flexible hedging instrument. The most

Table 10.4 An example of two interest rate collars (based on a yield curve of 5 per cent throughout)

	Example one	*Example two*
Currency	US$	US$
Notional principal	US$20 million	US$20 million
Period	5 years	5 years
Roll-overs	6-monthly linked to US$ LIBOR	6-monthly linked to US$ LIBOR
Strike rate under cap	5.50 %	5.50 %
Strike rate under floor	4.50 %	4.00 %
Premium payable	0.20 %	0.68 %

Table 10.5 The net borrowing cost on a notional US$20 million loan under different interest rate scenarios using an interest rate collar

	LIBOR at 6.0 %	*LIBOR at 4.75 %*	*LIBOR at 4.0 %*
Strike rate under cap/floor	5.50 %	5.50 %/4.50 %	4.50 %
6-month US$ LIBOR	6.0 %	4.75 %	4.00 %
Interest rate on underlying loan	6.00 %	4.75 %	4.00 %
(Receivable) under interest rate cap/ payable under floor	(0.50 %)	NIL	0.50 %
Net borrowing cost	5.50 %	4.75 %	4.50 %

usual exotic option that is marketed for interest rate management is the 'digital cap' (see Table 10.6). This gives a fixed payout if the strike rate is breached on one of the interest setting periods.

Payouts under different hypothetical interest rate scenarios for the above two instruments are shown in Table 10.7.

Digital options can be combined with standard options to produce different derivative structures. One example might be combining a digital cap with a standard floor to produce a zero-cost collar. In this structure, the digital cap buyer receives a fixed payout if the floating rate exceeds the cap level, and pays the difference between the floating rate and the strike rate under the floor if interest rates fall below the floor.

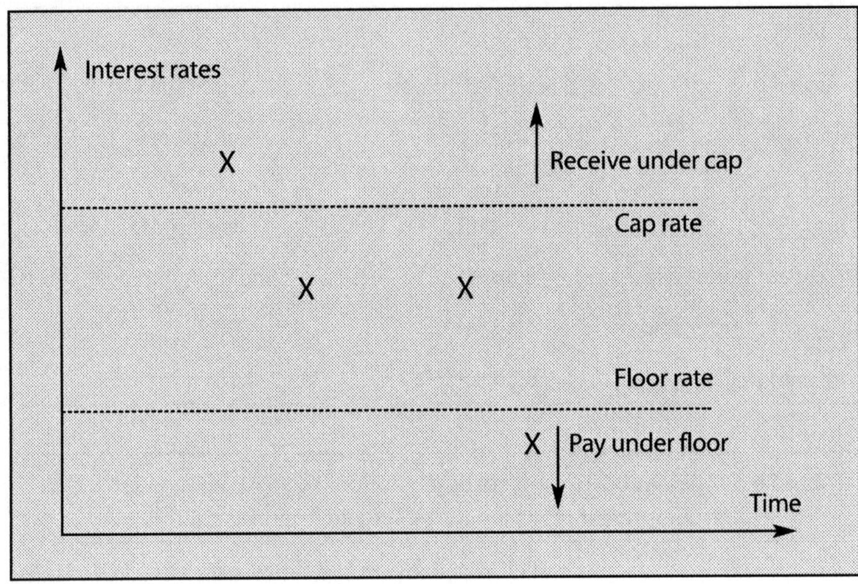

Figure 10.5 Operation of interest rate collar

Note: X = actual six-month LIBOR

Table 10.6 Comparison of a digital cap with an interest rate cap

	Standard cap	*Digital cap*
Currency	US$	US$
Notional principal	US$20 million	US$20 million
Period	5 years	5 years
Roll-overs	6-monthly linked to US$ LIBOR	6-monthly linked to US$ LIBOR
Strike rate under cap	5.00 %	5.00 %
Payout	6-month US$ LIBOR minus cap strike rate	50 basis points
Premium payable	1.81 %	1.20 %

Table 10.7 Payout under the digital in table under different interest rate scenarios

6-month US$ LIBOR	*Standard cap payout*	*Digital cap payout*
4.75 %	NIL	NIL
5.00 %	NIL	50 bps
5.25 %	25 bps	50 bps
5.50 %	50 bps	50 bps
5.7 %	75 bps	50 bps
6.00 %	100 bps	50 bps
6.25 %	125 bps	50 bps

SWAPTION

Definition

A swaption is a contract that confers on the buyer the right (but not the obligation) to enter into an interest rate swap on pre-determined terms at the end of a specified period (option period) in the future. The buyer pays the seller a premium for this right.

Elements to calculate the premium payable/receivable

A swaption is, as its name implies, an option on a swap. The premium payable is based on:

- the period of the option
- the period of the swap
- the fixed rate of the swap
- whether the option purchaser will be a fixed rate receiver or a payer
- the volatility of swap rates
- whether it is an American or European option.

Given the US$ yield curve shown in Table 10.8, a quotation for a six-month swaption on a three-year swap could be as shown in Table 10.9.

Table 10.8 Assumed US$ yield curve

Period	*Rate*
6-month LIBOR	1.40 %
1 year	1.55 % (s.a.)
2 years	2.25 % (s.a.)
3 years	2.75 % (s.a.)
4 years	3.25 % (s.a.)
5 years	3.40 % (s.a.)

Table 10.9 Quotation for a European swaption

Swaption details	
Expiry date of swaption	Today + 182 days
Currency	US$
Nominal amount	US$20 million
Swaption buyer	Fixed rate payer/floating rate receiver
Swap maturity	Today + 3 years and 182 days
Swap rate	3.30 %
Premium	49 bps (US$98,000)

If, in six months, the three-year swap rate has fallen below 3.30 per cent, then the treasurer would let the option lapse and take a swap out in the market. If the rate is above 3.30 per cent, the treasurer would exercise the option and take out the three-year swap at 3.30 per cent.

It must also be remembered that the yield curve is upward sloping, so the effective rate for a six-month forward starting swap is going to be higher than the current three-year spot rate. Hence the rate under the swaption (which would be equivalent to the rate for a three-year swap forwarding starting six months), is higher than the spot four-year rate.

Use of swaptions

Swaptions can often be used in a hedging programme where the treasurer is looking to 'buy some time' or add some flexibility into the programme. A typical situation maybe where the treasurer has to undertake a major hedging programme, but is hesitant about whether the current rates ruling may not be bettered in the market over the next six months or so. A swaption enables the treasurer to take out protection, but retain the opportunity to benefit from a substantial fall in long-term interest rates during the option period.

Swaptions also have their uses in managing the issuance of bonds.

THE EFFECTIVE USE OF DERIVATIVES

There are two ways in which the corporate treasurer can approach the use of derivatives to manage risk. The first is to wait for suggestions and proposals from banks. The treasurer lets the banks know what his or her hedging objectives are, sits back and waits for suggestions and proposals.

The second approach is for the treasurer to become very familiar with the various derivative instruments and to identify and work out which instruments and structures best suit the company and the particular exposures it faces. This puts the treasurer in control of exposure management. To take this proactive approach the treasurer will have need to have access to a derivatives valuation model. These can be purchased on a stand-alone basis, but can also be purchased as a separate module as part of a treasury management system.

There are two attitudes about the treasurer taking views on the direction of market rates. One is that it is the responsibility of the treasurer to take views on the direction of market rates, and to back those views with the timing of hedging programmes. For instance, a treasurer who has a strong view that interest rates will fall much more substantially than the market anticipates may either decide not to hedge, to postpone any hedging, or to purchase an out-of-the-money interest rate cap. Such a philosophy is consistent with the quasi-profit-centre treasury.

The alternative philosophy is that over a long period of time there is no evidence that the treasurer who takes views on the direction of market rates adds value (indeed this often subtracts value). If so, the role of the treasurer is to build a hedging programme that is flexible enough to respond to future changes in interest rates. Such a philosophy is consistent with a value-added treasury.

For those treasurers who like to consider the potential direction of interest rates on their hedging decision, which is applicable to both profit and value-added treasuries, Table 10.10, applicable to a treasurer trying to hedge floating rate borrowings, may help to clarify thoughts.

The table can be re-arranged or expanded to suit the treasurer's own preferences. For instance, instead of having headings for 'interest rates rising, remaining stable or falling', the table could be headed: 'interest rates rise rapidly and quickly, interest rates rise slowly and gently, interest rates remain stable'.

LONG-TERM CROSS-CURRENCY SWAPS

A long-term cross-currency swap can be defined as an agreement between two parties to exchange interest obligations or receipts in different currencies. With a typical cross-currency swap there is an initial exchange of principal and a re-exchange at maturity. The underlying interest payments can be fixed or floating. The need for cross-currency swaps arises from a number of different situations:

- to convert a loan raised in a foreign currency into the company's domestic currency
- to hedge a foreign-denominated asset into a domestic currency
- to convert foreign currency cash balances to a domestic currency for a period of time.

Table 10.10 Schedule for determining the appropriate interest rate derivative to use based upon specific views on interest rates

	Interest rates will rise	*Interest rates will remain stable*	*Interest rates will fall*
Strongly agree	Take out swap	Use collar or other combination of derivatives	Leave or purchase out of money cap
No view	Buy swaption	Use collar or other combination of derivatives	Buy swaption or interest rate cap
Strongly disagree	Buy cap	Take out swap or buy cap	Take out swap or collar

Example of use of long-term cross-currency swap

A Hong Kong-based company, with no US$ income, has access to the US private placement market. It raises US$50 million by means of a five-year private placement. Summary details are shown in Table 10.11.

However, the company's requirement is for HK$ at floating rate. If it sells the US$50 million it has raised for HK$ spot, then it is exposed to movements in the US$/HK$ exchange rate. This exposure occurs for two reasons. First, it has to finance the US$ interest payments out of HK$ income, and second, it has to repay the US$ loan on maturity from HK$ resources. To hedge these exposures the company enters into a five-year cross-currency swap. In this transaction the corporate pays floating HK$ and receives US$ interest at the current five-year swap rate. The swap can be seen diagrammatically in Figures 10.6, 10.7 and 10.8.

It can be seen that the Hong Kong company has effectively converted the US$ loan into a HK$ loan. All the liabilities in respect of the borrowing – the liability to pay interest and the obligation to repay principal on maturity of the loan – are now in HK$.

Table 10.11 Summary details for US$/HK$ long-term currency swap

Bond details	
US$ principal	50 million
Term	5 years
Fixed interest rate	4 %
US$ 5-year interest rate swap	3.25 %
US$/HK$ spot rate	7.7985

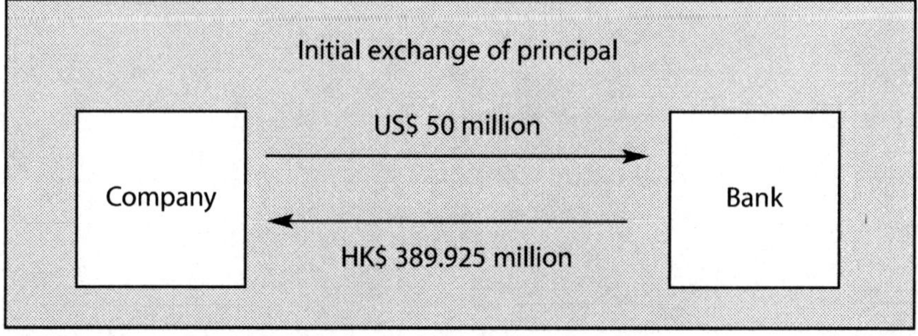

Figure 10.6 Step one in a cross-currency swap: exchange of principal

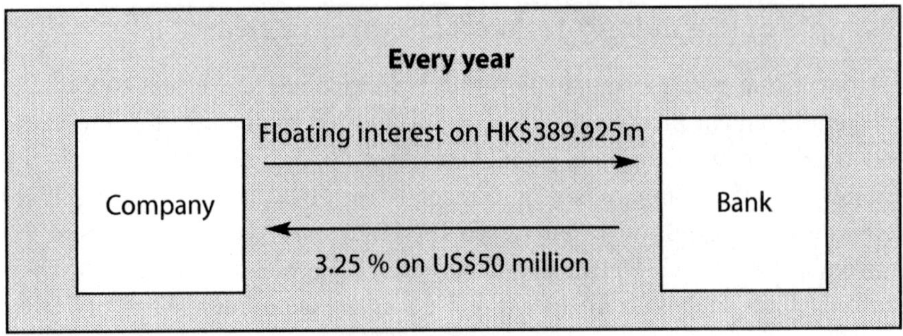

Figure 10.7 Step two in a cross-currency swap: exchange of interest throughout the life of the swap

Of course during the course of the cross-currency swap, the company will have to pay interest at 4 per cent on the US$ loan. This is partly financed by the receipt of US$ interest at 3.25 per cent under the interest leg of the swap. The remaining interest will need to be purchased forward at the time the swap is entered into.

Forms of cross-currency swaps

A cross-currency swap may be fixed–fixed, fixed–floating or floating–floating. A floating–floating swap is often called a basis swap. For this type of swap, a margin is typically put on one side of the deal in order to reflect market forces of supply and demand. For example, a bank may offer to receive euro LIBOR plus 0.03 per cent versus paying US$ LIBOR flat.

As a result of the margins embedded in basis swaps, the fixed rates used on a cross-currency swap may differ slightly from those used for a single-

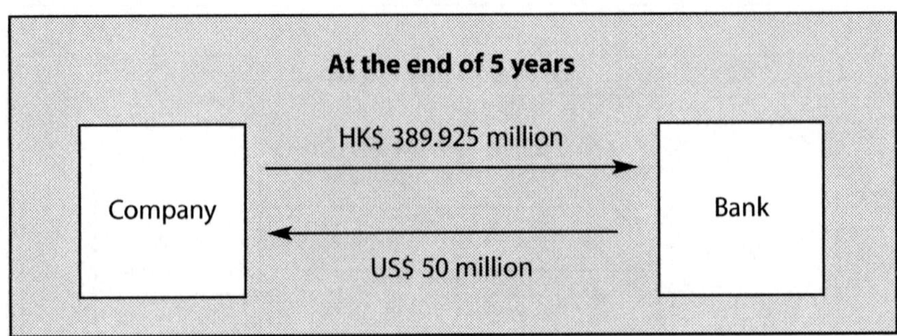

Figure 10.8 Step three in a cross-currency swap: re-exchange of principal at end of the swap

currency interest rate swap. To price a standard cross-currency fixed–floating or fixed–fixed swap, the fixed rates quoted in the market are adjusted by the basis swap margin. In the above case, if the euro five-year fixed rate was 3.75 per cent and a company wanted a cross-currency paying fixed euro versus receiving US$ LIBOR, then the fixed rate of 3.75 per cent together with the basis swap margin of 0.03 per cent is used. This gives a fixed euro rate under the cross-currency swap of 3.78 per cent.

EXERCISES

Interest rate swaps

Using the following US$ semi-annual swap rates:

Period	*Bank pays*	*Bank receives*
2 years	3.34	3.37
3 years	4.01	4.04
4 years	4.47	4.50
5 years	4.79	4.82
6 years	5.02	5.05

consider the following questions:

1. The treasurer of MultiMedia Inc. is concerned that US$ interest rates will start to rise. They have a US$250 million term loan on which they pay six-month LIBOR + 50bp, and which has a further four years to maturity.
   What will the swap structure look like, given the fact that a bank requires an additional 5bp credit risk return for this client?
   What is the company's cost of funds?

2. The treasurer of another company, a utility company, forecasts it will have core deposits of US$150 million for the next three years. They are concerned that interest rates will fall, and want to cover this risk for the next three years.
   What swap will the bank quote?
   What would be the fixed deposit rate the company would receive?

3. Five years ago a company raised US$300 million by means of a ten-year fixed rate bond.
   The semi-annual cost of this bond was 9 per cent and was swapped to floating whereby the company receives 9 per cent and pays LIBOR. What is the effective cost of funds for the remaining life of the bond if the company decides to re-swap into fixed payments at the current market rate?
   If the re-swap is effected with the original bank, which of the following statements is true:
   - Every six months the bank will expect to receive US$6,000,000 in advance.
   - Every six months the bank will expect to receive US$6,270,000 in arrears.
   - Every six months the bank will pay US$6,270,000 in arrears.
   - Every six months the bank will pay US$6,000,000 in advance.

Interest rate options

An alternative strategy for Multimedia might be to take out an interest rate cap. This way it has protection should rates rise, but can pick up the benefit of falling rates.

The market rates for four-year interest rate cap are:

Strike rate	*Premium*
4.75 %	2.75 %
5.00 %	2.40 %

How would you evaluate such an option strategy? The company's five-year borrowing cost is 5.25 per cent.

Application of interest rate derivatives

1. You are treasurer of a company that has a US$500 million floating rate loan. You want to protect your company against the effects of rising interest rates and wish to take out a cap. However you are concerned that inflation will stay consistently low over the next five years and want to design a structure whereby the option premium will be refunded if any of the option caplets are unexercised.
   How would you design such a structure?

2. Another thought you have is that you would like a structure whereby you could take out a five-year interest rate swap, but if the floating rate was below the swap rate on any roll-over date, you would be able to take the lower of the floating rates. You recognize that such a swap has option type characteristics, but you are not prepared to pay a full premium. You are however prepared to consider paying a higher fixed rate should LIBOR rates fall below a certain level. One of your thoughts is that, in return for such a five-year swap, if LIBOR fell below 3.90 per cent on any rollover date, you would be prepared to pay the current five-year swap rate of 4.82 per cent.

   How would you design such a structure?

Application of interest rate derivatives with bonds

Given the following information on interest rates and swaptions consider the questions below.

Swaptions

Exercise date	*Period (years)*	*Rate %*	*Receive fixed premium %*	*Pay fixed premium %*
1 year	9	5.5		2.0
1 year	9	5.0	2.2	3.5
1 year	9	4.5	0.93	
1 year	8	4.0	0.29	

Swap rates (semi-annual)

1 year	4.15 %	4.10 %
2 year	4.30 %	4.25 %
3 year	4.40 %	4.35 %
4 year	4.51 %	4.45 %
5 year	4.61 %	4.55 %
7 year	4.71 %	4.65 %
10 year	5.06 %	5.0 %

Note that three and six-month euro LIBOR is currently 3.75 per cent.

1. You are considering the issue of a bond for €100 million. Your objective is to keep the bond in fixed rate. However you are very concerned about forecasts for zero inflation, zero or negative real interest rates and stagnant economic growth. You therefore want the opportunity to be able to call the bond at the end of one year should long-term interest rates fall another 1 per cent.

   The bond will be a ten-year issue at 5.60 per cent all in. The swap curve for euros is attached. You determine that there is currently no investor appetite for a callable bond with the call date on the first anniversary of issue.

   How could you synthetically create a bond callable after one year? How expensive would your structure be?

2. You are considering the issue of a ten-year euro Eurobond. Your objective is to switch it into floating rates. On the evening before launch you are advised by the lead manager that the underlying government security is currently trading at 4.50 per cent, indicating a spread of 100 basis points over for your bond. What would you have to consider in calculating the floating rate cost of funds for the issue?

Long-term currency swap swaps

A French company issues a US$ five-year bond and decides to swap the interest exposure into floating euros. The rate in the currency swap market is 3.77–3.70 (annual 30/360). Spot €/US$ is .9734/.9738. Given that the US$ bond was issued at par in a nominal size of US$100 million with a yield of 4.4 per cent (annual 30/360), what is the effective euro cost of funds?

Fixed leg	*€ yield curve*	*US$ yield curve*	*Forward points*
1 year	1.53	2.75	0.0117/0.0127
2 year	2.10	2.94	0.0161/0.0184
3 year	2.64	3.22	0.0166/0.0201
4 year	3.05	3.48	.0.0163/0.0217
5 year	3.38	3.70	0.0152/0.0224

Discount any euro cashflows by the five-year euro swap rate.

SOLUTIONS

Interest rate swaps

1. MultiMedia

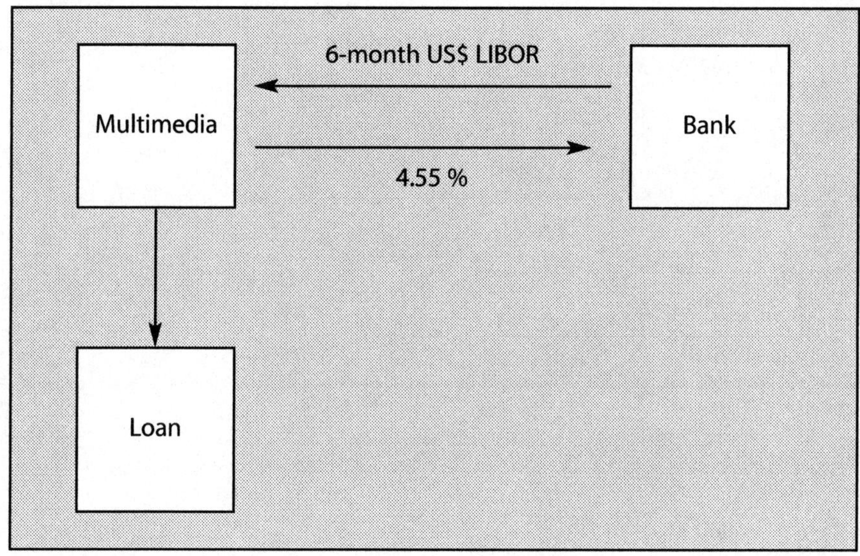

MultiMedia's net cost of funds for next four years:

IN	US$ LIBOR
OUT	(US$ LIBOR+50bp)
OUT	(4.55 per cent) (4.50 per cent + 5bp)
NET (cost of funds)	5.05 per cent

Interest rate swaps (contd.)

2. Utility Co.

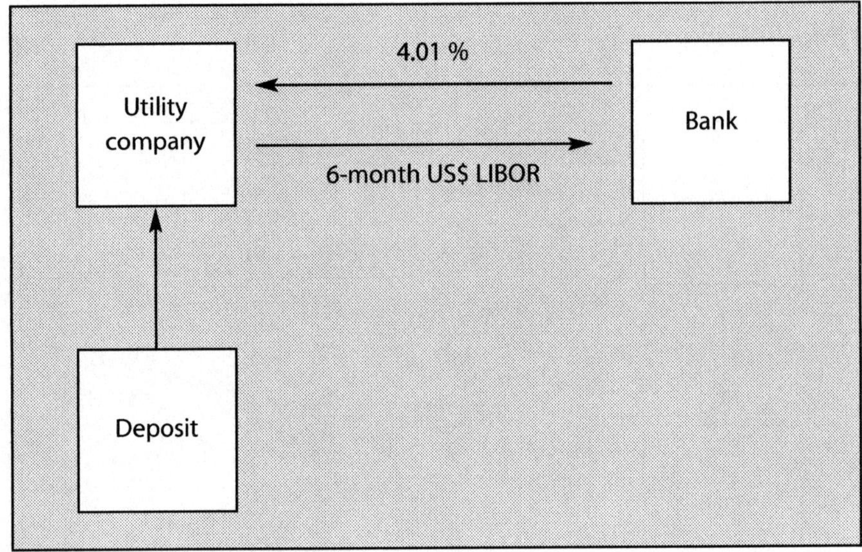

Utility company's deposit rate

IN	LIBID
IN	4.01 per cent
OUT	(US$ LIBOR)
NET	3.88 per cent s.a. (LIBID is generally 1/8 per cent lower than LIBOR)

Interest rate swaps (contd.)

3. A company

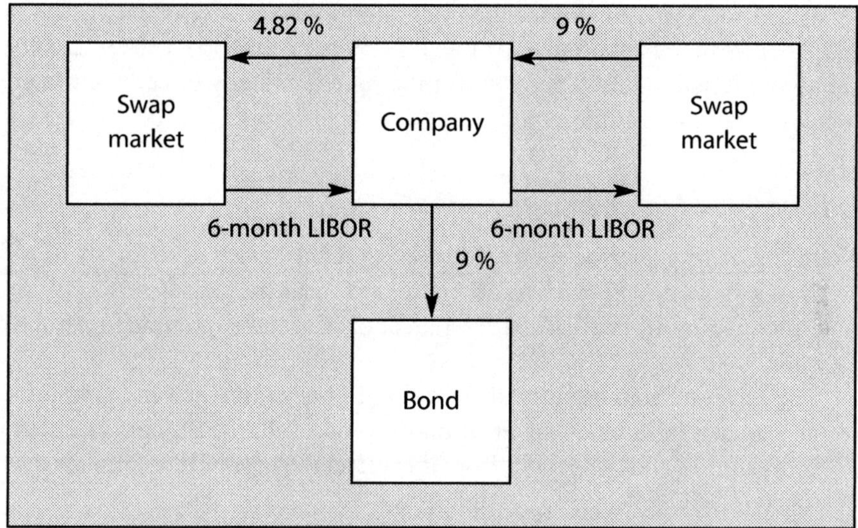

IN	9 per cent	*Initial swap*
OUT	(six-months US$ LIBOR)	
OUT	9 per cent	*Bond*
IN	six-months US$ LIBOR	*New swap*
OUT	4.82 per cent	
NET	4.82 per cent s.a. for 5 years	

Every six months the company will receive six-monthly in arrears:

$$\frac{300{,}000{,}000 * (9 \text{ per cent} - 4.82 \text{ per cent})}{2} = \text{US\$}6{,}270{,}000$$

Interest rate options

MultiMedia

For MultiMedia's option strategy to work interest rates have to fall to a level such that the lower borrowing costs enjoyed by the company on its debt offset the premium payable.

Taking the interest cap with a 4.75 per cent strike:

The upfront premium is US$6,875,000

The annual amount payable over the next four years, which at 5.25 per cent has a net present value of US$6,875,000, is US$1,950,103.

Therefore interest costs on the loan have to fall to US$11,250,000 – 1,950,103 = US$9,229,897 for the premium to be recouped.

This corresponds to an interest rate of 3.69 per cent. US$ LIBOR has to fall to and remain at 3.69 per cent for the option strategy to be better than taking out an interest rate swap.

Application of interest rate derivatives

1. In this particular case the basic building blocks are:
   Buy a standard cap with a strike rate at or near the money.
   Buy a digital floor with a strike rate at or near the strike rate under the cap.
   The payouts from the digital floor should be set to equal the premium under each individual caplet. If interest rates fall, the digital floor will be exercised and the payout from this offset the cost of premium for the unexercised caplets.
   However two premia are paid under this structure. Would the company be better off with, say, an out-of-the-money cap?

2. The building blocks here are:
   Purchase a standard cap with a strike rate close to the money.
   Sell a digital floor with a strike rate of 3.90 per and paying out 92 basis poiints when LIBOR falls below the strike rate.

Application of interest rate derivatives with bonds

1. If the company had issued a callable bond and had actually called the bond, then it would have had to re-finance it. This would have been done at floating rates. Therefore the company needs to purchase a derivative that would put it in the same position. This can be achieved by buying a swaption, giving the swaption buyer the right to receive fixed. Much depends on what the rate is under the swaption, but let us assume it is 5.0 per cent. Should the company decide to exercise the swaption its position will be the one shown at the top of the next page:

   It will be left with the bond effectively at floating rates, where it will be paying euro LIBOR + 60bp. However, the option premium of 2.2 per cent (€2.2 million) needs to be amortized over the life of the transaction. This equates to 29bp per annum.

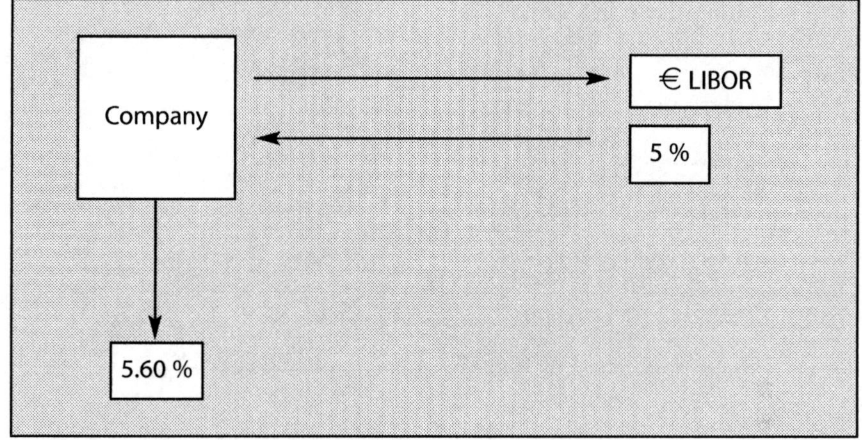

2 Calculating all-in cost of funds with a bond issue.

There are a number of steps here:

- Calculate the all-in cost of the issue. This primarily involves amortizing the lead managers' upfront fees and including them with the overall cost of funding. Lead managers' fees are usually 40bps for a Eurobond issue, which equates to 4 basis points a year (slightly more when the time cost of money is taken into account).

- The company will receive fixed under the swap, and the relevant semi-annual rate is 5.00 per cent. However the Eurobond market is an annual coupon. Therefore any swap will need an annual exchange of interest to match the coupon payments, and the semi-annual coupon will need to be adjusted for that. The calculation is:

  $$\left(1 + \frac{.05}{2}\right)^2 - 1 + 5.06$$

- Interest first starts to accrue on the bond two to three weeks after launch. Therefore the interest rate swap that will be taken out on the day of the launch will need to be forward starting to the first interest accrual date. Given the interest rate curve outlined, a three-week forward starting swap would give a fixed leg under the swap of 5.13 per cent (annual 30E/360))

- Putting these in a table:

	Yield
Underlying government security	4.50
Spread	1.00
Lead manager's fees	0.04
All-in fixed costs	5.54
Fixed rate under swap	5.13
Floating rate cost of funds	€ LIBOR + 41 bp

The above excludes rating agency fees, legal and printing costs.

- It should be noted that under a bond, if interest is due to be paid on a date that is a Saturday or Sunday, interest is delayed until the next business day but the interest amount is generally not adjusted. This is not the case in the swap market where the interest amounts are adjusted for the additional days.

Currency swaps

The bond and swap can be portrayed diagrammatically as below:

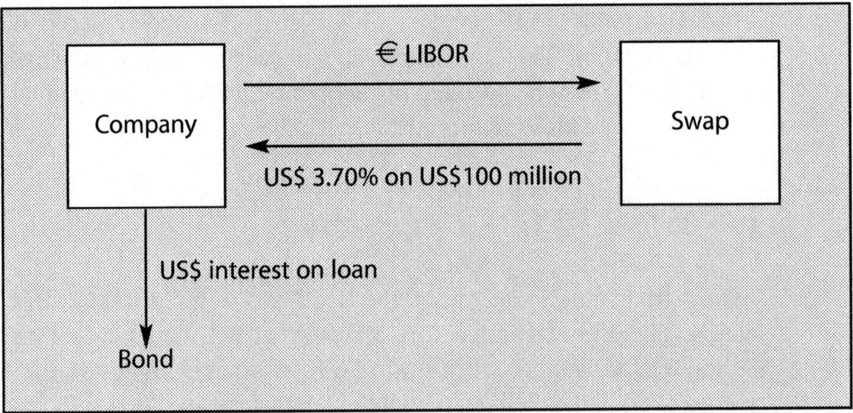

The issuer must pay an annuity of 70bp on US$100 million over the next five years. This does not translate into euro LIBOR + 70bp funding due to the FX risk on the US$ income stream. To calculate the true euro cost of funds, the US$ annuity must be translated into euros by buying the US$ forward, and the resulting euro cashflow must then be calculated as a euro annuity in terms of basis points.

0.7 per cent × US$ 100,000,000 = US$700,000

Time	*US$*	*Forward FX*	*€*	*PV (€)*
1	700,000	.9851	710,590	685,237
2	700,000	.9895	707,440	657,858
3	700,000	.9900	707,074	634,058
4	700,000	.9897	707,250	611,587
5	700,000	.9886	708,102	590,475
				3,179,214

Solving for an annuity that yields a present value of €3,179,214 at a discount rate of 4.4% over 5 years gives €722,182. On a principal of 1,026,905 million this translates to an annuity of 70.3 basis points.

The effective cost of funds to the issuer is therefore LIBOR + 70 bp.

CHAPTER 11

Zero-Coupon Interest Rates, Forward–Forward Rates, Counterparty Exposure for Derivatives and Contracts for Derivatives

ZERO-COUPON RATES AND FORWARD–FORWARD RATES

Introduction

In the chapter on bond valuation, the yield to maturity (YTM) method was explained. The yield was that single rate which discounted all future cash-flows arising on a bond back to the current market value (net present value). The advantage of YTM is its simplicity. Its disadvantage is that it assumes all coupons are re-invested at the single rate. The zero-coupon curve attempts to overcome this disadvantage.

Calculating zero-coupon rates

Using money market rates

Assume that that the US$ money market rate for borrowing for one year is 3 per cent.

Borrowing US$1.00 for one year at 3 per cent would involve only two cashflows. The first an inflow today of US$1.00 and secondly an outflow in one year of US$1 + (1 × 0.03) = US$1.03

The present value (PV) factor for year one is:

$$PVf_1 = \frac{1}{(1 + 0.03)} = 0.9709$$

If we multiply the cashflow at the end of year one by the PV factor it will bring us back to the first cashflow:

US$1.03 × 0.9709 = US$1.00

Using swap rates

It is important to remember that money market rates are zero-coupon interest rates. This simply means that with a borrowing for one year, all principal and interest is paid at the end of the period. Beyond one year however, interest rates quoted in the market are not zero-coupon rates, but are 'par-coupon' rates. For example, if bank quoted 3.25 per cent for lending US$ for two years, it will usually want an interest payment at the end of the first year of 3.25 per cent and another interest payment at the end of two years of 3.25 per cent plus the principal. Interest is thus paid twice over the life of the borrowing, once at the end of year one and once at the end of the second year.

In calculating zero-coupon rates beyond one year the market actually uses swap rates. Table 11.1 shows some hypothetical US$ swap rates going out to three years.

Table 11.1 US$ swap rates

Maturity years	*US$ swap rates*
0	
1	3.00 %
2	3.25 %
3	3.35 %

From the standpoint of the borrower the cashflows for borrowing 100.00 for one year is shown in Table 11.2.

Table 11.2 Cashflow for a one-year borrowing

	Year	*Amount*
Inflow	0	+ 100.00
Outflow	1	- 103.00

Calculating present value factors

The present value factor for year one is:

$$PVf = \frac{PV}{FV} = PVf_1 = \frac{1}{(1 + 0.03)} = 0.9709$$

Table 11.3 Cashflow for a two-year borrowing

	Year	*Amount*
Inflow	0	+ 100.00
Outflow	1	- 3.25
Outflow	2	- 103.25

Since the one-year discount factor has been calculated from the one-year cash rate (3 per cent), the discount factor for the second year can be found. The discount factor must be the rate that, together with the discount factor for year one (0.9709) will discount the flows for the two years to 100.

In other words $-r.df_1 - (100 + r)df_2 = -100$

Re-arranging this:

$$df_2 = \frac{100 - r.df_1}{100 + r}$$

$$df_2 = \frac{100 - 3.25 \times 0.9709}{100 + 3.25}$$

$$= 0.9380$$

Table 11.4 Net present value of cash outflow for a two-year borrowing

	Year	*Amount*	*Discount factor*	*Net present value*
Inflow	0	+ 100.00		
Outflow	1	– 3.25	0.9709	3.1554
Outflow	2	– 103.25	0.9380	96.8485
				100.00

Having solved the discount factor for year two, one can now solve the discount factor for year three, as in Table 11.5.

Table 11.5 Cash outflow for a three-year borrowing

	Year	*Amount*
Inflow	0	+ 100.00
Outflow	1	– 3.35
Outflow	2	– 3.35
Outflow	3	– 103.35

$$-\ r.df_1 - r.df_2 - (100 + r)df_3 = -\ 100$$

Which can be re-arranged again to create the following formula:

$$df_3 = \frac{100 - r.df - r.df_2}{100 + r}$$

$$df_3 = \frac{100 - 3.35 \times 0.9709 - 3.35 \times .9380}{100 + 3.35}$$

$$= .9057$$

Table 11.6 Net present value of cash outflows for three-year borrowing

	Year	*Amount*	*Discount factor*	*Net present value*
Inflow	0	+ 100.00		
Outflow	1	– 3.35	0.9709	3.2525
Outflow	2	– 3.35	0.9380	3.1423
Outflow	3	103.35	0.9057	93.6041
				100.00

This process of deriving the discount factor for a particular year from the discount factors for previous years is known as 'bootstrapping'.

This formula says:

$$PVf_n = \frac{1 - (PMT \times \sum_{t=1}^{n-1} PVf_t)}{1 + PMT}$$

- Calculate the sum of all previous present value factors.
- Multiply by the swap fixed rate.
- Subtract the results from 1.
- Divide by 1 + the swap fixed rate.

$$PV_3 = \frac{1 - (.0335(.9709 + .9380))}{1.0335}$$

$$= .9057$$

Calculating zero-coupon rates from PV factors

The respective zero-coupon rates can be obtained from the following equation:

$$r_{zero.n} = \left(\frac{1}{PVf_n}\right)^{\frac{1}{n}} - 1$$

Using the discount rates calculated above:

$$r_{zero.1} = \left(\frac{1}{0.9709}\right)^{\frac{1}{n}} - 1 = 3.0\ \%$$

As stated earlier, the zero-coupon rate for year one is the same as the par coupon rate:

$$r_{zero.2} = \left(\frac{1}{0.9380}\right)^{\frac{1}{2}} - 1 = 3.252\ \%$$

$$r_{zero.3} = \left(\frac{1}{0.9057}\right)^{\frac{1}{3}} - 1 = 3.3567\ \%$$

Understanding zero-coupon rates

Rational borrowers should not care whether or not they borrow at 3.25 per cent for two years or borrow at the zero-coupon rate compounded up $(1.03252)^2 - 1 = 1.0661$ per cent. Under either scenario their return is:

Years	*Normal coupon borrowing*	*Zero-coupon borrowing*
0	US$ 100	US$ 100
1	(US$ 3.25) × 0.9709	US$ 0
2	(US$ 103.25 × 0.9380	(US$ 106.61) × 0.9380
	NPV = 0	NPV = 0

If the cashflows of an instrument are known, its price in the current market environment can be calculated by using present value factors.

Forward yield curves

Calculating future interest rates from current market rates

In addition to information about rates for periods beginning today, yield curves provide information about rates for periods in the future. Forward interest rates are used to take views about where the yield curve might be at a forward date. This view can be used to price derivatives products, to evaluate re-financing decisions, and to lock in investment rates or borrowing costs that will only occur in the future.

Consider the case of a corporate that needs to borrow US$10 million in three months time for three months and that wants to lock in the borrowing cost now. The bank that will supply that transaction could do the following:

- borrow money for six months from today
- use the proceeds from the borrowing to deposit for three months
- at the end of three months use the proceeds of the maturing deposit to lend to the corporate for three months
- at the end of the six-month borrowing period, the maturing loan to the corporate will be used to repay the original borrowing.

This can be represented as in Figure 11.1.

Two questions arise out of this. First, how much will the bank need to borrow and lend? Second, at what rate should the bank lend to break even?

If the bank is giving the customer US$10 million on the three-month date, it requires an inflow of US$10 million on that date. The inflow is going to come from repayment of principal and interest on the maturing loan. The amount that the bank will deposit must therefore be the present value of the US$10 million inflow in three months time. This is also the amount the bank will borrow for six months.

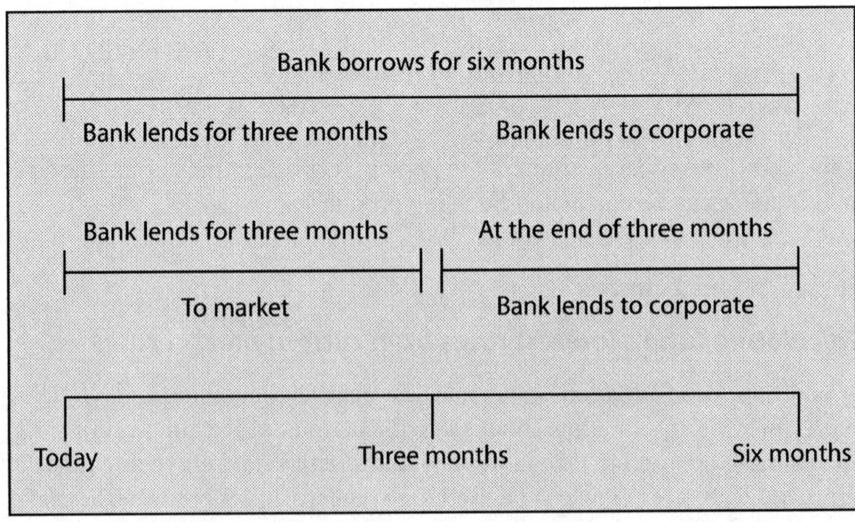

Figure 11.1 Creating a future loan from a simultaneous borrowing and deposit

Assume that the three and six month money market rates are:

3-month: 3.50–3.625 per cent.

6-month: 4.00–4.125 per cent.

The bank would therefore be borrowing for six months at 4.125 per cent, and depositing for three months at 3.50 per cent. To calculate the amount of money acting as the principal today, we must discount US$10 million at 3.5 per cent for (say) 90 days.

Formula for future interest rates

$$PV = \frac{FV.}{1 + (r \times {}^{d}/_{b})}$$

Where PV = the present value, FV = the future value, r = the discount rate, d = the number of days in the discounting period, and b = the day base for the currency.

$$PV = \frac{10{,}000{,}000}{1 + (0.035 \times 90/360)} = \text{US\$}9{,}913{,}259$$

If the bank borrows US$9,913,259 for six months at 4.125 per cent then it will have to repay:

$$\text{US\$}9{,}913{,}259 \times (1 + (0.04125 \times 180/360)) = \text{US\$}10{,}117{,}720$$

in principal and interest at the end of that six months. If the bank is lending US$10 million in three moths and repaying US$10,117,720 in six months, then it needs to generate US$117,720 from the loan to the corporate client. This can be turned into an annual rate by dividing the interest by the principal and re-annualizing:

$$\frac{117{,}720}{10{,}000{,}000} \times \frac{360}{90} = 4.71 \text{ per cent}$$

Essentially the calculation involved is one of compounding interest. Money invested for three months and then re-invested for a further three months will end up with the same amount as if it had been invested for six months. The equation can be re-arranged as follows:

$(1 + r_1 \,.\, d_1/b)\ (1 + r_F/b) = (1 + r_2 \,.\, d_2/b)$

Where r_1 = interest rate for the short period, r_2 = interest rate for the long period, r_F = interest rate for the forward period, d_n = number of days in the interest period, and b = day base for the currency.

$$\left[\frac{1+\left(r_2 \times \frac{d_2}{b}\right)}{1+\left(r_1 \times \frac{d_1}{b}\right)} - 1\right] \times \frac{b}{d_2 - d_1}$$

$$\left[\frac{1+\left(.04125 \times \frac{180}{360}\right)}{1+\left(.035 \times \frac{90}{360}\right)} - 1\right] \times \frac{360}{180-90}$$

= 4.71 per cent.

Forward rates beyond one year

Above, the short-term forward–forward rates were calculated from a series of money market interest rates. Exactly the same approach can be used for constructing long-term forward–forward yields from long-term zero-coupon yields. Using the same swap rates used for calculating zero-coupon rates used in the previous example, gives the result shown in Table 11.7.

An amount worth 1.03 after one year is worth $(1.0325)^2$ after two years.

Table 11.7 Three-year US$ swap rates and derived zero rates

Maturity years	*US$ swap rates*	*Zero rates*
0		
1	3.00 %	3.000 %
2	3.25 %	3.252 %
3	3.35 %	3.3567 %

The yield linking these two amounts over that one-year forward–forward period is:

$$\frac{(1.03252)^2}{1.03} = 3.505 \text{ per cent}$$

This represents the one-year versus two-year forward rate. Similarly, using the three-year zero-coupon rate of 3.3567 per cent gives the two-year versus three-year forward rate of:

$$\frac{(1.033567)^3}{(1.03252)^2} = 3.5662 \text{ per cent}$$

Significance of zero-coupon curve

Three yield curves have been discussed: that created from the yield to maturity (the par curve), that created from zero-coupon rates (the zero-coupon curve), and the forward rate curve.

Yield to maturity is used to value government securities and bonds. There is just one rate used to discount all future coupon and principal flows back to the net present value. It assumes that all coupons can be re-invested at the underlying yield.

The zero-coupon curve calculates discount factors to be applied to cash-flows on a loan from a series of rates or yields. The zero-coupon curve can only be established by a process of bootstrapping, each discount factor being calculated from the previous discount factor. The zero-coupon curve and associated discount factors are used to value derivative instruments such as interest rate swaps.

Forward rates show where the market anticipates interest rates will be in the future. Any set of forward rates can be calculated either for short periods of up to one year when money market rates are used, or for periods extending beyond one year when zero coupon rates are used.

When the yield curve is upward sloping, the zero-coupon curve will rise more steeply than the par curve, and the forward rate curve will rise more steeply than the zero-coupon curve. This can be seen by examining Table 11.8 on page 248.

In practice, while the treasurer needs to be familiar with all three curves, their actual calculation is performed by either modules on a treasury management system, or by stand-alone derivative and bond valuation models.

VALUING INTEREST RATE SWAPS

While most treasurers have access to derivative valuation models, a practical knowledge of how interest rate swaps and associated derivatives are valued is important. The following example takes the PV values, zero rates and forward rates calculated earlier in this chapter. The data for a three-year swap is shown in Table 11.8.

Table 11.8 Assumed swap rates, PV factors, zero rates and forward–forward rates

Years	*Swap rates*	*PVf*	*Zero rates*	*Forward rates 1 year maturity*
0		1		
1	3.00 %	0.9709	3.000 %	3.000 %
2	3.25 %	0.9380	3.252 %	3.505 %
3	3.35 %	0.9057	3.3567 %	3.566 %

The present value of the fixed flows for the three-year swap can be calculated by multiplying each fixed flow by the relevant PV factor taken from the above table. The same can be done for the floating flows (Table 11.9).

Table 11.9 Present value of fixed and floating legs under a swap

Fixed leg	*Floating leg*	*PV fixed leg*	*PV floating leg*
3.35 %	3.00 %	3.252 %	2.9127 %
3.35 %	3.50 %	3.1423 %	3.2830 %
3.35 %	3.57 %	3.0341 %	3.2333 %
		9.429 %	9.429 %

This swap has a value of zero because the present value of the fixed cashflows is exactly the same as the present value of the floating leg cashflows. This would always be expected at the start of a swap.

Assume that the three-year swap rate changes by one basis point from 3.35 per cent to 3.36 per cent. This will in turn change the PV factor and forward rate for three years (Table 11.10).

Table 11.10 Changing three-year fixed leg under the interest rate swap by one basis point

Years	*Swap rates*	*PVf*	*Zero rates*	*Forward rates 1 year maturity*
0		1		
1	3.00 %	0.9709	3.00 %	3.00 %
2	3.25 %	0.9380	3.252 %	3.505 %
3	3.36 %	0.9054	3.368 %	3.600 %

The three-year swap when marked to market no longer has a value of zero. If this was a swap for US$10 million, the swap would have lost US$2770.

Table 11.11 Present value of original swap after changing market rates by one basis point

Years	*Fixed leg*	*Floating leg*	*PV fixed leg*	*PV floating leg*
0	3.35 %	3.0 %	3.252 %	2.9127 %
1	3.25 %	3.505 %	3.1423 %	3.283 %
2	3.35 %	3.600 %	3.0331 %	3.2594 %
3			9.4274 %	9.4551 %
		Present value of basis point (PVBP)	– 0.002777 %	

The swap has lost money since the net present value of the fixed flows that are being received are worth less than the present value of the floating flows that are being paid.

In reality the swap rate could change by much larger amounts than one basis point. In addition the one and two-year swap rates could change.

COUNTERPARTY EXPOSURE

One of the significances of marking a derivative to market is to identify the level of counterparty exposure. In the above example, the present value of US$10 million swap is now US$2770. That is, the fixed rate payer to the swap would have an exposure of US$2770 to the counterparty. That is, should the counterparty to the swap no longer be able to meet its commitments under the swap, the corporate would lose the net present value of US$2770, since no other bank would enter into a swap where it was receiving less than the market rate for the fixed leg.

Exposure limits

To control counterparty exposure arising from derivatives, exposure limits need to be established for counterparties in much the same way they are established for deposits (see page 330). Exposure limits will be based on:

- The credit quality of the counterparty.
- The maturity period of the derivative. (In the case of interest rate derivatives, the longer the maturity period of the contract, the greater are the movements in present value for a given movement in interest rates.)

A way needs to be found for establishing limits on the level of derivative contracts that can be taken out with any one counterparty. Generally this limit will be based on the nominal value of outstanding contracts. Some corporates may look at the historic volatility of financial prices and from that calculate the potential movement in present value for particular derivatives. Other corporates may use a more basic calculation, which might broadly be as follows: the maximum movement in interest rates over a ten-year period may be 3 per cent. At current interest rates the impact of a 3 per cent movement in interest rates on a US$10 million interest rate swap is US$2.2 million. The maximum exposure we wish to have to a AA counterparty is US$50 million. Therefore the maximum in ten-year interest rate swaps, or equivalent in other interest rate derivatives, that we will have outstanding with any one AA counterparty is US$225 million (50/2.2 × 10).

Whatever method is selected, there needs to be some means of establishing the maximum exposure to any one counterparty. In addition, the longer the derivative contract, the higher the necessary credit quality of the counterparty.

Treasury policies

Treasury policies may be framed somewhat as follows. The maximum exposure under all derivative contracts is:

AAA/Aaa counterparties: US$ 4 billion.

AA/Aa counterparties: US$ 2 billion.

A counterparties: US$ 1 billion.

No derivates may be taken out with counterparties for whom there is no specific approved exposure limit.

Exposure is measured by the nominal value of contracts outstanding with the counterparty. In establishing the nominal value outstanding on interest rate swaps, the swap will be the total nominal value of each six-month interest rate fixing. For instance the nominal value of a five-year swap for US$10 million would be calculated as US$100 million. In calculating the exposure, offsetting contracts must be netted.

No derivative contract extending beyond five years may be taken out with an A rated counterparty, or beyond ten years with a AA/Aa rated counterparty.

The mark to market value of all derivative contracts must be calculated monthly and included in the treasury report. Mark to market value should not exceed:

AAA/Aaa: US$ 25 million.

AA: US$ 15 million.

A: US$ 10 million.

The regular treasury report may be as shown in Table 11.12.

Table 11.12 Possible format detailing counterparty exposures

Counter party	*Exposure limit*	*Nominal value of interest rate swaps outstanding*	*Nominal value of foreign exchange contracts outstanding*	*Total outstanding*	*Mark to market value **
	US$ Bn	*US$ Bn*	*US$ Bn*	*US$ Bn*	*US$ Mn*
Bank A	2.0	0.55	0.5	1.05	3.3
Bank B	2.0	0.3	0.3	0.6	(2.5)
Bank C	1.0	0.25	0.2	0.45	1.0

* Positive amounts are due to, negative amounts due from the company to the bank.

CONTRACTUAL TERMS FOR DERIVATIVE CONTRACTS

Background

The contractual terms governing over-the-counter (OTC) derivatives between a corporate and a bank are legally managed through documentation established by the International Swaps and Derivatives Association (ISDA). This documentation is intended to cover virtually all types of derivative trades that might possibly be contracted between the two parties, for instance: interest rate swaps, basis swaps, forward starting interest rate swaps, forward rates, commodity swaps, foreign exchange, caps, floors, collars, swaptions, currency swaps, cross-currency swaps, currency options and combinations of the above.

ISDA was established in 1985, and has tried to fulfil the need for standardization within derivative contracts. The first ISDA Master Agreement was published in 1987, and was followed by Addenda in 1989 and 1990 to cover interest and currency derivatives. The last major change to the Master Agreement was made in 1992, together with further changes in 2002. Some adjustments have led to the 2000 ISDA Definitions, which are intended for use in confirmations of individual transactions governed by the 1992 ISDA Master Agreement.

The ISDA documentation is perhaps among the most complex legal agreements that a treasurer has to be familiar with and negotiate. Its complexity is due partly to the fact that there are three separate documents involved, with each document referring to the other. They have been described as a 'mosaic' of documents.

ISDA Master Agreement

Central to the ISDA documentation is the ISDA Master Agreement. As its name suggests, it is a 'master' agreement and once signed it governs all past and future individual transactions between the parties.

The Agreement is split into two sections. The first section is a printed form, which basically is a set of standard definitions and terms ('Standard Terms'). This section is composed of five parts. They cover such points as interpretation, conditions precedent, netting, withholding tax, representation, events of default, termination events, early termination and governing law.

The Master Agreement is an open-ended agreement with no fixed term. If the parties want to end their relationship, they can either formally terminate the Master Agreement or simply not enter into any deals with each other in the future.

Schedule to the Master Agreement

The other section is the schedule to the Master Agreement. This tailors the terms defined in the Standard Terms to the relationship between the two parties. For instance, while the Standard Terms define how cross default occurs, the schedule to the Master Agreement agrees that cross default will apply to the contract and establishes a threshold level for it. It is this section that will prove to be most contentious and over which any negotiation will occur.

The treasurer is likely to be most concerned with three sections: termination provisions, payment provisions, and other provisions.

Termination provisions

These set out how existing derivative contracts between the parties may be terminated. There are three terms:

- *Default.* This gives the non-defaulting party the right to designate an early termination date. Cross-default automatically leads to an event of default.
- *Additional termination events* are often added to the schedule; this is particularly the case for weaker credits.
- *Threshold amount.* Defaults must exceed the threshold amount. Sometimes this is defined in absolute terms (e.g. US$20 million), or as a percentage – say 1 per cent – of net worth. (It should be noted that with some very large banks this may represent a very large absolute amount.)

Many banks are increasingly looking to have collateral posted, usually if the mark to market of the outstanding derivative transactions between the two parties exceeds a certain level.

Payment provisions

The section Payment on Early Termination establishes how payments due between the parties on early termination are to be calculated. Most market participants choose those described below.

Market quotation

This specifies that at least three arm's-length quotations are to be used for the calculation of the value of outstanding derivatives. This is compared to loss, where the non-defaulting party determines in good faith the losses and costs (minus its gains) in potentially replacing the derivative transactions.

Second method

The net close-out amount is always paid to the party to which it is due, regardless of whether it is the defaulting or non-defaulting party. (The first method is a method to withhold payments due under ISDA and set those off with other defaulted payments.)

Other provisions

Banks are increasingly concerned about deterioration in the credit standing of their counterparties (and arguably corporates should be so as well). Within the schedule to the Master Agreement there are a number of ways of handling this.

Material adverse change

This is usually applied where one of the parties is non-rated. It allows the bank to claim an early termination event if there has been a material adverse change in the counterparty.

Financial ratios

An early termination event can be claimed if certain pre-established ratios are breached.

Rating triggers

A fall in published ratings below a certain level can trigger an early termination event.

Collateralization

There can be two circumstances where the parties agree that collateral should be posted. The first is where breaches of financial ratios or rating triggers, instead of causing an early termination event, require the defaulting party to place collateral with the other non-defaulting party. This collateral is usually in the form of cash. The second is where the mark to market value of the transactions between the parties exceeds a certain value. In this case the party whose transactions are in deficit has to place collateral with the other party, who has an exposure. Obviously the collateral is adjusted as the mark to market value of the transactions changes.

2002 ISDA

The above describes the principal elements of the 1992 ISDA. The major changes implemented by the 2002 ISDA are outlined below.

Close-out amount

Market quotation and loss have been replaced by a single standard close-out amount. The new approach to closing out transactions is based on a standard of commercial reasonableness; it describes the type of information that can be used in valuing transactions and sets forth the procedures that can be followed in valuing those terminated transactions.

Other provisions

These include: *force majeure* type events, a reduction of grace periods, and the inclusion of set-off provisions.

Confirmation

Derivative contracts are usually dealt by both parties by telephone. The oral terms are then documented in a confirmation. The confirmation is usually produced by the bank, signed by the bank's signatories and then faxed or posted to the corporate. It is market practice for the company receiving the confirmation to check, sign and return it within 48 hours. All the terms agreed between the parties should be set out in it. In the case of an interest rate swap, for instance, the fixed rate payer, the fixed rate, the frequency of payment, the notional amount, the currency, the day convention, the floating rate payer, the floating rate basis (six-month LIBOR etc.), the notional amount, the currency, day convention and so on should all be set out in the confirmation.

Should the confirmation conflict with the schedule then the confirmation terms prevail.

SUMMARY

It is worth noting that it is usual for the bank to produce the schedule to the Master Agreement. In doing this, they will set out terms that have been established by their in-house legal department and are usually going to be very favourable to them. The treasurer should note that the schedule is a negotiable document, and needs to be aware of the terms that he or she is prepared to accept in these contractual agreements.

The ISDA documents are often so complex and time consuming that many treasurers adopt one of two approaches. The first is to refer all ISDA documents to their lawyers. A lower-cost option is to determine with their lawyers what terms they are prepared to accept on the ISDA schedule and stick rigidly to those terms. Either way, ISDA documentation needs some input from the company's lawyers.

ISDA documentation should be in place with potential counterparties before derivative contracts are entered into.

CHAPTER 12

Risk Management Summary and Use of Derivatives

SUMMARY

The different steps involved in managing financial risk should now be quite clear. They are as follows:

- Identify the treasury-related financial risks operating within the business. This exercise may be part of a much wider company or group-wide risk management exercise, or it may be a one-off exercise undertaken by the treasury department. In many cases, for instance in most large to medium-sized companies, the financial risks to which the company is exposed will be well known to the treasury department. In other situations, for instance in many multinational companies with complex intercompany and external flows, or where a company has not explicitly measured all its financial risks before, a separate exercise may be necessary to map and identify the quantum of financial risk.
- Measure the magnitude of these treasury-related financial risks. Before any action can be taken to manage financial risks, the size and timing of these risks must be identified. In addition, only those risks that are significant in the overall scope of the business need to be managed. Generally the treasury department's risk management will be set within the overall scope of the company-wide risk management programme.
- Establish the company's treasury risk policies. These determine how financial risks are to be managed by treasury, who have the responsibility

for their management and how they will be managed. Treasury policies should be ratified by the main board and periodically reviewed and re-ratified.

- Manage the risks in accordance with the company's risk management policies. This may involve the use of derivatives, but in many cases – for instance managing financing risks – other risk management procedures are relevant.
- Report regularly on the status of risk management. This report may be to a formal committee such as a risk management committee, or it may be a more informal report to the chief financial officer or finance director.
- Consider the use of performance measures to determine how effectively the risk management process is being operated.

SPECIFIC CONSIDERATIONS

While the section above sets out the general steps, there are a number of specific aspects to risk management that a treasury department will need to consider. These have been alluded to in previous chapters.

Understand the financial markets to which the company is exposed

The foreign exchange, interest rate and financing markets have been described. However, a company may be exposed to other financial markets, for example the commodity and equity markets. It is important that the treasurer fully understands how these markets operate, how assets are priced in that market, what kinds of derivatives are available to manage risk, and how these derivatives operate.

Surrogate derivatives

Do the derivatives that are available in a market exactly match the underlying exposure or is there a mismatch? A company may have an exposure to a particular kind of fuel: do the derivatives exactly correspond to that fuel or to some other fuel class? This mismatch is known as basis risk, the extent to which movements in the market value of the underlying risk may not be exactly offset by movements in the market value of the derivative.

Sometimes the company will accept this basis risk, since a perfect hedge using a derivative cannot be found. If so, it will need to understand the scale of the risk being run and have some plan of how to manage the basis risk.

In other cases a company may have an indirect exposure to financial risk. The purchaser of aluminium cans may consider that the price of aluminium is a significant part of its raw material cost. It may be able to require its supplier to hedge the cost of aluminium, or it may enter into long-term fixed-price contracts, or it may take out an underlying hedge itself. Each route has advantages and disadvantages.

A portfolio of risks, or offsetting risks

Most companies are aware of and are comfortable with the concept of portfolio theory. (Once a portfolio of equities exceeds approximately eight to ten equities, the returns from that portfolio will start to move broadly in line with the market as a whole. In other words, many stock-specific risks balance each other out.) However, do the financial risks being run by a company also operate like a portfolio? That is, do the financial risks to which the company is exposed broadly balance each other out?

In some cases a company may have exposures that historically have always offset. For example an Australian company may have receivables in US$ and payables in HK$, and history may show that the HK$ is linked to US$. Is the company prepared to accept this relationship, and net off the offsetting flows, or does it wish to hedge both exposures separately? Some companies believe that using past correlations is dangerous since these can often break down. Other companies believe that hedges using derivatives, once put in place, can in themselves introduce an element of rigidity and risk. (For instance a hedge could be put in place against a pre-transaction US$ receivable and HK$ payable, only for these risks to subsequently change in their scale, leaving the company with derivative hedges that are no longer required.)

Natural hedges

A further extension to the above is a consideration of the extent to which the company may have natural hedges that offset the financial risk being examined. One of the problems for many companies is that although natural hedges do exist, their relationship to the underlying financial risk cannot be quantified.

What is being hedged?

Is group income and cashflow being hedged, or is subsidiary or operating division income and cashflow being hedged? The answer to this may well determine whether a portfolio approach to risk management is appropriate or whether individual risks should be managed on their own. Much depends on how a company is managed. A decentralized company where each subsidiary is given cashflow and operating profit targets may find it difficult to implement a hedging programme where offsetting risks are netted.

A related question is: 'Should intercompany flows be hedged?' A US company has subsidiaries in Singapore and in Hong Kong. Should the Singapore subsidiary be permitted to hedge sales to the Hong Kong subsidiary? Some treasurers consider that such hedging is opening up a risk, others that the Singapore subsidiary should be allowed to hedge the HK$ income to protect its own income and operating results. Much depends on how a company is managed and what the functional currency for the subsidiaries is.

EXAMPLES OF OTHER DERIVATIVES

So far the derivatives examined have been broadly confined to foreign exchange and interest rate exposure management. Every treasurer, however, needs to be aware of the range of derivatives available in the market. There is a continual development of new derivatives and products designed to manage financial risk, and there may be instances when one of these is applicable to his/her company.

The following is a very brief summary of some examples of the other derivatives available in the market. The objective of this summary is to illustrate how a company may be subject to some risks, financial or otherwise, that may be capable of management with derivatives.

Credit default swaps

In return for a periodic fee (expressed in basis points per year on the nominal amount), the protection buyer receives from the protection seller a payment that is contingent on the occurrence of a credit event with respect to a reference entity. The credit event is various and can range from bankruptcy or failure to meet obligations when due, to obligation acceleration or obligation default (see Figure 12.1).

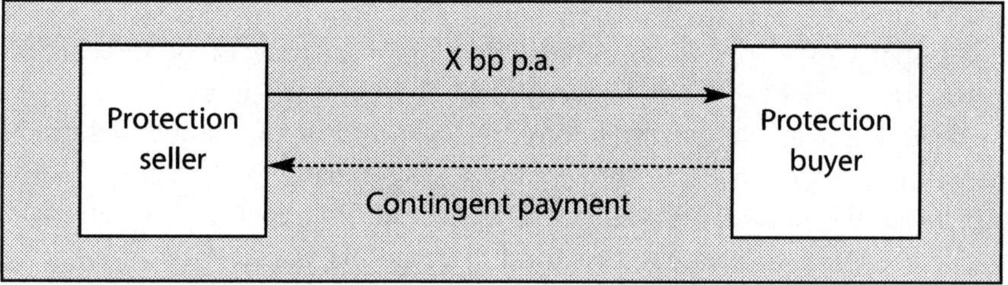

Figure 12.1 Credit default swap

When the credit event occurs, the swap terminates and final payment is made. Payment can take the form of:

- Physical settlement, where the buyer delivers the asset (as in the case of a bond) and receives the strike price.
- Cash settlement, where the buyer receives the strike price less the post-event market price. This is designed to mirror the loss incurred by a creditor of the reference entity following a credit event,
- A binary payment; i.e. a one-off lump sum payment.

Credit default swaps are part of a 'family' of credit-related derivatives and products, the market size of which has shown very rapid and substantial growth over the last few years. In the main, these products are used by banks and investment managers to manage the shape and credit risk of their portfolios. There may however be situations where a credit default swap may be applicable to a corporate environment. One example might be of a corporate who has an excessive credit exposure to a bank on one or more outstanding derivative transactions. Another example could be that of a corporate that has a major credit exposure to one large customer.

Property index forwards

Some organizations, property companies in particular, have substantial exposure to the commercial property market. Either these companies are trying to buy commercial property and are worried that prices may have risen before suitable properties are found, or they are considering selling properties and wish to lock in gains on the properties without having to wait for a buyer.

One of the parties to the contract assumes a long position and is the buyer of the underlying asset, while the counterparty is the seller. The particular asset is an index constructed from annual valuations of major UK commercial property investors. It is estimated that approximately 75–80 per cent of institutionally held property is incorporated within this index.

Assume a company wishes to buy UK£100 million of commercial property and wants to lock into prices now. They enter into a property index forward for a notional amount of UK£100 million. The index currently stands at 100, and the agreed forward price in one year is 105. Assume in one year's time the index has risen to 110, then the buyer of the property index forward receives:

$$\text{UK£}100{,}000{,}000 \times \frac{110}{105} - \text{UK£}100{,}000{,}000 = \text{UK£}4{,}761{,}900$$

The receipt from the contract offsets the loss incurred by purchasing the property at a higher price.

Weather derivatives

A number of companies can see a clear link between temperature and/or precipitation and cashflow and earnings. Such companies can include natural gas distributors, who are affected by unusually warm winters or cooler than normal summers, or agricultural concerns affected by adverse growing conditions.

An agricultural company wishes to obtain protection against both high temperatures and low cumulative precipitation. The derivative structure pays a fixed amount if defined temperature and precipitation conditions occur during a given season. The company pays a premium annually and receives contingent payments depending on the weather during the risk period. The weather conditions are based on data issued by a national weather service for a basket of locations representative of the company's production area.

CONCLUSION

The above is a very brief summary of some other derivatives that have been traded in the market in recent years. These derivatives have been used by some corporates to cover specific exposures. Other derivatives used by corporates are those related to commodities such as power and fuel and those related to equities. This highlights the importance of the treasurer remaining abreast of all the developments in the derivatives market in case company-specific opportunities arise.

PART IV

Cash and Liquidity Management

Cash management is one of the basic daily routines that every treasury department undertakes. While it is routine, efficiencies within this area can lead to significant cashflow benefits to an organization. Chapter 13 deals with the main domestic payment and collection instruments and how these instruments 'clear' and what the advantage and disadvantage of each instrument is. Chapter 14 deals with the mechanics of international payments and some of the instruments available, while Chapter 15 looks at two major cash management techniques: pooling bank account balances and intercompany netting systems. Liquidity management links cash management and debt management by managing the short-term cashflows of an organization.

CHAPTER 13

Domestic Payment and Collection Instruments and Domestic Clearing

CASH MANAGEMENT

The objectives of cash management are to:

- minimize the time involved in converting receipts into usable bank funds
- concentrate those funds into a central account where they can be most effectively managed
- control and minimize the cost of payments
- reduce or eliminate borrowings.

It is worth remembering that the treasury cash manager only manages cash at one narrow point of the company's business cycle. That is from the time that receipts become usable funds until the time those funds are used again to make payments. However, an organization is concerned with the effective management of cash at every point of the business cycle. For instance, efficient working capital management will in practice be linked to a company's production, sales and marketing and administrative controls. These are established to ensure an efficient control over the company's business processes and to minimize the use of working capital. A company will establish fixed asset controls to ensure not only that fixed assets are purchased and installed as rapidly as possible, but also that their cost is minimized (as far as is consistent with performance). Ultimately, every employee in an organization is a 'cash manager': cash is the lifeblood of every business.

The following three chapters examine cash management from the standpoint of the treasury department. They consider the principal domestic instruments for making payments and collecting receipts, and the way payments are made internationally, and conclude with a summary of aspects of cash pooling.

DOMESTIC COLLECTION AND PAYMENT INSTRUMENTS

Cash

Cash gives the recipient same-day value since it can be used immediately to make payments. If cash needs to be paid into a bank it does not normally become usable funds until the next day. Cash brings security and risk considerations, and its handling costs are comparatively high. The use of cash is in general decline, but in many countries it still accounts for 50 per cent of all retail spending.

Bank transfer or bank giro

A bank transfer is a written instruction by a payer to the bank to make a payment to a beneficiary. Bank transfers vary from the completion of a simple form that is lodged with the bank accompanied by a cheque or cash to 'accept' giros. The simple bank transfers require the payer to have the payee's bank account details, and since they are manually completed involve work in their preparation. Accept giros are completed by the beneficiary and sent to the debtor along with an invoice. The debtor accepts the giro by signing it and then forwards it to his/her bank.

Cheques

A cheque is an order to a banker signed by the bank's customer, and requiring the bank to make a payment to a named person. Payment to the payee is made immediately upon presentment of the cheque to the paying bank, and is made from funds held by the bank on the payer's behalf. A cheque must therefore specify the payee, the payer, the paying bank, the date, and the amount. In addition a cheque will specify the payer's account number and cheque number. In many countries cheques are still the main method of corporate to corporate payment, although the use of cheques is in decline.

Cheques gives rise to float. That is, there is a time delay between a company preparing a cheque to pay a supplier and the supplier having usable funds. This float arises from the time it takes to produce the cheque and post it, for it to be delivered, for the supplier to handle the cheque and pay it into the bank, for the cheque to pass through the clearing system, and finally for the supplier to get value from its bank.

The cost of cheques for the payer lies mainly in the preparation time and administration involved.

Banker's draft

A banker's draft is a written instruction, similar to a cheque but drawn by or on behalf of the bank itself rather than on a customer's account. Banker's drafts are payable on demand. Since the draft is drawn on a bank, it is regarded as cash once it is drawn (provided the drawing bank is of an appropriate credit quality).

Banker's drafts are usually used where the creditor demands guaranteed payment and where the size of the transaction makes cash too risky. Since a banker's draft is prepared by a bank on behalf of a customer, the customer's account is debited when the draft is prepared.

Credit cards and debit cards

Once the card is 'swiped' through a terminal, the retailer or supplier's account is credited automatically. However, a piece of paper is produced by the terminal, which the customer needs to sign to authorize the payment. The credit and debit card acquirer pays suppliers and retailers, and the value dating depends on the deal negotiated with the acquirer together with the systems used. Generally the retailer obtains value within one to three days.

In the case of credit cards, the card holder makes payment on receipt of a monthly statement. With a debit card, the card holder's account is debited electronically, usually within one to three days.

Telegraphic transfer

Also known as wire transfer. Provided the request to make the transfer is received before a stated cut-off time, same-day value is provided to the beneficiary. Full beneficiary bank details are required to effect the transfer. Since wire transfers are expensive, they tend only to be used for those payments where value must be received by the beneficiary on a specific day. This tends to confine wire transfers to financial transactions undertaken by a company: the payment of interest and principal, settlement of derivative contracts, and transfers within bank accounts.

Most wire transfers are initiated by companies using an electronic banking terminal, in which case the payment request is sent electronically to the paying bank. It is possible however for a written instruction to be sent to the bank, requesting that a wire transfer is made to a named beneficiary on a stated date.

Direct debit

Direct debits are payment requests submitted to the buyer's or debtor's bank by the seller for the payment of a particular sum of money. The paying bank is pre-authorized by the buyer or creditor to honour the payment request. For the originator, a direct debit gives cashflow certainty. Direct debits are often used by utility suppliers such as gas, electricity, water and telephone companies, but are now being used by an increasingly wide range of companies for regular commercial transactions.

Direct credit

Direct credits are requests submitted by the debtor to a bank, for payment to be made to a beneficiary's account. They are in a sense the reverse of direct debits, and are used in situations where regular amounts are due to a beneficiary. Examples of the use of direct credits include the payment of salaries, pensions and social security payments.

Standing order

A standing order is a written instruction to a bank to pay a specified person a regular amount of money on a periodic but recurring basis. Standing orders remain valid until cancelled. They are used for regular payments, including mortgage repayments, rental and life insurance payments.

HOW PAYMENTS CLEAR

Once a payment instruction has reached a bank, there needs to be some system for transferring money from the debtor's account to the beneficiary's. This process is known as clearing. The following describes the principal methods of clearing in most countries banking systems.

Wire payments

In the United Kingdom, same-day fund transfers can only be effected via CHAPS (the Clearing House Automated Payments System). There is no limit on the value of payments that can be made through this system, but due to the cost of CHAPS payments its use is typically reserved for financial and other large commercial payments where same-day value must be guaranteed.

Figure 13.1 shows how wire payments are made through the banking system. Company A is required to make a same-day value payment to Company B. Typical examples are the payment of interest on a loan or the repayment of a short-term advance. Company A remits details of the payment – amount and beneficiary bank account details – via its electronic banking system to its clearing bank (Bank A). The bank debits company A's account in its books and passes the payment into the CHAPS system. Banks communicate with each other on a real-time basis by means of standardized software in each bank, known as a gateway, through which all inward and outward messages pass. Gateways are connected by means of a packet switchstream (PSS). A sub-set of messages will be forwarded to the Bank of England for settlement. Once settlement has been effected, a confirmation is returned to the sender's gateway and the entire message is forwarded to the receiving bank (Bank B). Bank B will therefore receive a pre-settled payment and will credit its customer's account (Company B's account) in its books.

The CHAPS system in the United Kingdom is a real time gross settlement system (RTGS). The principal feature of a RTGS from the paying company's standpoint is that once payment has been entered into the system the beneficiary is guaranteed payment. Since a bank's balances with the Bank of England are typically quite small in comparison to the volumes of payments and receipts it makes through CHAPS, the Bank provides additional intra-day liquidity. This prevents gridlocks in the system. Since all payments are effected on a real-time basis, the receiving bank is obliged to give the beneficiary value by the end of the day.

In most countries with RTGS systems, the principles involved in making wire payments are similar.

Cheque clearing

Figure 13.2 shows the payment and document flow in a cheque clearing process. In this case a debtor mails a cheque, drawn on a particular branch of his/her clearing bank, to a supplier in settlement of outstanding invoices.

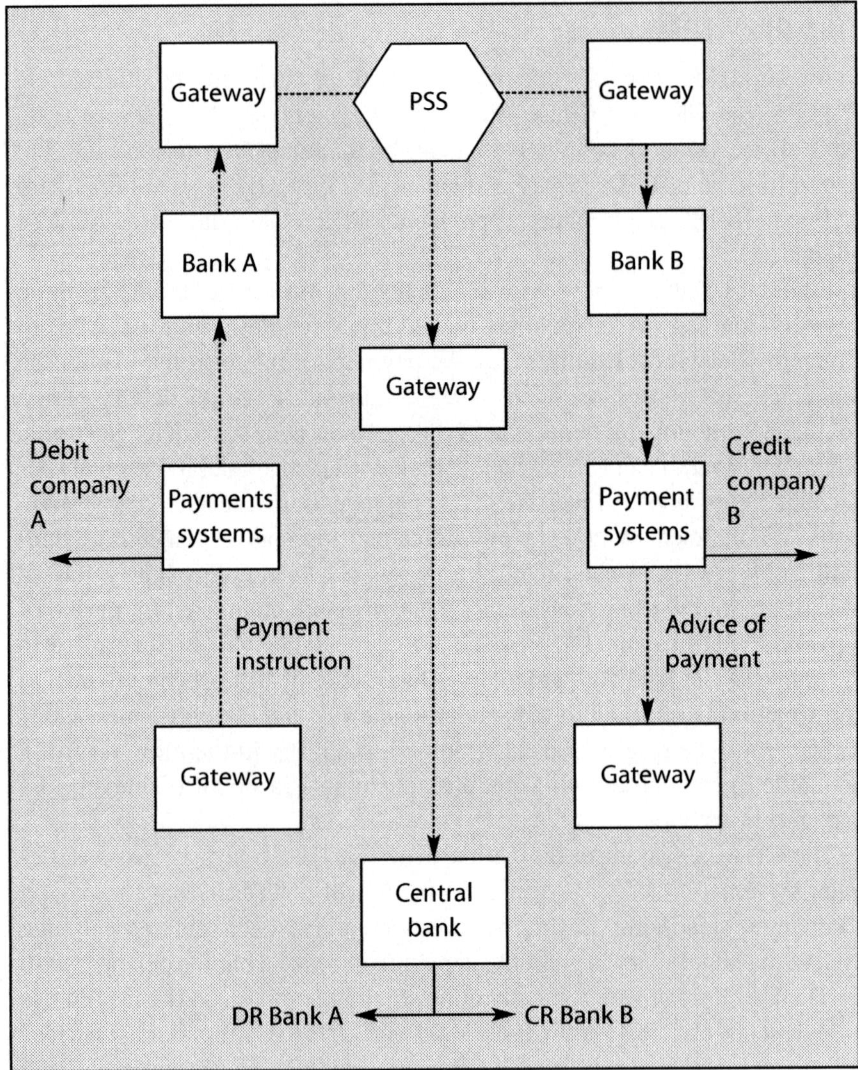

Figure 13.1 The message payment flows in a CHAPS payment

Day one

The creditor pays the cheque into his/her local bank (the collecting bank) together with all other cheques that have been received by the company that day. At the branch, all cheques received during the day from all local customers are sorted. There may be some cheques that are drawn on the local branch, in which case the drawer's and drawee's account with the

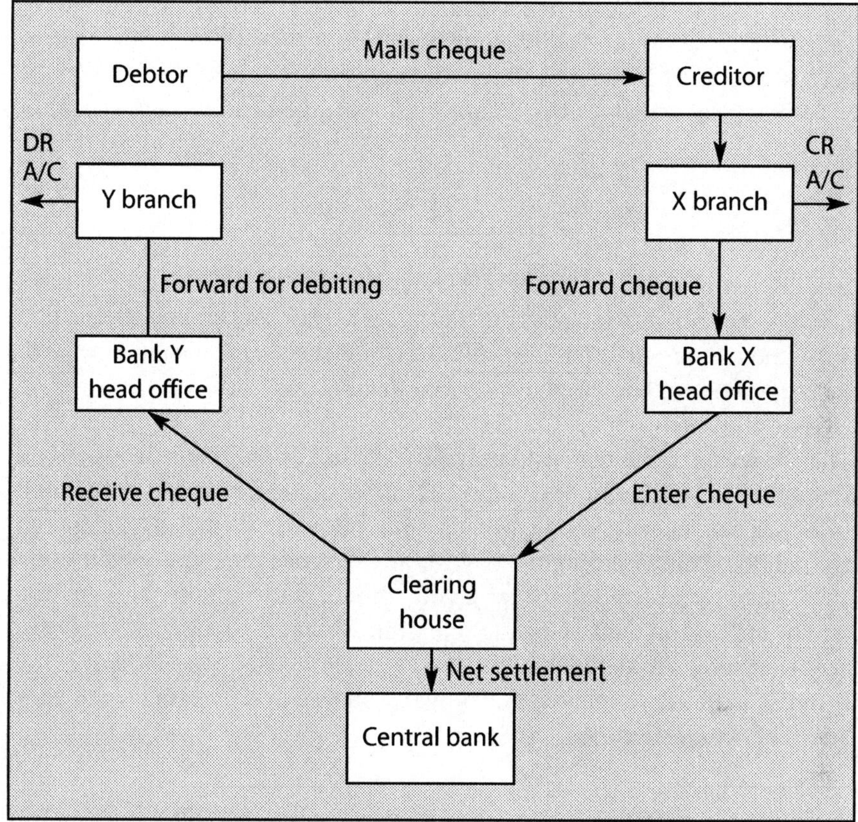

Figure 13.2 The document and payment flows for cheque clearing in the United Kingdom

bank are debited and credited. All other cheques are forwarded to the bank's clearing department, where they are merged with other cheques sent from other branches of the same bank. The bank will credit its customer's ledger with the value of the cheque that has been paid in. At this stage however, the customer does not have value for those funds.

Day two

The clearing house sorts all the cheques received into the different banks on which they have been drawn. Those cheques that have been drawn on other branches of the bank (Bank X) are put on one side, and customers' accounts with Bank X will be debited and credited. Details of other cheques are sent to the central clearing house. Here cheques are swapped between banks. There is a net settlement between banks (for instance Bank Y will be submitting some cheques drawn on Bank X, as well as Bank X submitting cheques drawn on Bank Y). The settlement is made by a transfer of balances that banks hold with the central bank (Bank of England).

Day three

Each branch of each bank will receive cheques drawn by their customers that were presented in the clearing the previous day. The branch checks that all the cheques are in order and will return any cheques that cannot be paid. The latter are sent back to the collecting bank.

In the above example the customer will have use of the funds deposited on day one at the beginning of day three. Thus customers normally have good value for cheques paid in on a Monday the following Wednesday, although they may be debited during the day for any cheques returned unpaid.

The above description is relatively broad, and certain parts of the system are automated. Cheque clearing in most countries that use cheques follows broadly the processes described above, although the degree of automation may vary, and value dating practices may also vary widely between countries.

Payments via the automated clearing house (ACH)

Virtually all countries have some process for clearing low-value high-volume payments. In the section on payment and collection instruments mention was made of direct debits, direct credits and standing orders. Payment of these instruments is effected via the ACH system.

The ACH system in the United Kingdom is called the Bankers Automated Clearing Services (BACS). Figure 13.3 shows how payments are effected through BACS. In this example an employer submits details of salary payments to be made to the employees' bank accounts. In the United Kingdom, BACS can be accessed directly by the corporate, who can download directly from its payroll systems via the appropriate interface. An input report is sent to the user to confirm that the file has been received and processed. If valid payment instructions are received at BACS on day one, all items will be processed overnight and distributed to banks on day two. These institutions will process the output from BACS on day two, and on day three the payments will be debited to the corporate's account with their bank and employees' accounts will be credited.

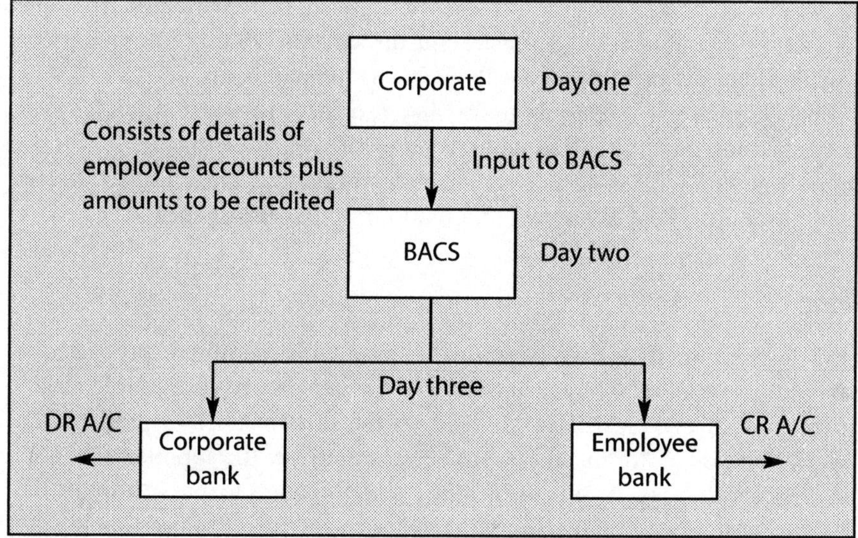

Figure 13.3 Information and payment flows with a direct credit through BACS

Significance of clearing systems and payment instruments for the treasurer

What has been described so far is, very broadly, the main payment and collection instruments found in different countries and the way payment is effected for these instruments in the United Kingdom. The description of the clearing process could be applied to a number of different countries around the world.

The significance of the different instruments and clearing systems for the treasurer lies in the aspects described below.

Cost

Wire transfers, although they can provide same-day value, attract the highest bank charges. For this reason they are generally used only for urgent payments or for commercial and financial payments where same-day value must be guaranteed (as otherwise the company would be in default of its obligations). Cheques are expensive payment instruments to use, not only because of the tariffs charged by banks for cheque clearance but particularly due to their costs of preparation. These costs lie in the time taken in preparation, checking, signature and dispatch, and security over blank cheques. Costs are highest when cheques are manually prepared, signed and dispatched. In comparison with cheques, the downloading of payment of direct debit files to an ACH can be effected automatically from the companies payment files. This straight-through processing is much more efficient than the processing involved in cheque payments.

The charges for ACH payments and receipts are substantially lower than cheques and wire transfers. While wire transfers in the UK cost approximately UK£8–10 per payment, and cheques are charged at 10p per transaction, BACS payments are about 2p per transaction.

Float

Float was defined as the time delay between a company preparing a payment instrument to pay a supplier and the supplier having usable funds. In the case of cheques, float arises from the time it takes to produce the cheque and post it, for the cheque to be delivered, for the supplier to handle the cheque and pay it into the bank, for the cheque to pass through the clearing system, and finally for the supplier to get value from its bank. Any one of these factors can cause float in respect of cheque payments to vary from four to ten days or more. When interest rates were generally high across the world, the float for the payer provided by cheques was comparatively valuable. Nowadays, with interest rates very low across the globe, the value of float has all but vanished.

The disadvantage of float is that it can make accurate cashflow forecasting and effective cash planning more difficult. With both wire transfers and ACH payments and receipts, there is no float. When payments and receipts are effected through these means, companies know when they will be debited or credited. Hence many companies are migrating to making as many payments through ACH as possible. This is due to:

- lower tariffs applied to ACH payments and the facility of straight-through processing to the ACH centre
- control over payment times
- improved cashflow forecasting.

Value dating practices

These can vary from country to country. For instance, in some countries a company may be debited for a payment through the ACH a day before the beneficiary is credited. In other countries the payee on a cheque may be credited some days after the drawer is debited. Understanding value dating practices enables the treasurer to make valid decisions about different payment instruments and when payments should be presented either to the supplier or to the bank.

Clearing cycle

Again these can vary among different countries. In some countries the cheque clearing cycle is less than the three days described for the United Kingdom; in other countries it can be considerably longer.

While the treasurer need not understand in detail how the clearing systems work for the various payment instruments available, an understanding of the cost, float, clearing cycle times and value dating practices attached to these different instruments are essential to enable a rational choice to be made between them.

CLEARING IN THE UNITED STATES

What has been discussed so far has been based on a country (the UK) where there is only one clearing house for cheques, and one for ACH payments. This is not always the case as a brief examination of the United States will demonstrate.

Cheque clearing

In the United States the Federal Reserve System consists of 12 regional Federal Reserve banks, which provide money transfer services and cheque clearing facilities as well as ACH systems. Thus a beneficiary whose bank clears through one particular Federal Reserve district may receive a cheque drawn on a bank that clears through another district. Banks use a number of channels for cheque clearing.

Principal clearing channels

- The Federal Reserve System provides a nationwide cheque collection facility. Each regional Federal Reserve bank clears cheques among its own member banks and forwards items to other regional 'Feds' that are drawn on their members. Settlement occurs through the members' reserve accounts held with the local Fed.
- Regional (local) clearing house associations provide cheque collection facilities for member banks. Banks in the same geographic area clear

with other banks in the clearing house. For cheques drawn on banks in another local clearing house, a bank will use a correspondent bank. Cheques are sent to the correspondent, which in turn collects the item through its local clearing house and credits the account of the sending bank. The regional clearing houses calculate the net settlement amounts due between members and debits or credits their reserve accounts at the appropriate Federal Reserve bank.

- Direct send networks are bilateral arrangements made between correspondent banks to exchange cheques drawn on each other, as well as items drawn on each other's clearing region. These networks are established to reduce the cost of clearing through the Fed or clearing house, and also to improve the availability of funds. Direct sends are used to achieve faster clearing times than are available by clearing through the local Fed. The sending bank maintains a deposit account with the relevant correspondent bank. The correspondent bank credits the account of the sending bank with the proceeds of the cheque.
- Cash letters consist of a number of cheques listed on a paying in/deposit slip, which is delivered directly to a local bank in the clearing district in which the cheques are drawn. Settlement is effected across correspondent accounts.

Any bank can present a cheque at any other bank if the cheque is presented to the drawee bank by 8.00 a.m. local time. If this deadline is met, the Federal Reserve requires the drawee bank to settle in same-day funds by the close of Fedwire.

With electronic cheque presentment, the MICR line on a cheque is captured by a reader/sorter at the depositary bank. The data is transmitted to the drawee bank who use this information to debit the funds from the payer's demand deposit account.

Availability

Selection of the appropriate cheque clearing channel is a function of deposit bank processing time, geographic location and the availability schedules of clearing agents. Availability is granted to the clearing bank if the cheque reaches the endpoint (or location established by the clearing agent) prior to a prearranged deposit deadline. Availability schedules define the number of days delay for each endpoint. The assignment is usually in whole business days, and cheques are generally assigned zero, one or two days availability. The Fed has availability schedules for banks, and banks have availability schedules for their customers. Many banks have multiple availability schedules.

To construct the availability schedule, the clearing bank examines clearing times for important endpoints, determines the clearing channels for each endpoint, calculates costs, and works back from deposit deadlines for those endpoints to establish its own deposit deadlines for customers.

The following factors influence the availability a bank assigns to a particular cheque:

- *Drawee location.* Cheques drawn on banks in remote locations generally have a longer availability time than those drawn on nearby banks.
- *Time of deposit.* Cheques must reach the processing centre by a certain time of the day in order to receive the designated availability.
- *Encoding.* If a company MICR-encodes the cheque dollar amount on the cheques it deposits, the bank may gain faster availability, or a later cut-off time.

Automated clearing house (ACH)

An ACH is a network of regional associations, inter-bank associations and private sector processors. Most regional ACHs are operated by the Fed. The ACH system is a batch process, store and forward system. Transactions received by the bank during the day are stored and processed in batches later that day. Transactions are settled one or two days after the file is released to the ACH operator, with both the receiver and the originator being settled on the same day. Credits are entered into the system two banking days prior to settlement, and debits are entered on the banking day prior to settlement (see Figure 13.4).

The most frequently used corporate applications are in cash concentration and disbursement funding. Many companies use ACH debits to consolidate funds deposited in field banks. This is particularly suited to corporate lockboxes (see page 279).

Fedwire

Fedwire is a real-time fund transfer system. The transaction is final once it has been sent to the originating bank and receipt is confirmed by the Fed. Fedwire hours are 12.30 a.m. to 6.30 p.m. Eastern Time. Banks establish earlier cut-off times for customers.

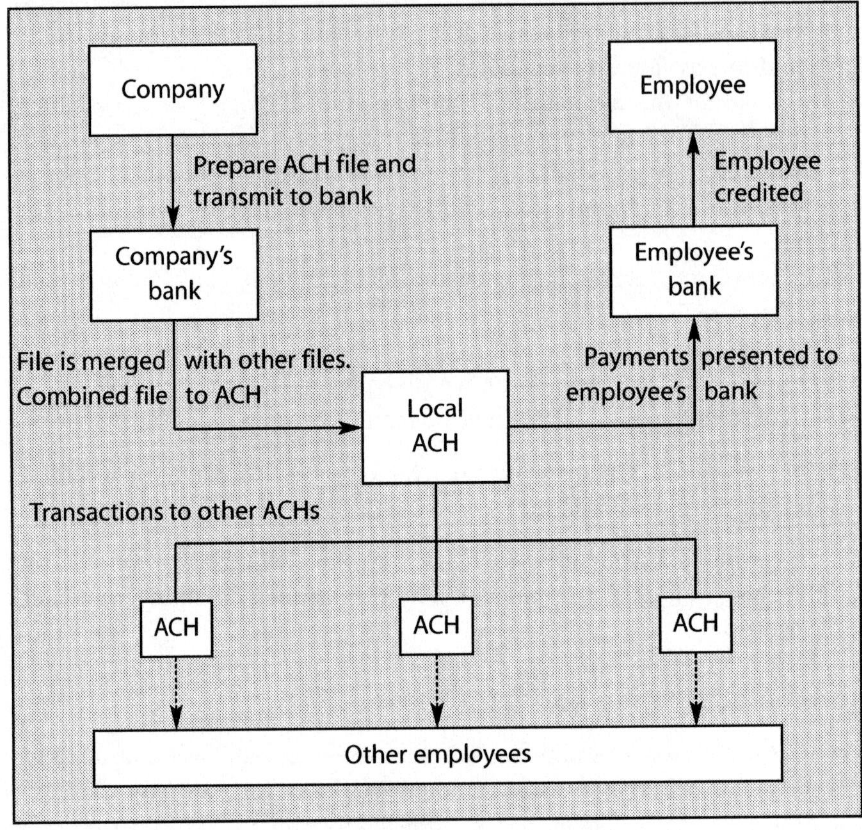

Figure 13.4 ACH system in the United States

Clearing House Inter-bank Payments System (CHIPS)

CHIPS is an independent large-dollar funds transfer network operated by the New York Automated Clearing House. It was established for foreign exchange settlements between foreign and American banks. It is also used for payments under letters of credit and documentary collections and for third-party transfers.

Transfers between member banks are received and authenticated during the day. Transfers are batched, and at the end of the day net amounts due to or from each settling participant are settled using clearing banks or the Fed. Non-settling banks settle via corresponding banks.

Transfers are executed on a same-day basis and may be unwound only if a member bank cannot honour its net deposit position. A receiving bank that credits a customer and allows use of the funds bears the risk that the sending bank will not settle. A fund consisting of collateral posted by all members has been established to insure against the failure of a participant.

Collection

Four features distinguish the US payments system from that of most other countries. They are:

- the widespread use of cheques for the majority of payments
- unpredictable delays in the mail system
- a large number of small banks
- a lack of comprehensive branch banking.

Collection systems have been designed in the light of the above characteristics.

Lockboxes

Companies receive cheques from customers in the mail or through lockboxes. With a lockbox a processor receives mail at a specified lockbox address, processes the remittances and deposits them in the payee's account. There are a number of advantages to lockboxes as opposed to receiving cheques through the mail.

- Mail float is usually reduced because a processor uses its own unique ZIP code to speed mail delivery. A lockbox processor may also make more frequent mail pickups.
- Processing float can be reduced because cheques are mailed directly to the lockbox processor. This eliminates company handling time. Also many processors operate 24 hours a day, seven days a week. In effect, they specialize in the efficient processing of receipts and deposits.
- Availability float is also reduced because the processor works to meet critical availability deadlines. These are deadlines by which cheques must reach the bank's proof and transit area. For example, 8 a.m. could be the deadline for receiving same-day availability for cheques drawn on banks in the same city. Different processors will have different availability schedules.

- In addition lockboxes provide efficient processing through economies of scale, and an audit trail and control.

Lockbox costs

These consist of a fixed monthly cost and a variable cost, which may be a per-item deposit and processing charge.

Collection studies

The location of lockboxes and the choice of lockbox processor are established after a collection study. The following data are analyzed: location and geographic concentration of remitting customers, location of customers with largest payments, intercity mail times, bank availability schedules and administrative costs associated with using lockboxes.

Lockbox networks may involve several processors in different cities or a single processor with multiple locations.

CLEARING IN OTHER COUNTRIES

Clearing in other countries around the world can vary. In some countries such as India, where there are 14 clearing houses in the major urban centres and cities and over 800 local clearing houses set up in towns, clearing a cheque can take from a few days to over a month. In other countries cheques are not used for corporate payments and most payments take place through bank transfers and the giro system. The important concern for the treasurer is to understand the payment and collection instruments available in his/her country, how quickly value can be obtained for different instruments and the relative cost of each one.

Importance of payment instruments and clearing processes

Treasurers and cash managers must familiarize themselves with the payment and collection instruments available to them, and how these instruments clear. Table 13.1 is based on the clearing systems within the United Kingdom. It illustrates the benefit of using ACH for payments and receipts where possible. With the fall in interest rates the benefit of float has become less important.

Table 13.1 Cost and availability for ACH, cheques and wire transfer in the United Kingdom

Instrument	*Available to beneficiary*	*Payor debited*	*Cost per transaction*	*Possibility of float*
ACH – direct debit, direct credit	2 days from transmission to clearing house	2 days from transmission to clearing house	2p per transaction	No
Cheques	2 days from depositing with local clearing branch	2 days after customer deposits with local clearing branch	Varies from 10p to 20p	Yes
Wire transfer	Same day	Same day	£10	No

SOME TECHNIQUES FOR MANAGING PAYMENTS AND RECEIPTS

Electronic cheques

The cost of issuing a single cheque has been variously calculated at between UK£5 and UK£10. The cost is not incurred in the bank charges for clearing cheques but in the cost of producing and processing the instrument. The more manual the work involved in cheque production, signing and dispatching, then the greater the cost. Some banks have developed outsourcing facilities for cheque production, where they will print, mail and post the cheque (including the remittance advice) to the customer. Typically a data file of payment instructions would be sent to the bank. Authorization is carried out electronically.

Banks that have developed this service may try to debit the customer at the time the cheques are dispatched as opposed to when the cheque is actually cleared.

Bank reconciliation

Automation of bank reconciliation processes should be made a priority. All transaction data required to perform effective reconciliation can be downloaded from the organization's electronic banking terminal and directly matched against internal records via a matching in the company's mainframe computer or PC. If the organization's accounting package lacks the functionality to automatically undertake the reconciliation of balances using information downloaded from the bank, a proprietary reconciliation package can be purchased. If cheque preparation is outsourced then the bank will also undertake cheque reconciliation.

Company purchase cards

The use of purchase cards is designed to reduce the cost of managing the cost of purchasing orders for small value items (see Figure 13.5). The cost of managing purchases has been calculated at anything up to UK£50 per order.

The controls over company purchase cards are:

- Purchase cards can only be used for authorized items with authorized suppliers.
- Purchases must fall within card control parameters such as transaction and monthly spend limits.
- The card holder must obtain a tax invoice.
- The card holder checks the statement and passes it to his/her manager for approval.
- The bank providing the cards will often also provide an MIS statement allocation costs to sites/departments or contracts.

CASE STUDY

Receipts

UptoDate Fashions plc is a high street retailer with 100 sites in most of the major towns and principal suburbs in the United Kingdom. Its cash profile is as follows:

- Annual Turnover £500 m
Profits before tax £ 25 m
- Takings:
Cash 25 per cent
Cheques 10 per cent

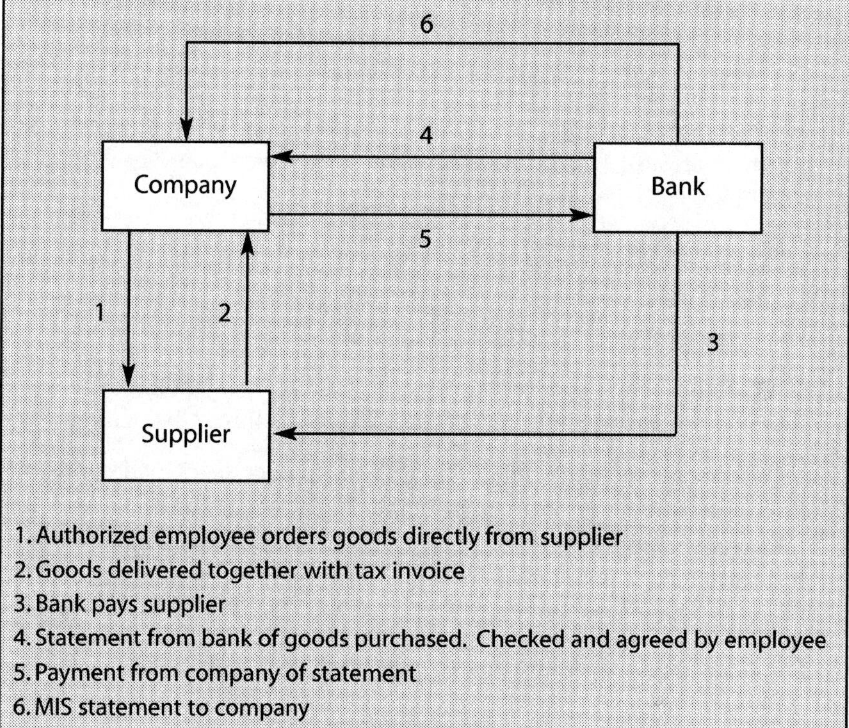
6
4
Company
Bank
5
1
2
3
Supplier
1. Authorized employee orders goods directly from supplier
2. Goods delivered together with tax invoice
3. Bank pays supplier
4. Statement from bank of goods purchased. Checked and agreed by employee
5. Payment from company of statement
6. MIS statement to company

Figure 13.5 A company purchase card scheme

Debit cards	30 per cent
Credit cards	35 per cent

- 50 per cent of the trade takes place on a Friday and a Saturday. The average transaction size is UK£25
- Costs of bankings:

	Main banker Per item
Cash	15p per £100
Cheques	7p per transaction
Debit cards	10p per transaction
Credit cards	1.15 per cent

- Cash and cheque bankings can be made either by an employee or by a security firm that collects, sorts, counts and banks the cash at the nearest bullion centre.

The security company charges UK£15 + 3p per UK£100

When cash is banked by employees, value is received:

Cash	Deposit day
Cheques	Deposit day + 2 working days

Since the security company collects takings later in the day and does not deposit until late in the day value is received one day later than when banked by employees.

Credits on statements are charged at 20p per credit slip.

- Credit cards
  There are two types of terminal available:

  PDQ equipment. The rental cost is UK£25 per month. Value is obtained on Day + 3 for credit cards. There are three tills per site.

  EFTPOS. There is no rental as the equipment is owned; costs of purchase are UK£22,500 per machine. Value is achieved Day + 1 for both credit cards. EFTPOS record sales data for management control purposes and is integrated into the information reporting structure. There are three tills per site.

- The marginal cost of borrowing is 6 per cent.

Question

What are the company's costs of obtaining value for takings?

SOLUTION

UptoDate Fashions

Average turnover per site	£5 m
Banking costs per site per annum:	(£)
Credit cards: UK£5 m × 35 per cent × 1.15 per cent	20,125
Cheques:	
Average number of transactions per site	200,000
Cost of cheques: 200,000 × 10 per cent x7p	1,400
Debit cards: 200,000 × 30 per cent × 10p	6,000
Cash UK£5 m × 25 per cent × .15	1,875
	29,400
Total for all sites	**UK£ 2,940,000**

Cost of using security company:	
Say two bankings a week: UK£15 × 2 × 52	1,560
Cash and cheques per site:	
UK£5 m × 35 per cent = UK£1,750,000 Charge 3p per UK£100	525
Loss of value on cash: UK£1,250,000 × 6 per cent × 1/365	205
	2,290
Per 100 sites	**UK£229,000**

Costs of different terminals PDQ vs EFTPOS	
Per site rental costs p.a.	900
Loss of value two days for PDQ: UK£5 m × 65 per cent × .06 2/365	,068
Cost of EFTPOS equipment: UK£22,500 × .063	(4,050)
	2,082
100 sites	**UK£208,200**

General

It is important that the treasurer knows what the cost is of making payments and obtaining value for receipts. This enables an informed decision to be made about:

- negotiating banking fees and tariffs
- changing clearing banker
- using alternative payment instruments.

Note:

The company is faced with a number of challenges.

- As with most retailers, obtaining value for takings can be expensive: in this case, over 10 per cent of profits before tax. The major cause is the cost of accepting credit cards. Can a lower fee be negotiated or could the use of a store credit card for customers be an opportunity?
- The cost of using a security company must be set against the implications of sending employees to the bank with takings.
- Although EFTPOS equipment is more expensive, it represents significant benefits by being integrated into the information reporting structure.

CHAPTER 14

International Payments and Receipts

CORRESPONDENT BANKING

When considering an international transaction – for example a payment in US$ by a Singapore company to an American company – a payment process needs to be used that can be cleared through the American banking system. This is because the American company needs to get value in US dollars. However since the Singapore company's bank accounts are in Singapore dollars and are all maintained in Singapore, there also needs to be a way to make payments from Singapore to the United States. The means of effecting this is the correspondent banking system and the SWIFT message system.

Example

Correspondent bank relationships are normally relationships between two banks, with each bank holding a bank account in its own country for use by the other. In the above example, the Singapore company's bank will have a correspondent bank in the United States. This US correspondent bank will have a bank account in US$ for the account of the Singapore bank (and the Singapore bank will likewise have an account in SG$ for the account of the US bank). To monitor the entries that pass through the bank account, the account holding bank (the Singapore bank) will open a mirror account in its own books against which it will reconcile its bank statements. Correspondent bank accounts are known as 'nostro' accounts and mirror accounts held in account holder's own books are known as 'vostro' accounts.

Assuming the Singapore company needs to pay US$10,000 to the American company the entries in both the Singapore and American banks books are as follows:

Singapore bank's books (remitting country)

Customer account SG$

DR	
18,000	

Due to (vostro) US$

	CR
	10,000

American bank's books (receiving country)

Due from account (nostro)

DR	
10,000	

Customer's account

	CR
	10,000

This example shows the entries that may be passed in a transaction where a Singapore company remits US$10,000 to an American supplier by telegraphic transfer. The Singapore company instructs its bank to send US$10,000 to a beneficiary in the United States and to debit its account with the SG$ equivalent. The accounting entries in Singapore bank's books will be a debit to the customer's account and a credit to the vostro account. A SWIFT message (see next section) will be sent to the American correspondent which will in effect say 'debit my account with you with US$10,000 and pay US$10,000 to the beneficiary company'.

In the above example the Singapore bank held its US dollars with the same bank that the beneficiary banked with.

SWIFT (THE SOCIETY FOR WORLDWIDE INTER-BANK FINANCIAL TELECOMMUNICATIONS)

SWIFT is a telecommunications network, owned and used by 6000 banks and certain types of financial institutions for the exchange of financial data between members. SWIFT is not a payment system. The SWIFT system uses a strict set of standards that enable standardized messages to be generated, received and interfaced by bank computers and local clearing systems in a fully automated way. Banks use SWIFT to send messages to each other in respect of inter-bank business, and they also use it to transmit information regarding corporate business. The most commonly used message relating to corporate business is the international funds transfer message (MT100), followed by the 'advice to receive' message (MT210). SWIFT is also used for reporting customers' bank account details between banks (MT940 message).

In many countries electronic interfaces exist between SWIFT and the local electronic clearing system.

Message series

SWIFT has developed sets of standards covering various types of bank transactions. There are a number of message series covering different types of transactions:

Message series	Types of transaction covered
100	customer payments
200	bank-to-bank applications
300	foreign exchange and money market transactions
500	securities transactions
700	trade transactions (letters of credit etc.)
900	balance and transaction reporting.

SWIFT and international payments

Refer back to the earlier example of a Singapore company that needs to remit US$10,000 to their American supplier. SWIFT will be used in the transaction as described below and in Figure 14.1.

Once the Singapore bank has received instructions from its customer it will generate a SWIFT message to its local SWIFT centre. Local centres are linked into the SWIFT network via the appropriate SWIFT operations centre. The operations centre sends the message to the appropriate operations centre that handles messages for the country of the beneficiary. This centre will then pass the message to the local SWIFT centre used by the receiving bank. The various links within in the system work on a real-time basis, and therefore the messages take only a few seconds to reach the receiving bank.

Cover payment method

So far, this example has covered a situation where the US correspondent bank for the Singapore company is the same as that used by the ultimate beneficiary. However this is usually not the case. In the following example

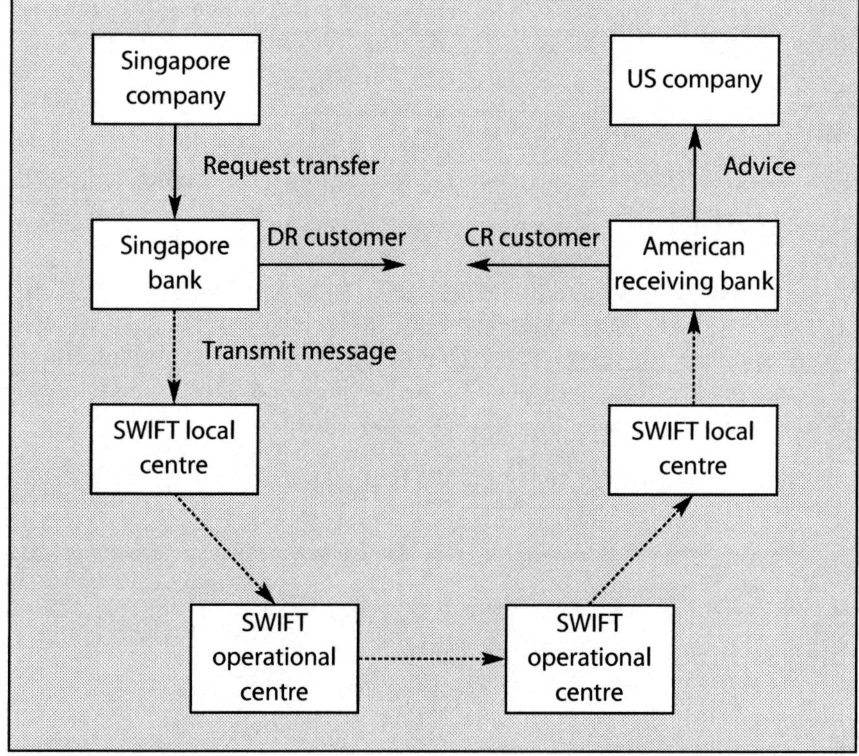

Figure 14.1 Simple international payment using SWIFT network

it is assumed that the beneficiary banks with a Chicago bank that is not a member of CHIPS or Fedwire.

The Singapore bank will carry out the foreign exchange transaction, debit its customer's account with the Singapore dollars and will credit its US$ vostro account. It will then send a payment order MT100 to the beneficiary's Chicago bank, which will in effect say: 'when you receive US$10,000 from Singapore bank please pay to your customer – Company A – on behalf of Company XYZ, Singapore'.

Since the Singapore bank does not have a relationship with the Chicago bank, it will send a cover payment message MT202 to its New York correspondent. The MT202 in effect says: 'debit our account with you and pay US$10,000 to Chicago bank, for the account of Company A'. If the Chicago bank has no correspondent relationship with the Singapore bank's New York correspondent, payment will have to go to the bank with which the Chicago bank clears its dollars in New York.

On receipt of US$10,000 by the Chicago bank's New York correspondent bank, an advice of credit is sent to the Chicago bank, which will match this with the original MT100 and credit Company A's account (Figure 14.2).

Implications for the treasurer

The questions for the treasurer making a number of foreign currency payments are as follows:

- Is there any timing difference between being debited by my bank for the domestic currency equivalent of the foreign currency payment and my supplier receiving value? One common reason for timing differences is due to the number of banks involved in an international payment, which can slow the transaction down.
- What charges will be applied to the transaction? It may not be unusual

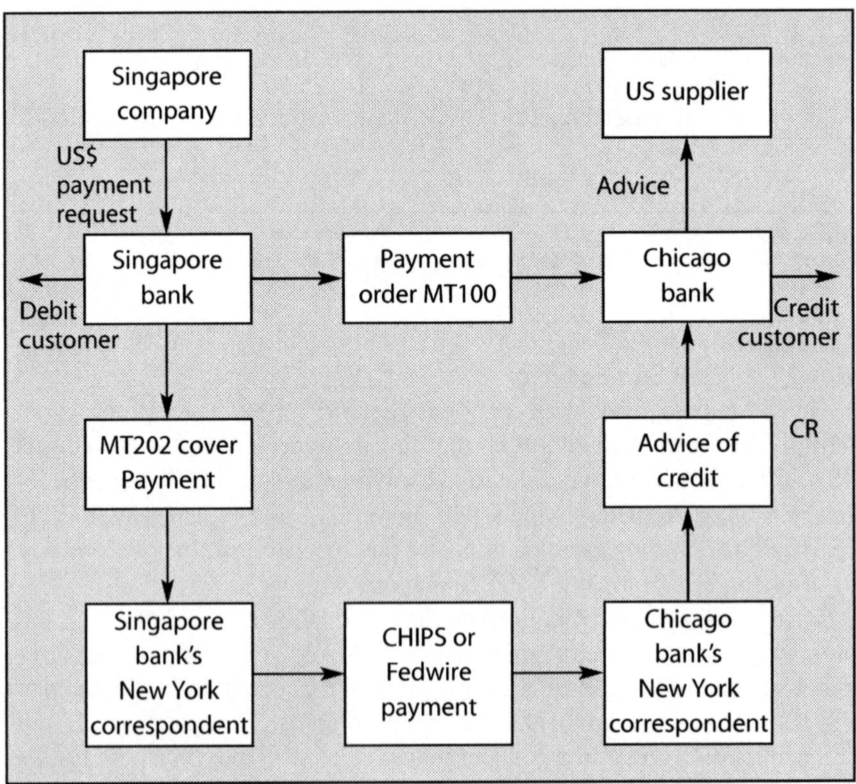

Figure 14.2 Illustration of a foreign payment using the SWIFT and correspondent banking systems

for the correspondent bank used by the treasurer's domestic bank to levy charges, together with the beneficiary's bank and any correspondent bank used by the beneficiary's bank.

- Is the payment being made through the cheapest clearing channel consistent with the date the treasurer's company needs the supplier to receive value?

All in all the treasurer is concerned with one question: 'Can I be satisfied that I will receive a consistent, efficient and cost-effective service and that any fees to be levied can be identified in advance?'

FOREIGN CURRENCY ACCOUNTS

In the previous example, the Singapore company's local bank account was debited with the SG$ equivalent of the US$ payment. However a company can open up a foreign currency account in much the same way that a local resident can. For example the Singapore company could open a US$ bank account and transact business in US$ using that account. Such accounts are subject to the laws of, and exchange control existing in, the account holder's country (Singapore) as well as those in the United States. Sometimes prior approval is required from the central bank, and sometimes local taxes can make such accounts uneconomic.

It is possible to hold currency accounts located either in the centre of the currency concerned (e.g. a US$ account held in New York), in another major financial centre (e.g. London) or in the company's domestic country (in this case, Singapore). When a Singapore company opens up a US$ foreign currency account with a local bank in Singapore, the US$ in that account will still be held in the United States. In this situation the Singapore bank would maintain the US$ account in the United States with its US correspondent. If an amount is paid into the Singapore company's US$ account, the US correspondent will credit its nostro account with the Singapore bank, who will in turn credit its Singapore customer's US$ account in their books. It is important to recognize that wherever the foreign currency account is located, the actual currency will be held in the country of the currency.

Advantage of foreign currency accounts

Foreign currency accounts are used when there is a large enough volume of the relevant foreign currency receipts or payments. Overseas customers may be invoiced in their domestic currency, and overseas suppliers paid in theirs. It may be more appropriate for a company to use a foreign currency account to handle such receipts and payments, and periodically sell or buy the necessary foreign currency to manage the overall balance in the account. This may be done by periodic spot transactions where the foreign currency amounts involved are small. However, where the transaction or pre-transaction exposures that they represent are more significant, the foreign currency accounts may be used to receive or pay away for forward hedges taken out to eliminate such exposures.

Costs of maintaining foreign currency accounts

There are a number of matters to be considered in determining whether foreign currency accounts will be an effective way of handling foreign currency receipts and payments.

- There may be requirements for minimum balances to be maintained. If so what size are these balances?
- Will credit interest be applied on any balances and if so what rate will it be? How will credit interest be calculated?
- What debit interest will be charged on overdrafts?
- How will bank charges be established? Will they be transaction-based or turnover-based? Will lifting charges apply to transactions going through the account, and will an account maintenance fee apply?

The costs of maintaining the foreign currency accounts need to compared to the risks and inefficiencies involved in handling foreign exchange receipts and payments without such accounts.

Location of foreign currency accounts

Companies need to decide where to locate their foreign currency accounts. Generally the consideration is: should the accounts be maintained in the country of currency or should they be maintained at the local branch of the company's domestic bank? There are advantages and disadvantages to each, as laid out in Table 14.1.

The location of a foreign currency account will therefore depend on a number of considerations. However most treasury departments opening up foreign currency accounts will open them at the local branch with their domestic bank, since administration of the account is that much easier.

Table 14.1 Advantages and disadvantages of location of foreign currency accounts

Local branch of domestic bank	*Account in country of currency*
Foreign currency cheques and drafts easily paid into the bank.	Some process needs to be established for paying in cheques (e.g. lockboxes).
Cheque/draft clearing times may be longer since they have to be sent to country of currency.	Cheques/drafts clear more quickly.
Cut-off times to receive same-day value on funds will be earlier.	Later cut-off times for achieving same-day value on transactions.
Queries can be more easily dealt with. In addition bank statements are easier to obtain promptly, and there are no language problems in resolving queries.	More problems in dealing with queries, and in some countries language problems may be severe.
Value for direct credits can take longer.	Value for direct credits received earlier.
Cheques drawn on this account may be less acceptable to an overseas supplier.	Cheques drawn on local account may be more acceptable to supplier.
If a number of different foreign currency accounts are being maintained, they can all be opened with one bank.	May need to be opened with different banks.

The foreign currency accounts and their location are further discussed in the next chapter.

INTERNATIONAL PAYMENT METHODS: NON-ELECTRONIC

There are two principal ways of making international payments and effecting collections: electronic and non-electronic. This section examines the principal non-electronic international payment and collection methods.

Foreign currency cheques

If a company holds a foreign currency account, either domestically or in the country of currency, then provided cheques are acceptable and local banking regulations apply, they may have the opportunity of raising cheques on that account. This enables them to make international payments in exactly the same way that they make domestic payments.

There are a couple of conditions to the above. First, in some countries cheques are not a common method of payment. Such countries include many European countries, such as Germany, Netherlands and Poland. These countries tend to use the automated clearing house for making commercial payments. Second, the viability of cheques may depend on where the foreign currency account is located. Cheques drawn on foreign currency accounts located outside the currency centres can be expensive to collect and take a long time to clear. For example a Singapore company that must make a US$ payment to a Hong Kong company provides a US$ cheque drawn on a US$ account located in Singapore. Such a cheque may not be well received by the Hong Kong company. This could be particularly so if the Hong Kong company's US$ account is located in Hong Kong.

Cheques for collection

A company receiving a foreign currency cheque will pay the cheque into its local branch. The bank's head office will send the cheque together with other cheques in the same currency received from other customers to its correspondent bank in the relevant country. On receipt of the cheques, the correspondent will put them into the domestic clearing system. When the cheques are paid, the correspondent will credit the amount (less any applicable charges) to the presenting bank's nostro account in its books and notify the bank. One receipt of notification the presenting bank will debit the nostro account in its books and credit the customer's account. If the company maintains only bank accounts in local currency, the collecting bank will convert the foreign currency amount to local currency.

With cheques for collection, the company is only credited once the funds have been received.

Cheques for negotiation

In this process the domestic bank will purchase the foreign currency cheque and credit the customer's account immediately with the local currency equivalent. The purchase is subject to recourse and the customer receives the discounted value representing the interest on the value of the cheque while the bank is collecting it. The amount of interest depends on the currency of the cheque and the estimated amount of time to clear the cheque and allow the collecting bank to be given good value.

Reducing costs and collection times

There are certain basic procedures that companies which periodically receive foreign currency cheques for substantial amounts can take. These can include:

- Either deliver the cheque directly the local bank's international branch or consider sending it direct to the local bank's correspondent bank in the country of currency.
- Use couriers where local postage is known to be slow or for large amounts drawn on overseas centres.
- Consider opening a foreign currency account where the amounts are regularly received. Either net off the amount received with payments being made in the same currency, or handle foreign exchange directly rather than leaving it to the bank.

Banker's draft

A buyer or importer can purchase a foreign currency draft from his/her bank drawn on a bank in the exporter's country. The banker's draft enables the exporter to be guaranteed payment and to obtain funds faster and at less cost. The buyer of the draft will be debited when the draft is raised.

Documentary collection

Documentary collection is a method that is used to restrict the possibility of non-payment and is often used where there is no existing commercial relationship between two companies. The steps in documentary collections are as follows:

- The buyer and seller agree on the terms of sale and also agree that payment will be made on a documentary basis.
- The exporter arranges for delivery of the goods to the port or airport.

- The freight forwarder prepares the necessary documents of title based on information received from the exporter.
- The documents of title are delivered to the exporter's bank. This may be done by either the exporter or freight forwarder.
- The bank processes the documents and forwards them to the collecting bank.
- On receipt of the documents the buyer's (importer's) bank will contact its customer and request payment or acceptance of the draft.
- After payment or acceptance of the draft, the documents of title are released to the customer, who utilizes them to arrange delivery.
- The importer's bank remits the funds to the exporter's bank or advises that the draft has been accepted.

Letter of credit

A letter of credit (L/C) contains all the following elements:

- A payment undertaking given by a bank (issuing bank) on behalf of a buyer (applicant).
- The payment undertaking is to pay a seller (beneficiary) a given amount of money.
- Payment is made on presentation of specified documents representing the supply of goods within specified time limits.
- The documents must conform to the terms and conditions set out in the letter of credit and must be presented at a specified place.

A letter of credit is an extension of documentary collection whereby the seller exchanges the buyer's credit for that of a bank. The steps involved in a letter of credit are shown in Figure 14.3:

1. Buyer and seller agree terms of sale, including means of transport, period of credit and latest date of shipment.
2. The buyer applies to its bank (issuing bank) for the issue of a letter of credit (L/C).
3. The issuing bank issues an L/C, and sends it to the seller's bank (Advising bank) by airmail or, more commonly, by electronic means such as SWIFT.

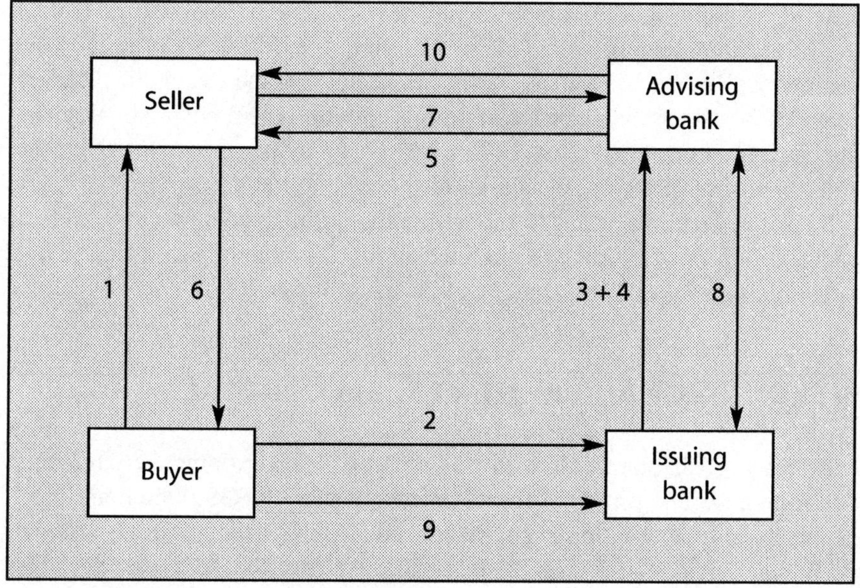

Figure 14.3 Steps in the preparation and payment under a letter of credit

4. The advising bank establishes the authenticity of the L/C, using signature codes or test codes, and then informs the seller (beneficiary).
5. The seller checks that the L/C matches the terms of the commercial agreement and that all its terms and conditions can be satisfied. If there is anything that may cause a problem, an amendment may be requested.
6. The seller ships the goods, and then assembles the documents called for in the L/C.
7. Documents are presented to the advising bank together with a draft drawn under the L/C.
8. The issuing bank now checks the documents and if they are in order reimburses the seller's bank.
9. The issuing bank debits the buyer and releases the documents, so that the buyer can claim the goods from the carrier.
10. The seller is paid by the advising bank.

Letters of credit may be issued for one single transaction or for a number of transactions. In the latter case the buyer can issue letters of credit up to a facility amount. Letters of credit can be revocable or irrevocable. If they are irrevocable, then provided all the required documents are presented the issuing bank must honour all drafts presented by the seller. In addition letters of credit can be guaranteed. In this situation the advising bank guarantees payment under the letter of credit. This may be important where the seller is unsure of the credit quality of the issuing bank.

It is of course important to recognize that strictly documentary collection and letters of credit are not international payment instruments, but mechanisms whereby payments can be made internationally.

INTERNATIONAL PAYMENTS: ELECTRONIC

The previous chapter dealt with methods of clearing domestic payments electronically. The principal forms discussed were RTGS, which are used for high-value low-volume payments, and ACH, used for high-volume low-value payments. It was also mentioned that the ACH is ideal for handling direct debits and direct credits. The first part of this chapter discussed SWIFT and correspondent banking, and how these two elements of international banking interlink for making and collecting payments internationally.

Making international payments electronically, therefore, effectively means connecting domestic electronic payments with the elements of international banking. Most treasury departments use electronic banking to send payment requests to their clearing banks. These electronic banking systems allow customers to compile files of payments on personal computers and transmit the files directly their bank. These payment requests may cover domestic or international payments. Furthermore, most banks now have the facility of sorting the international payments and determining from their size and required value dating which particular medium for domestic payment should be chosen: transfer via RTGS or via ACH. In addition, some of the major banks also have systems that allow direct credits and direct debits to be included in these payment requests.

Furthermore, some global banks are members of the clearing system in most countries around the globe. This enables their customers to connect to the bank's global network to make a payment in any country where the global bank has a clearing presence. The bank takes the payment request and converts it into the format required for it to pass on a fully automated basis into the clearing system in the beneficiary's country. This is effected by the payment request being transmitted to the global bank in the beneficiary's country and then being entered into the relevant clearing system

(RTGS or ACH). Some banks have the capability to input the payment directly into the clearing system. The system is shown in Figure 14.4.

The advantages of using a global bank are standard service standards, later cut-off times for payments, guaranteed value dating and a single transfer price.

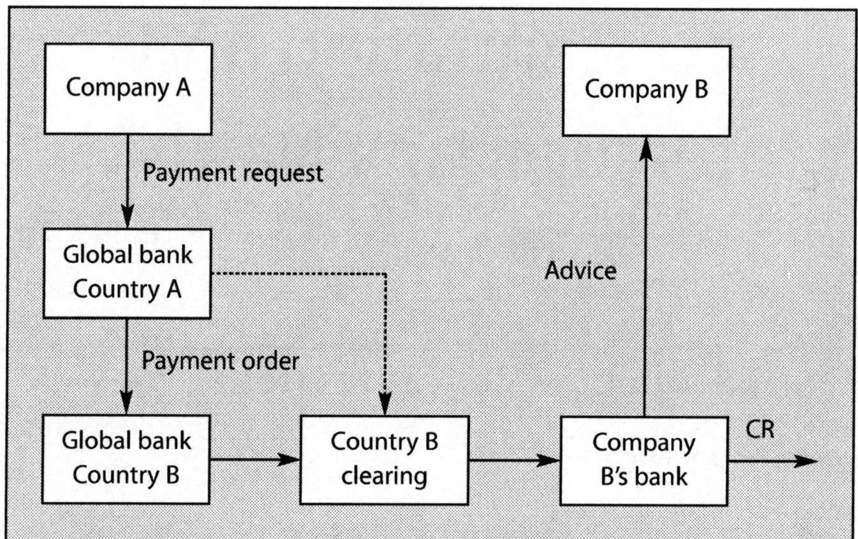

Figure 14.4 International payments using a global bank

CHAPTER 15

Pooling and Cash Concentration and Intercompany Netting

POOLING AND CASH CONCENTRATION

Domestic pooling

Notional pooling

Pooling is the offsetting of the credit balances on certain accounts against the debit balances on other accounts, with interest being charged or credited on the resultant net balance. With true pooling (known as notional pooling) there is no movement or co-mingling of funds.

The benefits of pooling can be illustrated as follows. The current interest charged by the bank overnight on accounts in debit is 5 per cent, while the interest credited on accounts in credit is 3 per cent. In the case shown in Table 15.1, the total net annual interest charged on the accounts is UK£30,000 without pooling. However with pooling, as shown in Table 15.2, the net interest charged on the four accounts has fallen from UK£30,000 to zero, since all the accounts are now netted off in calculating the interest charge for the accounts.

Pooling is desirable because the overdraft interest rate that a bank applies to accounts that are in overdraft is substantially greater than the market rate; likewise, the credit it gives on accounts in credit is substantially below the market rate. The bank does this because overdrafts are a 'convenience' product and the company often provides no notice of the overdraft that will exist on an account at the end of the day.

Table 15.1 Interest cost without pooling. The daily interest charge amounts to an annual cost of UK£30,000

	End of day cleared balance on account UK£	*Daily interest charge UK£*
Subsidiary 1	250,000	20.55
Subsidiary 2	(500,000)	(68.49)
Subsidiary 3	1 250,000	102.74
Subsidiary 4	(1,000,000)	(136.99)
Total	Zero	(82.19)

Note: Brackets represent negative balances and interest charged.

Table 15.2 Interest benefit with pooling

	End of day cleared balances on account	*Annual interest charged*
Net pool	Zero	Zero

Benefits of notional pooling

Among the benefits are:

- minimizing the day-to-day borrowing requirements
- reducing the exposure to any one bank
- maximizing the interest earned on credit balances, and minimizing the interest charged on accounts in overdraft.

For notional pooling to work, all the accounts need to be with the same bank. This needs to be borne in mind since there will be an exposure to the service levels and pricing of one bank.

Application of interest

In the above example, the net balance on the four accounts was zero. However the balances for each individual subsidiary were either credit or debit balances. Without pooling, subsidiaries one and three would have received interest on their credit balances, while subsidiaries two and four would have needed to pay interest on their debit balances. Some companies have internal accounting processes that allocate interest to companies with credit balances and charge those with debit balances, even though their bank accounts are pooled. The object of these allocations is to put the subsidiaries in the same position as if they were stand-alone companies without access to group resources, and to create greater cash management awareness on their part.

If the company has no allocation process then often, if necessary, the bank can provide some shadow administration. This involves allocating interest to companies in the pool according to some set of agreed rates. In the above example the agreement may be that the bank will calculate interest on credit balances at 3.5 per cent and at 4.5 per cent on debit balances. This gives subsidiaries in credit a better rate than they would have achieved on a stand-alone basis, and those in debit a lower rate.

Management of the pool

One of the objectives of pooling is to fund the liquidity position of the group in an effective manner, or to deposit net surpluses. One of the cash manager's first jobs in the day is to calculate the end-of-day cleared position (see the chapters on liquidity management and treasury systems). This calculation will show either a surplus in the pool (which will need to be deposited), or a deficit (which will need to be funded). In such a situation it is usual for the cash manager to use a treasury account to effect the movement of funds. This account will be credited with any funds raised to finance the pool, or debited with any deposit of funds (Table 15.3).

Table 15.3 Projected end-of-day balances on the pool

	Projected end-of-day cleared balance
Subsidiary 1	(2,000,000)
Subsidiary 2	1,500,000
Subsidiary 3	(3,000,000)
Subsidiary 4	1,000,000
Treasury account	(500,000)
Net pool	(3,000,000)

In this situation the projected balance on the pool is (3 million) and the cash manager will need to fund that shortfall. As discussed earlier the reason for this is that better rates are available on the money markets than are available from the bank on the pool. (This funding will be done using the instruments and cash forecasting described in Chapter 16, Liquidity Management.) If the cash manager borrows 3 million, that amount will be credited to the treasury account, and the projected net balance on the pool will be zero.

Overdraft limits gross and net

It is common treasury practice for the pool to have an overdraft limit. There are two reasons for this.

Market rates versus overdraft rates

It can sometimes happen, though rarely, that the money market rates are above the overdraft rate. In such an event it is cheaper to fund any shortage for the day through the overdraft rather than borrowing overnight on the money markets.

Accuracy of end-of-day cash forecast

No matter how carefully the calculation of the projected end-of-day balance is prepared, it will never be totally accurate. There will always be small credits and debits going through accounts in the pool that cannot be forecast with total accuracy. In addition, some groups have a large number of subsidiaries or divisions, all of which have the authority to make same-day value payments. There is always the chance that a subsidiary may make a same-day value payment from an account within the pool without notifying central treasury. Finally, there is the possibility of overseas payments being made in a domestic currency from one of the accounts in the pool. For some reason it may be that this payment is made before its anticipated date.

The existence of the overdraft means that any net debit balance on the pool that has not been separately funded can be financed via the overdraft attached to the pool. The size of the overdraft is obviously a function of the nature of the company's cashflows, the size of daily shortages and the extent to which unplanned payments could hit accounts within the pool.

While the pool itself will have an overdraft based on the net balance on the pool, the bank providing the pool will insist on overdrawn limits on each account within the pool. These are referred to as gross and net limits. For instance there may be an overdraft limit of 5 million for the pool as a whole, with a stipulation that no account can be overdrawn by more than 10 million.

Interest on credit balances

In addition to an overdraft attached to the pool, the treasurer will want to ensure that idle credit balances earn interest. The pool could be in net credit for much the same reason that it could be in debit. It should be noted however, that in some countries banks are not allowed to pay interest on credit balances on current accounts.

Cross-border, cross-currency pooling

So far we have considered domestic pooling. This is an example of single-currency, one-country pooling. International companies may need to consider the availability of three other types of pooling:

- *Single-currency, cross-border pooling*. This type of pooling may be sought by a company that, for instance, has US$ in a number of accounts in different countries and is seeking a pooling arrangement for these accounts.
- *Cross-currency, one-country pooling*. This reflects a situation where a company has a number different foreign currency accounts all positioned at one location. It is important to ensure any pooling product offered is genuine pooling and not a sharing of the spread between the borrowing and deposit rate for each currency.
- *Cross-currency, cross-border pooling*. A multinational company with domestic and foreign currency accounts in different currencies and in different countries may seek to pool all these accounts.

These structures are discussed later in the chapter.

Cash concentration: single currency

In some countries notional cash pooling is prohibited, in others regulatory reasons may make pooling economically unviable, while in others the banks may not be able to achieve legal right of set-off. In such cases, concentration is used to transfer funds to one central account.

Cash concentration is also referred to as sweeping, and can be managed in different ways.

- *Zero balance accounts*. In this situation the balance on designated accounts is transferred to a central account (concentration account).
- *Target balance accounts*. A bank transfers all funds over a specified limit. This technique may be employed where there is the likelihood that same-day value debits may hit the account after the transfer has been effected.
- *Threshold zero balancing*. Funds are only transferred out of an account once a certain balance has been reached. This prevents transfers of small amounts, where the cost of the transfer is greater than the interest benefit of concentrating the cash.

Using the example at the beginning of the chapter, concentration would operate as shown in Figure 15.1 (an example of zero balance cash concentration). The balance on all the relevant subsidiaries' accounts is either transferred to a central account (in the case of credit

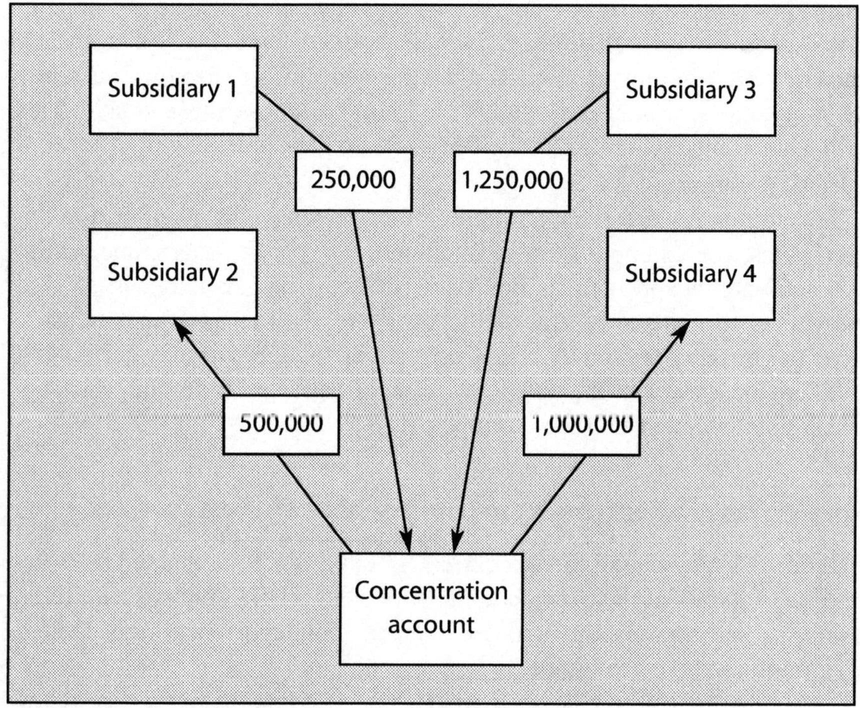

Figure 15.1 Zero balance cash concentration

balances) or transferred from a central account to fund debit balances. The resulting balance on the concentration account is either funded by borrowing in the market (net debit position) or is invested (net credit position)

The control account and subsidiary accounts may be with the same bank or held with a different bank. The concentration account may be interest bearing or may have an overdraft limit attached to it to cater for the pool running into deficit. In some countries where credit interest on current accounts is prohibited, balances are concentrated and then swept offshore overnight. This technique has been in place for a number of years in the United States.

Foreign currency accounts

As discussed in the last chapter, foreign currency accounts are used when there is a large enough volume of receipts or payments in the relevant foreign currency. There, however, foreign currency accounts were looked at from the standpoint of a company with purely domestic operations, but making foreign currency payments to suppliers or receiving foreign currency payments from customers. When a company acquires overseas subsidiaries, which in turn have foreign currency receipts and payments to handle, the pattern of foreign currency accounts can become more complex. This is because these subsidiaries will also want foreign currency accounts to manage their own foreign currency transactions.

In addition such a company may either be financing itself in foreign currencies, for example through a commercial paper programme whose proceeds are swapped to its domestic currency, or borrowing in foreign currencies to manage its translation exposure. To manage these transactions the treasury team may also need a set of foreign currency accounts.

There are a number of possible ways of managing these foreign currency accounts, three of which are outlined below.

Foreign currency accounts in country of operation

In the first approach, all foreign currency holdings are maintained by overseas subsidiaries in their own country. Consider a US company with three overseas subsidiaries situated in Canada, Singapore and the United Kingdom, as shown in Figure 15.2.

Such a structure may be used where balances held in foreign currency accounts are small or minimal and local subsidiaries have substantial local

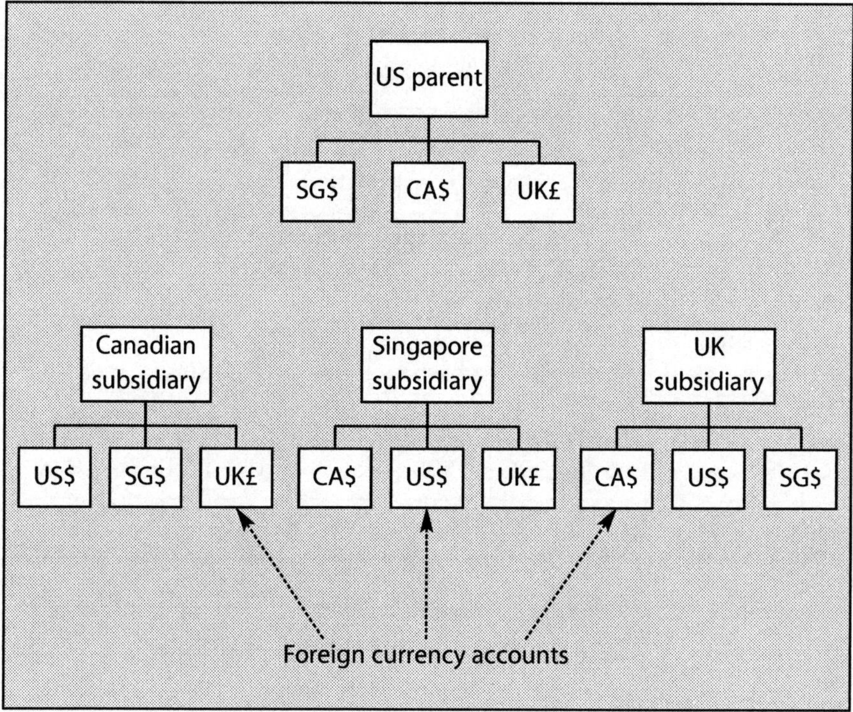

Figure 15.2 US parent with three overseas subsidiaries, each with its own foreign currency account in country of operation

autonomy. This structure has all the benefits of local administration. However, the problem that this structure presents for the treasury team is identifying and maintaining a record of the balances held in the individual foreign currency accounts. Usually the treasury team is reliant on daily or weekly faxes or e-mails from the subsidiaries, although some treasury systems have the capability of reporting on bank balances in overseas subsidiaries.

Foreign currency accounts in country of currency

If balances held in the accounts or transactions passing through them are more substantial, however, consideration may need to be given to whether any of these accounts should be pooled, as shown in Figure 15.3. This may more easily be achieved if foreign currency accounts are situated in the country of the currency. In that case they may be available to be pooled between themselves and with local balances. The management

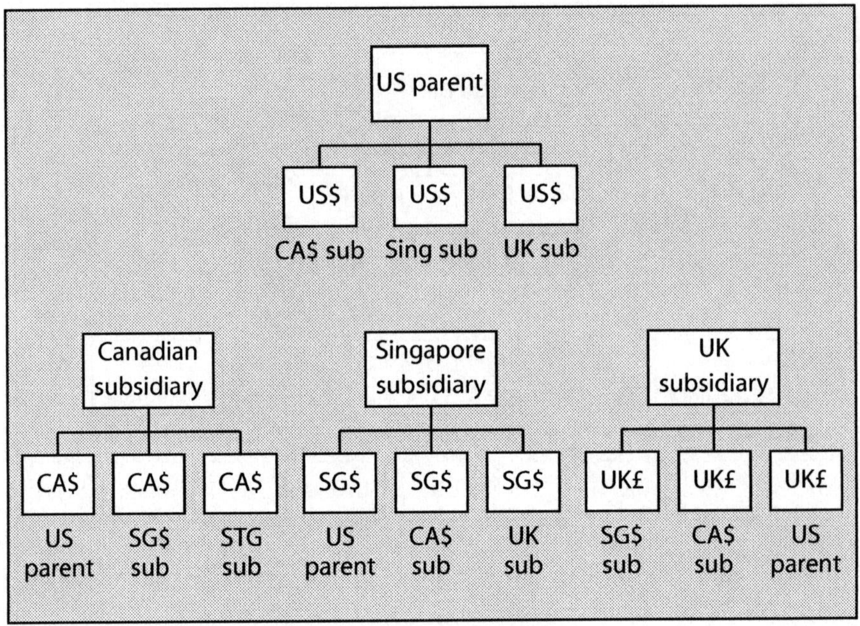

Figure 15.3 US parent with three overseas subsidiaries, each with its own foreign currency account maintained in the country of currency

of bank accounts is then often under the control of the local cash manager (Figure 15.4).

The advantage of such a structure is that, provided it is permitted by the regulatory authorities of both the currency country and the relevant subsidiary, the foreign currency accounts can all be pooled and also pooled with the local balances. However, good cash forecasting and communications are important. When managing the liquidity position of the pool, the local pool controller needs to be certain that accounts will not be hit with same-day value payments or receipts after action to fund or deposit the liquidity in the pool has been taken.

With such a structure a number of considerations need to be taken into account. As already explained, notional pooling results in any interest charge or credit being applied to the net balance in the pool, regardless of the balances on individual accounts. Assume that the net balance on the UK£ pool was virtually zero, but that the Singapore subsidiary UK£ account was in credit and the US subsidiary was in debit. In this case effectively the Singapore subsidiary would have lent money to the UK£ banking pool and the US subsidiary will have borrowed from the same banking pool. As a result:

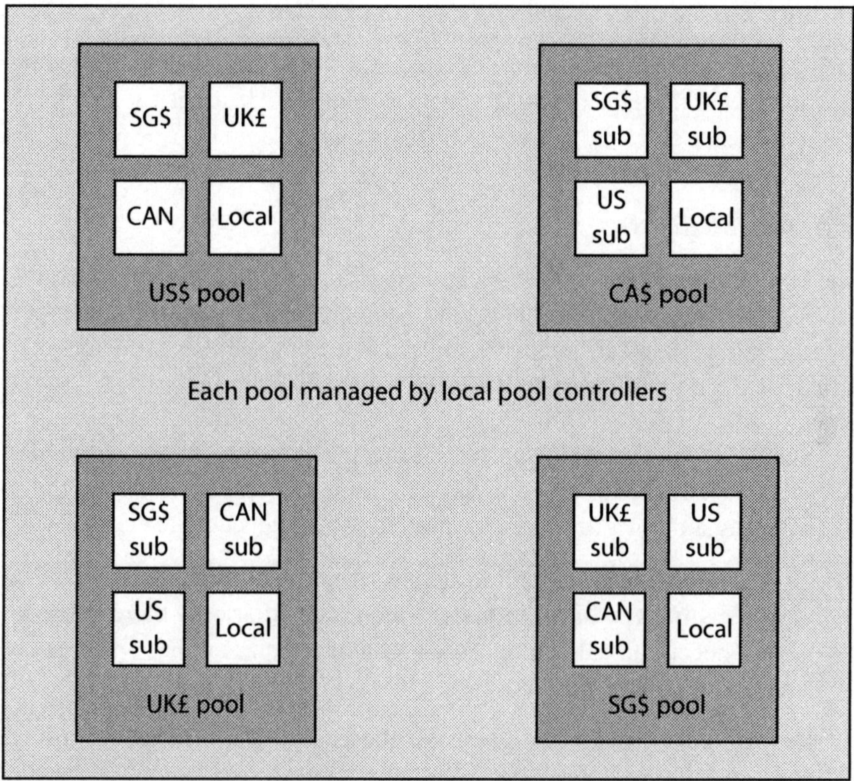

Figure 15.4 Foreign currency accounts belonging to subsidiaries and US parent opened in country of currency and pooled with local balances

- The interest in respect of these loans needs to be recorded. Who will maintain these records and calculate interest due and payable from members of the pool? Very often this is a service that can be offered by the bank.
- The tax authorities in Singapore will want to be sure that the Singapore subsidiary is receiving a proper rate of interest on its UK£ balances. Equally the US tax authorities will want to ensure that the rate of interest charged on the US subsidiary overdraft is not excessive.
- Thin capitalization rules limit the extent of borrowing by a subsidiary with an overseas parent. This limit is normally set in relation to the company's capital and reserves; for instance debts cannot exceed six times share capital and reserves. The implications of thin capitalization rules need to be borne in mind when managing currency pools.
- Reports may need to be delivered to the central bank.

Foreign currency accounts at treasury centre

In this case all the foreign currency accounts would be opened at the same location as the treasury centre (regional or global). The treasury may have a much greater control over the company's bank accounts.

Different structures

The choice of different structures and permutations of different structures is obviously very wide. Examples have been given above of just three types of international bank account structures. There are a number of factors that influence the type of structure a company may choose.

- Size of balances. How substantial are the balances in the individual accounts and the flows going through those accounts? The greater these balances and flows, the more the need to pool or concentrate the balances.
- Company organization and structure. A company that operates on a very decentralized basis with stand-alone subsidiaries is more likely to have a decentralized bank account structure than one that operates on a highly centralized basis.
- Reporting systems. How good are the company's internal recording and reporting systems? The better the company's systems, the more likely the treasury department is to want to take control of bank accounts and balances throughout the countries in which the company operates.
- Regulatory environment. What is the regulatory environment in the countries in which a company operates as regards the pooling of resident and non-resident accounts?
- Tax. The company's own particular tax structure will have a bearing on the bank account structure finally adopted.

Managing surpluses and deficits in local banking pools

A mechanism needs to be found for extracting surpluses and reducing overdrafts in the local banking pools as well as in the foreign currency accounts. Companies adopt a number of different approaches. They may leave local subsidiaries to deposit surplus funds or finance any shortfall on the local money markets. This approach works quite well when local balances are small or surpluses and overdrafts are temporary. Alternatively, a regional or group treasury may operate an account within the banking pool. This enables it to extract funds from the pool or transfer funds into it according to local cash forecasts (Figure 15.5).

The treasury maintains an account within the banking pool (in this case SG$), enabling it to extract funds from the pool or fund any shortages. FX swaps are used to manage the foreign exchange exposure that would otherwise result from such a transaction.

Alternatively, on the basis of local cash forecasts, the group or regional treasury request transfers to be made from local banking pools or foreign currency accounts. These transfers are made to local foreign currency accounts maintained by the treasury department (Figure 15.6).

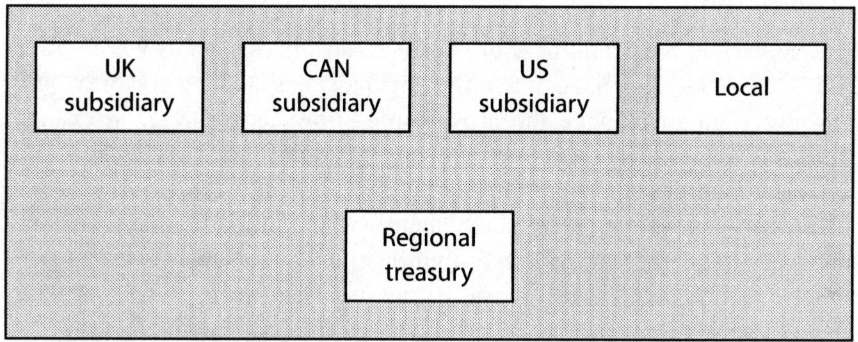

Figure 15.5 Structure of pooled accounts for SG$

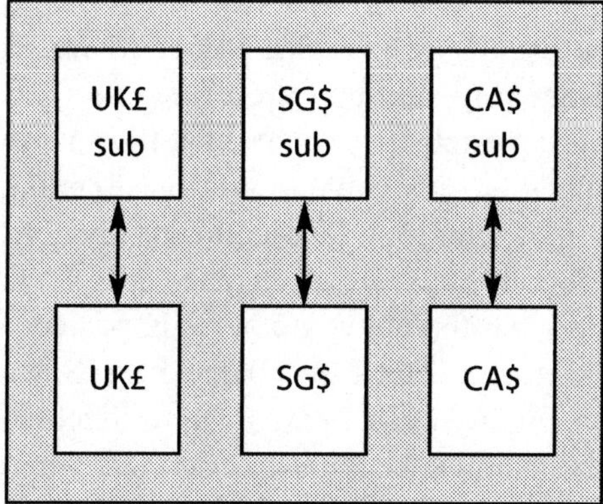

Figure 15.6 Transfers to/from currency accounts maintained by treasury

Intercompany loans

It should be noted that all transfers between subsidiaries give rise to intercompany loans. Exactly the same considerations apply as those applying to the loans arising on banking pools. However there are two further considerations. First, with intercompany loans the administration must be maintained by the company. The company needs to be sure it has the infrastructure to do this. Second, witholding taxes often apply to interest paid on these intercompany loans. This gives rise to identifying the company's ability to reclaim these taxes.

NETTING

Introduction

Companies that have a number of overseas subsidiaries, all of whom trade with each other and have intercompany payables and receivables, will probably want to manage the cross-border flows and foreign exchange exposures inherent in such intercompany relationships. This section is a very brief overview of intercompany netting.

Netting systems can be either bilateral, where amounts due from one subsidiary to another are netted, or multilateral, where subsidiaries participating in the netting make or receive one payment in respect of all their intercompany payables and receivables. Multilateral netting requires a netting centre that coordinates the process and manages the purchase and sale of the necessary foreign exchange.

Outline of multilateral netting system

Netting systems are usually receivables-based, where participants notify the netting centre what they are due to receive from other participants, or payables-based, where participants report what they are due to pay.

Consider the payable/receivable situation existing between four subsidiaries shown in Table 15.4. The company indebtedness represents intercompany transactions that have taken place over the last month and are now due to be settled. All the above amounts have been converted into a single common currency, in this case UK£. These flows are represented diagrammatically in Figure 15.7. Intercompany indebtedness can be put into a spread sheet, as shown in Table 15.5. In this very simple example, use of netting has reduced currency flows in and out from UK£11,400 to UK£5600.

Table 15.4 Intercompany payables and receivables stated in a common currency

Payer → / Receiver ↓	*UK*	*Euro zone*	*USA*	*Japan*
UK		1600	3000	
Euro zone	200		2000	1400
USA		200		2400
Japan	400	200		

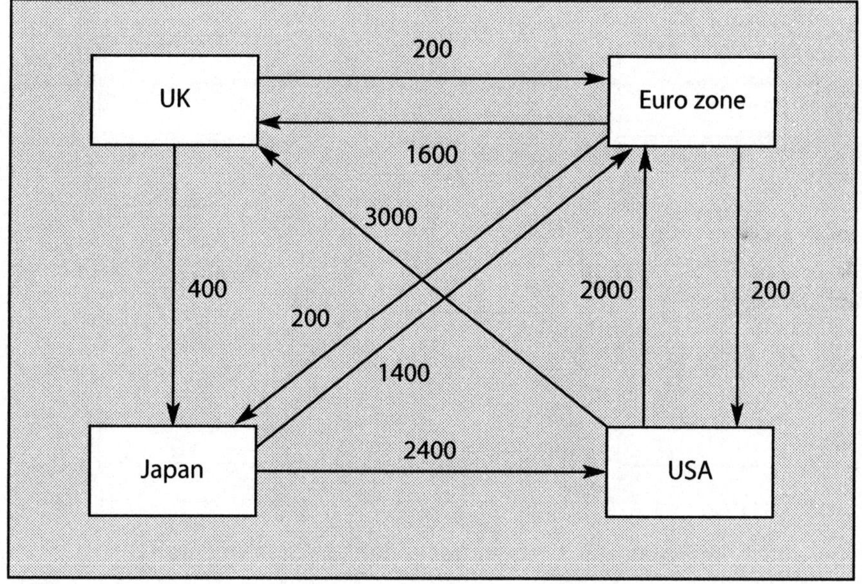

Figure 15.7 Intercompany flows

Benefits of netting

In the above example, the number of intercompany flows has been reduced from nine to four, and the value of these flows has been reduced from UK£11,400 to UK£5600 (see Table 15.5). Benefits include:

- A reduction in foreign exchange costs. Without netting, the amount of currency bought and sold with the banks would have amounted to

Table 15.5 Netting of intercompany indebtedness

Participant	*Payments*	*Receipts*	*Net flows*	*Flows eliminated*
UK	600	4600	4000	600
Euro zone	2000	3600	1600	2000
Japan	3800	600	(3200)	600
USA	5000	2600	(2400)	2600
TOTALS	11,400	11,400	+ 5600	5800
			– 5600	

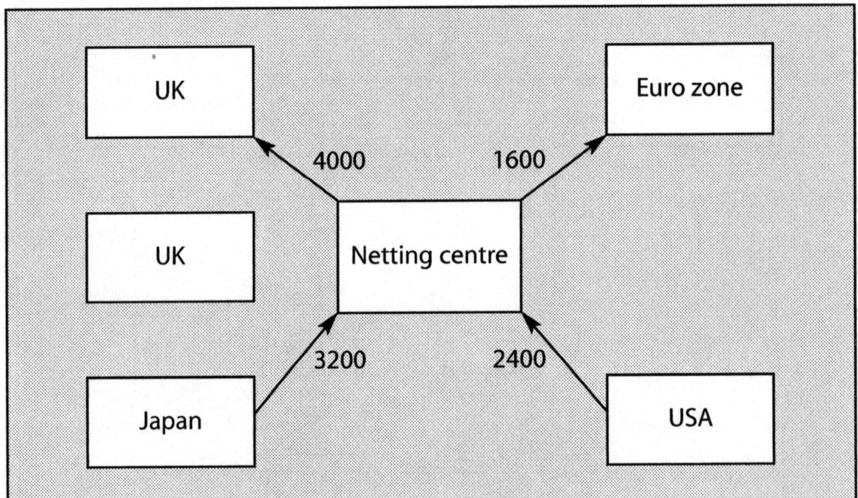

Figure 15.8 Intercompany indebtedness netted to four payments

UK£11,400. The reduction in the volume of foreign exchange represents a saving on the bid offer spread. Moreover, many small subsidiaries would probably purchase or sell the currency with their local bank, where they would receive below market rates. Experienced treasury professionals at the netting centre would be able to use their expertise to buy and sell currency at the best market rate. They would also be buying and selling larger blocks of currency.

- A saving in cross-border transfer costs, including any lifting fees, and a possible saving on float.

- A disciplined control over intercompany settlements. Considerable costs could be incurred if there is a lack of discipline over the timing of intercompany payables. For example, in the case above, if the UK settled their liability to euro-country subsidiaries before those subsidiaries settled with the UK, the group would be exposed to foreign exchange movements in €/UK£ between those two dates.
- A reduction in the number of foreign currency accounts held by subsidiaries.

Aspects of netting systems

- Some companies include third-party trade payables in their netting systems, with a payment to the creditors being made directly from the netting centre or being channelled via a group participant. Third-party trade receipts are more difficult to include in the system, although some companies have developed techniques to include them. Increasingly, companies are adding financial flows such as foreign currency purchases and sales (subsidiaries buying and selling foreign currency via group treasury and settling through the netting), settlement of intra-group loans, and payment and collection of interest and principal on intercompany loans.
- Credit periods need to be established. Ideally all participants should have the same credit period, but leading and lagging techniques may be introduced where some subsidiaries are cash poor.
- All participants must be aware of netting settlement dates. These are usually published well in advance. Netting periods can vary, with monthly settlement being the most usual. Large companies sometimes run their settlements weekly or every two weeks.
- A method of calculating the exchange rates needs to be identified. Some groups use the spot rate taken two days before settlement, other groups might use a rate fixed for a period.
- A netting centre needs to be established. This is usually the treasury centre, which is staffed with treasury professionals. Some companies run global netting systems, while others use regional netting.
- Banks will operate netting systems for customers, or a company may decide to operate the netting itself. Where companies operate netting themselves, this may vary from spreadsheets on a PC to modules available with most treasury management systems.

CASE STUDY

Pooling

Your company intends to implement a pooling of bank accounts, both domestic and foreign currency.

1. What do you think the benefits of pooling might be?
2. What due diligence questions should you ask?
3. What kinds of documentation would you expect to have to undertake?

Netting

Monthly amounts in 000s

Payer ⟶	*UK*	*USA*	*Euro zone*	*Japan*
Receiver				
UK		867	926	542
USA	1897		1085	
Euro zone		1335		789
Japan	195,000		156,600	
Australia		924		

- Spot rates versus UK£

UK£/US$	1.6563
UK£/JPY	217.6
€/UK£	.7093
UK£/AU$	2.2634

- Borrowing costs in UK are 5.5 per cent.
- Transaction costs are UK£6 per transfer.
- FX spread is .01 of 1 per cent.
- Paying countries pay in the currency of creditor (receiver) country.

Questions

1. What is each county's net position (calculate in UK£)?
2. What are the annual cost savings from the introduction of a netting system?

SOLUTIONS

Pooling

Benefits

- Reduction of interest charges.
- Fewer banks used by a company with less use of resources to manage those relationships and accounts.
- Single funding decision.
- Opportunity for book transfers between two pooled accounts – important where cross-border payments involving some of the less developed clearing systems are involved.
- Increased liquidity for subsidiaries, who effectively access the pool for funds.
- Parent can access the pool to pay down borrowings.

Due diligence questions would comprise

- Is pooling permitted? Pooling is not a product that can be offered by banks in all countries (e.g. the United States).
- Can resident and non-resident accounts participate in the pool? A company may have a number of domestic (resident) bank accounts that it wishes to pool, and include in the pool bank accounts in the same currency but held by an overseas subsidiary (non-resident).
- What rules apply to resident accounts and to non-resident accounts? In some countries interest may be paid on non-resident accounts but not on resident accounts, or vice versa.
- Tax issues:
  - As mentioned, members of a domestic banking pool may receive interest on accounts within the pool that are in credit. In turn, interest may be charged to pool members on debit balances on accounts within the pool. (If any member of the pool is non-resident, the tax authorities of the pool member's country will want to ensure that interest at a market rate is paid on accounts in credit.) What is the withholding tax treatment for such interest payments and receipts?
  - If pool members with accounts in debit are charged interest, will it be tax deductible?

- Is there a possibility of contravening thin capitalization rules in certain countries? (Thin capitalization rules require a minimum of equity capital in the financial structure of a company owned by a foreign parent.) Pool members with accounts in debit (overdraft) will be increasing their debt levels. What impact will this have on the company's debt/equity?
- Stamp duty.

- Do the regulatory authorities allow cross-border, cross-currency pooling? Do the regulatory authorities allow the pooling of accounts in the same currency but belonging to non-resident companies? In other words, if central treasury is located in Singapore, can central treasury pool all US$ foreign currency accounts owned by overseas subsidiaries but located in Singapore?
- The ability to apply legal right of offset to accounts may affect the pooling objectives a company has. If, for instance, a company wants to apply pooling to euro accounts held in London by a UK subsidiary and to euro accounts held in France by a French subsidiary, does the bank have a legal right of setoff of the balances held by the UK subsidiary with those of the French subsidiary in the event that one of the entities goes into liquidation?
- Are there any restrictions on intercompany lending that effectively apply when subsidiary balances are pooled?
- How are banks obliged to calculate the reserve ratios imposed on them by their central bank, on a net or gross basis? To make pooling effective, the bank must be able to report a customer's balances on a net basis. If they have to report on a gross basis, the cost of lodging free or low interest deposits will have to be passed on to the customer.
- Does the company want to make same-day value payments from accounts in the pool, and if so what cut-off times need to be available? Consider, for instance, a euro pool managed from London with balances that must be invested or funded in the money markets.
- If funds are to be moved across borders then a consistent value dating practice from the bank needs to be available.
- Financial benefits:
  - How much money is on the table?
  - How badly do we need to capture it?
  - How capable are we of capturing that money (consider, for example, systems, company structure and philosophy)?

Documentation and agreements

Once the financial case has been made for pooling and the necessary due diligence has been undertaken, then certain documentation and agreements need to be put in place for pooling to become effective.

- Pooling Agreement This will contain a number of clauses, among the more significant being:

  Representations and warranties. Parties to the agreement warrant that they are not violating any law or regulation, or breaching any covenants by entering into the pooling arrangement. In addition they will confirm that there are no prior liens on any credit balances.

  Agent or lead company. One company in the group will need to act as a pool manager and coordination point with the bank. This is likely to be the treasury centre.

  Agreement on interest calculation. How will interest be charged or credited? In the United Kingdom, overdraft interest is charged by reference to the bank's base rate plus a certain percentage (e.g. base rate + 1 per cent). Credit is usually calculated by reference to the base rate minus a percentage. The frequency and dates of interest charging will also be established.

  Set off. This clause enables the bank to set off any balances in the pool.
  There will also be sections on: waivers, assignments, notices and demands, provision for changing agreement and signatories.

- Cross guarantees. These are guarantees given by each of the participating members of the pool, guaranteeing the other pool members.

- Legal right of set off. The bank will need assurance that if a member of the pool with a debit balance goes into liquidation they can claim the credit balances from other members of the pool.

- Tax indemnity. Should the tax authorities for some reason claim that the bank is due to pay tax on the structure, they are indemnified. This is normally provided by the legal entity that houses the relevant treasury operation.

- Interest apportionment. Where the bank apportions interest among the pool members, there needs to be agreement on how this is to be done.

Netting

Figures in UK£000s

Payer ⟶ Receiver ↓	*UK*	*USA*	*Euro zone*	*Japan*	*Total*
UK		867	926	542	2335
USA	1145		657		1802
Euro zone		947		560	1507
Japan	896		720		1616
Australia		408			408
	2041	2222	2303	1102	7668

	Payments	*Receipts*	*Gross*	*Net*	*Flows saved*
UK	2041	2335	4376	296	2041
USA	2222	1802	4024	(420)	1802
Euro zone	2303	1507	3810	(796)	1507
Japan	1102	1616	2718	514	1102
Australia		408	408	408	
	7668	7668			6452

Savings:

Transactions	Original	10		
	Now	5		
		5	@ UK£6 per transfer	30
Float saved	7,668,000 *.055 *2/365			2311
FX	6,452,000 * .0001			645
		Monthly		2986
		Annual		UK£35,832

CHAPTER 16

Liquidity Management

INTRODUCTION

Liquidity management involves the management of day-to-day cash deficits and surpluses. A company's cashflow is never stable from one day to another, one week to another or one month to another. Payrolls and suppliers may be paid at the end of the month, but payments from customers not received until the beginning of the following month. Capital expenditure programmes, taxation and dividend payments often result in lumpy expenditure patterns, and the cash outflows that they represent are offset fully or partly by the regular cash inflows from the company's underlying business. Some companies have a seasonal business, with cashflows from the business being stronger at certain periods of the year.

A company whose financing structure consists partly of debt will usually have a level of 'core' debt. This is represented by bonds (public and private), together with various forms of bank debt. The purpose of this core debt is to fund the long-term development of the organization. However the swings and fluctuations in a company's cashflow also need to be managed.

Effective liquidity management involves an efficient information system that can answer the following questions:

- How much cash does and will the company have?
- Where is the cash?
- When will the cash become available to the company?
- What are the different interest costs/opportunities available?
- In which direction are interest rates and cash positions likely to move?

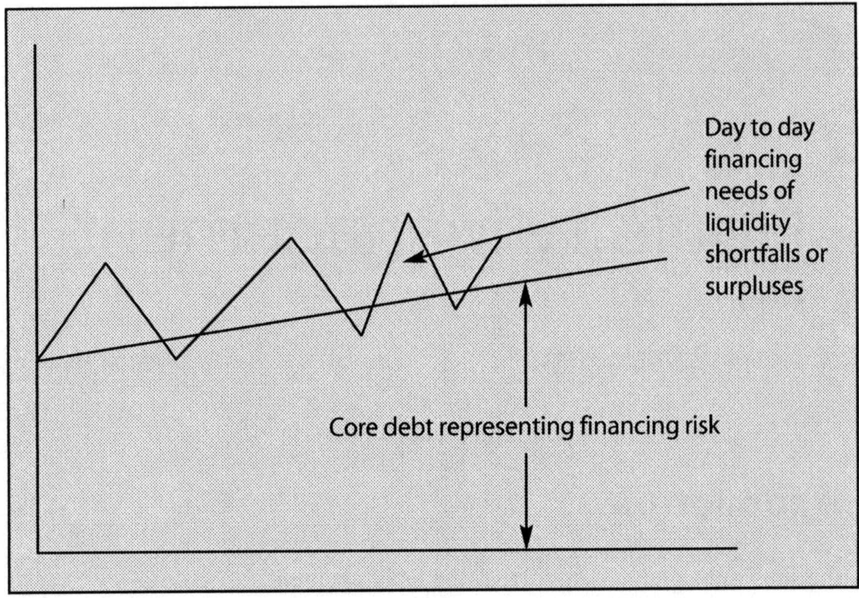

Figure 16.1 Core debt versus short-term liquidity fluctuations

Signs of poor liquidity management, as discussed in Chapter 1, are:

- A company having insufficient resources to pay liabilities when they fall due, resulting in penalty costs or loss of reputation.
- A company simultaneously making both cash deposits and short-term borrowings. This means that cash resources are not being used to reduce short-term financings. The resulting cost is the difference between the deposit rate and the cost of borrowing.
- An organization incurring losses as a result of deposits being made with financial institutions that fail, or the purchase of financial instruments that cannot be subsequently sold or realized to meet cash needs.
- Idle cash balances.
- Too many or an insufficient number of credit lines.

Effective liquidity management involves processes and systems for determining and predicting the timing and duration of cash surpluses and deficits (cash forecasting) together with procedures for their management (liquidity instruments).

CASH FORECASTING

Cash forecasts are generally made over three time horizons: short, medium and long term.

Short-term cash forecasts

Generally these cover approximately 30 days. Short-term forecasts are usually used exclusively by the treasury department to manage liquidity on a day-to-day basis. Their purpose is to aid decisions on the management of short-term borrowings and deposits, to ensure that there are no idle balances sitting in bank accounts and that shortages are detected and financed in the most cost-effective manner.

Short-term cash forecasts are generally prepared on a daily basis for the following five to ten days. Opening cleared cash balances at banks are calculated and adjusted for anticipated daily cash receipts and cash payments. This day-by-day forecast is ideally updated daily. The following 20 days are often prepared on a week-by-week basis, since trends, as opposed to daily movements, are more important.

Short-term forecasts are usually prepared by the treasury department from records at their disposal, or information supplied by other parts of the business. Those companies with stable and predictable cashflows sometimes prepare parts of these forecasts from historic data, updated for known circumstances.

Preparation of short-term cash forecasts

It is normally the responsibility of the cash manager to prepare short-term cash forecasts. An example of a daily cash worksheet is shown in Table 16.1.

The opening balance will be the cleared balance reported through the company's bank balance reporting system. It will represent the total of cleared balances at the start of the day on the banking pool, or the net of different individual accounts with a particular bank. The bank balance reporting system will also inform the company of those payments or receipts that are being cleared through the clearing system that day, and for which their accounts will be debited or credited by the end of the day.

In the example in Table 16.1, the net total of opening cleared balances for Bank A on the 15th was UK£0.5 million. The bank balance reporting system also informs the cash manager that UK£10.5 million of payments (either cheques or payments through the ACH system) will clear that day and will be debited to the company's bank accounts. In addition there are UK£11.1 million of receipts clearing through the system. The treasury

Table 16.1 Bank A: 30-day forecast at 15 February 20– –

February	*15th UK£ million*	*16th UK£ million*	*17th UK£ million*	*18th UK£ million*
Opening balance	0.5*	–	–	–
Payments clearing through clearing system	(10.5)*			
Cheques		(5.0)	(2.5)	(1.5)
ACH payments		(5.0)	(1.3)	
Receipts clearing through clearing system	11.1*			
Receipts ACH		2.5	2.0	1.5
Receipts cheques		3.0	2.5	1.0
Same-day transfers	(5.5)		(10.0)	
Maturing deals	10.0	(5.0)	(2.5)	(25.0)
Maturing overnight deal		5.1	(4.4)	(16.2)
Closing balance	5.1	(4.4)	(16.2)	(40.2)
Deposit/fund – overnight	(5.1)	4.4	16.2	40.2

* Established from bank balance reporting system

department have been requested to make telegraphic transfers totalling UK£5.5 million. Finally there is a maturing bank deposit for UK£10.0 million. The cash manager therefore knows that, at the end of the day, there will be an estimated UK£5.1 million of funds in the pool accounts held with Bank A that will need to be deposited.

For the other days of the forecast the cash manager will have different sources of information for compiling the cash forecast. Some companies, for example, have built up quite accurate data on how quickly a 'cheque run' will clear through the banking system. For instance they may have historic data showing that for a batch of cheques prepared and dispatched on day one (say a Monday), approximately 50 per cent will clear five working days later, 25 per cent eight working days later, 10 per cent nine working days later and the balance over the following three days. Payments through the ACH can be accurately managed. If the cash manager is informed that the payroll will be submitted to the ACH on the 25th day of the month, then the payments will be debited to on the 27th (if the ACH works to a three-day clearing cycle).

Income can be more difficult to predict accurately, since the payments are being made by third parties and the company has no control over when these will be made. In these circumstances the cash manager usually has to work from historic data and trends. In addition, the cash manager will have to forecast other non-operating cash receipts and payments. Here the manager's forecasting skill is often dependent on his/her relationship with other company departments and the ability to identify potential transactions in the company. Sometimes treasury will be requested to make these payments telegraphically or will be told they will be received telegraphically. Such payments may be intercompany funding requests and payments on acquisitions and disposals.

Finally information on maturing deals is available from the treasury management system.

Uses of short-term cash forecasts

In the above example, the cash manager can tell that at the end of the day there will be UK£5.1 million of cleared funds in the pool of bank accounts held with Bank A. These funds will need to be deposited, or transferred to another bank where accounts at the close of day are forecast to be in deficit.

The cash manager can also see that there is a growing deficit on the accounts with Bank A over the next four days. The decision needs to be made as to how that deficit should be funded. It may be that it will be reversed by some inflows over the following few days, in which case the decision may be made to fund the deficit on a day-to-day basis with uncommitted funds. It may be however that the deficit will not be reduced in the short term, in which case the cash manager may consider drawing down on committed funds or taking surplus funds from an overseas subsidiary using a short-term FX swap.

Medium-term forecasts

If short-term cash forecasts are generally prepared by the cash manager in the treasury department for treasury purposes, the medium-term cash forecast is generally prepared for financial management purposes by the various finance departments within the organization. Equity analysts are putting more and more emphasis on cashflow as an indicator of the financial health of a company. Company directors also are seeing cash control as one of the primary tools in the creation of value. As a result the management of cash, effected through a whole series of controls over every aspect of working capital and capital expenditure, becomes a key management issue. Central to these controls is the efficient and effective forecasting of cash over the budget or current financial year and beyond.

Most companies will produce medium-term cash forecasts on a month-by-month basis, which are then updated at regular intervals. Many will produce medium-term cash forecasts that cover a rolling 12–18 months. Such rolling forecasts ensure that the control of cash does not just go from financial year to financial year, but that a consistent control is taken over a 12-month cycle.

Medium-term cash forecasts are usually prepared on a receipts and payments basis, with emphasis being placed on the key drivers in cash management.

Use by treasury of medium-term forecasts

Medium-term cash forecasts are used by the treasury department for a number of purposes, such as the management of headroom within medium-term banking facilities and forecasting the observance of key financial covenants within borrowing instruments. Treasury also uses medium-term forecasts to:

- Strategically manage short-term liquidity. For instance a treasury department with some cash surpluses, if it believes interest rates may decline more rapidly than the market predicts, may use the medium-term cash forecasts in determining whether to deposit those funds for a more extended period than usual.
- Manage the actual interest cost, which for many treasury departments is one of their annual objectives. The medium-term forecast aids the management of derivative and liquidity instruments to meet this objective.

Long-term cash forecasts

Long-term cash forecasts generally cover a period of three to five years and are produced during the strategic planning process. These cash forecasts are only indicative of the likely trend of a company's cash generation. Long-term cash forecasts are little used in the management of liquidity, but have a greater significance in the management of a company's debt structure.

Aspects of cash forecasting

Most companies accept the need for accurate cash forecasts but few are able to produce them on a consistent basis. One of the main reasons for this is the difficulty of forecasting the timing of certain major items of cash expenditure and receipt. For instance, a company may have planned the purchase of certain items of capital equipment, but identifying the exact timing of the payments for the plant may be extremely difficult. If the assets are being specifically manufactured, timing of payment depends on delivery of the order by the company, the design and production at the supplier, and then delivery, testing and acceptance by the company. Alternatively, expenditure may relate to the development of freehold premises, with all the problems of planning consent and construction progress. Working capital in some companies can fluctuate quite substantially. While companies can forecast the total cash outflow or inflow for the year as a whole, it is extremely difficult to achieve the same accuracy on a month-by-month basis. There are however, a number of general principles that, when applied, can lead to more efficient cash forecasting:

- Are full variances produced of actual cashflow against that budgeted or most recently forecast? This analysis should give an understanding as to permanent variances and those that are due to timing. What lessons for cash forecasting can be learned from these variances?
- Are the forecasts being prepared in sufficient detail to enable meaningful variance analysis to be undertaken? Is there a continual review of the underlying assumptions used in the preparation of the forecasts? Who vets and reviews these assumptions?
- Is sensitivity analysis used to determine the possible boundaries of cash inflows and outflows? Is the sensitivity analysis sensible and related to the historic volatility of the business?
- Who prepares the forecasts and for what purpose? Sometimes medium-term cash forecasts are prepared for treasury by the finance function. If the finance function has no involvement in managing actual cashflow to that budgeted, then it is unlikely they will give the exercise high priority and may not be too concerned with its accuracy.
- Are the time horizons used in the forecast appropriate? This very much depends on the volatility of the cash cycles in the business.
- How frequently are forecasts, actual cashflow and variance analysis reports prepared? The more regularly they are undertaken, then generally the more accurate they become.

- Specific forecasting techniques should be applied to each component of the cash forecast. For instance, to forecast the timing of cash receipts from customer trade payments requires an understanding of the payment methods used by customers (ACH, cheque, bill of exchange etc.), the company's payment terms and billing cycle, and the payment routines on their receivables ledger used by customers. It may also require an analysis of the comparative importance of different customers and different payment terms attached to different groups of customers.
- Do other related items need to be forecast? This may include foreign exchange receipts and payments that are related to forecasts for overseas sales.
- Are incentives aligned to the management of cash against that budgeted and forecast, and does a cash management culture pervade the whole organization?

It needs to be remembered that successful cash forecasting is often heavily reliant on the individuals preparing the forecasts, and their experience, skill and knowledge of the business and its current operations.

INTEREST RATE DERIVATIVES

Forward rate agreements

Many companies manage the interest rate exposure presented by fluctuations in cashflow by the use of forward rate agreements (FRAs). An FRA is an agreement between two parties that determines the interest rate that will apply to a notional future loan or deposit of an agreed amount and specified period.

The FRA essentially allows the forward fixing of interest rates on money market transactions. Settlement is by the payment of a compensating amount from one party to the other so that both parties are effectively locked into the fixed rate specified in the FRA. In terms of its end result, the FRA achieves the same purpose as the forward–forward arrangement described in Chapter 11 (the creation of a fixed-rate borrowing for a defined period in the future using a borrowing and a deposit), but without the undesirable balance sheet effects.

The market uses a convention for describing the period for which the interest protection applies. It can be written in a number of ways: for example, 3–6, 3 × 9, 3 vs 6. It is spoken of as either '3s', '6s' or '3s against 6s'. The first figure denotes the period in months to the start of the period for which interest protection is sought. The second figure is the time in months to the end of that period. In British Bankers Association guidelines these are referred to as the 'settlement date', 'maturity date', and 'contract period', which is the period of the FRA.

Prices of FRAs are quoted on the same basis as money market interest rates, as a percentage per annum figure.

Parties to an FRA are either buyers or sellers. The buyer is seeking protection against a rise in interest rates, while the seller is seeking protection against a fall.

Settlement arrangements

Settlement takes place at the start of the contract period. Since FRAs are based on money market cash advances in which interest is due at maturity, the settlement amount is discounted (at the reference rate) back to the settlement date.

The following formula is used to calculate the compensation due:

$$\frac{(L-R) \text{ or } (R-L) \times D \times A}{[(B \times 100) + (D \times L)]}$$

where L = Settlement rate (LIBOR), R = Contract reference rate, D = Days in contract period, A = Notional principal amount, B = Days basis (360 or 365).

Example

A company forecasts a liquidity shortfall of US$50 million in six months' time. The shortfall is forecast to extend for a further six months, after which it will be eliminated by positive movements in working capital. To cover the interest rate exposure, the company buys a 6–12 FRA at 3.00 per cent for US$50 million. In six months, six-month US$ LIBOR has risen to 3.5 per cent. The company will receive on the FRA contract (assuming a contract period of 181 days):

$$\text{US\$50 m} \times (3.5\text{–}3.0) \times 181/360 = \text{US\$125,694.44}$$

Since this amount will be settled at the beginning of the contract period, it must be discounted using the formula above. The net settlement is thus:

$$\frac{(3.5-3.0) \times 181 \times 50\text{m}}{[(360 \times 100) + (181 \times 3.5)]} = \text{US\$123,520.82}$$

THE MANAGEMENT OF CASH SURPLUSES

Treasury policies

Treasury policies need to address a number of specific issues relating to the management of cash surpluses.

Security

The minimum short-term credit rating attached to any instrument that treasury is authorized to purchase, together with the minimum short-term rating for any financial institution that cash may be deposited with, must be specified. Policies will also specify if there are any circumstances in which an unrated financial instrument may be purchased. Additionally:

- The maximum investment period applicable to different credit ratings. For instance, a treasury department may be permitted to invest in A–1+/P1 rated instruments for periods of up to six months, and A–1/P1 rated instruments only for periods of up to three months.
- The maximum amount to be deposited with any one financial institution, and the maximum amount of financial instruments issued by any one institution that can be held. The policy may specify for instance, that the maximum deposit with any bank rated A–1/P1 is US$50 million and that the maximum outstanding instruments issued by an A–1/P1 institution or company and held by the company cannot exceed US$50 million. Credit limits for individual institutions will need to be listed, either in the treasury policies or elsewhere, so that exposures can be tracked by dealers and the middle office.

Tenor or maturity

It is a specific principle for most companies that they will not purchase any financial instrument with a maturity extending beyond the forecast period of available funds. If a company forecasts having US$20 million available for investment for three months, any instrument they invest in must mature on or before the expiry of that forecast period.

Permitted instruments

The policies should specify the instruments that the treasury department can purchase or invest in managing cash surpluses. These will cover government securities, bank CDs, commercial paper, bank deposits and money market funds.

Marketability

Cash forecasts are not always accurate and unforeseen demands may arise for that surplus cash. Some companies' treasury policies cover the marketability of any permitted instruments.

Reporting

The monthly treasury report will specify how cash surpluses have been managed with investments analyzed between: instrument, counterparty. maturity period or tenor, and value of investments.

Treasury policies example

Management of cash surpluses

The following is an abbreviated example of treasury policies covering the management of cash surpluses. The company is naturally short of funds; however the following policies are designed to manage temporary cash surpluses that arise from disposals or corporate restructurings.

- Authorized instruments:
  - money market funds
  - cash deposits
  - commercial paper
  - corporate bonds.
- Rating
  The maximum permitted investments are shown in Table 16.2.

  The company will not purchase instruments issued by, or deposit with, entities with a rating below A.

  A separate list of all approved financial institutions or corporate entities is attached. No investment or deposit can be made with a financial institution or corporate entity that is not on the list, even if they meet the approved rating.
- No investments can be made for maturities which extend beyond available cash surpluses as established by the latest cash forecasts.

Table 16.2 Excerpt from treasury report relating ratings to permitted investment

Rating	*Maximum investment*	*Maximum period*
AAA/Aaa	US$50 million	6 months
AA/Aa or above	US$25 million	3 months
A/a or above	US$20 million	1 month

In managing the interest rate exposure arising from short-term cash surpluses, treasury may use forward rate agreements. No hedges may be taken out for any periods extending beyond 12 months without the prior approval of the risk committee.

A typical report may look like that in Table 16.3. Where substantial surpluses exist, the report is often accompanied by a bar chart showing the maturity of current deposits and investments. Many companies may also include the current medium-term cash forecast.

Table 16.3 Excerpt from treasury report regarding the management of surplus funds

Instrument	*Counter-party*	*Credit rating*	*Remaining tenor/ maturity*	*Value US$ million*	*Interest rate*
Commercial paper					
	Company A	A1/P1	30 days	5.5	3.3 %
	Company B	A1/P1	25 days	10.2	3.35 %
Total CP				15.7	3.33 %
Bank deposits					
	Bank A	A1+/P1	56 days	15.0	3.25 %
	Bank B	A1/P1	48 days	10.0	3.30 %
	Bank C	None (deposit overnight)	1 day	2.5	2.75 %
Total deposits				27.5	3.22 %
Grand total				43.2	3.26 %

INSTRUMENTS FOR MANAGING LIQUIDITY SURPLUSES

Treasury bills

Treasury bills are short-term government securities issued in the government's domestic currency and with maturities of up to one year. The most frequent issuing periods are 91 and 182 days. Treasury bills are negotiable and can always be sold in the market before maturity.

Because treasury bills are government securities, in most developed economies they carry the highest rating. However because it is the 'risk free' debt security in such countries, it also provides the lowest return. Few corporates purchase treasury bills, preferring to deposit funds or buy instruments with maturities that match more precisely their own cashflow forecasts, or to obtain a higher yield by investing in safe but riskier instruments.

Certificates of deposit (CDs)

A CD is no more than a piece of paper evidencing a bank deposit. The piece of paper is tradable, so that to realize the capital the investor can simply sell the CD to a third party instead of closing a bank deposit, which may involve interest penalties. CDs are a popular source of short-term finance for banks, which are often not allowed to issue commercial paper in their own domestic markets (although they are not prohibited from issuing in the euro commercial paper market).

Many countries have domestic CD markets, while international markets for dollar CDs have developed in the main financial centres round the world. The largest international market is in London where US$, UK£, €, JPY, AU$ and CA$ CDs are issued. London CDs must conform to rules laid down by the Bank of England and maturities may not exceed five years. The majority are issued for under one year.

Since CDs are negotiable they offer a slightly lower yield than a conventional bank deposit. Again CDs do not appear to be a popular instrument for corporates to invest cash surpluses.

Bank deposits

For many corporates, a bank deposit is the most popular route for handling short-term cash surpluses. Deposits have a number of advantages. Among these are the ease with which they can be effected and the comparatively large size of deposits that can be made. A company that has a forecast cash surplus of US$50 million for a month can deposit the surplus with two banks by making two telephone calls in the space of five minutes. Companies can also deposit for periods of their choosing – six weeks, one month etc. – rather than the investment period being partly dictated by the counterparty.

Bank deposits can suffer from a number of disadvantages however. Banks with the highest credit quality will often offer interest rates below the market rate. This is because their credit standing attracts such a high inflow of funds that they are usually 'long' of cash. Furthermore, in some countries domestic banks are long of their domestic currency for regulatory capital reasons, and hence offer deposit rates below the market. In addition the surplus funds are 'tied up' for the period of deposit, and cannot be realized before maturity without suffering penalty charges.

Money market funds (MMFs)

While there has been widespread use of MMFs in the United States for some time it is only comparatively recently that they have appeared in Europe. MMFs offer a number of advantages over the traditional overnight bank deposit.

- More flexibility. Funds can be deposited and withdrawn from MMFs on a daily basis.
- Higher returns than those available on the traditional bank deposit.
- Better security. Most MMFs are rated AAA, a much higher rating than that currently enjoyed by virtually all banks.

MMFs are essentially pooled investment vehicles. Since they invest in a wide range of liquid assets, including certificates of deposit, treasury bills and short-dated commercial paper, they offer the advantage of a widely diversified portfolio of investments. Since investors redeem their investments at different times, a MMF can invest further along the yield curve, and as a result achieve higher returns than an overnight deposit.

To achieve a AAA rating, the profile of the MMFs investments needs, among other things, to meet the following broad criteria:

- A weighted average maturity not exceeding 60 days.
- No single security has a maturity of more than 13 months + 1 day.
- Exposure to any one counterparty cannot exceed 5 per cent.

- At least 50 per cent of investments must be with AAA rated securities.

In examining the opportunities offered by a MMF, the treasury will need to consider the points outlined below.

Performance returns

Different funds will have different return performances. As mentioned they can offer daily withdrawal of funds together with higher returns than those available on bank deposits because they can invest along the yield curve. However it should be remembered that performance returns are judged against an overnight deposit. This may or may not be relevant for a corporate.

In addition, the treasurer needs to find some simple and easy means of comparing performance and returns available from MMFs. There are some websites that provide average returns in seven and 30-day yields as well as monthly, year-to-date and one-year returns.

Liquidity

Many treasurers are not concerned to have daily access to their investment and are prepared to sacrifice liquidity for return. There are a number of funds that offer T+3 and T+5 return of funds (funds are returned three and five days after notice)

Pricing

An investor in a MMF receives 'shares' or units in the fund. Shares are often priced at 'constant net asset value', which means that the fund operates in the same way as a bank deposit. Income is compounded daily and paid out monthly. Income can be taken as cash dividends or re-invested in new shares. Alternatively, some liquidity funds offer accumulation – or 'roll up' – shares, where income is accrued daily but not distributed. There may be something specific in a company's tax position that makes one pricing mechanism superior to another.

Cut-off times

MMFs impose cut-off times for same-day dealing. The treasurer needs to ensure that this cut-off time meets his/her own internal cash management procedures. Most cut-off times range between 12 noon and 2 p.m.

Minimum investment

MMFs impose a restriction on how much cash can be placed with them. Current minimums however are well below the level at which most corporates operate. For instance, in the UK the current minimum investment applied by many funds is UK£50,000. However in the UK some funds apply minimum deposits of UK£6 million.

Size of fund

To avoid problems if clients wish to withdraw large amounts at short notice, most funds ensure that no more than 10 per cent of the total value of the fund is represented by one investor. Conversely, most investors will wish to ensure that their investment in a fund is not significant.

Fees

Currently, management fees are usually around 12 to 15 basis points. It may be that fees are negotiable for larger investments, or where returns are lower than expected.

Conclusion

MMFs offer substantial advantages over other traditional forms of cash investment: security, liquidity and return. However there are a number of other factors to consider. One is that, by investing in a MMF, the treasurer is losing control of the investment period. Treasurers with surplus funds available for months rather than days may want to make fundamental decisions about the course of interest rates and the period of deposit or investment. This ability is lost with MMFs. Second, a treasurer with substantial funds to invest may be able to replicate the diversification effects of a MMF by investing in a wide range of instruments with different counterparties. Lastly, the use of MMFs involves a certain amount of initial due diligence work, together with the need to track returns offered by different funds.

Commercial paper (CP)

Commercial paper is discussed in more detail later in the chapter. For the investment of surpluses, CP has the following advantages:

- Rated paper is always available.

- The investor can specify the maturities required.
- Yields can be better than those available from bank deposits.

INSTRUMENTS FOR MANAGING LIQUIDITY SHORTAGES

Treasury policies

Most of the considerations regarding treasury policies and the management of short-term cash shortages are covered in the chapter on debt management. This will ensure that the company has sufficient headroom in revolving facilities to cover fluctuations in working capital and the cyclicality of the cashflow of the business over the year. The treasury policies sometimes cover matters such as cash forecasting.

Overdraft

An overdraft is a short-term loan facility from a bank that can be drawn as required without giving prior notice. Overdrafts are attached to bank accounts or to a pool of accounts. Essentially they represent the extent to which any debit balances on an account have not been funded by the company. Overdrafts have limits, say, UK£5 million or UK£25 million. Overdrafts will fluctuate from day to day in accordance with the cash fluctuations in the business.

Interest on overdrafts is charged at the bank's base rate plus a margin. Generally overdrafts are the most expensive form of funding for short-term liquidity management, since no notice has to be given to the bank of intended use. This is reflected in the margin charged by the bank.

Interest is usually paid quarterly in arrears. Overdrafts in most countries are technically repayable on demand, although they are reviewed and renewed annually by the bank.

It is worth noting that in many countries, for instance the United States, overdrafts are not permitted.

Cash advance

A cash advance is a short-term loan from a bank. It differs from an overdraft in that it is for a defined period. Cash advances can vary from one day (overnight) to 365 days. Principal and interest are repaid at the maturity of the advance.

Cash advances can be made under uncommitted facilities, in which case the interest rate is agreed between the parties when the cash advance is made and will be related to the inter-bank rate. Alternatively, cash advances will be made under committed facilities, in which case interest will be paid according the process for identifying the inter-bank rate (LIBOR, SIBOR, HIBOR etc.) (see Appendix) for the period of the advance plus the margin established in the facility.

Acceptance credits

In some countries drawings under bank facilities may be made by issuing acceptance credits. An acceptance credit is a bill of exchange issued and signed by the company. In the United Kingdom, while it is essential that the finance raised is used to fund working capital, it does not have to be directly linked to a specific transaction.

Acceptance by a bank denotes that the bank will redeem the bill if the issuer fails to do so. Acceptance enables the bill to be discounted in the discount market. The bills are issued at a discount and are usually for periods of one, three or six months.

Commercial paper

Commercial paper is simply a short-term IOU issued by a company. CP has long been a source of short-term finance in the United States, but was introduced into the Euromarket (ECP) only in 1984. There is no direct supervision in the ECP market, but domestic markets are regulated by the relevant local authorities (for instance the Securities and Exchange Commission (SEC) regulates the CP market in the United States). There are domestic CP markets in many countries round the world, each with their own rules and practices.

With approximately US$1.3 trillion in outstandings, the US is the deepest and most liquid of the CP markets. CP can be issued in the Euromarket when it is commonly called Euro-commercial paper or ECP. ECP can be issued in a range of currencies, though issues are increasingly denominated in euros. Due to its size and liquidity, issuers in the US CP market generally receive more aggressive pricing for dollar issues in the US market than for a similar issue in the Euromarket.

CP can be issued at a discount to face value or be interest bearing. US CP is issued at a discount and so usually is ECP, but interest-bearing ECP can be issued. CP is issued pursuant to a programme that will set an overall maximum for oustandings.

CP is typically used to meet short-term liquidity requirements. However, some larger companies with sound credit ratings may use CP as a near-long-term source of funding.

Issuing mechanics of CP

CP is sold through a dealer panel of banks that place the paper with their 'investor base'. Selecting the appropriate dealers is often one of the issues a treasurer faces in establishing a CP programme. Generally three to four banks that cover most big investor accounts make a quite adequate dealer panel. Banks should be selected according to the breadth of the salesforce coverage, the number of dealerships they have and feedback from their investors and other issuers. Generally a treasurer will want to establish a dealers' group that has complementary as opposed to overlapping investors.

The maintenance of a successful programme means a company must be able to issue a consistent level of paper. This consistency in issuing ensures that the treasurer will receive due and regular attention from the company's group of dealers. Dealers need to be reassured that they will be able to obtain a regular supply of paper to meet demand from their investor base. The issuer pays a fee to the dealer based on the value of paper placed with investors.

The marketing of CP is usually done on a same-day basis, so dealers must be able to establish how much supply they will receive each day to enable them to plan their marketing effort. Again, treasurers need to recognize this and plan their cash and liquidity management efforts accordingly.

Rating and backup lines

Many institutional investors require any CP they purchase to carry a rating from two recognized agencies. These are usually Standard and Poor's and Moody's. Although the relationship between long and short-term ratings is not mechanistic, Figure 16.2 shows the correlation between Standard and Poor's long and short-term ratings.

Most maturing paper in the CP market is redeemed by the issue of new CP. Due to this the rating agencies deem it prudent for companies to ensure that they have alternative sources of 'backup' liquidity, which protect them from defaulting were they unable to roll over their maturing paper with new notes. These backup lines cater for situations where issuers may find themselves excluded from issuing new CP due to a shrinkage in the market or some credit event or 'cloud' affecting the company.

The standard for commercial companies is generally 100 per cent of the maximum anticipated outstandings under a programme. Companies that are rated A–1+ can provide 50–75 per cent coverage, the exact amount being determined by the issuer's overall credit strength and access to capital markets. The agencies expect backup lines to be in place and confirmed in writing. This backup is normally in the form of contractually committed revolving facilities from an investment grade bank. The cost of this backup facility, usually in the form of commitment charges or fees, needs to be factored into the overall cost benefit analysis of establishing a programme.

Extendable commercial notes (ECN) provide 'built-in backup' by allowing the issuer to extend for several months if there is a difficulty in rolling over the notes. Accordingly there is no need to provide backup for such notes.

Advantages of CP

CP can often provide the issuer with more attractively priced funds to manage liquidity shortages than those available by drawing on revolving facilities. Drawings under revolving facilities will always carry a margin, which is not present in CP issuance.

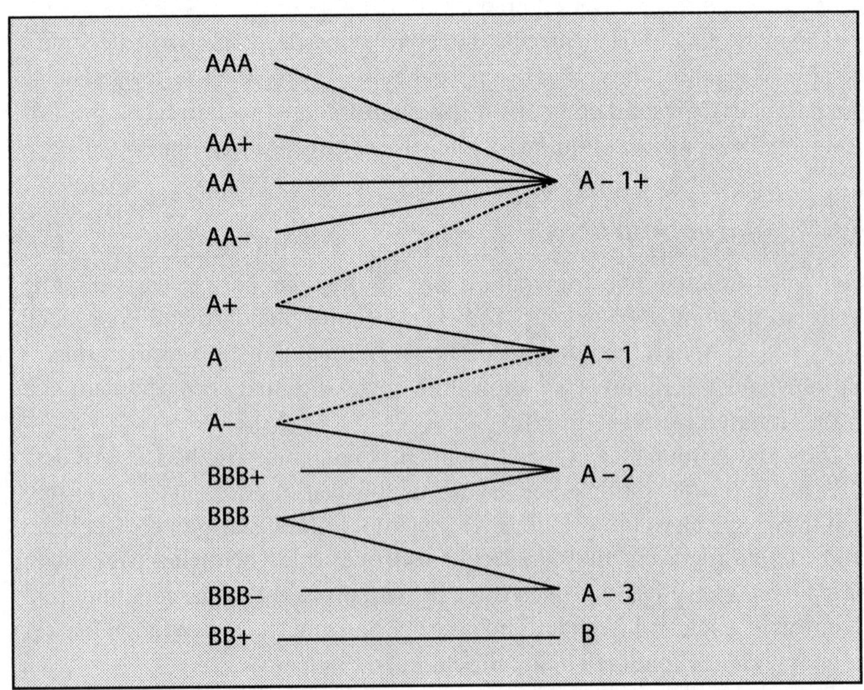

Figure 16.2 Broad relationship between long and short-term credit ratings

INTEREST CALCULATIONS

True yield versus discount

Some financial instruments pay interest on the instruments maturity. The amount of interest payable is calculated as follows:

$$I = \frac{P \times R \times D}{DB \times 100}$$

where I = interest amount, P = principal, DB = day basis (360 or 365), R= interest rate, and D = tenor (number of days).

Company A draws a cash advance of US$5 million for 91 days bearing interest at 4 per cent. Interest payable at maturity of the advance:

$$I = \frac{5m \times 4 \times 91}{360 \times 100} = \text{US\$50,555.56}$$

Other financial instruments such as commercial paper, treasury bills or acceptance credits are issued at a discount and redeemed at face value.

A company issues commercial paper with a face value of US$5 million. It matures in 91 days and is issued at a 4 per cent discount rate.

PV = US$ 5 m × (1.0 – (.04. × 91/360)) = US$4,949,444

In this particular case interest is paid on issuance of the instrument, since the issuer of the commercial paper only receives US$4,949,444
To compare the two interest rates the following formula converts a discount rate to true yield:

$$\text{TRUE YIELD} = \frac{DiscountRate(DR)}{1 - \left(\frac{DR \times No.of\ Days}{100 \times DB}\right)}$$

$$= \frac{4}{1 - \left(\frac{4 \times 91}{100 \times 360}\right)}$$

$$= 4.04 \text{ per cent}$$

360 days versus 365 days

Some money markets calculate interest based on 365 days (ACT/365) in a year while others use 360 (ACT/360) days. For instance the UK, Australian, and Canadian domestic money markets use ACT/365, while the main Euromarkets (with the exception notably of the UK£ and HK$), United States and euro zone use ACT/360. An example is given in Table 16.4.

Table 16.4 Different interest accruals for 365 and 360 day conventions

First day of interest period	*Last day of interest period*	*Interest accrued on 10 million ACT/365*	*Interest accrued on 10 million ACT/360*
15th May	31st August	108/365 × 10m	108/360 × 10m

To convert from an interest rate quoted on a 360-day basis (i) to an interest quoted on a 365-day basis (i*):

$$i^* = i \times 360/365$$

CASE STUDY

Corporate liquidity management checklist

You have just been appointed group treasurer of a large international company, operating in the engineering sector. The company operates three manufacturing plants in the United Kingdom, together with one plant in the United States and one in Germany. The UK operations export around the world. You know from your interviews that the company has experienced substantial liquidity problems in recent months.

You are about to have a discussion with your deputy treasurer to discuss liquidity management. Please make a checklist of what you consider to be appropriate questions.

Money market comparison

You have been given the job of investing your company's short-term funds, and up until now you have only placed in the inter-bank deposit market.

A broker keeps suggesting that you try other possibilities, and as you are not as busy as usual, you have decided to investigate the products available.

You have about US$10 million to invest for three months (91 days), although sometimes unexpected costs occur. Below you are given current quotations. The instruments have a three-month maturity. Which product would you choose?

Available investment opportunities

Investment	*Price*
T-bill	5.25 %
Interbank deposit	5.75 %
Negotiable CD	5.35 %
USCP	5.40 %
Corporate bond-coupon yield to redemption	5.6 %
Bankers acceptance	5.30 %

FRAs

You are treasurer of a company that forecasts it will have a liquidity shortage of US$100 million in six months' time. The shortage is forecast to last for six months, after which time the company will become cash rich again. In conjunction with the finance director you agree that the interest rate exposure should be hedged. You are presented with the following FRA prices. Which one would you select?

3 vs 6	3.03–2.97	3 vs 9	3.05–3.00
4 vs 7	2.99–2.93	4 vs 10	3.06–3.00
5 vs 8	2.90–2.85	5 vs 11	2.96–2.90
6 vs 9	3.05–3.00	6 vs 12	3.09–3.03
9 vs 12	3.07–3.01	7 vs 13	3.26–3.20

SOLUTIONS

Corporate liquidity management checklist

No check list can be exhaustive, but the following are some of the most pertinent questions relating to corporate liquidity management.

Committed bank facilities

1. How much headroom is there in the company's committed banking facilities?
2. Are the committed facility levels regularly monitored against cash forecasts?
3. How are drawings planned under the committed facilities?
   (They should be planned against a cashflow forecast to ensure that drawings made are not subsequently deposited.)
4. Are there clear company policies regarding the level of headroom required within the committed facilities?

Overdrafts

1. Are all bank accounts with the company's principal bankers pooled?
   Are there any accounts in regular use that are not pooled?
2. Do all the principal banking pools have overdrafts?
   Are the limits appropriate?
   How is the appropriateness measured?
3. What is the history of utilization of overdrafts?
   (Since overdrafts are comparatively expensive this utilization should be minimal.)

Uncommitted bank facilities

1. What are the levels of uncommitted facilities?
   How are these levels established?
2. Are the costs of drawing under uncommitted lines regularly compared with the marginal costs of drawing under committed lines?
3. Do uncommitted facilities cover the company's needs for foreign exchange and foreign currency borrowings?

Commercial paper (CP) programme

1. Has the company considered a commercial paper programme? What are the cost/ benefits of a programme?

Use of uncommitted lines

One option for a company with a substantial proportion of its core debt represented by revolving facilities is to finance drawings with uncommitted lines or CP since these are marginally cheaper than drawings under committed facilities. Does this create any liquidity exposures?

Cash forecasts

1. Are cash forecasts regularly prepared? Minimum requirements might be considered:
   - daily forecasts of closing cleared balances
   - weekly forecasts of daily cash positions
   - monthly cashflow forecasts
   - rolling annual forecasts, updated quarterly.
2. Who prepares the forecasts, and what are they prepared for? (Forecasts prepared by the finance team may be quite inappropriate for use by the treasury team to manage liquidity.)
3. How accurate are the forecasts? What variances are produced?
4. A number of other subsidiary questions arise, e.g.:
   - What is the source data for preparing cash forecasts?
   - If the source data are accounting records, how are these records reconciled to cleared balances?
   - Who reviews the forecasts?
   - What is the cost of getting the forecast wrong?

Deposits/investments

1. Are there clear treasury policies covering:
   - approved counterparties
   - approved instruments and investment instruments
   - approved investment periods?
2. Are these policies approved by the main board? How often are these approvals established?

Overseas operations

1. How do overseas operations manage liquidity? Exactly the same questions and considerations raised above apply to the overseas operations (other than those applying to committed facilities).
2. Do we ever have to provide finance for overseas operations on an emergency basis? If so, why? How does the company handle thin capitalization rules and withholding tax in such circumstances?
3. How are surplus overseas funds handled?

General

1. In selecting borrowing or depositing instruments, does the company adjust for the difference of instruments issued at a discount and those issued on a true yield basis?
2. Are there circumstances where it may be cheaper to raise finance in a foreign currency – e.g. US commercial paper – and swap the proceeds to sterling (or vice versa)?

Money market deposits

Investment	*Price*	*True yield*
T-bill	5.25 %	5.32 %
Interbank deposit	5.75 %	5.75 %
Negotiable CD	5.35 %	5.35 %
BA (Corporate)	5.30 %	5.37 %
USCP	5.40 %	5.48 %
Corporate paper	5.6 %	5.6 % (YTM)

Among some of the other considerations to be considered are:

- How will documents of title be held? What administration needs to be set up to hold these documents securely?
- What is the negotiability of the instrument should it need to be sold to meet cash shortages? Or will we be better borrowing separately to meet any cash shortages that arise during the period of the investment?

- What is the credit rating attached to the different instruments?
- Are all the instruments permitted within the treasury policies?

FRAs

The relevant FRA is an FRA starting in six months' time and maturing in 12 months time: a 6 vs 12. Since you want protection against a rise in interest rates you are purchasing an FRA. Therefore the relevant FRA is 6 vs 12 – 3.09 per cent.

PART V

Managing the Treasury Department, Treasury Systems, Tax and Accounting

Treasurers are concerned with how a department should be managed: what its structure should be, what internal controls should be in place to manage treasury activities, and how bank relationships should be managed. The board of directors is also concerned with what is expected from a treasury department: should it operate for profit or should it merely provide services to the rest of the company? How should the performance of the treasury department be measured? Finally, the question of outsourcing is also examined. Does a company in fact need to maintain an in-house treasury department, and what are the considerations involved in outsourcing the treasury department?

Treasury systems are very much the hub of a treasury department, providing information for reports and for treasury transactions, and enabling cash management activities to be undertaken. In many cases treasury systems are linked into a company's general ledger.

The final chapter deals with tax and accounting. Virtually no treasury transaction can be contemplated without the tax and accounting implications being considered.

CHAPTER 17

Managing the Treasury Function

INTRODUCTION

This chapter considers the question of how the treasury function is managed and controlled. It examines the management of the function from the standpoint of the main board and chief financial officer as well as those internal controls that are necessary to achieve an efficient and secure treasury department. It addresses a number of questions that boards, chief financial officers and corporate treasurers are often asked: 'Should our treasury department be a cost centre or profit centre?' 'How do we measure the performance of the treasury function?' 'Should we operate with a centralized or decentralized treasury function?' 'How should we manage our banking relationships?' 'Are there some treasury activities that could be outsourced?'

In addressing the questions, the principles and processes outlined in previous chapters will be drawn on.

Managing the treasury function

Treasury objectives

From the standpoint of the main board, one of the principal controls over the treasury function is the existence of a comprehensive set of treasury policies. These cover various topics discussed in the previous chapters: the organization's principal financial risks, the ways they can be identified and measured, and the company's policies for dealing with the risks so identified. In addition, they address the management and reporting of specific financial risks such as financing, interest rate, liquidity and foreign exchange risk.

In establishing parameters for treasury policies, however, the main board will first need to consider the question: 'What are the primary objectives of the treasury department, and what is the role of the treasury team?' There are four broad approaches.

Hedge risks as soon as they arise

In this approach the treasury department has as its principal objectives the minimization of the financial consequences of an adverse movement in financial exposure. With this type of treasury department, financial risks that can be measured with an appropriate degree of accuracy are hedged as soon as they are identified.

Such a department would be the classic 'cost centre' treasury department. Very often the philosophy behind such objectives is the belief that the company, and in particular the treasury team, are unable to create any value through the timing of hedges. The view would be that, over time, hedging will sometimes be advantageous for the company when hedge rates are subsequently compared with market rates. This will occur when financial prices and markets move adversely and resulting losses are offset by gains on the hedges. At other times, however, hedging will be disadvantageous for the company, when financial prices and markets move in the company's favour. Although over time the favourable and adverse movements in financial rates will balance out, the view is taken that the financial and operational effects of adverse movements are worse than the benefits of favourable movements.

Add value through the treasury department

Few departments within an organization would subscribe to the view that they are solely cost centres. Many organizations believe that their treasury team should add value through their activities. This value addition comes from the department providing a proactive service to operating units, subsidiaries and other departments within the organization. These services will vary according to the activities of the company, and can cover a wide range of potential areas. Examples are:

- Working with subsidiaries/divisions to help them identify ways of reducing their banking costs (for instance the use of lockboxes where the company receives a substantial volume of cheques overseas on a regular basis).

- Helping sales teams develop, in conjunction with relationship banks, financing packages to assist sales efforts. These packages may comprise loans or leasing where the bank takes the primary risk.
- In the case of a retailer the development, in conjunction with relationship banks, of a company store card that offers customers a credit facility.
- Assisting the tax department to reduce the corporate tax charge through the identification of tax efficient financing structures.

The concept of the treasury department adding value to operating units through its knowledge of financial markets fits more closely with today's service culture than the cost centre operation. The value-adding treasury function may still manage financial exposures in the same manner as the cost centre operation: they are hedged as soon as they are identified. The department's role however is to seek out and implement service and value-added opportunities.

A quasi-profit centre treasury

Once financial exposures have been identified and measured the treasury team can chose, within bands, the timing of hedges. Financial market prices never move in a straight line, and there are periods of short-term peaks above and troughs below the trend line. The philosophy of the quasi-profit centre treasury is that the treasury team, through its involvement in these markets, is well positioned to identify such peaks and troughs, and can time hedging programmes appropriately.

Clearly the activities of such departments need to be monitored more closely and the effectiveness of their timing decisions needs to be measured constantly.

A profit centre treasury

Profit centre treasury departments are empowered to take bets with the company's money. This is an extension of the philosophy of the quasi-profit centre treasury. However, the profit centre treasury is able to buy or sell financial assets or instruments, depending on their view of financial markets. For instance a treasury team may believe that short-term Japanese market interest rates may rise. Although the company has no borrowings in Japanese yen, the treasury department is authorized (within strict parameters) to buy yen FRAs to back its view.

True profit centre treasuries are few and are usually confined to the largest multinationals with substantial cross border flows.

Summary

The precise nature of the objectives of the treasury department will vary according to the business philosophy and activities of the company. Most companies feel very uncomfortable with the concept of the quasi-profit and full profit centre treasuries. This is usually due to the belief that the organization's skills lie in the businesses they operate and not in the financial markets. Furthermore, many companies also believe that they do not have the required controls and expertise to manage quasi and full profit centre treasuries. Finally there is also a belief that if their treasury departments engage in such profit-orientated activites, this would be contrary to the views of their shareholders.

Currently most companies take the value-added approach to their treasury departments. However, as in all things, there are substantial areas of grey. A treasury department that funds liquidity shortages by borrowing overnight on the money markets will probably use its judgement about when to time the daily transaction (and probably would be expected to do so). Many exposures, such as financing risks and interest rate risk, do not arise suddenly but tend to be identified over time. An organization would probably use its judgement about when the appropriate time was to eliminate financing and interest rate risk. Among items included in making this decision would be the state of the financial markets and advice received from its core bankers.

Even foreign exchange transaction risks, which usually arise once a commitment is incurred, may require time for their precise timing and magnitude to be measured. This can be due to product specification changes, order cancellations, and re-arrangement of delivery schedules. While a treasury team may not make judgements about when to take out a hedge once the transaction risk has been properly measured, it will use its judgement about what type of instrument to use, on the basis of its view of foreign exchange markets and prices in particular. If options are being used, a decision needs to be made about where to establish the exercise price and whether and when an option should be closed out and replaced with a forward transaction. Often, by its very nature, pre-transaction risk requires a judgement regarding foreign exchange markets and prices before hedges are taken out.

The above considerations point to the need for clearly worded treasury policies setting out the objectives of the treasury department, and the importance of reporting fully on treasury activities.

Most treasury departments therefore use substantial judgement about the timing and scale of hedges taken out.

INTERNAL CONTROLS

While the treasury policies and authority levels help to manage the treasury department in an overall context, certain controls and division of duties are necessary to ensure effective control over the company's assets and the smooth running of the day-to-day operations within the department. The following questionnaires address some of the controls that ensure the efficient running of the department.

Controls over dealing, deal recording and confirmations

These controls ensure that the company obtains the best available prices for its transactions, and that all dealing activities are properly recorded and accounted for.

- Are two quotes always obtained whenever practicable to ensure that the company pays the best price? A record of all quotes obtained should be maintained, indicating which ones were accepted. This record ensures that no one bank is being favoured. (Some treasury management systems have the facility for the dealer to record details of quotes received for a particular transaction, with the ability to 'hit' a particular quote and for that to be automatically input as a deal.)
- How does the dealer record deal details? Sometimes deals are input directly into the treasury management system, where they will automatically be given a sequential deal number. Other dealers record details in a diary or on pre-numbered deal tickets, for subsequent input into a treasury management system. Some formal system for recording deals as soon as they are undertaken needs to be established.
- Is tape-recording used? If so how long are tapes retained (they should be kept until confirmations are received)? Tapes provide a record if there is a dispute concerning a counterparty.
- When deals are separately recorded (for example, in a diary or on deal tickets) is there a check to ensure that all deals have been recorded in the treasury management system?
- Are deal confirmations produced by the treasury management system and not on a separate system? This ensures that confirmations are produced for all deals recorded in the treasury management system.

Where deal tickets are used, are they checked confirmations? Is this done by someone other than the dealer?

- Are deal confirmations sent out immediately, that is, on the same day?
- Is electronic deal confirmation used? Electronic deal confirmation is a process whereby banks post all deals undertaken with specific counterparties on a secure website. Counterparties can access this website and confirm all deals posted. Confirmation should not be undertaken by anyone connected with dealing.
- If electronic deal confirmation is not used, who receives incoming deal confirmations? Is that person quite separate from the dealer?
- Do incoming deal confirmations go directly to the treasury department back office? If that department is too small to support a separate back office, do deal confirmations go to a separate function such as financial accounts? Banks should be instructed that confirmations or faxes should not go to the dealers.
- How are discrepancies reconciled? Generally discrepancies should be reconciled with the counterparty, as opposed to help being sought from the dealer.
- Are all counterparties subject to mandates and ISDA documentation (where relevant) to ensure that all transactions are properly authorized?

The objective of these controls is to ensure that the dealer has no responsibility for the recording of the transaction, and procedures are designed to ensure that deals are accurately recorded in the system. Ideally there should be a separation of duties between the dealers and those persons responsible for recording the transactions, for checking counterparty confirmations and resolving discrepancies, and for settling transactions.

Where the treasury department is too small to allow such a division of duties, then the company should consider using a separate department to handle some work such as checking counterparty confirmations and resolving discrepancies. Should the company decide not to effect such a division of duties, it should be aware of the risks that it is running.

It is also worth considering whether the dealer(s) should work on his/her (their) own or in company, and whether access to dealing facilities and payment facilities should be restricted. This prevents people from attempting to deal on their own behalf.

Controls over mandates

The purpose of bank mandates is to define the authority of banks to accept the company's instructions, and to establish the authorities required for bank transactions. All counterparties should be subject to full and correctly worded dealing mandates and these mandates should be subject to approval by board resolutions. The following points consider some of the more common controls relating to mandates and related board resolutions.

- Are mandates split between cash management mandates and dealing mandates? This prevents mandates being too long and complex.
- Do board resolutions that create mandates specify:
  - who is authorized to commit the company
  - accounts into which funds will be received
  - how deals can be undertaken and payments made (for example, by telephone or electronically)
  - who is authorized to sign confirmations
  - that the bank should confirm that it has received and is acting on the mandates
  - that call back procedures should be used
  - transaction limits
  - where confirmations are to be sent to
  - that the company will not deal at non-standard rates?
- Who is responsible for producing board resolutions? Ideally this should be someone in the legal and secretarial department.
- Who maintains specimen signatures? These should be held separately from the treasury.
- Do mandates exist for all banks the company deals with?
- Who is responsible for requesting changes to the mandate? All requests should come from the treasury department to the individual responsible for producing the board resolutions.
- Is there a record for every facility accepted by the company?

Procedures

In addition to controls over dealing and mandates there are a number of procedural controls that a company should observe. These ensure that the administration of the department is efficiently conducted.

- Is access to the treasury department limited?
- Are there job descriptions detailing individual responsibilities and authorities?
- How are holidays, promotions and resignations catered for, to ensure that all individuals take holidays and that holidays cause the minimum of disruption?
- Are there facility denial procedures in operation? (Facility denial is the situation where due to some unforeseen circumstance such as fire, the treasury area is not accessible.)
- Are procedures for coping with facility denial fully recorded, and are these procedures regularly practised?
- What insurance policies covering the treasury function are in place? Do they cover losses from fraud and error by treasury staff?
- Are procedures within the department such as cash management recorded, to ensure that absences, holidays and resignations can be handled efficiently?

Payment controls

Finally there are a number of controls over payments. Most companies make treasury payments, such as interest and principal payments and settlement of derivative contracts, via an electronic banking system. Access to these machines needs to be strictly controlled.

- Are all electronic payments made by the treasury? If subsidiaries use electronic banking systems how is their use controlled?
- How does the treasury receive requests for payment? Payment requests should be written and appropriately authorized.
- Are requests reviewed by the treasury to ensure they are properly authorized?
- Are different people responsible for input, verification and authorization of payments into the electronic banking systems? It is important to ensure that no one person can make payments without proper supervision and checks.
- Are pre-formatted input screens used for regular payments? Is the level of non-regular payments limited?

- How are cash books written up and by whom? (Cash books should be maintained outside the treasury department.)
- Who reconciles the bank accounts? This should be undertaken by a function outside the treasury. Bank reconciliations should be produced daily for all treasury accounts and discrepancies investigated immediately.
- Are machines for payment subject to restricted access? Ideally they should be in a separate room with access restricted to authorized individuals. Users should log out of systems when they leave their desks.
- Who is the systems administrator? Is that person independent of those authorized to input verification and authorization?
- What control is there over passwords? All systems should have passwords and personal computers should be locked if unattended.
- What are the authority levels for payments? All large payments should need the authority of senior people.

Reporting

The regular treasury reports discussed in Chapters 1 and 2 need to be prepared. These reports cover the principal treasury-related financial risks that face the company and the action the treasury has undertaken to manage these risks. It is good practice if this report is prepared by the treasury middle office. However in the vast majority of treasury departments this is not feasible, in which case consideration should be given to the preparation of this report by another function such as financial accounts.

CENTRALIZE OR DECENTRALIZE TREASURY?

Sometimes the decision needs to be made about the degree of centralization within the treasury function.

Decentralized treasury

In a true decentralized treasury, all treasury activities are carried out at the business unit or subsidiary level in the case of a domestic company, and in the case of an international company at the country level. In practice true decentralized treasury functions rarely exist, since there are some activities such as financing or foreign exchange translation management that must be carried out centrally. However some companies leave various treasury activities, such as the management of liquidity and foreign exchange, to be managed by local units and subsidiaries.

Advantages of a decentralized treasury

When treasury operations are decentralized there is a belief that local units can react more closely and rapidly to local needs. In addition treasury activities are handled by individuals with a knowledge of local company needs and the local business environment. Since treasury is handled at the unit or subsidiary level there is more autonomy and sense of ownership over treasury activities.

Disadvantages of a decentralized treasury

With a decentralized treasury there is no overall control of risk. Some risks may be ignored or mismanaged, since there is no centre of expertise or any function that can take a group perspective. A decentralized treasury operation cannot take advantage of group-wide activities such as netting or intragroup funding, and the costs of treasury activities such as foreign exchange transactions may be higher.

Decentralized treasury – central responsibility

While many treasury activities are carried out on a decentralized basis, a group treasury department sets guidelines, policies and instruct local staff on the management of risks. The local treasury staff report to group treasury and local line management.

Advantages of central responsibility

This structure is designed to overcome some of the disadvantages of the true decentralized structure while retaining its flexibility. An experienced central treasury can take a global view of the group's financial exposures, yet actions are still left to local staff.

Disadvantages of central responsibility

One of the disadvantages of this type of structure is that group treasury is responsible for the actions of others. Group treasury have to rely on the full cooperation of the local treasury staff in identifying exposures, reporting cash forecasts and taking out appropriate hedges. Moreover, no benefit is gained from the economies available when treasury operations are centralized.

Full centralization

The fully centralized treasury function aims to eliminate many of the disadvantages of decentralized treasury operations. Centralized treasury operations aim to reduce the overall cost of treasury operations through some of the following activities:

- efficient and effective international cash management structures
- optimizing groupwide liquidity through offsetting surpluses and shortages
- netting intercompany flows
- managing financial risks on a group-wide basis.

Advantages of a treasury management centre (TMC)

A TMC can gain economies of scale by maximizing individual transaction volumes. In addition, when cash management is centralized, subsidiaries are able to obtain higher rates for lending cash surpluses to the TMC rather than depositing locally. Other subsidiaries can obtain short-term finance from the TMC on more favourable terms than those available in local markets. The TMC acts as a centre of expertise and can manage group-wide exposures in the best interests of the group. The centre of expertise can purchase treasury products more cost effectively than they can be purchased in a decentralized structure.

Disadvantages of a TMC

Local involvement in treasury activities is reduced, and hence interest in treasury activities is reduced. Local units still have to provide forecasts, identify exposures and comply with TMC instructions; as a result, information supplied to the TMC may lack accuracy and timeliness of delivery.

Structure of TMCs

Many TMCs are structured on a regional basis, as with the example shown in Figure 17.1.

The regional operations in Europe would probably cover Europe, including Scandinavia, along with the Middle East and Africa. The Americas would cover the United States, Canada, South America and the Caribbean, while the Far East centre would cover South East Asia, Australasia and Japan. The regional treasury centre is often confined to cash and liquidity management. Its geographical position enables it to manage funds effectively within the region due to common time zones.

The role of the regional operation is usually to:

- centralize and optimize the regional liquidity position
- manage the centralized liquidity
- centralize and coordinate intercompany and major third party foreign exchange exposures
- manage local banking relationships, charges and accounts.

The in-house bank

The objective of the in-house bank is to provide services to subsidiaries and units that are both as efficient as those of local banks and priced competitively with them. The in-house bank provides deposit opportunities to group companies with surplus funds, and borrowing opportunities to subsidiaries with shortages. It provides foreign exchange services, intercompany funding and netting of intercompany flows.

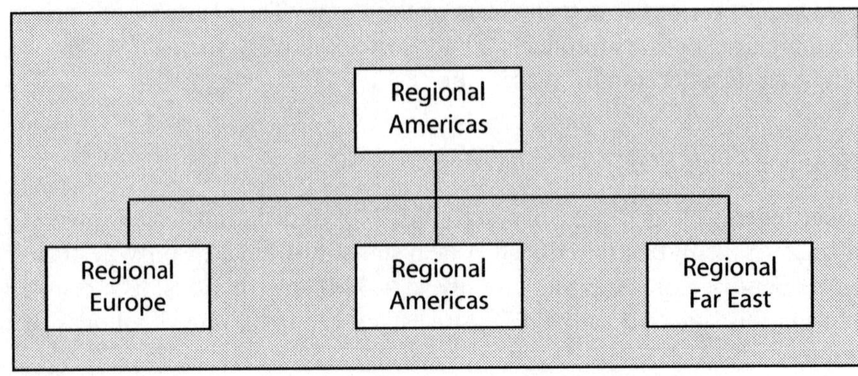

Figure 17.1 Typical treasury structure for a multinational company

The in-house bank normally aims to provide these services at a profit. Clearly the ability to operate effectively depends on the standard of internal accounting and systems.

The relevant structure

Companies determining the relevant structure will bear the following in mind:

- Does the company operate on a highly decentralized basis, giving subsidiaries and operating units substantial independence providing they meet certain financial targets? If so the decentralized structure may have some relevance. On the other hand, a company that operates a highly centralized control structure with centralized finance may find the centralized structure more relevant.
- Does the company have substantial financial exposures? This would tend to argue for a centralized treasury to ensure these exposures are properly and effectively managed.
- Does the company have substantial intercompany transactions that a centralized treasury can profitably manage?

BANK RELATIONS

Why are bank relationships important?

Most companies subscribe to the concept of relationship banking: that a company should have a small number of banks from whom it purchases all its banking products. The company may go through good times when its credit is strong and bad times when its credit is much weaker. The argument is that it needs banks on which it can rely when it is going through bad trading conditions and its credit standing is suffering. If a company has done a good job in relationship building, then its relationship banks will continue to support the company through such difficult economic circumstances.

Selection of banks

A company needs a small number of relationship banks from whom it can purchase its treasury products. The products that these banks offer need to be strongly differentiated between the individual banks that offer them. Some banks for instance bring powerful balance sheets and the ability to provide substantial amounts of finance at short notice. Others have very extensive capital market distribution capabilities and hence, in addition to providing effective delivery for capital market transactions, are able to provide constructive advice on the appropriate capital market products for a company. Others may have very efficient derivatives businesses or specialization in certain derivative products that meet the company's particular needs.

The essence of good banking relationships is for the company to exploit the favoured products and market positions of banks to both the company's and the banks' mutual benefit.

Building and maintaining relationships

Selecting the right relationship banks and establishing the correct 'cocktail' of banks is very important to the standing of a company and its efficient and effective financing. It needs a combination of commercial and investment banks that are able to service the company's needs at a reasonable cost and on reasonable terms and conditions.

Building bank relationships is best done in good times when the company's business is healthy. This enables it to choose its relationship banks more freely. A corporate treasurer, having selected the relationship banks, needs to maintain and foster the relationship. This will comprise: providing annual and half yearly report and accounts, along with other textual information about the company that the company's investor relations department may from time to time produce, ensuring that senior officials of the bank are able to meet members of the company's board, and inviting the bank's relationship managers to investment presentations. In addition, day-to-day contact between the treasury team and the bank's relationship team cannot be overemphasized.

The objective of the relationship building exercise is to ensure that relationship banks understand the company's business, strategy, financing structure and objectives. This ensures that banks can identify the appropriate products in their portfolio to offer and discuss with the company's treasury team. It also means that the company can rely on the support of its relationship banks when it makes major strategic moves, such as an acquisition or disposal, or embarks on a major capital expenditure programme. It also means that the company has support from the banking community when or if the company's business suffers a reverse or business goes into a cyclical downturn.

How many relationship banks?

A company probably needs at least one house bank in any territory where it has major operations. This bank will need to be able to offer the administration of current accounts, short-term credit facilities and efficient international payments. There is no rule for the number of relationship banks but Table 17.1 gives an indication.

Many treasury teams believe that there is no point in establishing relationships with investment banks. Should major acquisitions or disposals be effected, then advice will come from the company's merchant banks where officials are close to the company's senior executives. This is probably true, but today most banks that have advisory arms to their business are also part of a large banking group. In these circumstances the company should be able to 'lever off' the existing relationship to access products that interest and concern it.

Relationships are never stable. Rightly or wrongly, a bank usually achieves the status of a relationship bank by participating in one of the company's major bank financings. This financing for most companies is a revolving credit that provides the company's core finance to meet working capital, capital and small acquisition needs. Banks are continually changing the perception of their desire to be involved in such financings. In addition they are continually comparing the return from the total business generated by the relationship with the cost of capital required to support it. If banks consider the returns are inadequate they will reduce support to the company. As a result of this a treasurer needs to be continually open to new potential relationships, and ever sensitive to which of the existing relationships may wither.

Most banks that participate in a major financing maintain that the returns from traditional bank lending are insufficient to cover the cost

Table 17.1 Structure of relationship banking group for major and large companies

	Major company	*Large company*
House banks: domestic	1–3	1
House banks: international per territory	1	1
Secondary banks*: in home country	8	5
Investment banks: in home country	2	1

* Will include branches of major international banks.

of capital required to support their commitment. As a result they are continually looking for ancillary business from a company to subsidize the bank lending activities effectively. This is a real problem for many treasurers since many companies do not have that volume of ancillary business. Unfortunately there is not much that can be done other than to be extra sensitive to ensuring that all treasury business goes to relationship banks. Additionally, treasurers need to ensure that relationship banks have, wherever possible, an opportunity to bid for all relevant treasury business.

What each side must give the relationship

Most treasurers would probably see the key elements to a successful relationship as being:

- product compatibility
- personal chemistry
- integrity: the ability to see each other's point of view
- open information and understanding
- credit standing by the bank and credit consciousness by the company.

PERFORMANCE MEASUREMENT

Measuring the performance of the treasury department is another key control that management exercises over the function. However few companies seem to be able to find simple key performance indicators (KPIs) that can accurately measure the performance of the treasury team. This is usually because most treasuries are service orientated, and simple KPIs for a service function do not apply directly to most treasury departments. There are a number of different ways that treasury teams have tried to manage performance measurement.

The annual treasury plan

Most treasury teams produce an annual operating plan setting out the objectives of the department for the coming year. Usually this plan forms part of the individual achievement targets for the team's members over the coming year. It is common for this annual plan to be the basis for assessing the treasury team.

One of the problems with the annual treasury plan is that, in today's volatile business environment, what is planned often never occurs and what occurs is often never planned. Opportunities for acquisitions and disposals and the treasury activities that flow from them can often never be planned. Changes in capital markets can nullify the timing of planned capital market transactions to be undertaken by the company. Very often the treasury team is finally assessed against what it actually achieved against events occurring during the year, as opposed to what it achieved against the plan.

Sometimes the annual treasury plan does have some objective measurements such as a reduction in banking charges or the financial benefits from the establishment of a cash pooling system.

Projects actually undertaken

The treasury department is assessed against projects actually undertaken during the year. This is a version of the annual treasury plan, but instead of targets being set at the beginning of the year the treasury team is assessed against actual achievements. A number of companies adopt this approach.

The underlying philosophy is that in a large organization there are always profitable projects arising during the year that can be undertaken by the treasury team, although it may not be possible to identify these projects at the start of the year. A good treasury department will be able to seek these projects out during the course of a year, and successfully complete them.

Targets set by the board

Sometimes the board will set targets for the treasury team based on budgeted and planned activities. For instance a target may be set that the actual interest cost for the financial year must not exceed budgeted interest cost by a certain amount. The treasury is then tasked with ensuring that the company benefits from falling interest rates while protecting the company from increasing rates.

There are certain disadvantages with this kind of target setting. First, in the example above the treasury team could meet the objective by covering all exposures using options. Some quantification therefore needs to be brought in for the cost of alternative instruments. Second, the company may have a substantial part of its interest rate exposure covered with swaps and options that extend beyond a year. In this case the treasury team's ability to manoeuvre is severely restricted. Finally, this kind of target is influenced not only by interest rates but by the actual level of borrowing during the year, and so a treasury team can only be assessed against rates achieved on budgeted borrowings.

Assessment against a benchmark

Quasi-profit centre treasuries that are timing hedges to be undertaken against their view of the market should be assessed against a benchmark. Take, for instance, a treasury team that deposits surpluses and funds shortages on the overnight money market; it will be assessed against an overnight money market rate taken at a fixed time during the day, for example 11 a.m. A treasury team that has flexibility about the timing of interest rate hedges could be assessed on the actual rate achieved at the end of the year against the market rate established when the budget is finally concluded.

Service quality

Treasury teams that act as service centres have to determine by what standards their service should be measured. Such a department has to identify who its customers are, what service they require, and how that service will be provided. Measurement is generally achieved by customers providing feedback through the medium of questionnaires.

For instance, a treasury team may determine that divisional finance directors are among its group of customers. They may also determine that one of the principal services they can offer these directors is assistance with the preparation of cash forecasts and foreign exchange exposures. They may deliver this service by meeting regularly with divisional finance staff and helping on the preparation of these forecasts. Questionnaires sent to divisional finance directors will identify the extent to which the divisional staff felt that a positive service had been delivered during the year.

Cost data

Typical data might be the overall cost of the company's bank charges for clearing or bank charges on a per transaction basis, such as cost of charges for obtaining value for collections. Such data may need to be examined over a course of time, or may be used in benchmarking surveys.

Performance against treasury policies

This would seem to be the minimum in terms of performance measurement: that treasury is implementing the treasury policies and all the hedging policies and other actions that flow from it. Many companies would regard this as the minimum that a treasury department should achieve, since it is no more than the team is paid to do. However, the full implementation of treasury policies, together with best standards of internal control and administration, would be a natural starting point in measuring treasury performance.

Other measures

Large treasury departments may use other, perhaps more sophisticated, measures such as value at risk or cashflow at risk.

Summary

Any performance measurement needs to be related to the objectives and structure of the treasury department. Is it a cost centre, a service centre, a value-added treasury or a profit centre treasury? What are the nature of the risks it is managing? Does it operate on a centralized or a decentralized basis? If it is a service centre treasury, what is the service culture of the organization as a whole and how are other corporate departments measured? Any performance measure should be not only relevant to the department but also simple to establish and within the capabilities of the information systems within the department.

OUTSOURCING

Application Service Providers

The term 'application service provider' (ASP) is applied to companies that supply software applications and/or software services over the Internet. The most common features of an ASP are:

- The ASP owns and operates a software application.
- It owns, operates and maintains the servers that run the application. It also employs the people needed to maintain the application.
- It makes the application available to customers everywhere via the Internet, either in a browser or through some sort of 'thin client'.

- The ASP bills for the application either on a per-use basis or on a monthly/annual fee basis.

Application to treasury

Many treasuries are faced with the problems of size, cost and complexity, and much of their work may be routine.

Size

As already mentioned, the typical treasury department would have perhaps three or four staff. This creates problems in maintaining a satisfactory division of duties and appropriate internal controls

Cost of treasury management systems

Many treasury management systems are costly. A treasury department can find itself faced with the problem that its existing systems are inadequate but the cost of a new system is unacceptable.

Complexity of systems

In addition someone in the department has to maintain a knowledge of the attributes and capabilities of the system. There has to be someone capable of extracting the necessary reports. With staff turnover this can be a burden in a small department.

Routine tasks

A number of tasks undertaken within a treasury department are routine; they consist of collecting, maintaining and extracting data and different reports.

From what has been described about ASPs, it is clear that an ASP could maintain a treasury management system for access by corporate treasuries. In addition a number of ASPs maintain a dedicated staff of treasury professionals and as a result have very effective internal controls and division of duties. It is possible therefore for corporates to consider the outsourcing of a large part of their treasury functions, to overcome some of the problems outlined above.

The following case study is designed to highlight some of the issues to be considered when a corporate is considering outsourcing some or all the treasury function.

CASE STUDY

Outsourcing

You are the treasurer of a mutinational company with its headquarters in Singapore. In Europe you have a small regional treasury centre that handles cash management activities for European operations. The centre consists of four people and you have long wondered whether there might be benefits from outsourcing the cash management activities undertaken by the treasury centre.

The principal activities undertaken by the centre are:

- managing the euro cash pool
- managing the sterling cash pool
- transferring cash from the euro pool to the sterling pool using FX swaps
- making bank transfers for short-term borrowings and deposits and maturing FX swaps
- arranging deposits of surplus funds
- cash forecasting.

Your boss the finance director is interested in the concept, and asks you to set down the principal points to be considered.

What do you think these points would be?

SOLUTION

Typical points to be considered would be as follows:

1 *Benefits*

- What are the financial benefits of outsourcing likely to be?
- Will internal controls be improved? If so, how?
- Will the company avoid the necessity of maintaining existing treasury management systems? This should bring us more flexibility since the agent manager has responsibility for managing resources.
- Will the company have access to more professional expertise?

2 *Issues to be managed*

- How do we ensure that the proposed agent manager has the competence to deliver the people, the expertise, systems, communications and management?
- How do we avoid any conflicts of interest, to make certain that the agent manager is working for us and not acting in his own interest?
- How do we ensure that the agent manager's control and security framework is adequate?
- How can we ensure that data transmitted to and maintained by the agent manager on his/her database is secure?
- How can we ensure that the outsource agent will be in business in the long term? What is its client list? What backup procedures can we implement should it go out of business?
- What treasury systems does the agent use? Is there long-term commitment by the software company to maintain the system, and what kind of global support system is there?

3 *Matters to be implemented before 'transition'*

- The agent manager should not have access to client funds or financial assets.

- The agent manager should have an effective front, middle and back-office structure. There should be adequate internal controls.
- A comprehensive policy, including authority and limits, must be agreed.
- An effective suite of bank mandates must be in place.
- What procedures are in place to ensure adequate and effective auditing?
- What is the level of insurance cover for errors, fraud and the like?
- What reports will we need from the outsource agent, how often and in what detail and so on?

4 *Management of the transition*

The migration of activities from the treasury centre to the outsourcing agent needs to be managed properly. This means that it should be managed along regular project management lines:

- Terms of reference. These include:
  - authority and project sponsor
  - definition of the customer
  - objectives of project (measurable, achievable, consistent, understandable and few in number)
  - scope of the project (What will be outsourced?)
  - costs/budget (How much will the project cost?)
  - resources available to implement the project must be sufficient
  - deliverables (What will these be? How will the success of the project be measured?)
  - project phases and timescale
  - risks to be managed (How are the various risks that will arise be managed?)
  - roles and responsibilities.
- Project organization
  - work breakdown structure (breaking the project down into units of work)
  - project organization (Who is going to do elements of the project and how they should be organized?)
  - the milestone.

- Detailed planning
  - estimating
  - identifying dependencies
  - constructing the dependency network
  - assigning responsibilities
  - allocating resources
  - producing a Gantt chart.
- Controlling projects
  - time, cost and quality.

CHAPTER 18

Treasury Systems

TREASURY MANAGEMENT SYSTEMS

Treasury management systems (TMS) are essentially large databases of treasury transactions. They enable the treasury department to collect information on treasury transactions, and to facilitate the calculation and monitoring of positions and exposures by currency, maturity and type of instrument. In addition, they enable varying levels of analysis either based on the transaction detail stored or using decision support and modelling techniques.

Risk management support is now a standard feature of treasury management systems and capabilities include value at risk and counterparty exposure risk as well as the ability to measure exposure to interest rate movements and compliance with regulatory requirements such as FAS133.

Cash management is now no longer left to a specialist cash management system, as more treasury management system suppliers add their own multilateral netting capability together with cash forecasting and management tools.

Treasurers are also seeking a fully integrated solution with seamless interfaces, for example, to electronic banking technology employed within the treasury for balance and transaction enquiry purposes, automatic reconciliation with data in the TMS and payment initiation.

Interfaces to external general ledger applications, third-party netting software, other internal spread sheet applications and perhaps desktop foreign currency dealing systems are also becoming common.

With the ever increasing use of the Internet, many treasury systems can be deployed within a globally based corporate treasury function using web-browser technology. Such an environment has the advantage of enabling overseas-based operating units to submit cash forecasts, for example, or requests for funding electronically into Group Treasury without the need to install direct remote links.

Calculation and monitoring of positions

Most treasury departments are faced with undertaking a number of routine administrative tasks. Some of these tasks are described below.

Liquidity and derivative transactions

- Recording the due date and amount for settlement of money market transactions, foreign exchange and derivative transactions. Ensuring that interest payments receivable and payable and amounts due under derivative transactions are correctly settled.
- Ensuring that transactions with counterparties are within the appropriate limits.
- Tracking liquidity positions of overseas subsidiaries.

Debt management

- Calculating interest payments and principal repayments due under loans, and maintaining due date for payment of interest and principal. Ensuring that liabilities for interest and principal are correctly settled.

Accounting

- Computing the interest costs for money market transactions and long-term debt financing. Analyzing this interest cost between accounting periods.
- Reconciling treasury transactions with those recorded in the accounting ledgers.
- In addition, the accounting implications of derivatives transactions have to be determined. Principally this consists of allocating payments or receipts under derivative contracts to the appropriate accounting periods.

Reporting

- Calculating performance measurement data.
- Undertaking what-if analysis.
- Preparing the monthly treasury report.

Cash management

- Identifying the current cleared balances and the projected cleared balances for the end of the day for the different banking pools.
- Identifying current day's liquidity shortages or surpluses.
- Making all necessary payments in connection with liquidity, debt and risk management transaction.
- Preparation of longer-term cash forecasts.

Alternative types of TMS

The TMS is the principal instrument used for undertaking most of the above routine tasks. There are alternatives to the type of TMS to be used.

Office applications: This consists of single or multiple spreadsheets. This is often a quite acceptable route for a treasury department that only has a very small number of treasury transactions to record. Spreadsheets are still used in companies where dedicated treasury management systems are used, usually for one-off what-if analysis or some irregular tasks that are considered to be best handled as separate exercises. As treasury activities grow, however, increasing the workload of the corporate treasurer, the sustained use of spreadsheet-based applications presents increased risk as, by their very nature, multiple linked spreadsheets are unstable and prone to failure.

In-house solutions: This approach was widely adopted by companies with the resources to build and maintain an in-house system. Although no longer so common, in-house systems are still used, with the objective being a high degree of specification. For most companies the in-house solution is generally both too long to develop and expensive.

Single dedicated TMS: This is probably the most common route taken to meet treasury software needs. The architecture of most of the major dedicated TMS is similar. Most of the systems are modular in design, enabling users to buy just the modules that they require. The basic modules most companies need are:

- foreign exchange and money markets
- bank accounts and cash management
- administration and correspondence
- report generator.

Other modules comprise:

- risk management
- investment management
- debt management
- netting
- accounting
- link to banks from balance reporting
- links to banks for electronic funds transfer
- modelling, decision support and what-if analysis.

Treasury modules of group-wide ERP systems: Many enterprise resource planning (ERP) systems now include a treasury module. The advantage is that the treasury system is part of the same platform as the financial and other systems.

Straight-through processing (STP)

STP represents the ability to produce different reports and data, usually relating to the same transaction, without the necessity for the constant re-keying or re-inputting of the same information. Table 18.1 gives a short summary of some of the reports and data that need to be produced in connection with their routine transactions by a treasury department. STP reduces the amount of clerical intervention in the processing of data thereby savings costs and improving accuracy. STP is also known as connectivity, meaning the connection between different systems used by treasury, or into which treasury has an input.

An example of how STP can be achieved in a treasury department from the TMS is summarized in Table 18.1.

ELECTRONIC BANKING (EB) SYSTEMS

Most companies communicate with their bank via an electronic banking system. The basic service allows a corporate to do two things: first, to obtain information regarding account balances and transactions flowing through accounts, and second, to initiate payments.

Table 18.1 Benefits of straight-through processing illustrated with money market and derivative transactions

Money market transactions and derivative transactions are entered into the TMS. The following are prepared directly from the TMS:	Money market and derivative transactions entered into the TMS
• Maturity ladders showing the principal and interest due, and amounts due under derivatives transactions.	• TMS prepares maturity schedules and amounts due/receivable under money market and derivative transactions
• Input to the accounting system where amounts due/receivable under derivative trades and interest payable/receivable are recorded and allocated to the respective accounting periods	• Input to the accounting system is done via journals prepared from output from TMS
• Preparation of the liquidity management sections of the treasury report showing interest payable/receivable, and amounts due/receivable under risk management transactions, together with outstanding derivative trades matched against exposures	• Preparation of reports is done from spreadsheets with input from reports generated from TMS
• Marking derivative instruments to market for internal and external reporting purposes using direct feeds from Reuters or Bloomberg	• Mark to market exercises carried out via separate stand alone systems Input of all derivatives extracted from the TMS and market rates recorded manually from Reuters or Bloomberg and manually input into valuation system

Balance and transaction information

EB systems access an 'electronic banking computer' which sits in front of the bank's internal application system. This computer provides customers with mirror copies of the account information that is held on the bank's internal systems (Figure 18.1).

The information required by a treasury department falls into two categories.

1. Prior day and historical information. This includes:
   - Information regarding current ledger and cleared balances by currency by account. (In some countries ledger balances are analyzed between one and two-day float.)
   - Where relevant, net ledger and cleared balances on a pool of accounts.
   - Details of transactions going through individual accounts.
   - Information on the clearing status of cheques that have been issued.

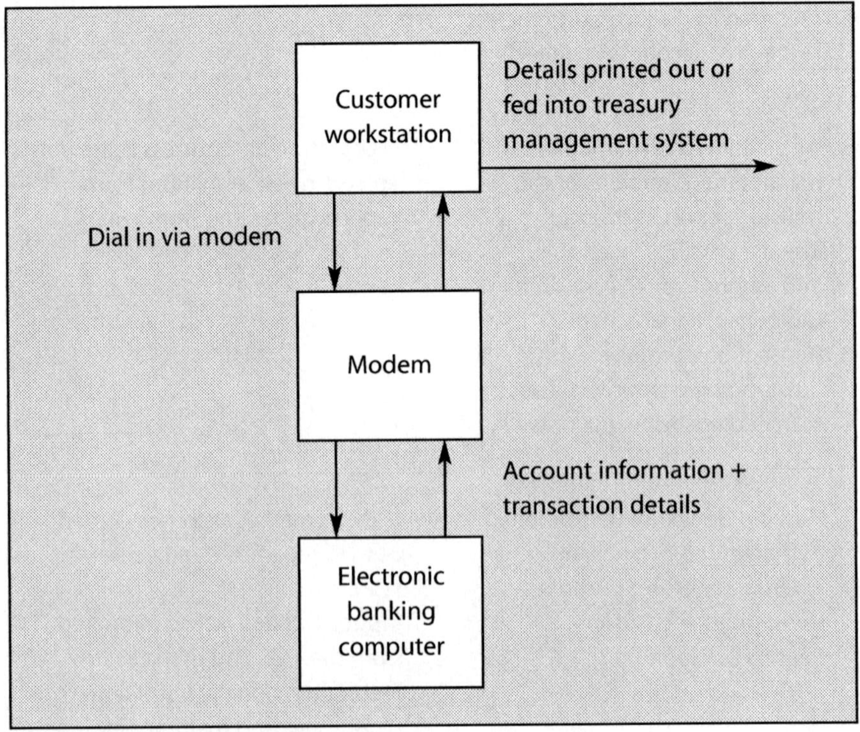

Figure 18.1 Standard EB systems

- International transaction activity including wire transfers, drafts, and letters of credit.

2. Current day information:
   - Details of payments clearing that day and being debited to accounts in respect of both cheques and payments through ACH.
   - Details of items to be credited, including credits through ACH.
   - Projected cleared balance account, and projected cleared balances on pools of accounts.

A typical bank report receivable in many countries such as the UK is shown in Table 18.2. It shows the ledger balance, the cleared balance at the end of the day and the projected cleared balance for certain accounts. The totals relate to the pool of accounts, which contains other accounts than the five illustrated. The difference between the cleared balance and projected cleared balances represents net amounts being cleared that day and being debited or credited to accounts.

EB systems will also provide information of transactions that have cleared or failed since the opening update. These include:

- items that failed autoclearing
- manual items that would not clear automatically
- returned/unpaid items
- items passed across accounts during the current day.

Reporting balance and transaction information from other banks

Most EB systems can report balances on accounts held at other banks and in other countries (at their lead bank or otherwise). However, there are

Table 18.2 Typical bank balance report

Account	*Ledger balance*	*Cleared balance*	*Projected cleared*
137606A	26 102 DR	26 107 DR	49 109 DR
137607A	89 750	100 867	155 867
137608A	90 862	121 620	175 909
137609A	1 378 756 DR	1 400 850 DR	2 769 870 DR
Total	27 867	49 807	2 030 795 DR

often difficulties for the treasurer in receiving information via one EB system. First of all, from a competitive and operational point of view, banks would rather not implement such third-party functionality. Companies may find themselves paying extra for the privilege. Second, companies holding accounts at other banks overseas may find that, due to the different technical platforms and account information standards used by other banks in other countries, feeding information to their own EB systems is not straightforward. The result is that the level of detail received on accounts held with another bank will not be the same as that held at the bank that supplied the EB system.

Use of more than one EB system inevitably complicates attempts by international companies to manage cash balances and is one of the reasons why an increasing number of companies are moving towards as few suppliers of cash management services as possible.

Payment initiation

When initiating a payment using an EB system, a member of staff will complete a series of fields preformatted by the bank.

Most treasury departments only use the payments initiation module of an EB system for urgent domestic payments (such settling financial obligations) and international payments. In terms of international transfers, the user can choose between an urgent (same or next-day value) and non-urgent (two or three days' value) international payment, but the actual route of the transfer once it is received by the bank will depend on whether the EB system is supplied by a bank that uses correspondents or its own branch network (or a combination of both) to meet the cross-border requirements of its clients.

For the majority of companies, most payments are generally made to a small number of regular suppliers. Users may wish to establish a set of predefined beneficiaries in a restricted-access basis library. This allows authorized users to call up a template and enter non-static data such as currency amount and value date.

Cut-off times

Banks' cut-off times for effecting payments for same-day value (or indeed for forwarding any payment into the clearing process on the same day as received from the customer) are generally later for payments submitted from their electronic banking system than by other means (e.g. paper-based instructions or fax). Thus the corporate that uses its EB system to effect a payment bypasses some of the manual processes within the bank and is given more time in which to receive funds and assess ongoing funding/depositing needs before submitting its final payments for the day.

Connectivity

In large companies it is usual to see EB systems being used by the accounts department to make payments and receive information. Connectivity is the interface with other treasury and finance systems. Increasingly, information is being downloaded from the EB systems into a company's accounting, account receivable and payable systems for reconciliation purposes.

An important aspect of EB systems is the ability to match transaction records maintained in accounts payable and receivable systems to the balance and transaction information supplied by the banks. Matches can be made against:

- exact amounts
- close amounts
- value dates
- reference fields
- combinations of the above.

Banks will make reconciliation data in a standard format that is then forwarded to the company's accounts system via a customized link.

For corporates with high volumes of transaction data, it is possible to establish a direct link to collect data from the bank's internal systems, effectively bypassing the EB service.

CHAPTER 19

Tax and Accounting

GENERAL

In all the preceding chapters, treasury activities have been approached from the standpoint of economic value. Do the treasury activities protect the company from financial risk and do they add value to the organization? The question of adding value is usually tackled from the standpoint of reducing costs and giving greater certainty to cashflow and earnings numbers.

Tax and accounting can have major influences on the activities of a treasury department, the instruments it uses and on a number of treasury processes such as cash management. Tax can have a significant effect on treasury activities, since it can change the whole dimension of the economics of a transaction. A transaction will not always be taxed according to its economic structure. This can work either to the advantage the disadvantage of the treasurer.

Accounting also has a major influence on treasury activities. Most organizations try to ensure the accounting represents what they consider to be the economic reality of a transaction. Some argue that if the accounting does not represent this reality, the transaction should be undertaken anyway. The argument is that accounting results can have no long-term influence on the value of a company. Others argue that if a transaction initially gives adverse accounting results, this does have an impact on the value of a company, since the market reacts negatively to the accounting results and a company's share price is marked down, with unforeseen consequences arising from that.

The basic rule for the treasurer must be that tax and accounting are specialist areas, and that before considering any fund raising operations or any new approach to hedging or cash management, contact should always be made with the tax and accounting specialists. In most organizations, queries can be dealt with by the tax and accounting departments themselves.

A discussion of tax and accounting is outside the scope of this book. Tax regimes vary considerably from country to country, and within each country different companies' tax positions vary. Accounting rules are continually changing, their application varies from country to country and every company and its auditors may have different interpretations. The following is a very brief checklist of some of the questions that the treasurer will need to discuss when considering some of transactions outlined in this book.

Taxation

Some of the questions that a treasurer may need to ask are listed below.

Fund raising

- Eurobond coupons are rounded down to the nearest 1/8th and issues are made at a discount to par. Medium-term notes may be capable of being issued with many different structures such as zero-coupons structures, amortizing coupons, issues at a discount or a premium to par and so on. Is tax relief for interest based on the underlying yield to maturity of the bond or notes?
- Is tax relief available for the upfront costs of the lead manager in the case of a bond issue and arranger in the case of debt finance?
- Are legal, printing and other costs incurred in fund raising tax deductible?
- Are there any value added tax implications?

Special transactions

- If a special transaction is being considered, what are the consequences of any asset sales to another company?
- Will assets be sold at a premium or discount to current book or tax value? What are the implications for any sale in terms of taxation on any capital gains?
- Does stamp duty apply to any asset sales or to any aspect of the transaction?
- How are legal and set up costs treated? Are they tax deductible in the originator or the SPV?

- What is the tax status of the SPV and where should it be established?
- What is the taxation of any surplus in the SPV at the end of the transaction, both in the SPV and when received by the originator?

Cash management

- Will withholding tax apply on any intercompany loans? Is it recoverable?
- Is interest calculated on an 'arms length'? Will interest payable on intercompany loans be tax deductible?
- Will stamp duty apply to any intercompany loans?
- Is there a possibility of contravention of any thin capitalization rules?

Accounting

Generally accounting should follow the economics of a transaction.

Funding

All financing transactions should be accounted for at the underlying yield of the transaction. Upfront costs are normally amortized over the anticipated life of the transaction.

Special transactions

In the case of special transactions such as asset securitization or project finance, a lot of effort will be put into determining whether the assets are genuinely owned by the vehicle company, or whether the originator still retains an interest in the assets. Much is determined by whether the transferee has the right to sell or pledge the assets and whether the transferor does not have the right to re-acquire the transferred assets.

Hedging

European listed companies are affected by International Accounting Standard (IAS) 39, which the European Commission has proposed should be used for all accounts beginning on or after 1 January 2005. American companies are already affected by FAS 133.

Both standards are very similar. A very brief summary of IAS 39 is as follows:

- All financial assets and liabilities will be recognized on the balance sheet. Certain derivative instruments will have to be recorded at fair value.
- Where an asset or liability is recorded at fair value, changes in fair value from one period to another will be recorded in profit and loss or in equity according to the nature of the financial asset or liability.
- IAS 39 defines four categories of financial asset:
  - those held for trading
  - those held to maturity of investment
  - loans and receivables originated by the company and not held for trading
  - financial assets available for sale.

  The first and last category should be accounted for at fair value, and the second and third at amortized cost.
- Derivative financial assets and liabilities are always assumed to be held for trading unless specifically designated as an effective hedge.
- All other financial liabilities should be measured at amortized cost.
- For a derivative to be classified as an effective hedge, the hedging relationship must be clearly defined. The risk that is being hedged and the expected relationship between that risk and the hedged instrument must be defined. The above should be fully documented, and documentation should include the firm's risk management objective and strategy for undertaking the hedge. In addition the hedging relationship must be measurable, and the company must define the technique to be used for assessing hedge effectiveness.

Companies may well need to examine their existing hedging policies and the instruments they use to effect that policy, and study the impact that IAS39 will have on these hedging policies. This may have implications for a company's treasury policies.

APPENDIX

LIBOR Fixings

In syndicated banking facilities and derivative contracts, there must be some objective way of determining the rate of interest to be applied. For instance, under interest rate swaps, at each roll-over or interest rate fixing, the floating interest rate has to be established for the next period. At the end of that period a net settlement will be made, consisting of the difference between the floating and fixed rate under the swap. With a syndicated loan, either when advances are rolled over or when new advances are requested, the interest rate has to be determined for the relevant period.

BBA (British Banks' Association) LIBOR is the BBA fixing of the London Inter-Bank Offered Rate. It is established each day for a number of different maturities. LIBOR is based on a panel of contributor banks contributing the rate at which they could borrow funds in reasonable market size just prior to 11 a.m. The contributor banks are chosen on the basis of reputation and scale of activity in the London market, and perceived expertise in the currency concerned.

The contributed rates are ranked in order and the middle two quartiles are averaged arithmetically. The LIBOR fixing process is managed on behalf of BBA by Moneyline Telerate. Once the LIBOR for the currencies' fixing date and maturities are determined, they are released and distributed among a number of major information vendors such as Reuters and Bloomberg.

LIBOR fixings are calculated for a whole range of maturities, from one week to 12 months. BBA LIBOR is fixed for the following currencies: UK£, CA$, €, US$, AU$, yen and CHF. All are fixed on spot apart from UK£, which is same day. Maturity dates are subject to the modified following business day convention.

Official fixings are made for a number of markets in other countries. SIBOR is the Singapore Inter-Bank Offered Rate, and HIBOR the Hong Kong Inter-Bank Offered Rate. EURIBOR is the fixing that has been established by the European Banking Federation to benchmark in-zone rates.

Glossary

Accreting swaps An interest rate swap where the notional principal of the swap increases at each interest fixing.

Accrued interest Interest earned but not due and payable. Interest is accrued according to different conventions depending on the particular market.

ACH A US money transfer system, similar to the BACS system in the UK.

Administrator In a securitization, the task of an administrator is to collect the cash from the underlying assets and maintain all appropriate asset records. The weaker the credit standing of an administrator, the more likely it is that some actual or standby agreement is required for the administrator to be replaced by a more creditworthy party.

Agency fee The fee paid to the bank that acts as agent for a syndicated facility.

American option An American option can be exercised at any time during the option contract period.

Amortizing loan A loan repayable by instalments over a period of time. Such loans are typical of leasing and terms loans.

Arrangement fee The fee paid to the arranger for arranging the syndication of a committed facility. It may also include an underwriting fee if the facility is being underwritten. An arrangement fee is an upfront fee.

Arranger The bank responsible for syndicating a committed facility. The arranger is responsible for advising on the price and terms at which a facility can be successfully syndicated and for inviting participation.

Assignment A method for the transfer of receivables together with associated rights and interests. In the case of an unconditional assignment, the assignee has direct legal rights against the underlying receivables and the obligors are informed. Alternatively, it may be conditional, in which case recovery by the assignee requires the completion of the necessary steps to make it absolute, or the assignee is required to join in any action the assignor takes against the underlying receivables and obligors.

At the money There would be neither gain nor loss in exercising the option. The exercise price is equal to the current market price of the asset.

Automated investment of surplus funds Standing instruction to move all or some end-of-day balances from an account to an investment vehicle. Transaction initiation is normally based on credit position of accounts.

Average rate option Market prices of the underlying asset are averaged over the option period. At the end of the option period, the average of the prices is compared with the strike price in determining whether the option can be exercised.

BACS (Bankers Automated Clearing Services.) BACS is a low value, bulk clearing system that handles automated credits, debits and standing orders. BACS provides an automated clearing house service in the UK for the clearing of transactions originated by settlement members or others sponsored by them to use the service. Similar systems exist in most countries, such as ACH in US and Autopay in Hong Kong.

Bank relationship risk The risk that a company could suffer loss as a result of having inadequate banking relationships.

Bank transfer An instruction from a payer to a bank to debit his/her account with a specific amount and pay money directly to the account of a third party. Bank transfers may be by wire or telegraphic transfer, or transfers via the bank giro.

Banker's drafts Essentially a cheque drawn by a bank on itself. Banker's drafts are regarded as cash, since the beneficiary has high confidence he/she will be paid.

Bankruptcy remote The SPV is structured to ensure that bankruptcy of the originator does not result in the bankruptcy of the SPV.

Basis point 1/100 of one per cent (0.01 per cent).

Basis risk The risk that changes in the value of a derivative do not exactly match changes in an underlying exposure. Basis risk arises where it is not possible to find a derivative that perfectly matches the underlying exposure.

Basis swap Enables a treasurer to change the interest basis of a loan.

Bearer security A negotiable security whose title is to the bearer; that is, it is presumed in law to be owned by the holder.

Beneficiary The individual with the right to receive value (payment) under a payment instrument; for example, the beneficiary under a cheque is the payee on the cheque.

Beta A measure of the riskiness of a company's equity against the market as a whole. The shares of company with a beta of two is twice as risky as the market, when risk is measured by volatility of a shares return.

Bid	Price at which the market maker is prepared to buy a financial asset.
Bid offer spread	The difference between the market makers buying and selling price. The size of the spread usually denotes the liquidity in the market.
Bilateral lines	A facility arranged between just one bank and the borrower. A number of bilaterals can be arranged by a borrower, each with its own margin and terms.
Book value	The value of assets as recorded in a company's financial records and stated in its financial statements.
Bookbuilding	The process whereby the lead manager to a bond issue receives indications of the amount that investors will buy of a bond and the price they are prepared to pay. Bookbuilding takes place during the bookbuilding period prior to launch.
Bought deal	The lead manager to a bond issue buys the whole of the issue on predetermined terms and price and then places the bonds with his/her own customers.
Bridge facilities	Facilities intended to bridge the borrower from one event to another, such as the maturity of a loan and a fund raising exercise in the capital markets.
Bullet loan	A loan that is repayable on one date.
Business day	The period from 00.01 to 24.00 on any working day. It is used to determine the settlement date of financial transactions.
Business risks	Those risks that arise from being in a particular industry and geographical area.
Call option	The option holder has the right to buy an asset at the underlying exercise price.
Capital asset pricing model (CAPM)	A model in corporate finance theory that seeks to calculate the minimum return that should be

generated by a company's projects. CAPM is also used to calculate a company's weighted average cost of capital.

Cash Legal tender in notes and coins.

Cash concentration As opposed to cash pooling, which involves no movement of funds, cash concentration involves the transfer of funds from accounts in credit either to a central account, or to other accounts which are in debit. In countries where cash pooling is unavailable, such as the United States, cash concentration or sweeping is used to manage liquidity.

Cash pooling See notional pooling.

Cash settlement The settlement of option contracts for cash instead of settlement involving the physical transfer of assets.

Central bank reporting A requirement in many countries to report cross-border and currency transactions to the local monetary authority.

Certainty of funds A rule applicable in many countries where the advisor to the offeror in an acquisition has to certify the offeror has resources to satisfy full acceptance of the offer.

Certificates of deposit A certificate evidencing a bank deposit. The certificate is a bearer instrument that is capable of being traded.

Charges Arise when a bond is issued or loan established with security over certain assets. If the borrower defaults on the bond or loan the charged assets can be sold and the proceeds used to repay the debt.

Cheque A payment instrument, drawn by the payer and ordering a bank to make a specified payment to the person named on the cheque. Payment is made immediately on presentation of the cheque from funds standing in the payer's account.

Cheque truncation Instead of the physical cheque being passed through the clearing system, the details of the cheque are captured electronically at the point of deposit.

Cleared funds Funds for which the beneficiary has value; in other words, if they were placed in an interest-bearing account, interest would be paid thereon.

Collar A combination of a call option and a put option. The holder of a collar has purchased either a call or put option and has sold a countervailing put or call. Collars can be constructed so that there is no premium payable. The holder of a collar is protected against an adverse movements in rates or prices, but forgoes some the gains of a favourable price movement.

Commercial paper A short-term promissory note issued by a company. Commercial paper is normally issued at a discount.

Commitment fee The fee paid on the unutilized portion of a committed facility. Commitments fees are calculated daily on unutilized amounts and normally paid quarterly.

Committed bank facility A facility where, provided the terms and conditions of the loan agreement are observed, the bank or syndicate is obliged to provide finance to the borrower.

Commodity risk The risk that operating costs or revenues of a company will fluctuate as a result of movements in the market price of commodities. Some companies have commodity sales risk, where their revenues may fluctuate as a result of movements in the market price of the commodity. Others have commodity purchase risk, where costs may increase as a result raw material price increases.

Compliance risk Compliance with laws and regulations which, if infringed, can damage a company.

Conduit A particular type of SPV that is designed to finance, usually through commercial paper issuance, receivables portfolios typically purchased from a number of originators.

Confirmation The confirmation outlines the terms of derivative or money market trades.

Corporate credit rating (CCR) The rating nominally assigned to the obligor of a debt security. The CCR is then adjusted to reflect the specifics of any issue to arrive at the rating for that issue.

Correspondent bank A bank in another country, through which a bank is able to pay funds to a beneficiary in that country. For instance, if a UK company wants to pay yen to a supplier in Japan, their UK bank will instruct their Japanese correspondent to make the payment and debit their yen account held with that correspondent bank.

Counterparty risk The risk of losses being sustained on derivative contracts, financial instruments or deposits as a result of the counterparty failing to meet its obligations.

Coupon The rate of interest payable on a bond. The nominal annual rate of interest expressed as a percentage of the principal value. The coupon is payable annually, semi-annually or quarterly, depending on the type of security.

Covenants Essentially undertakings by the borrower to observe certain conditions. The purpose of covenants is to ensure the ongoing ability of the borrower to meet its obligations.

Credit card A card allowing the holder to purchase goods on credit.

Credit enhancement In a securitization, credit support which may come from one or more sources that provides a buffer for the investors against losses on the securitized assets.

Credit rating An independent third-party assessment of the creditworthiness of an obligor with respect to a specific financial obligation.

Credit research Research undertaken by the major investment houses on the respective credit quality of bonds. Some investors will want to see credit research published by the lead manager prior to purchasing a bond at launch.

Credit watch A security is placed on credit watch when an event has occurred to the obligor that may change its credit rating. Further information is required before making a rating decision.

Cross-border concentration Cash concentration carried out over national boundaries. Generally cross-border concentration has to be effected using FX swaps.

Cross default An event of default arising under a financial contract that enables lenders, or counterparties under derivative contracts, to claim default on another separate facility or transaction. An example might be a default under a term loan, which enables the banks with commitments under a revolving syndicated facility to claim default under that facility.

Cross guarantees If the bank accounts of a number of different legal entities are involved in cash pooling, then guarantees are required from all individual legal entities to each other. The purpose of the guarantees is to ensure that the bank does not suffer loss should one of the entities go into bankruptcy or insolvency.

Cross rates Currency pairs that do not include US$.

Currency cheque A cheque payable in another currency to the payee's domestic currency; for instance a German company receiving a cheque payable in US$.

Cut-off time Times after which a bank's customer is unable to effect transfers for value on specified days. For example, if the cut-off time for a RTGS is 4 p.m., then transfers after that time cannot be effected that day and must be made the following day.

Daylight overdraft An exposure one bank may have to its customer or to another bank during daytime operations. For instance a bank's customer may have many transactions, both debit and credits, on its accounts during the day. The customer may make payments in anticipation of receipts coming in. Although the account may end the day with a zero balance, during the day the account may have been in substantial deficit. Banks will impose limits on daytime exposure.

Debt gearing Calculated as: net borrowings/net assets. It is a crude measure of a company's financial gearing.

Default Failure by a party to fufil its obligations under the terms of a loan, bond or derivatives contract. Defaults usually enable lenders or counterparties to claim repayment of loans or termination of the derivatives contract.

Derivative A financial instrument whose performance is based on the price of an underlying asset. No movement of principal funds is required.

Digital option The payout under a digital option is a fixed amount, regardless of how far the option is in the money at expiry.

Direct debit A system whereby creditors request their bank to debit the bank account of their debtors directly. Approval of the debtor is necessary.

Discount The difference between par and the price of a financial instrument. Many instruments such as commercial paper and bills of exchange are issued at a discount, the discount representing the interest payable on the paper or bill.

Distribution A term used in the placement of bonds. It is used to denote the geographic placement and investor type.

Documentary collection An exporter ships goods and then entrusts the documents needed by the overseas buyer to a collecting bank for delivery in accordance with detailed instructions. In contrast to a documentary credit, the banks involved in a documentary collection have no liability to make payment for the documents presented.

Documentary credit A conditional undertaking issued by a bank, at the request of one of its customers, to pay a named beneficiary a specified amount of money upon presentation of documents that comply with the terms and conditions stated therein. Also called letter of credit (LC).

Drawdown period The period in a term loan during which funds must be drawn. Drawdown periods are usually comparatively short.

EBITDA Earnings before interest depreciation and amortization. EBITDA/net interest expense attempts to overcome some of the shortfalls in interest cover by adding back two significant non-cash items charged in calculating operating profit.

Economic exposure The impact that exchange rate movements may have on a company's cashflow. Economic exposure is outside transaction and pre-transaction exposure.

EDI Electronic data interchange. It is the intercompany electronic transmission of business transactions in a standard format. There are three essential elements to EDI:

- It is intercompany.
- It deals with day-to-day business transactions; it is not electronic mail.
- It works to a set of closely defined standards.

Most basic EDI networks are between industry groups; the motor industry, for instance, has a closed user group between the major manufacturers such as Ford and General Motors.

EFT Electronic funds transfer. The process whereby funds are transferred electronically by one company either to another company or to a third party using a bank's proprietary system.

EFTPOS Instead of signing a form at the point of sale, the card holder authorizes payment by inputting the PIN into a terminal connected to the card reader. The EFTPOS system first checks to see if there are sufficient funds, and if so, immediately debits the card holder's account and credits the retailers.

Enterprise risk management A corporate-wide, risk management programme that covers the management of risks throughout the organization.

Equity Share capital and reserves.

Equity premium The premium over and above a risk-free asset (government bonds and treasury bills) that a holder of a company's share needs to compensate for the risks of holding that share. Equity premiums are normally calculated over time and are represented by some long-term average.

Equity risk The risk that a company may suffer losses as a result of adverse movements in equity prices.

Eurobonds Bonds issued for international distribution and hence outside the regulatory scope of the country of issue.

European option A European option can only be exercised at the maturity date of the option contract period.

Excess spread The difference between the gross yield on securitized assets and the costs of the finance.

Finality The date after which a payment is considered final. If finality has occurred, banks cannot refuse value to the beneficiary.

Financial covenants Normally financial ratio tests such as a certain minimum level of interest cover or EBITDA/net interest that the company must observe.

Financial gearing A measure of the extent to which a change in interest rates may affect a business's financial viability. Financial gearing is usually measured by ratios such as EBITDA/net interest, operating profits before interest/net interest (interest cover).

Financial risk The risk that a company may suffer loss as a result of an adverse movement in financial prices or rates, or an adverse change in financial markets.

Financing risk The risk that a company may either be unable to finance itself in its chosen debt markets or pay too high a price for its finance.

Fixed re-offer price The price at which the bonds are purchased from the issuer and offered to investors. The purchase and sale price is identical.

Float The time which elapses between incurring an obligation to make a payment and the beneficiary obtaining value in settlement.

Foreign currency draft A banker's draft drawn in a currency foreign to that in the relevant domestic market.

Forward foreign exchange The exchange of two currencies on any date beyond spot, with the rate agreed at the deal.

Forward–forward rates The rate of interest applying to a period of time in the future. Forward–forward rates are calculated from money market rates for short periods of up to a year, and from zero-coupon rates for periods beyond a year. They demonstrate the market's view about the future level of interest rates.

Forward points The difference between spot and forward rate of exchange for two currencies.

Headroom A company's financial resources to meet unexpected fluctuations in working capital expenditure and small acquisitions. The financial resources are usually the unutilized portion of a committed facility such as a revolver. A company will normally want sufficient headroom to cover a projection of cashflow over a future period of time (say 12 to 18 months).

Hybrid options The combination of two options, or options and forwards, to create another option.

In the money An option contract can be profitably exercised.

Interest compensation Compensation of the difference of interest calculated on the total pool balance as compared with interest calculated on the individual pool accounts.

Interest cover Profit on ordinary activities/net interest. A measure of a company's ability to meet ongoing interest expense. It suffers from the shortfall that operating profits may contain significant provisions, charges and credits of a non-cash nature.

Interest rate cap An interest rate option that protects the buyer from a rise in interest rates.

Interest rate floor An interest rate option that protects the buyer from a fall in interest rates.

Interest rate risk The risk that the interest cost of borrowings will increase or returns from deposits will fall as a result of movements in interest rates.

Interest rate swap An agreement between two parties to exchange interest rate payments or receipts on a notional principal amount, for a specific period of time. Interest exchanges are netted. There is no exchange of principal.

International direct debit A direct debiting system that operates internationally. For an international direct debiting system to work effectively, the bank operating the system needs to have access to ACH systems in the relevant countries.

Intrinsic value The difference between the market price of the underlying asset and the option strike price.

Investment grade Typically credit ratings of BBB (Baa) or above. Its significance lies in the fact that securities with credit ratings lower than investment grade have speculative characteristics and are not available for purchase by many funds.

ISDA (International Swaps Derivatives Association.) The ISDA document is designed to cover the terms of all types of derivative trades that could be contracted between two counterparties.

Knock-in option An option that does not become effective unless the market price of the asset breaches a certain price level (barrier).

Knock-out option An option that expires worthless if the market price of the asset breaches a certain price level (barrier).

Launch date The day on which a new issue is offered to investors.

Lead manager The leader of a new issue responsible for the overall coordination, distribution and documentation of a primary market issue.

Ledger balance The balance on an account, reflecting transactions that have been processed through it. The ledger balance on an account is not necessarily the same as the cleared balance.

LIBOR The average rate at which certain banks can borrow on the London market at 11.00 am. LIBOR is fixed for UK£ and euro currencies.

Lifting charges Charges that are levied by banks when payments are made internationally. For instance a UK company making a payment to a customer in Tokyo may find that its domestic bank's correspondent has applied charges to the payment.

Liquidity risk The risk that a company has insufficient financial resources to meet day-to-day fluctuations in working capital and cashflow.

Loan maturity profile An analysis of the maturity dates of a company's borrowings. The analysis is usually done on a year-by-year basis, with amortizing loans being split over the years in which the individual tranches are repayable.

Lockbox A mailing address to which cheques are sent. Lockboxes are widely used in the United States but may be also used in other countries; for instance, a German publishing company with substantial magazine sales in Canada may request readers to send annual subscriptions to a lockbox in Toronto. A bank in Toronto may periodically open the lockbox and pay the receipts into a local CA$ account in the name of the publisher.

Long-term currency swap An agreement between two parties to exchange interest payments or receipts in different currencies for a specified period. There is usually an exchange of principal at the beginning of the swap and a re-exchange at the end.

Margin The amount added to the underlying interest rate for an advance under a committed facility. Margins are usually fixed for the period of the facility, although they can increase or decrease depending on the credit rating of the borrower or the amount drawn under the facility.

Multi-currency account An account denominated in a particular currency that can be used to make payments and take receipts in different foreign currencies.

Natural hedge The extent to which a financial risk may be offset by a countervailing gains within a company's business. For instance, a company's exposure to increases in interest rates may be offset by increased sales and margins that apply in its business when economic activity is higher and that is reflected in the need for higher interest rates.

Negative pledge An undertaking by the borrower not to raise secured debt.

Notional pooling A bank account structure whereby all the balances on specified accounts with a particular bank are offset. Overdraft interest is only charged on the resulting net debit balance, or if interest is to be paid on accounts in credit, it is paid on the net credit balance.

Obligor The party that has the obligation to make payment under the assets subject to a securitization.

Offer Price at which a market maker is prepared to sell a financial asset.

Offering circular The prospectus for a bond issue.

Operational gearing The level of fixed costs within a company's cost structure.

Operational risks The risks arising in the various administrative and operational procedures that a business uses to manage its business, such as production control, stock control and quality control.

Option premium The price paid by an option buyer for the rights under the option contract.

Originator The entity that originates an asset-backed security transaction.

Out of the money The option cannot be profitably exercised.

Overlay An additional layer of bank accounts between operating company local accounts and group treasury accounts.

Par In reference to the price of a security, 100 per cent of the principal value of a debt security. Usually the face value of a bond, or the coupon of a bond.

Pari-passu An undertaking by the borrower that all unsecured creditors will rank equally.

Participation fee The fee paid to banks for participation in a committed facility. It is an upfront fee and is usually paid out of the arrangement fee.

Paying agent A bank responsible for the task of making

payments of principal and interest to the holder of a security.

Pre-transaction risk Contingent foreign exchange exposures arising before entering into a commercial contract that would turn them into transactional exposures.

Price discovery The process whereby the book runner receives indications of the price at which individual investors will purchase amounts of a bond that is to be launched.

Price/yield relationship The relationship between price and YTM on a security. If the market price of a bond rises then the yield will fall and vice versa.

Private placement A privately agreed issue of debt, where the terms are directly agreed and negotiated between the investor(s) and issuer. The bonds issued are not traded and are purchased by a very small group of investors.

Put option The option holder has the right to sell an asset at the exercise price.

Rating outlook Assesses the potential for a future change in a rating.

Receipts and uses Cashflow forecasts based on forecasting cash receipts and cash uses.

Representations and warranties A section in a loan document where the borrower effectively represents and warrants that it has due authority and power to enter into the agreement, and has suffered no adverse events that could lead a bank to refuse the advance of funds.

Revolving facility A facility where multiple advances can be drawn by the borrower for different periods and amounts. Not all the facility needs to be drawn.

Roadshow A series of investor presentations at a number of major financial centres to market a bond issue.

RTGS The inter-bank settlement is effected electronically item by item, as they occur, across the settlement bank's account held at the Central Bank. RTGS systems guarantee payment as soon as they enter the system.

Rule 144A This allows the issue of a bond in the US domestic market without full SEC registration. Rule 144A restricts investors to qualified institutional buyers.

Same-day value The beneficiary receives value the same day that the payer tenders payment.

Secondary market The term used to describe the market where investors trade securities among themselves. It is distinguished from the primary market where the issuer originally issues securities to the investor.

Security The provision of some form of charge over a company's assets, usually provided in conjunction with the undertaking of a borrowing.

Special presentation Short-circuiting of the cheque clearing system. A bank couriers the cheque to the paying branch. On receipt of the cheque, the paying branch will debit the payer's account and make payment.

Spot foreign exchange The exchange of two currencies for settlement in two days' time.

Spread The difference between the yield on a corporate bond and the yield on a government bond for the same currency and maturity.

SPV (Special purpose vehicle.) A vehicle, in a variety of legal forms including corporate, trusts and partnerships, that is set up with a strictly defined and limited purpose.

Standby facilities Facilities that back up a cheaper source of finance such as commercial paper, and can be used should that cheaper finance no longer be available.

Standing order Instructions given by the debtor to a bank to make a payment of a specified sum to a specified beneficiary on stated dates.

Strike price Exercise price under an option contract. The difference between market price and strike price identifies whether a contract can be profitably exercised.

Subscription agreement The agreement between the issuer, lead manager and co-managers that sets out underwriting terms and fees.

Swap spread Difference between the fixed swap rate for a particular maturity and the yield of the underlying government security.

Swaption The buyer of a swaption has the right to enter an interest rate swap at some date in the future.

Sweeping The process whereby balances on sub-accounts are transferred to a master account in order to reduce those sub-accounts to zero or some pre-defined balance.

SWIFT (Society for World Inter-bank Telecommunications.) A means of communicating information and exchanging transactions between banks. SWIFT's objective is to provide a method for members to effect financial transactions between themselves that is timely, secure, standardized, auditable and controllable.

The system only moves data not funds. SWIFT operates on standard message formats relating to different kinds of bank operations.

Syndicated loans A facility arranged with a number of banks. Syndicated facilities have a common loan agreement, and each bank contributes to advances in proportion to its individual commitments.

Term loan Funds are advanced for the period of the loan.

Term structure of interest rates Another term for yield curve.

Time value The difference between the fair value of an option and its intrinsic value.

Transaction risk The risk that a company's cashflows and realized profits may be affected by movements in foreign exchange markets. Transaction risk represents definite foreign currency receipts or payments where a clear obligation to make a payment or a right to receive a payment has arisen.

Translation risk The risk that the domestic value of the assets and liabilities and the revenue of foreign subsidiaries will fluctuate with exchange rate movements.

Treasury bills Short-term government securities.

Treasury policies A document that establishes a company's approach to managing the significant financial exposures facing a company.

Trust deed Sets out the powers and duties of the trustee.

Uncommitted facility A facility where the bank is not obligated to advance funds.

VaR (Value at risk.) VaR measures the possible adverse change in market value of a financial instrument, based on what is regarded as the largest likely adverse move in rates or prices over a given timeframe. It also includes the correlation between different financial instruments to measure the volatility of a financial portfolio of instruments.

Value dating The date at which a beneficiary can use funds received from a debtor. In the case of funds paid into an interest-bearing account, it is the date at which the funds start to earn interest.

Volatility A measure of the variation in the market price of the underlying asset in an option contract.

WACC (Weighted average cost of capital.) The average of the cost of a company's equity and debt weighted according to their respective market values.

Yield curve A graph showing the relationship between yields and maturities for a set of similar securities.

YTM (Yield to maturity.) The return a security earns on the price at which it was purchased if held to maturity. YTM assumes that coupons can be reinvested at the same underlying yield.

Zero-coupon rates The rates earned on a zero-coupon bond. A zero-coupon bond pays no interest during its life; all interest is compounded and paid at maturity of the bond. Zero-coupon rates avoid the question of reinvestment risk of coupons that YTM raises.

Index

SPREADSHEETS

The spreadsheets on the attached CD are designed to provide some further assistance to the reader regarding some of the principles discussed in this book. The CD contains the following spreadsheets:

- *Bond valuation.* This spreadsheet calculates either the market price or fixed re-offer price for a ten-year bond with a given yield, or the yield on a ten-year bond for a given market price. The spreadsheet can be used to calculate price and yield for shorter dated bonds.

- *Foreign exchange risk.* This is designed to provide some practical guidance in the selection and use of derivatives to manage foreign exchange exposures to meet certain strategic objectives.

- *Interest rate risk.* As above but for interest rate exposures.

- *Zero coupon and swap valuation.* How to calculate zero coupon rates and use these rates to value an interest rate swap.

- *Short-term interest rate risk.* Covers the aspect of managing the interest rate risk inherent in liquidity management.

- *FX swaps.* How to determine whether an FX swap is viable.